Writing the Nation in
1530-

For PHIL *and* ELLEN

Writing the Nation in Reformation England 1530–1580

CATHY SHRANK

OXFORD
UNIVERSITY PRESS

OXFORD
UNIVERSITY PRESS

Great Clarendon Street, Oxford OX2 6DP

Oxford University Press is a department of the University of Oxford.
It furthers the University's objective of excellence in research, scholarship,
and education by publishing worldwide in

Oxford New York

Auckland Bangkok Buenos Aires Cape Town Chennai
Dar es Salaam Delhi Hong Kong Istanbul Karachi Kolkata
Kuala Lumpur Madrid Melbourne Mexico City Mumbai Nairobi
São Paulo Shanghai Taipei Tokyo Toronto

Oxford is a registered trade mark of Oxford University Press
in the UK and in certain other countries

Published in the United States
by Oxford University Press Inc., New York

British Library Cataloguing in Publication Data
Data available

Library of Congress Cataloging in Publication Data
Data available

Typeset by Cambrian Typesetters, Frimley, Surrey
Printed in Great Britain
on acid-free paper by
Biddles Ltd, King's Lynn

ISBN 0–19–926888–6   978–0–19–926888–7
ISBN 0–19–921100–0 (Pbk)   978–0–10–921100–5 (Pbk.)

1 3 5 7 9 10 8 6 4 2

Preface

This book began as a Ph.D. project at Cambridge, where I benefited from the knowledge and insight of my supervisor, Colin Burrow. I am also indebted to all those who read the work in its various stages and encouraged both me and the project, including Sylvia Adamson, Stephen Alford, Marie Axton, Tom Betteridge, James Carley, Peter Davidson, Barbara Fennell, Andrew Gordon, John Guy, Andrew Hadfield, Robert Maslen, Jennifer Richards, James Simpson, Quentin Skinner, Blair Worden, and Rivkah Zim; Alex Gillespie, Dermot Cavanagh, and Jessica Winston were also generous with references. The book would have been a far poorer piece of scholarship without their contributions: any errors that remain are—naturally—my own. In addition, I am grateful to the input of audiences of conference and seminar papers, especially in Cambridge, Newcastle, and Oxford, and to fourth-year students at the University of Aberdeen who took my 'Forging the Nation' course (many of whom shared my enthusiasm for Andrew Borde). During the evolution of this book, I have also enjoyed the advice and support of colleagues and former colleagues at Aberdeen and King's College London. Besides those named in the list of readers, Mary Morrissey and Gordon McMullan are owed especial thanks. Sophie Goldsworthy and Frances Whistler, my editors at OUP, and Jacqueline Harvey, my copy-editor, proved supportive in the latter stages of the project, when the encouragement and advice of my anonymous readers at OUP were also immensely helpful. Nor would the work in this book have been possible without the help of numerous library staff, particularly at the British Library, Cambridge University Library, the Public Records Office, and the Queen Mother Library and Special Libraries and Archives at the University of Aberdeen: much thanks is due to them.

Various parts of this book appeared in print in different, but recognizable, guises. Earlier drafts of sections of Chapter 1 were published as 'Andrew Borde and the Politics of Identity in Reformation England', in *Reformation*, 5 (2000), 1–26. Some of the material on language in Chapters 4 and 5 appeared in

'Rhetorical Constructions of a National Community: The Role of the King's English in Mid-Tudor Writing', in Alexandra Shepard and Phil Withington (eds.), *Communities in Early Modern England* (Manchester: Manchester University Press, 2000). Earlier thoughts about Wilson and civil speech appeared in 'Civil Tongues: Language, Law and Reformation', in Jennifer Richards (ed.), *Early Modern Civil Discourses* (Houndmills: Palgrave, 2003). I would like to thank the editors of these books and journals, and the respective presses, for permission to reproduce this material.

My greatest debts are, of course, to my family: to my parents, Alan and Lucy Shrank, for their long-term encouragement (and, more recently, babysitting); to Lesley Hamilton for always managing to sound interested; and to my brother, Alex Shrank, for much-needed advice about technology. Finally, to Phil Withington, the most thanks of all: your support, advice, knowledge, and belief have been essential.

Contents

List of Abbreviations

BL   British Library
CUL   Cambridge University Library
DNB   *Dictionary of National Biography*, ed. Leslie Stephen and Sidney Lee (Oxford: Oxford University Press, 1921–2)
EETS   Early English Texts Society
ELR   *English Literary Renaissance*
ERO   Essex Records Office
HLQ   *Huntington Library Quarterly*
LP   *Letters and Papers, Foreign and Domestic, of the reign of Henry VIII, 1509–1547*, ed. J. S. Brewer, 21 vols. (London: Public Records Office, 1862–1932)
OED   *Oxford English Dictionary*, ed. J. A. Simpson and E. A. Weiner, 2nd edn. (Oxford: Oxford University Press, 1989)
PRO   Public Records Office
SEL   *Studies in English Literature*
STC   *Short Title Catalogue*, ed. A. W. Pollard and G. R. Redgrave, 2nd edn., rev. W. A. Jackson, F. S. Ferguson, and Katharine F. Pantzer (London: Bibliographical Society, 1976)
VCH   *Victoria County History*

Note on Transcriptions, Translations, and References

Original spelling has been maintained in all quotations (including i/j and u/v), except for thorns and yoghs, which have been transcribed as Roman characters. Superscript letters have been lowered and abbreviations silently expanded. The tironian *and* is represented by the ampersand. The initial *ff* is reproduced as F. Where necessary to the argument to indicate afterthoughts or corrections, inserted words and phrases are enclosed in insertion carets (for example, ^inserted text^). Square brackets enclose any interpolated characters, including ellipses.

Since the practice of early modern punctuation differed substantially from our own, I felt it desirable to alter punctuation to aid the comprehension of the modern reader. My additions are indicated by their enclosure in square brackets.

Unless otherwise stated, translations are my own.

In the bibliography and notes, place of publication for books printed 1450–1800 is London, unless otherwise stated.

Introduction

In 1590, Edmund Spenser issued the first three books of his imperial epic, *The Faerie Queene*. Spenser's fairy world is famously populated by a number of national symbols, including Arthur, the archetypal British hero; the Redcrosse knight, who bears the arms of St George; and Britomart, 'this Briton Mayd'.[1] As Spenser's knights move across the fairy landscape towards the court of Gloriana (Elizabeth I), the poem holds England and Faery Land in parallel, endowing the former with mythic status, and—in habitual Tudor style—appropriating the terms 'Britain' and 'British' for English ends. Read as historical allegory, the journey of Redcrosse in Book I also represents Spenser's interpretation of the English Reformation, as Redcrosse (England)—separated from Una (the 'true' church)—is seduced by the false allure of Duessa (the Roman Church), before reunion with Una saves him from fatal despair and brings him to the house of Holiness.[2] It is after he is restored to the true church that Redcrosse also discovers his real identity, hitherto unknown to him. Redcrosse not only wears St George's cross, he is 'Saint *George* of mery England', 'thine own nations frend' (I. x. 61. 9, 7). Redcrosse's adoption, as an abandoned infant, by a 'ploughman' (I. x. 66. 3) further links the revelation of Redcrosse's identity with the Reformation and sixteenth-century readings of William Langland's *Piers Plowman* as a proto-Protestant text. By the 1590s, that is, Spenser was able to conceptualize England as a nation whose identity was bound up with the experience of Reformation. The connection between the Reformation and Spenser's vision of England is significant. As Patrick Collinson suggests, 'the Protestant Reformation was *thought* to have made a great difference to national self-esteem, not least by those who were themselves caught up in it; and that fact, an illusion though it may

[1] Edmund Spenser, *The Faerie Queene*, ed. A. C. Hamilton (London: Longman, 1977), III. ii. 4, 5.

[2] Duessa's identification as the Roman Church is signalled by her appearance with a papal 'triple crowne' (I. viii. 16. 3–4).

have been, is important in itself.'³ What this current book traces is the development of a rhetoric of English nationhood over the course of the sixteenth century, the age of Reformation, and the means by which Tudor England was, like Redcrosse, instructed in its Englishness.

Whilst it is undeniable that national sentiment existed in sixteenth-century England, as a text like *The Faerie Queene* testifies, for most historians of the modern era, nationalism is, in Elie Kedourie words, 'a doctrine invented in Europe at the beginning of the nineteenth century'.⁴ Nationalism is distinct from national consciousness, however, as John Breuilly argues. Where the former is a political movement, harnessing national feeling with 'the objective of obtaining and using state power', the latter is a means through which members of a race, territory, or language identify themselves as a group.⁵ A strong sense of national identity is prerequisite to nationalism: it is not synonymous with it. Nevertheless, there is a tendency amongst many historians of the modern era to regard the development of nationhood as a nineteenth- and twentieth-century phenomenon.⁶ Even the 'primordialist' Anthony D. Smith, who seeks to recover continuities between the modern and pre-modern periods, lapses into modernist assumptions. When he writes, for instance, that 'the "past" that is to serve modern purposes must not only be "full", it must be well preserved—or it must be "reconstructed" ', 'modern' serves as synonym for 'national'.⁷ Yet that need for, or reconstruction of, 'national' history is not restricted to the modern age. The desire to

³ Patrick Collinson, *The Birthpangs of Protestant England: Religious and Cultural Change in the Sixteenth and Seventeenth Centuries* (Basingstoke: Macmillan, 1988), 1.

⁴ Elie Kedourie, *Nationalism* (London: Hutchinson, 1960), 9. Cf., amongst others, Aira Kemilainen, *Nationalism: Problems concerning the Word, the Concept, the Classification* (Jyväskylä: Jyväskylän Kasvatusopillinen Korkeakoulu, 1964); Hans Kohn, *Nationalism, its Meaning and History* (Princeton: Princeton University Press, 1955); Eric Hobsbawm, *Nations and Nationalism since 1780: Programme, Myth, Reality* (Cambridge: Cambridge University Press, 1990).

⁵ John Breuilly, *Nationalism and the State*, 2nd edn. (Manchester: Manchester University Press, 1993), 3–4.

⁶ For a useful brief overview of this phenomenon, see Colin Kidd, *British Identities before Nationalism: Ethnicity and Nationhood in the Atlantic World, 1600–1800* (Cambridge: Cambridge University Press, 1999), 1–5.

⁷ Anthony D. Smith, *The Ethnic Origins of Nations* (Oxford: Blackwell, 1986), 178. For the term 'primordialist', see Kidd, *British Identities*.

refashion the past—particularly pressing at moments of change—can be seen, for example, in Shakespeare's English histories, written when England was both expanding its territories abroad and faced the end of the Tudor dynasty at home. Similarly, *King Lear* revisits early British 'history' at a time when the English were required to confront notions of Britishness in the years immediately after the accession of the Scottish James Stuart to the English throne.

Investment in national language, recurrently distinguished as a key characteristic of the 'national' project, is often similarly and erroneously viewed as the sole preserve of modernity. For Benedict Anderson, 'the "choice" of language' before the nineteenth century 'appears as a gradual, unselfconscious, pragmatic, not to say haphazard development', and 'there was no idea of systematically imposing language on the dynasts' various subject populations'.[8] His assessment of the uniqueness of post eighteenth-century attitudes to language overlooks the undeniable linguistic colonialism practised in areas such as Tudor Wales and planned for Ireland by writers such as Spenser.[9] In the process, Anderson also defines all national linguistic programmes as imperialist. Within Anderson's scheme, there is no recognition of language standardization as a means to national unification: it becomes a way of imposing an alien identity on a conquered territory, rather than a strategy that can also be used to enhance a sense of identity amongst a group that already sees itself as a national community.

That areas such as sixteenth-century England are deemed to lack 'national consciousness' is partly due to a misreading of early modern political processes. Craig Calhoun has defined ten 'features of the rhetoric of nation'. Few would dispute that, of these, Tudor England possessed at least seven: namely, (1) 'boundaries, of territory, population, or both'; (2) 'the notion that the nation is an integral unit' (the 'hole realm' that recurs throughout sixteenth-century legislation); (3) sovereignty, or 'aspiration to sovereignty'; (4) a common 'culture' (including 'language, shared beliefs and values, habitual practices'); (5) 'a notion of the nation [. . .] existing

---

[8] Benedict Anderson, *Imagined Communities: Reflections on the Origin and Spread of Nationalism*, rev. edn. (London: Verso, 1991), 42. Cf. Smith, *Ethnic Origins*, 133.
[9] Edmund Spenser, *A View of the State of Ireland*, ed. Andrew Hadfield and Willy Maley (Oxford: Blackwell, 1997).

through time, [. . .] and having a history'; (6) 'common descent';
and (7), 'historical or even sacred relations to a certain territory'.[10]
All these constituents are present in sixteenth-century writings
about the nation, as can be illustrated by John of Gaunt's 'This
England' speech in Shakespeare's *Richard II* (*c.*1595). Here Gaunt
celebrates England in a periphrastic list that grants sovereignty to
the land itself as 'this sceptered isle' and eulogizes its protective
isolation and territorial boundaries, describing the nation as a
'fortress built by nature for herself' and 'this precious stone set in
the silver sea'.[11] As Gaunt asserts a common descent, he aligns 'this
happy breed of men' (45) with 'this blessèd plot' (50). Land and
people are thus yoked together within a sequence that celebrates
England as 'this other Eden, demi-paradise' (42) and captures—in
Calhoun's terms—the 'sacred relations' of the English people 'to a
certain territory'. Calhoun's sense of the past, and of the nation
existing through history, is conjured by Gaunt's appeal to lineage,
with England appearing as a 'teeming womb of royal kings' (51),
whilst the work itself, as an English history play, further demonstrates the existence of Calhoun's 'shared culture', as at least part
of its audience appeal is based on the exposition of a common
heritage.

   Less established in current historiography are claims that the
early modern period is characterized by 'popular participation in
collective affairs' and 'the idea that government is just only when
[. . .] it serves the interests of "the people" or "the nation" ' (two
further features of Calhoun's 'rhetoric of nation'). Whilst it is only
a 'preponderance' of these rhetorical features that, under
Calhoun's scheme, identifies a nation, it is worth examining Tudor
England's claims to popular legitimacy and participation, not least
because of the importance of an enfranchised, politicized populace
to the arguments of historians such as Anderson, for whom
national consciousness only occurs with the destruction of 'the

----

[10] Craig Calhoun, *Nationalism* (Buckingham: Open University Press, 1997), 4–5.
The 'features' listed here are numbered 1–3, 7–10 in Calhoun's order. The fourth,
fifth, and sixth 'features' are (respectively): 'the idea that government is just only
when supported by popular will or at least when it serves the interests of "the
people" or "the nation" '; 'popular participation in collective affairs [. . .] (whether
for war or civic activities)'; and 'direct membership, in which each individual is
understood to be immediately a part of the nation'.
[11] William Shakespeare, *Richard II*, in Gary Taylor and Stanley Wells (eds.), *The
Oxford Shakespeare* (Oxford: Clarendon Press, 1986), ii. i. 43, 46.

divinely-ordained, hierarchical dynastic realm'.[12] Anderson's is a
very 'presentist' perspective, where political participation is
equated with late Western democracy and the right to vote. It also
transforms early modern monarchies into rather more monolithic
polities than they actually were. The inhabitants of early modern
monarchies were not passive subjects. Social historians in particular have shown the geographical range and social depth of political
participation and the forceful articulation of legally based rights.[13]
Indeed, the English system of incorporated towns and boroughs
seemed sufficiently familiar to one sixteenth-century Venetian (an
inhabitant of one of early modern Europe's most famous republics)
to induce the comment in 1557 that, 'in matters of justice', England
was not, 'like other kingdoms and Christian provinces, governed
by civil and imperial laws, but by municipalities, almost like a
republic' ('nelle cose di giustizia non è, come gli altri regni e provin-
cie cristiane, governato da leggi civili ed imperiali, ma da muncipali
quasi come repubblica').[14]

There was also an enduring belief in this period that just
monarchs did not rule alone and for themselves: they had a duty to
take counsel from the honest and experienced, an advisory role
that is recurrently justified 'in terms of public service and love of
country'.[15] As can be seen from texts such as John Bale's *King
Johan* (c.1537), or Bernadino Ochino's *Tragoedie [...] of the
vniuste vsurped primacie of the Bishop of Rome*, translated by
John Ponet in 1549, monarchs were also regarded as being obliged
to protect their people and country and to rule for the common
good. This is a far more reciprocal relationship between king and
country than that perceived by Anderson. In its logical extreme,

[12] Anderson, *Imagined Communities*, 7.
[13] Phil Withington, 'Citizens, Community and Political Culture', *Historical Journal*, 44 (2001), 239–67; Andy Wood, *The Politics of Social Conflict: The Peak Country, 1570–1770* (Cambridge: Cambridge University Press, 1999). Cf. Patrick Collinson, '*De Republica Anglorum*: or History with the Politics Put Back', in Collinson, *Elizabethan Essays* (London: Hambledon Press, 1994), 1–30, at 11–27.
[14] Giovanni Micheli, *Relazione d'Inghilterra*, in Eugenio Alberi (ed.), *Relazioni degli ambasciatori veneti al Senato*, serie 1, vol. ii (Florence, 1840), 291–380, at 315. Cf. Polydore Vergil, *Polydore Vergil's English History, from an early translation*, ed. Henry Ellis (London: Camden Society, 1846), 13.
[15] Richard Rex, 'The Role of English Humanists in the Reformation up to 1559', in N. Scott Amos, Andrew Pettegree, and Henk van Niewp (eds.), *The Education of a Christian Society: Humanism and the Reformation in Britain and the Netherlands* (Aldershot: Ashgate, 1999), 19–40, at 35.

this belief in the primacy of the 'commonweal' legitimated theories
of rightful resistance propounded by Ponet (amongst others) in the
1550s.[16] Anderson's top-down model thus diminishes the complex
and proactive identity of sixteenth-century citizen-subjects. Nor
did the presence of a monarch on the throne necessarily deaden a
concept of national community. Indeed, it could even become a
focus for it, as Hugh Seton-Watson comments in regard to
sixteenth-century France and England, where 'there was a much
stronger and wider sense of community [than elsewhere in Europe].
Englishmen and Frenchmen recognised themselves as such;
accepted obligations to the sovereign; and admitted the claim of the
sovereign on their loyalty at least in part because the sovereign
symbolised the country as a whole'.[17] In negative cases, the desire
to remove the monarch for 'the commonweal' also heightens
national consciousness, as potential regicides justify their actions
by appealing to the interests of the wider, national body, whose
rights transcend those of the monarch.[18]

   Despite his modernist assumptions, Anderson's much cited definition of the 'nation' nevertheless holds true for sixteenth-century
England. In Anderson's terms, a nation is 'an imagined political
community', '*imagined* because the members of even the smallest
nation will never know most of their fellow-members [. . .] yet in
the minds of each lives the image of their communion'; '*limited*'
because 'no nation imagines itself coterminous with mankind'.[19]
Anderson's definition, which draws on Seton-Watson's opinion
that 'a nation exists when a significant number of people in a
community consider themselves to form a nation', focuses attention on the importance of boundaries: it is crucial for a sense of
nationhood that members of a nation know where theirs begins,
and another ends.[20] The inhabitants of Tudor England belonged to
such an entity. They possessed a shared history, which they could
read, for example, in 'the comyn Chronycles of Englande' printed

---

[16] John Ponet, *A shorte treatise of politicke power* (Strasburg, 1556).
[17] Hugh Seton-Watson, *Nations and States: An Enquiry into the Origins of
Nations and the Politics of Nationalism* (London: Methuen, 1977), 8.
[18] J. W. Allen, *A History of Political Thought in the Sixteenth Century* (London:
Methuen, 1928), part II, ch. 2; Quentin Skinner, *The Foundations of Modern
Political Thought*, 2 vols. (Cambridge: Cambridge University Press, 1978), ii. 77–81
and passim.
[19] Anderson, *Imagined Communities*, 6–7.
[20] Seton-Watson, *Nations and States*, 5.

by William Caxton in 1498; they regarded England as an economic unit, collectively enriched or denuded, as can be seen at least as early as 1436 in the *Libel of English Policy*; and there were—as we shall see in Chapters 2, 4, and 6—concerted efforts to create a national language and national canon. Further to that, the English were conscious of common customs that distinguished them from other nations. Indeed, by the 1540s these national 'characteristics' were sufficiently established to warrant their depiction in graphic form in Andrew Borde's *Fyrst Boke of the Introduction to Knowledge* (discussed in Chapter 1).

My study of English identities begins in the 1530s. This is not to say there was no conception of national identity before the sixteenth century. Such a theory is disproved by the work of historians such as John Gillingham and Francis-Xavier Martin on English colonialism in medieval Ireland, or by the poetry of John Skelton (?1460–1529), with its loud celebrations of his self-awarded laureateship for English poetry and vituperative poems against the Scots.[21] Nevertheless, the period 1530–80 was a crucial time for forming the image of England found in texts such as *Richard II*, where it appears as an island nation, held in privileged and sovereign isolation. These decades witnessed a 'Tudor revolution' that stretched beyond the administrative centralization identified by Geoffrey Elton, or the extension of taxation and governance outlined by Michael Braddick.[22] Besides the development of the 'state' during these years, England consolidated its power over Wales, assimilated into England by the second Act of Union in 1543; emerged as a naval power; enjoyed a net increase in foreign trade; and saw the rise of its vernacular as a national

---

[21] John Gillingham, 'The English Invasion of Ireland', in Brendan Bradshaw, Andrew Hadfield, and Willy Maley (eds.), *Representing Ireland: Literature and the Origins of Conflict, 1534–1660* (Cambridge: Cambridge University Press, 1993), 26–42; Gillingham, 'Images of Ireland, 1170–1600: The Origins of English Imperialism', *History Today*, 37 (1987), 16–22; Francis-Xavier Martin, 'The Image of the Irish—Medieval and Modern—Continuity and Change', in Richard Wall (ed.), *Medieval and Modern Ireland* (Gerrards Cross: Smythe, 1988), 1–18; John Skelton, *The Complete English Poems*, ed. John Scattergood (Harmondsworth; Penguin, 1983); Andrew Hadfield, *Literature, Politics and National Identity* (Cambridge: Cambridge University Press, 1994), ch. 1.

[22] Geoffrey Elton, *The Tudor Revolution in Government: Administrative Changes in the Reign of Henry VIII* (Cambridge: Cambridge University Press, 1953); Michael J. Braddick, *State Formation in Early Modern England, c.1550–1700* (Cambridge: Cambridge University Press, 2000).

language of literature and learning.[23] Through the break with the Roman Church, England also detached itself (or was detached) from Continental Europe, a process of separation compounded by the loss of Calais, its last French territory, in 1558.

Of all these processes, the split from Rome, effected by a series of parliamentary acts between 1533 and 1536, had arguably the greatest influence on the construction of English national identity. Besides its impact on political and religious culture, it also acted as a spur to other facets of nation-building, not least investment in sea fare and the vulgar tongue: the former necessary to defend a realm now at odds with the Holy Roman Empire; the latter given extra impetus by worship in the vernacular (rather than Latin, as under the Roman Church), the publication of an authorized English Bible in 1539, and—under Edward VI—the dissemination of the Book of Common Prayer and Book of Homilies. Unification with Wales was similarly a direct result of, or at least accelerated by, the break with Rome: Parliament was needed to legitimize the renunciation of the Roman Church; if the Henrician Reformation was to be enforced in Wales, as it must, then Wales had to be brought under the jurisdiction of the English parliament which had endorsed the royal supremacy.[24]

The statutes that severed England from Rome were published from 1533 onwards by the king's printer, Thomas Berthelet. Collectively, they propagate a potent vocabulary of imperial sovereignty, focusing on the kingdom as an entity bound together by law and history. A key part of these proceedings was the Act in Restraint of Appeals in 1533. Its opening declaration, that 'by divers sundry old authentic histories and chronicles it is manifestly declared and expressed that this realm of England is an empire', highlights three factors that characterize the national identity of Tudor England.[25] First, it reveals the role of 'history', the longevity

[23] Elaine W. Fowler, *English Sea Power in the Early Tudor Period, 1485–1558* (Ithaca, NY: Cornell University Press, 1965); Craig Muldrew, *The Economy of Obligation: The Culture of Credit and Social Relations in Early Modern England* (Basingstoke: Macmillan, 1998); Richard Foster Jones, *The Triumph of English: A Survey of Opinions concerning the Vernacular from the Introduction of Printing to the Restoration* (Stanford, Calif.: Stanford University Press, 1953).

[24] Philip Edwards, *The Making of the Modern English State, 1460–1660* (Basingstoke: Palgrave, 2001), 121.

[25] G. R. Elton (ed.), *The Tudor Constitution: Documents and Commentary*, 2nd edn. (Cambridge: Cambridge University Press, 1982), 353.

of which is synonymous with, and a guarantee of, its authenticity. Secondly, the pronouncement demonstrates the importance of definable limits: the jurisdictional boundaries of 'empire' (in its pre-modern sense of 'supreme political dominion') within which the sovereign could rule without foreign interference.[26] The jurisdictional power of the monarch is thus drawn from, distinguished, and protected by the 'limits' of the realm, boundaries that do not restrict, but prescribe and defend English law and customs. Further to that, the act asserts the supremacy of indigenous common and statute law over canon law.

The effect of Reformation on the nation as a whole was undeniably gradual and piecemeal, and 'Reformation' England is, of course, a different entity from 'Protestant' England, the birth of which Collinson dates 'some considerable time' 'after the accession of Elizabeth I'.[27] It is not until 1547 that we can even talk of 'English Protestants': the word *Protestant* originally referred to Lutherans (*OED* 1), and whilst Henry VIII had renounced the Church of Rome, his English church did not accept the doctrines of the man who had previously been attacked in print in Henry's name.[28] It is not until the Edwardian period that Protestant doctrines began to be instituted in the English church, and it took the reign of Mary and her Spanish husband Philip to crystallize an association between Englishness and Protestantism, Catholicism and foreignness. This connection between Protestantism and national identity was further strengthened in 1570 by Pius V's bull, *Regnans in excelsis*, excommunicating Elizabeth and denying her claim to the throne.[29]

It is nonetheless evident that the effects of the Reformation were more immediate than those described in Collinson's nationwide narrative tracing the emergence of England as a Protestant country. As revisionists such as Richard Rex and Greg Walker have shown, the history of the English Reformation is not merely a Protestant

---

[26] *OED* 1. Cf. *OED* 7: 'a country of which the sovereign owes no allegiance to any foreign superior'. The *OED* cites Act in the Restraint of Appeals as the first usage of sense 7.

[27] Eamon Duffy, *The Stripping of the Altars: Traditional Religion in England, c.1400–c.1580* (New Haven: Yale University Press, 1992); Collinson, *Birthpangs*, p. ix.

[28] Henry VIII, *Adsertio VII. Sacram. adv. Luth.* (1521).

[29] David Loades, 'The Origins of English Protestant Nationalism', in Loades, *Politics, Censorship and the English Reformation* (London: Pinter, 1991), 39–55.

story.[30] It can be traced from the 1530s onwards in the multitude of texts that react to, resist, or accommodate religious and cultural changes already under way. My use of 'Reformation England' or 'English Reformation', therefore, does not discount Christopher Haigh's enlightening work, which has done much to remind us that the Reformation in England is a process, not an event, and that the Henrician Reformation was very different from its Edwardian or Elizabethan counterparts.[31] My choice of phrase simply takes it as given that one of the defining characteristics of the English Reformation was its fitful, ad hoc nature. Despite this, the Reformation gave those who were committed to it a vital resource and impetus for shaping their national identity: the belief that England was especially blessed by God. This rhetoric appears strikingly early in the history of Protestant England. It is found, for example, in 1549, in the prayers of Thomas Smith, a man deemed by contemporaries 'neutrall' in religion.[32] As Smith writes, 'this Realme, o Lord, shuld be and is a chosen Realme to thee, to which thou haest vouchsaved to give the true knowledge of thi veritie and gospel, first by the late King of most famous memorie, Henrie the Eight, and now more amply by his most swete sonne'.[33] England might not yet be seen as the one elect nation, but it is certainly viewed as a recipient of particular favour, and Smith's words make a connection between that favour, the break with Rome, and the arrival of the 'true' religion.

While literary critics acknowledge the political significance of the Henrician era, all too often they deny any literary impact until the late Elizabethan period. The neglect of pre-Elizabethan writing owes much to the hold of orthodox aestheticism, which finds little of any worth in early Tudor literature, and still less in that of the

---

[30] Rex, 'Role of English Humanists', and Greg Walker, 'Dialogue, Resistance and Accommodation: Conservative Literary Responses to the Henrician Reformation', in Amos et al (eds.), *Education of a Christian Society*, 89–104.

[31] Christopher Haigh, *English Reformations: Religion, Politics, and Society under the Tudors* (Oxford: Clarendon Press, 1993).

[32] Thomas Smith to the Duchess of Somerset, July/August 1549, BL Harleian 6989, 146ʳ; cited by Mary Dewar, *Sir Thomas Smith: A Tudor Intellectual in Office* (London: Athlone Press, 1964), 39.

[33] Thomas Smith, *Certaigne Psalmes or Songues of David translated into Englishe meter*, in *Sir Thomas Smith, Literary and Linguistic Works*, i, ed. Bror Danielsson, *Stockholm Studies in English*, 12 (Stockholm: Almqvist and Wiksell, 1963), 33.

reigns of Edward and Mary. At best, Thomas Wyatt, and to a lesser extent Henry Howard, Earl of Surrey, are seen as anomalous bright spots; Skelton as a curiosity. Despite the important work of critics such as Andrew Hadfield and John N. King, the spectre of C. S. Lewis's categorization of the mid-sixteenth century as 'a drab age' still looms large.[34] Lewis insists that the label is not intended to be a 'dyslogistic term'.[35] Nevertheless, by contrasting what he represents as 'an earnest, heavy-handed, commonplace age' against 'the last quarter of the century' when 'the unpredictable happens' and 'with startling suddenness we ascend' (1), and by his anachronistic reaction to, and rare enthusiasm for, a snippet of Henrician verse as 'an Elizabethan moment' (226), his work helps perpetuate the continued neglect of the period in favour of his 'golden' age of the 1580s and 1590s (318). New Historicists, for all their desire to challenge canonicity and read 'literary' and 'non-literary' texts alongside each other, have—for the most part—accepted the aesthetic paradigms epitomized by Lewis. By perpetuating the neglect of the earlier decades of the sixteenth century, influential, and otherwise admirable, monographs such as Richard Helgerson's *Forms of Nationhood* or Claire McEachern's *Poetics of English Nationhood* consequently risk creating the impression that pre-Elizabethan writing is of little scholarly interest: as McEachern unguardedly writes in her preface, 'no one would read' a book about a pre-Elizabethan like Bale.[36] Further to that, through omission, they also imply that processes such as the emergence of nationhood are solely Elizabethan phenomena.

One immediate problem facing the reader of much mid-sixteenth-century work is its apparent lack of what we would now call 'literariness' or 'fictionality'. Alistair Fox discerns a 'retreat from fictive literature' from the late 1520s, the years leading up to the break with Rome, a time when 'the energies of humanist writers were almost completely diverted away from imaginative writing

---

[34] Hadfield, *Literature, Politics and National Identity*; John N. King, *English Reformation Literature: The Tudor Origins of the Protestant Tradition* (Princeton: Princeton University Press, 1982).

[35] C. S. Lewis, *English Literature in the Sixteenth Century, excluding Drama* (Oxford: Clarendon Press, 1954), 64.

[36] Richard Helgerson, *Forms of Nationhood: The Elizabethan Writing of England* (Chicago: University of Chicago Press, 1992); Claire McEachern, *The Poetics of English Nationhood, 1590–1612* (Cambridge: Cambridge University Press, 1996), 1.

to the compilation of moral, pedagogical, political, medical, and
pietistic treatises and translations'.[37] His term 'fictive', though,
inscribes its own elusiveness: its suffix (*-ive*) suggests 'tending to', a
state not yet fully accomplished (*OED*). In the case of early modern
studies, such flexibility is an essential critical tool. There was no
concept of 'literature' in the period: we can see Sidney groping
towards some such understanding in his *Apology for Poetry* in the
1580s as he talks about verse as 'an ornament and no cause to
Poetry' and the 'many most excellent poets that never versified'.[38]
Such 'poetry', moreover, can be found in history and philosophy,
genres we would now broadly categorize as 'factual', even by our
sceptical, postmodern parameters. The limits of what constitutes
'literature', the product of Fox's 'fictive powers', are not fully
established in the sixteenth century: when reading the works of
that period, we should consequently be receptive to the inventive-
ness, subtexts, and even playfulness of seemingly 'factual' or
prosaic genres.

   Fox's own hesitation in pursuing a Protean literary beast into
writing after 1535 is surprising, considering the sensitively adapt-
able boundaries that he has hitherto recognized, finding and
substantiating flashes of 'fictive talent' in such superficially
improbable sources as Edward Hall's chronicles and Simon Fish's
Supplycayon for Beggars. 'Imaginative writing' is not deadened,
however, as Fox suggests, by the demands of religious and political
controversy on English pens. These later writers pour their 'fictive
energies' into the very treatises and translations Fox posits as the
cause of the demise. The pages of medical handbooks—regarded by
Fox as symptomatic of a retreat from fictive writing—can suddenly
veer into vivid portrayals of Italianate debauchery prefiguring
Elizabethan and Jacobean caricatures, as in the case of Andrew
Borde (Chapter 1). The selection of a particular text for translation,
with its necessary adaptation, accompanying apparatus of dedicatory letters and prefatory matter, can constitute a conscious,
crafted, and 'fictive' act, as seen in the writings of William Thomas
(Chapter 3). Purportedly pedagogical manuals, such as those of

---

[37] Alistair Fox, *Politics and Literature in the Reigns of Henry VII and Henry VIII*
(Oxford: Blackwell, 1989), 207, 126.
[38] Philip Sidney, *An Apology for Poetry*, ed. Geoffrey Shepherd (Manchester:
Manchester University Press, 1973), 103.

Introduction

Thomas Wilson (Chapter 5), are no less riven by doubts and signallings of their authors' scepticism than the Lucianic writings that Fox finds characteristic of earlier Tudor humanism. The period, then, did not witness a decline, as Fox argues, in 'creative' humanism. Rather, the movement changed direction, as internationalists such as More and Erasmus, for whom learning transcended territorial boundaries, were replaced by new generations of writers who used their humanist education to nurture national pride.

Despite the apparent introspection of English letters during this period, however, Elton's statement that, after 1536, England 'retreated within its own borders' is not strictly correct.[39] Even as later English humanists, such as Wilson, Smith, or John Cheke, used their learning for national ends, it was classical and Continental culture that provided the means and inspiration. They asserted the worth of the vernacular, and invested and published in it, but Latin continued to dominate their mindset, both as a model and a medium. Latin might be tainted by its association with the Roman Church, but it was still the language of Cicero, which Tudor schoolboys were brought up to revere and emulate. The sixteenth century is now regarded as the age of vernacularization, but as Françoise Wacqueath points out, throughout that century, knowledge of and ability in Latin increased in England as well as elsewhere in Europe.[40] Smith (the subject of Chapter 4) consequently published two Latin treatises—*De recta et emendata linguae anglicae scriptione, dialogus* and *De recta et emendata linguae graecae pronuntiatione*—in 1568 and much of his personal correspondence to other Englishmen, such as William Cecil, is in Latin; Wilson, although he chose to publish exclusively in English (bar one early work), continued to write letters in Latin and based his English *Arte of Rhetorique* (covered in Chapter 5) on Cicero and Quintilian.

Just as Latin retained its influence, so too did the Continent. English writers might continually celebrate their 'island' status (a

---

[39] G. R. Elton, *Reform and Reformation: England, 1509–1558* (London: Edward Arnold, 1977), 179.

[40] Françoise Wacqueath, *Latin, or the Empire of a Sign from the Sixteenth to the Twentieth Centuries*, trans. John Howe (London: Verso, 2001), 125. Cf. James W. Binns, *Intellectual Culture in Elizabethan and Jacobean England: The Latin Writing of the Age* (Leeds: Francis Cairns, 1990), 297–306.

geographical falsification which shows the age-old English tendency to appropriate Scotland). Nevertheless, Englishness was not constructed in isolation from the rest of Europe. Not only was it fashioned in distinction from its European counterparts, it also aped them, consciously following Italy's lead, for example, in using and 'improving' the vulgar tongue (see Chapter 3). Indeed, the very process of self-reflection and self-improvement in which the English were involved in the sixteenth century can be seen to spring from concern about what other nations thought, and their awareness of their stigmatization as 'beasts', to quote the sculptor Benvenuto Cellini, who refused Henry VIII's invitation to work in England on the grounds that he could not bear to live among such people.[41] To counter such insults, educated Englishmen tended to choose one of two paths: to out-Latin the practitioners of classical humanism and prove their compatriots' competence in Latin and Greek, or to champion the capabilities of their native tongue and prove that it could produce proficient examples of humanist genres, such as the dialogue or familiar letter. Neither option— writing in Latin, or showing how English can emulate Latin— shakes off the influence of the classics or the Continent, where Italy in particular set the pattern for improving the vernacular tongue.

Although religion, culture, and politics are difficult to segregate fully in this period, it is important to remember that the motivation behind, and impact of, the break with Rome was not purely doctrinal.[42] This book consequently moves away from the explicitly religious territory previously explored in John N. King's extensive study of Protestant literature and David Norbrook's examination of evangelical writing in his chapter on Edwardian poetry.[43] Just as Protestantism had an international side that did not equate Protestantism with Englishness, so too Tudor images of Englishness developed along contours other than those of evangelical Protestantism. As English anxieties about their 'barbarous'

---

[41] Cited by Neville Williams, 'The Tudors: Three Contrasts in Personality', in A. G. Dickens (ed.), *The Courts of Europe: Politics, Patronage and Royalty, 1400–1800* (London: Thames & Hudson, 1977), 147–67, at 155.

[42] Peter Lake and Maria Dowling (eds.), *Protestantism and the National Church in Sixteenth-Century England* (London: Croom Helm, 1987).

[43] King, *English Reformation Literature*; David Norbrook, *Poetry and Politics in the English Renaissance* (London: Routledge & Kegan Paul, 1984), ch. 2.

reputation show, areas such as language and the literary canon proved crucial to the construction of English identity in this period. This is not to negate the impact or importance of reformed religion on Tudor constructions of the nation. The following chapters echo with motifs of papal corruption and attacks on religious idolatry and superstition, and—by the 1570s—we can see an explicit link for committed Protestants between their religion and version of Englishness. Indeed, historical, literary, or linguistic issues are often consequent to, or intertwined with, religious turmoil. For example, the investment in the English tongue was, in part, a reaction against Latin, the language of the Roman Church, and a necessary step in achieving Protestant, text-based worship, comprehensible to the whole congregation, learned and unlearned alike. Nevertheless, the rise of the vernacular has secular manifestations as a language of literature and government, uniting a nation of language-users and differentiating them from Continental Europe. In Hadfield's words, 'the break-up of the Latinate culture of the late Middle Ages' is linked 'to the development of national language which should become expressions of a territorial integrity'.[44]

Twentieth-century linguists have repeatedly linked language standardization to the administrative needs of emergent empires, and Tudor governments were certainly alert to the crucial role played by language when attempting to impose an English identity on their Celtic fringes.[45] The early modern perception of Roman history gave precedent to the premise, since, as Paula Blank explains, 'the dominion of Latin [. . .] was widely envisioned [. . .] not only as a historical consequence of the Roman conquest of England and the continent, but as a means by which that conquest was achieved'.[46] Legislation for Ireland in 1537 consequently forbade diversity of language, dress, and manners (albeit unsuccessfully);[47] the Acts of Union for Wales in 1536 and 1543 were accompanied by regulations enforcing the use of English in the law

[44] Hadfield, *Literature, Politics and National Identity*, 9.
[45] See Dieter Stein, 'Sorting out the Variants: Standardization and Social Factors in the English Language, 1600–1800', in Dieter Stein and Ingrid Tieken-Boon von Ostade (eds.), *Towards a Standard English, 1600–1800* (Berlin: Mouton de Gruyter, 1994), 1–17.
[46] Paula Blank, *Broken English: Dialects and the Politics of Language in Renaissance Writings* (London: Routledge, 1996), 126.
[47] PRO State Papers, 27 Henry VIII c. 63.

courts.[48] Access to the law thus depended on access to the English
language, and arguably one of the major reasons for the acquies-
cence of most Welsh elites to the union was the advantage of
English laws of inheritance, which—operating by primogeniture—
allowed estates to be bequeathed in their entirety, where the Welsh
system of gavelkind divided property equally between male heirs,
to the eventual impoverishment of the estate.[49]

The link between language and identity goes deeper than administrative convenience, however. Language was also seen to express,
and even shape, national character. As Smith wrote in the early
1560s, 'the Dutchman and the Dane and all suche countries as
draweth in language and condition towards them [share] the great
loue which they haue to drink'.[50] Language and behaviour go hand
in hand. The Welshman William Salesbury tapped in to this
rhetoric in 1547, when, in the response to the second Act of Union,
he published his English–Welsh dictionary, 'moche necessary to all
suche Welshemen as wil spedly learne the englyshe tongue'.[51]
Dedicated to Henry VIII as a means of consolidating the union, it
clothes opportunism in rhetoric that subscribes to the unifying
properties of language. 'The communion of one tonge' offers 'a
bonde and knotte of loue and frendshyppe', resolving the 'great
hatred[,] debate & stryffe' caused by the current 'dyuersitie of
language' (A1ᵛ–A2ʳ). Salesbury's prospective readers are both individual, biological bodies with tongues and hearts, and metaphorical limbs ('membres') of a larger national body. It is by using their
actual tongues (to express hearts that 'agree in loue and obedience
to your grace') that they will become one figurative body, with the
monarch at its head. The drive towards unity works on an oral as
well as a semantic level, with the dictionary 'prefixed [by] a litle
treatyse of the englyshe pronunciacion of the letters' (A1ʳ). The

[48] Cited by R. Brinley Jones, *The Old British Tongue: The Vernacular in Wales,
1540–1640* (Cardiff: Avalon, 1970), 33.
[49] See Glanmor Williams, *Welsh Reformation Essays* (Cardiff: University of
Wales Press, 1967).
[50] Thomas Smith, *A Communicacion or Discourse of the Queenes highnes
mariage* (c.1561), BL Add. 48, 047, 123ʳ.
[51] William Salesbury, *A Dictionary in Englyshe & Welshe moche necessary to all
suche Welshemen as wil spedly learne the englyshe tongue thought vnto the kynges
maiestie very mete to be sette forthe to the vse of his graces subiectes in Wales:
wherevnto is prefixed a litel treatyse of the englyshe pronunciation of the letters*
(1547), A1ʳ.

Welsh were not only to be taught how to speak English, but to speak English like the English, knitting them into a seamless community of undifferentiated speakers. Language is not solely a means of defining a nation: it is a means of creating one, overriding issues of blood or longstanding alliances by its ability, practically and rhetorically, to gather potentially disparate groups into one cohesive national community, using and understanding one tongue. There was a further issue surrounding English as a national language in the sixteenth century, however. Although it had been used as a language of government since the reign of Richard II, it was still seen as inferior to Latin (and, for that matter, less polished than French and, above all, Italian). English had to act as one language for one people. Beyond that, it had to be a language of which its users could feel proud, and sixteenth-century writers, as we shall see, were dogged by insecurity about the status of their vernacular.

Just as the English language came under scrutiny during the sixteenth century, so too did its history. The renewed emphasis placed on history in the wake of the break with Rome—like the investment in English—is poised between religious and secular demands. Despite its authoritative appeal to 'divers sundry old authentic histories and chronicles', the declaration on which the Act in Restraint of Appeals depended ('that this realm of England is an empire') was historically unfounded. England needed a remodelled history to bolster its protestations of ancient autonomy from the Roman Church and to strip that church of its claims to spiritual leadership. History also offered Tudor authors the means of establishing a longstanding literary tradition. The cultural power of history, and of literary history in particular, is well documented. Ernest Renan is just one among many to deem 'a heroic past, great men, glory' 'the social capital upon which one bases a national idea'.[52] As Arthur Quiller-Couch told a lecture hall in Cambridge in 1916:

Few in this room are old enough to remember the shock of awed surprise which fell upon young minds presented, in the late 'seventies and early 'eighties of the last century, with Freeman's *Norman Conquest* or Green's *Short History of the English People*; in which as through parting clouds of

---

[52] Ernest Renan, 'What is a Nation?', trans. Martin Thom, in Homi K. Bhabha (ed.), *Nation and Narration* (London: Routledge, 1990), 8–22, at 19.

darkness, we beheld our ancestry, literary as well as political, radiantly legitimised.[53]

His words illustrate the 'legitimating' force of a past packed with literary achievement. His idiom, moreover, is that of the sixteenth-century bibliophiles, John Bale and John Leland, for whom (as will be seen in Chapter 2) the literary past was a potent national artefact waiting to 'be brought from darknesse to a lyuely lyght'.[54] The bibliographical endeavours of Bale and Leland were thus given impetus by the need to establish a glorious past on which to found the English nation, which was being fashioned as not only as a country *re*liberated from the tyranny of Rome to enjoy its ancient laws and customs, but also as a nation with a venerable literary tradition.

In the words of Colin Kidd, however, early modern England 'fits neatly into neither of the main categories of classification identified by political scientists, being neither indisputably ethnic nor exclusively civic-territorial'.[55] Talking about the past in relation to sixteenth-century England subsequently raises the question of what, or whose, past. For writers such as Caxton and Bale, 'England' and 'Britain' were interchangeable: Caxton offers a 'descrypcyon of this londe whiche of olde tyme was named Albyon And after Brytayne And now is called Englonde'; Bale elides 'oure Englyshe or Bryttyshe nacyon'.[56] Theirs is a 'thoroughly Anglocentric idea of Britain', a lingering tendency later highlighted in the decades either side of the accession of James VI of Scotland to the English throne, when 'whereas the endeavour to be both Scots and Britons was a genuine challenge north of the border, in the south the idea of being both English and British was simply tautological'.[57] These flexible labels consequently allow writers like Bale and Caxton to enrich their store of Renan's 'great men' and 'glory' in a period when 'the co-opting of British history

[53] Cited by Brian Doyle, *English and Englishness* (London: Routledge, 1989), 21.

[54] John Leland, 'A newe yeares gyfte', in John Bale, *The laboryouse Iourney & serche of Iohan Leylande for Englandes Antiquitees* (1549), B8^r.

[55] Kidd, *British Identities*, 75.

[56] William Caxton, *The descrypcyon of Englande [. . .] taken out of Polycronycon accordynge to the translacon of Treuisa* (1498), A1^r; Bale, *Laboryouse Iourney*, B3^v.

[57] Roger A. Mason (ed.), *Scots and Britons: Scottish Political Thought and the Union of 1603* (Cambridge: Cambridge University Press, 1994), 7, 13.

as English was almost *de rigeur*'.[58] The variety of ethnic identities available to Tudor writers also enabled a degree of selectivity: when an 'English', Anglo-Saxon past seemed undesirable, owing to its associations with paganism and pillage, affinity with Christian Britain could always be foregrounded instead. Generally, it is the invaders who are stigmatized: once settled, within generations they are seen to acquire rights of habitation. Thus sympathies lie with the Britons displaced by the Angles and Saxons, and with the Anglo-Saxons subjugated by the Danes and Normans.[59]

This book aims to fill a gap in the history of English writing, and the writing of England, by examining the rhetoric, motifs, and themes of nationhood in the work of seven authors active between 1540 and 1580, who were, or wanted to be, close to the circles of power: these are the medical writer and former Carthusian Andrew Borde; John Leland, the self-styled 'kinges antiquary'; William Thomas, clerk to the Privy Council under Edward VI; Thomas Smith, a leading Cambridge academic in the 1530s and 1540s, later secretary of state under Elizabeth I; Thomas Wilson, like Smith, an Elizabethan secretary of state; the poet Edmund Spenser; and the courtier Philip Sidney. All these writers—bar Spenser—spent time on the Continent, an experience that influenced the way in which they viewed their native country. As Bernadette Cunningham has written of Irish students in the late sixteenth century: 'living abroad', 'their sense of home was no longer focussed exclusively on a particular locality [. . .]; they developed a more abstract sense of [. . .] their homeland.'[60] The writers studied here might not be representative of the English 'everyman' in terms of their education, close acquaintance with Continental customs and ideas, and metropolitan outlook. Nevertheless, as Nicholas Tyacke has pointed out in his critique of Reformation historiography, the Tudor intelligentsia played a crucial role in the development of the

[58] Andrew Hadfield, 'Translating the Reformation', in Bradshaw et al (eds.), *Representing Ireland*, 43–59, at 48.

[59] John Leland, *Commentarii de Scriptoribus Britannicis*, ed. Anthony Hall, 2 vols. (Oxford, 1709); Stephen Gardiner, *A Discourse on the Coming of the English and Normans to Britain*, in Peter Samuel Donaldson (ed. and trans.), *A Machiavellian Treatise by Stephen Gardiner* (Cambridge: Cambridge University Press, 1975).

[60] Bernadette Cunningham, *The World of Geoffrey Keating: History, Myth and Religion in Seventeenth-Century Ireland* (Dublin: Four Courts Press, 2000), 105.

English Reformation.[61] This intellectual elite is all the more important because of the impact it was perceived to have by those involved in, or resistant to, processes of Reformation. As Bale comments, 'we had neuer good worlde (saye they) sens thys newe learnynge came in'.[62]

Humanism, or Bale's 'new learnynge', thus plays a key part in the story of the English Reformation and the formation of English identities during this period. It was humanistic education that gave the authors studied here (Borde apart) the tools with which to express, promote, interrogate, and define their own relationship with a national identity that was founded on questions of literature, history, language, topography, economics, law, and statecraft, no less than those of religion. In doing so, these authors reapplied their learning to national ends, a shift away from Morean or Erasmian humanism that also demonstrates the increasing secularization of learning during the sixteenth century.[63] More defended humanism by insisting on the Christian benefits of a humanist education.[64] In contrast, the learning of the authors examined here is employed (as Gilles advises Hythloday in Book I of *Utopia*) in service of the state. In particular, it is used to create and perpetuate a rhetoric of English nationhood that celebrates England's self-sufficiency. This vaunted independence is based on a perception of England as Gaunt's fertile island 'fortress', and is buttressed by a transfigured history authorizing English autonomy from the Roman Church.

The story this book traces is also one of 'self-fashioning'. This is not in Stephen Greenblatt's sense, which—with its interest in the struggle between the 'executive power of the will' and the social forces that mount a 'sustained and relentless assault' upon it— focuses on the creation and expression of personal identity.[65]

[61] Nicholas Tyacke, 'Introduction: Re-thinking the "English Reformation" ', in Nicholas Tyacke (ed.), *England's Long Reformation, 1500–1800* (London: UCL Press, 1998), 3.

[62] Bale, *Laboryouse Iourney*, A4r.

[63] Paul Oskar Kristeller, 'The Cultural Heritage of Humanism: An Overview', in Albert Rabil Jr. (ed.), *Renaissance Humanism: Foundations, Forms and Legacy*, 3 vols. (Philadelphia: University of Pennsylvania Press, 1988), iii. 515–28, at 525.

[64] Thomas More, 'Letter to Oxford University', ed. Daniel Kinney, *The Complete Works of St. Thomas More* (New Haven: Yale University Press, 1963), 15 vols., xv; cf. Kinney, introduction, xv, pp. xlvi–lxxi.

[65] Stephen Greenblatt, *Renaissance Self-Fashioning: More to Shakespeare* (Chicago: University of Chicago Press, 1980), 1.

Rather, it is the self-fashioning—what Joseph Loewenstein redescribes as 'self-composition'—explored by Lisa Jardine in *Erasmus, Man of Letters*, where publication is used to mould an authorial identity.[66] Where Jardine and Loewenstein concentrate on print, however, this book follows Harold Love's lead in viewing manuscript as a publishing medium that continued alongside print and which was therefore used by authors for self-construction no less than the newer technology of the printing press.[67] As these sixteenth-century writers engage with, and promote, concepts of national identity, their works in manuscript and print are used to project an image of themselves as authors, playing—and fitted to play—their part in the public domain.

The approach taken by this book—in which chapters are devoted to individual authors (Chapter 6 aside)—has been selected because it gives the space necessary to examine these writers as writers and not, as is often the case, as sources to be mined for historical colour. However, the method risks making the chosen authors seem more isolated than they in fact are. There are plenty of other figures, excluded from this book owing to restrictions of space, who—seething with their own 'fictive energies'—would have merited discussion: among them, Bale with his vituperative pen and fine turn in insult; John Heywood, noted in *The Arte of English Poesie* for 'myrth and quicknesse';[68] Arthur Golding, the translator of Ovid; or the poet and dramatist George Gascoigne. One figure regrettably excluded from this work is William Tyndale. There is no doubt that Tyndale's translation of the Bible, which forms the heart of all subsequent English translations, has had a profound and lasting impact on the English language (a key concern of this book), not least because Tyndale was able to merge native idioms with philological learning, the very combination of vernacular and classical cultures achieved by the authors studied here. Choices have to be made, however, and Tyndale is not included, partly because the majority of his works were written

---

[66] Lisa Jardine, *Erasmus, Man of Letters: The Construction of Charisma in Print* (Princeton: Princeton University Press, 1993); Joseph Loewenstein, *Ben Jonson and Possessive Authorship* (Cambridge: Cambridge University Press, 2002), 146.

[67] Harold Love, *Scribal Publication in Seventeenth-Century England* (Oxford: Clarendon Press, 1993).

[68] George Puttenham, *The Arte of Englishe Poesie*, ed. Gladys Doidge Willcock and Alice Walker (Cambridge: Cambridge University Press, 1936), 60.

before the chosen chronological boundary of 1530 (admittedly, a moveable starting point), but—more pertinently—because Tyndale's appearance alongside the authors dealt with here would have been anomalous. As a translator of holy text, Tyndale was concerned with the product, not (as these other writers) with constructing an authorial identity; further to that, while his work was produced for his nation and left an enduring impression on its language, England itself is not treated directly within it. This book, then, is not a comprehensive survey of English writers between 1530 and 1580; it merely offers a series of snapshots of various authors working within those dates, using an examination of a range of these writers' works to illustrate the overlooked vitality and even 'fictiveness' of English writing in this period; what it meant to be an English writer at this time; and how they engaged with, and helped form, images of English nationhood.

These 'snapshots' begin with a chapter on Andrew Borde (?1490–1549), his use of linguistic expansion and material culture, and manipulation of the genres of travel writing and medical treatises to promote England, still then suffering under the dictum 'bona terra, mala gente' (great land, pity about the people), as a country of learning and civilized living. These spirited constructions of Englishness are also used to counter lingering accusations of Borde's own disloyalty and 'papistry'. Like Thomas Elyot, Borde belongs to that earlier generation of Tudor linguists who championed the enrichment of English by frequent Anglicization of classical words. Borde's neologisms are complemented by his efforts to portray England as a land of linguistic and material plenty. He boasts of England's agricultural, mineral, and cultural wealth in a literary style that favours accumulations of synonyms and frequent doublings and triplings of words. His style thus serves as proof of an abundant material culture manifested in verbal copiousness. Borde's own adherence to the rituals and practices of the 'old' faith, and simultaneous endorsement of the royal supremacy, moreover, are a timely reminder that English national identity was not always defined along doctrinal lines.

Chapter 2 examines the significance of history, and literary history, in the construction of national identity, and the application of neo-Latin learning to promote and shape national consciousness. Looking at the works of John Leland (?1506–1552), the chapter highlights the use of topography, rewriting history, and the search for a national literary canon as necessary elements of nation-building. Leland himself is aware of the imperialist role of the historian: for him, classical Romans not only conquered territory; they also subjugated the history of those territories, their multitude of authors obliterating the pasts of other countries in favour of their own. Preservation or reconstruction of a nation's history is—in Leland's view—integral to its sense of identity and pride. Topography, meanwhile, lends Leland the resources to mould his England into a distinct, cohesive, and imaginable entity, suppressing in particular any troublesome dynamics between England, Wales, and Cornwall. Although a champion of native letters, however, Leland is still part of a neoclassical tradition. His public works are written in Latin, magnifying England's charms for an international audience, and it is in, and through, Latin that he competes with Continental humanists in order to claim intellectual laurels for his homeland.

The second half of the book turns from Borde and Leland and their promotion of England as a second Rome to the next generation of writers and the pursuit of a culture that—although indebted to both classical and Continental traditions (especially those of Italy)—is nevertheless invested in the English vernacular. Chapter 3 focuses on the rise of English as a language of scholarship, science, and literature, as reflected in the works of William Thomas (*fl.* 1530–54), one of the first writers to call for education in the English tongue. His depictions of England as an island of plenty echo those of Borde. The inspiration he draws from the achievements of the Italian vernacular, though, demonstrates the change in emphasis away from the purely classical traditions, whilst his shrewd readings of Machiavelli, adapted to suit England's particular political circumstances, throw light on the pressures of portraying a defiantly independent nation in an age of minority, a time of obvious weakness. The Welsh-born Thomas here exemplifies the eagerness with which many of the Welsh gentry embraced union with England. In his English–Welsh dictionary, Thomas's compatriot Salesbury utilized a rhetoric of cultural cohesion, whereby Welsh and English 'hertes', already 'agreed in loue and obedience to [the king's] grace', might be complemented by 'tongues agreeyng in one kynd of speche & language' (A2^r). Thomas goes further still: it is for being born an Englishman that Thomas gives 'contynuall and most hertie thankes' to God, as his learning is used in the service of an increasingly centralized and metropolitan English government.[69] As a Welshman, Thomas thus epitomizes the integration of Wales with England after the second Act of Union in 1543; as a committed Protestant in the Edwardian era, he is also a fitting example of a period in which partisans began to draw national identity along confessional lines.

Chapter 4 concentrates on the work of Thomas Smith (1513–77), focusing on the continued use and development of humanist dialogue as a political and literary form, and Smith's commitment to 'civil conversation' and debate amongst learned men as the proper means of formulating policy, a belief in counsel all the more pressing in an age of minority or the childless reign of an ageing queen. Smith's works, produced in response to specifically English issues, demonstrate the goal-orientated nature of his humanistic output and his conviction that scholarship should be put to public use. The circulation of most of his writings in manuscript, not print, also reveals his conciliar outlook: aimed at government circles, Smith's works did not seek or need a wider audience.

Chapter 5 investigates the literature of regulation, necessary to control and consolidate a potentially anarchic and geographically fragmented population. It focuses on the works of Thomas Wilson (?1525–81), which attempt to fashion a readership of 'right-thinking' (that is, loyal, Protestant) compatriots. Wilson's works seek to combat inner divisiveness through establishing standards of language, thought, and social behaviour. Rhetoric, logic, and humanist education become tools of nation formation and social control. Wilson's writing is also placed in the context of Tudor centralization as, in the course of his literary career, he became increasingly dissatisfied with the concept of the commonweal (the standard translation of *res publica* in the period) and turned instead to that of the state, a semantic development that can be traced to his exile in Italy during the Marian regime and the influence of Italian political thought. The seeming confidence of Wilson's promotion of rhetoric as an instrument of government, however, is undercut by the potential failings, or inadequacies, of eloquence that his own works explore, especially his *Discourse*

---

[69] William Thomas, *Jos. Barbaros Voiages to Tana and Persia* (c.1551), BL Royal 17. C. x, 1ʳ.

vppon Vsurye, which can be seen to revisit the Lucianic writings of More.

A number of key themes run through the book. It argues that nationhood was not an Elizabethan phenomenon, and that the 'triumph of English'—manifested in the literary achievements of Spenser, Shakespeare, Sidney, and their contemporaries—was not as sudden as it appears to a critic like Lewis, if we look to the writings of the earlier years of the sixteenth century. The writing of this period was much more interesting and complex than has been appreciated by many, and feeds directly—in its concerns, practices, and ambiguities—into the 'high' Elizabethan period. These concerns include the use of the physical appearance of the book as a means of fashioning the reception of text (and author); a commitment to counsel and direct engagement with politics; an awareness of the benefits and pitfalls of rhetoric and dialogue; a belief in the place of the writer within the national community; and the search for a national language and literary style. This emphasis on the vernacular, like the assertion of nationhood, was not simply a process of turning inward (looking to English traditions) and backward (looking to an English past). Both these strains were important. Nevertheless, the writing of this period, and the means by which English identities were forged, never broke away from Latinate or Continental culture. Even as Tudor writers asserted their Englishness, they did so in relation to Latin and the Continent: they emulated them, learnt from them, and fused their traditions with their own.

In order to explore the continuity of tradition between the more familiar field of later Elizabethan literature and earlier sixteenth-century writing, Chapter 6 takes a different approach from previous chapters and looks at how the themes outlined above are manifested in two more canonical works: Spenser's *Shepheardes Calender* (1579) and Sidney's *Old Arcadia* (c.1580). As they blend the native, classical, and Continental, and consciously craft an English literary style and language, both texts are very much in keeping with, and a culmination of, the writings of the preceding decades. Like them, they are politically engaged; attuned to the interpretive significance of the form in which a work is produced (in manuscript or print); and eager to assert the capabilities of the English tongue, even as it is indebted to borrowings from Latin and the Continent. Written in reaction to Elizabeth's potential marriage to a French Catholic—the Duke of Alençon—both texts also show a definite alignment of Englishness and Protestantism, at least within the rhetoric deployed by some Protestant factions.

Between them, these seven authors—Borde, Leland, Thomas, Wilson, Smith, Sidney, and Spenser—run the gamut of Tudor literary media, encompassing medical handbooks, historiography, dialogue, manuals of logic, language, and rhetoric, neo-Latin poetry, travel literature, translation, topography, prose romance, and pastoral poetry. The generic range demonstrates the ubiquity and variety of the 'fictive impulses' resulting from the period's constructions of Englishness, which prove central to all these authors' works. The different careers pursued by each (as, respectively, a monk turned physician, an antiquarian, a bureaucrat, two lawyers, a courtier, and, in 1579, a household retainer) allow us to see the use made of varied pools of knowledge to fashion versions of English nationhood. This process was both of lasting cultural consequence, and a key to understanding the rich, untapped vein of literature from the period itself.

Andrew Borde:
Authorship and Identity in
Reformation England

It shall pleace your lordship to vnderstand that the monkes of the charter-house here at london whiche wer committed to newgate for thair traitorus behauor long tyme continued against the kinges grace be almost dispeched by thand of god [. . .] (considering thair behauor and the hole mater I am not sory but wold that al such as loue not the kinges highnes and his worldly honor wer in like caas).[1]

I am, as I am, but not as I was.[2]

The introduction argued that the break with the Roman Church impacted on the literary culture of mid-Tudor England. This first chapter assesses the immediacy of its effect on the author Andrew Borde, whose works are shaped by his experiences in the years directly following Henry VIII's rejection of the authority of Rome. Owing to his connections with the Charterhouse during 1530s, Borde would have felt the aftershocks of the split with Rome more keenly than many. This London base for the Carthusian order gained a dangerous notoriety during the mid-1530s, due to a number of its members' refusal to swear the oath of allegiance required by the Act of Succession of 1534. These Carthusians were consequently grouped with Thomas More and John Fisher, Bishop of Rochester, as highly visible dissenters, whose resistance to the royal supremacy—and increasing fame across Europe—caused considerable concern for the English crown and its agents, not least

---

[1] BL Cleopatra E. iv, 256[r].
[2] Andrew Borde, *The Fyrst Boke of the Introduction of Knowledge* (c.1549), E1[r].

because of the perceived disquiet of the London crowds, with rumours that Fisher's head—fixed to London Bridge—refused to putrefy, fuelling belief in the bishop's sanctity.[3]

The mood amongst the members of the Carthusian order, meanwhile, seems no less heady, a feverish environment in which visions became a matter of political record, such as that of John Darby, who related how, in late June 1535, the ghost of a fellow Carthusian appeared in a dream to express solidarity with the resistant monks.[4] Strict measures were taken against the Charterhouse. Secular 'governors' were appointed, of which two were to be present overnight and at every meal. These governors were to exercise a coherent programme of 'reformacon', sequestering the monks from the outside world, monitoring their reading, and removing 'all maner of boks, wherein errors be conteyned, & to let them haue the olde testament and the new testament'.[5] Other measures included inducing them to amend their religious practices and 'forsake all suche ceremonyes that be nought', and pressurizing them to subscribe to the royal supremacy. Those monks who proved 'obstynate' were to be imprisoned.[6] The lengths to which the English authorities were prepared to go in their campaign against what E. Margaret Thompson calls this 'hot-bed of Romanism' is suggested by a letter from Thomas Bedyll to Thomas Cromwell, the king's chief minister, on 14 June 1537, in which Bedyll states that the nine Carthusians committed to Newgate two years previously 'be almost dispeched by thand of god', for which he professes he is 'not sory'. The appended bill makes the manner of their dispatch all too apparent, as it lists the 'departed', the 'syck', and those 'enew at the poynt of dethe'.[7] It was in connection with this hostility and persecution that Borde experienced the Henrician Reformation.

Although a name now unfamiliar to many scholars, Andrew Borde (or Boorde) was not a marginal writer. There was consistent demand for his two major works, *The Breuiary of Helthe* (1547) and *A Compendyous Regyment or a Dyetary of Helth* (1542), which by 1598 had gone through seven and eight editions respectively. He

[3] See, e.g., *LP*, VIII. i. 726, 846, 1096; ii. 588, 873.
[4] BL Cleopatra E. iv, 160[rv].   [5] Ibid. 256[rv].
[6] Ibid. 27[rv].
[7] E. Margaret Thompson, *A History of the Somerset Carthusians* (London: John Hodges, 1895), 312; BL Cleopatra E. iv, 256[rv].

himself was a figure of sufficient prominence to catch the eye, amongst others, of Angel Day, John Ponet, and Thomas Wilson.[8] According to autobiographical references, Borde was born at Board Hill in Sussex and brought up at Oxford, before joining the Carthusian order, apparently under age. In 1529, when he was probably in his mid to late thirties, he was granted dispensation from his vows to study medicine abroad, returning to England in 1530 and acting as physician to the Duke of Norfolk. After another sojourn abroad between 1531 and 1532, he returned to the Charterhouse, where he was still resident in 1534, registered as a priest. He took the oath of allegiance on 29 May 1534,[9] and subsequently left for the Continent, where he acted as a government informant, reporting to Cromwell on the state of feeling regarding Henry VIII and the 'great matter' of his divorce. By 1536, Borde was studying medicine at Glasgow, disguised as a Scotsman under the pseudonym Karre, and again reporting to Cromwell.[10]

Despite Borde's royal service, however, his association with the Carthusians left his own loyalties open to question. This chapter begins by examining Borde's private correspondence, in which he was concerned to counter any lingering suspicions regarding his political and religious affiliations. It then traces those same preoccupations in his printed texts, analysing the ways in which he attempted to forge an appropriately conformist persona with which to weather the predominantly anti-papal climate of the 1530s and 1540s. As such, Borde's works reveal some of the strategies with which writers reacted to the uncertainty and confusion of those years, as English identities were refashioned in the spirit of long-standing independence from the Roman Church suggested by the Act in Restraint of Appeals in 1533, even though many practices of the 'old' religion, and the mindset that accepted them, remained in place.

---

[8] *STC*; Angel Day, *An Englishe Secretarie* (1586), 38–9; Thomas Wilson, *The Arte of Rhetorique* (1553), 89ᵛ; John Ponet, *An Apologie fully aunsweringe by Scriptures and aunceant Doctors / a blasphemous Book gatherid by D. Steph. Gardiner* (Strasburg, 1556), 48–9.

[9] Thomas Rymer, *Foedora* (1704–35), 20 vols., xiv. 492.

[10] For biographical details and their sources, see F. J. Furnivall (ed.), *Andrew Boorde's Introduction and Dyetary with Barnes in the Defence of the Berde*, EETS, extra series, 10 (1870), introduction.

'I DO WRYTE THIS BOKE FOR A COMON WELTH':
FASHIONING A PATRIOTIC PERSONA[11]

In 1535, Borde served abroad as a spy, 'coactyd' (as Borde puts it
in his distinctive, highly Latinate style) 'to geue [. . .] notycyon of
certyn synystrall matters, contrary to our realme of ynglond'.[12]
Within the ensuing correspondence, Borde endeavours to endorse
his newfound loyalties, not merely by fulfilling his duties as agent,
but also by promoting the devoted self-image required to negate
any suspicions regarding the wholeheartedness of his subscription
to the royal supremacy and alignment with 'our realme of ynglond'
as opposed to former, now conflicting, allegiances to Rome. As he
writes to Cromwell from Scotland in April 1536, 'yff I myght do
ynglond any seruyce, specyally to my soueryn lorde the kyng & to
yow, I wold do ytt to spend & putt my lyff in danger & Iuberdy as
far as any man.'[13] These vows of fealty and service to the nation
are more than courteous commonplaces. When the ex-monk
proclaims that 'god be my Iuge, yow haue my hartt & shalbe sure
of me to the uttermust off my poer power', it is both in remem-
brance of, and an attempt to erase, a past rendered suddenly undesirable by recent history. National loyalty is expressed as a gesture
of reparation, announced because he is 'neuer able to mak [. . .]
amendes'. This sentiment, moreover, is focused on the bodies of the
king and his chief deputy. On Borde's pages, to be true to your
country is to be a dedicated subject and (unlike his former companions, the recusant monks) obedient to the wishes of your king.

The time-span of Borde's correspondence allows us to trace the
processes by which he constructed this loyal identity, as he writes
and rewrites versions of his past in response to his perceptions of
the political situation. His first extant letter to Cromwell, written
from Bordeaux on 20 June 1535, reveals Borde still willing to be
associated with the Carthusians. He even draws attention to his
relationship with them in a postscript, as he 'humyly &
precordyally desyre[s] [Cromwell] to be good master (as [he] euer

---

[11] Andrew Borde, *The Breuiary of Helthe, for all maner of sycknesses and
diseases the whiche may be in man, or woman* (1547), B2ᵛ.
[12] PRO State Papers, Henry, 1/93/119. Borde's letters are reproduced by
Furnivall (ed.), *Boorde's Introduction*, 47–62.
[13] PRO State Papers, Henry, 1/103/61.

ha[s] byn) to [his] faythfull bedmen master prior of the cherter howse of london & to master doctor horde prior of hynton'.[14] Surprising as it may seem, considering the notoriety of the case across Europe, Borde must have somehow failed to hear about both the execution of the very prior (John Houghton) to whom he refers, and the disfavour into which the whole order had fallen, with nine of its members detained in Newgate and the rest of his former convent under surveillance and virtual house arrest.[15] The allusion to Edmund Horde also indicates that Borde was still concerned to maintain connections with the order. Besides being a personal acquaintance from their residence at the Charterhouse in 1520s, Horde was also one of the more prominent English Carthusians, recommended to Cromwell for his 'virtue and learning' and as a key figure to win to the royal cause, since the Carthusians would 'give him more credence and rather apply their conscience to his judgement than to any other'; it was also Horde to whom Borde himself felt it necessary to excuse and explain his departure from the order in May 1534.[16]

Certainly, in his next letter, written after his return to England in August 1535, Borde is much more circumspect. Letters 'browth [. . .] from by yend see' are withheld from Cromwell until he has 'suffycyentt record' that Borde has long been released from his monastic vows.[17] Before Borde dispatches these letters (and the information contained within them), the minister is requested to acknowledge 'that the prior off chartterhowse off london last beyng / of hys owne meere mocyon gaue [Borde] lycence to departe from the relygyon', and that, in addition, Borde 'was also xv yeres passyd dyspensyd with the relygyon by the byshopp of Romes bulles'. By April 1536, Borde's position was more clear-cut still, as he prostrates himself in gratitude to Cromwell for rescuing him from what he now portrays as spiritual and physical incarceration: 'for wher I was in greatt thraldom both bodyly and goostly[,] yow

[14] Ibid. 1/93/119.

[15] The 'prior of the cherter howse' must refer to Houghton: a new prior was not appointed until William Trafford took up the post in early 1536 (Gerald S. Davies, *The Charterhouse in London* (London: John Murray, 1921), 101).

[16] Thompson, *Somerset Carthusians*, 320–1; *LP*, VIII. i. 1011; ii. 49; XI. 75; PRO State Papers, Henry, 1/84/87. Borde's letter is catalogued twice in *LP*, appearing as VII. 730 (May 1534) and VIII. ii. 12 (Aug. 1535). Since Borde left the order in May 1534, it makes more sense to follow the earlier dating.

[17] PRO State Papers, Henry, 1/96/43.

of your gentylnes sett me att liberte & clernes off consyence[.]'[18]
His liberation assumes a religious tenor, with Borde released from
'the yngnorance & blyndnes that [the monks] & [he] war yn'.
Even while he admits to writing supportively to 'the prior of
london when he was in the tower' (where he had been imprisoned
in May 1534 after refusing to take the oath of allegiance), Borde
sloughs off responsibility for his actions, declaring that he was
kept in deliberate and total ignorance by the monks he now
depicts as his jailers: 'for I could neuer know no thyng of no maner
off matter butt only by them, & they wolde cause me wrett such
incypyently'.

The letter endorses the version of events Borde presented in
another letter, written the previous summer. This earlier letter
serves a dual purpose. First, by accusing the monks of enrolling
him illegally, 'vnder age contrary to [their] statutes', it annuls all
ties of allegiance to the Carthusian order, not only current, but
previous.[19] Secondly, it depicts Borde acting on behalf of his new,
royal master. Not only does he state that the Grand Chartreuse,
supreme head of the order, believes that the English Carthusians
should submit to their king, he himself assumes the role of moral
tutor to his former superiors, 'aduertysyng [them] that [they] loue
god, & [. . .] obay [their] soueryn lord the kyng'. He thus distances
himself from a party known to be resistant to the crown, whilst
simultaneously proving himself actively loyal to that body by offering evidence of his attempts to persuade these rebellious subjects to
obedience. Borde's allegiance to the crown is further signalled by
his reference to the pope—in approved reformist terms—as the
'bysshop of Rome', and by the coup he seems to have achieved in
persuading the Grand Chartreuse of the justice of Henry's cause,
action which is corroborated by a fire-damaged fragment of a letter
to this effect from the Grand Chartreuse to the English
Carthusians.[20] Borde's letter to the Carthusians is not private,
moreover, but is an expressly open address, directed 'to all priors
and conuentes off the sayd order in ynglond'.

During the late 1530s, these self-advancing representations
were confined to the medium of correspondence, in which—like

[18] PRO State Papers, Henry, 1/103/61.   [19] BL Cleopatra E. iv, 70[r].
[20] David Knowles, *The Religious Orders in England*, iii: *The Tudor Age*
(Cambridge: Cambridge University Press, 1959), 234.

Thomas Wyatt's parody of the devoted royal servant 'runnyng day and nyght / From Reaulme to Reaulme'—Borde breathlessly lists his 'perlustrat[ions]' through 'normandy[,] frawnce[,] goscony & lyon[,] the regions also of castyle[,] byscay[,] spayne[,] paarte of portyngale & [. . .] Aragon, Nauerre & [. . .] burdoyse'.[21] After the execution of his patron Cromwell in 1540, however, Borde found another means—the printing press—through which to declare his devotion to the royal cause. Within two years of Cromwell's death, Borde had no less than four books either published or in preparation for publication: the *Dyetary*, the *Breuiary*, *The fyrst boke of the Introduction of Knowledge*, and a lost treatise against beards.[22] These works recycle the experiences of the previous decade: as the preface explains, the *Dyetary* evolves from Borde's attendance on the Duke of Norfolk in 1530, 'the yeare in the whiche lorde Thomas cardynal bishop of york was commaunded to go to his see of york', a reference which locates the book within the political upheavals caused by the break with Rome and the fall of Cardinal Wolsey;[23] the *Breuiary* harks back to Borde's residence in Scotland in 1536; his travels as a Cromwellian agent on the Continent form the basis of the *Introduction*, a travel-guide cum phrasebook for Europe and the Near East. It is notable that, in all these works, Borde chooses to demonstrate his loyalty through noisy protestations of his own Englishness. 'Compyled by Andrew Boord of phisicke Doctour[,] an englysh man', the authority of the *Breuiary* rests as much on Borde's nationality as on his medical credentials ($A1^r$), and whilst it was common for a Latin title page to indicate the nationality of its author, this is rare in the vernacular, where the very act of writing in English indicates the author's, or translator's, Englishness. Beginning with the *Introduction*, this next section examines Borde's systematic attempts to portray England as a rich, cultivated, cohesive, and easily defensible realm. Borde's audience here is threefold: first, the compatriots whom he hopes to educate,

---

[21] PRO State Papers, Henry, 1/93/119; Thomas Wyatt, 'A spending hand', in *The Collected Poems of Sir Thomas Wyatt*, ed. Kenneth Muir and Patricia Thomson (Liverpool: Liverpool University Press, 1969), ll. 12–13.
[22] The existence of the second and third books, although unpublished until later in the decade, is confirmed by Borde's continual reference to them and their contents throughout his *Dyetary*, published by Robert Wyer in 1542.
[23] Andrew Borde, *A Compendyous Regyment or a Dyetary of Helth* (1542), π1^v.

inspire, and reassure; secondly, the European readers 'of what nacyon souer' (E1^v) whom he wishes to impress with the picture painted of his homeland and its capacities, and rebuff England's image as the rude man of Europe; and thirdly, the audience for whom both these enterprises are primarily enacted: the king and those to whom Borde's loyalty might still seem suspect.

REBUTTING PROVERBS AND THE
SIGNIFICANCE OF STYLE

Written in 1542 and first published *c.*1549, Borde's *Introduction* is broken down into chapters, each focusing on one country and headed by a woodcut representing its inhabitants (with varying degrees of specificity). Each chapter begins with some self-confessedly crude doggerel spoken by a stereotypical representative of each nation, outlining their compatriots' characteristics, followed by a prose account of the country in question, describing its nature, diet, currency, sites of interest, and ending with a rudimentary language lesson, detailing how to ask for food, drink, accommodation, and other practicalities. Borde here blends two literary traditions. On the one hand, the practical nature of much of his advice is akin to that found in works such as William Caxton's *Instructions for Travellers* (*c.*1483), which 'consists chiefly of colloquial phrases and dialogues' for the English journeying in France, or the anonymous *Informacon for pylgrymes vnto the holy londe* (*c.*1500), itself an example of a genre of pilgrims' guides stretching back to late antiquity, with its tips on foreign travel and brief word lists of 'the langage of Moreske', 'Greke', and 'the langage of Turky'.[24] On the other, like Caxton's *Descrypcyon of Englande* appended to John Trevisa's translation of the *Polycronycon* (1498), it is part of a topographical tradition that aims to raise English self-esteem. Borde shares both Caxton's ambition to set forth the hitherto unrecognized 'noblenesse & worthynesse' of 'Brytane', 'necessarye to all Englysshmen to knowe', and the means by which Caxton does so, through short descriptions of

---

[24] William Caxton, *Dialogues in French and English*, ed. Henry Bradley, EETS, extra series, 79 (1900), p. v; Anon., *Informacon for pylgrymes vnto the holy londe*, ed. George Henry Freely (London: William Nicol, 1824), E2^v, E3^{rv}.

the land, commodities, and people of Britain and Ireland.[25] Even Borde's use of doggerel finds precedent in Caxton's *Descrypcyon*, where the majority of the section on Wales is delivered in verse (D6^v). The *Introduction*, that is, serves a hybrid purpose. It offers practical advice—'necessary thynges to be knowen' (E1^v)—and affirms cultural stereotypes which, naturally enough, promote an idea of England's wealth and cultivation.

Borde's *Introduction* is, however, written in direct response to the poor opinion in which the English were then held by their European contemporaries. As Borde himself puts it in his opening confession, 'The Italyen and the Lombarde say Anglia terra[:] bona terra[,] mala gent. That is to say, the land of England is a good land, but the people be yl' (A4^v). The subsequent work is a concerted effort to rebuff this disparaging statement by advertising the virtues of England and the English whilst denigrating the inhabitants and assets of other nations. Borde eulogizes England as a land of material riches and handsome, cultured people, 'as good as any people in any other lande, and nacion that euer I haue trauayled in, yea and much more better in many thinges'. When Borde declares that 'the noble citie of London precelleth al other', elevating it above 'Constantynople, Venis, Rome, Florence, Paris [and] Colyn' (B1^r), his promotion of London as proof of English accomplishments also reveals a willingness to identify with national, rather than regional, symbols, and an admiration for the metropolis that displays none of the satirical impetus identified by Andrew McRae in the late sixteenth century, or Paul Slack in the seventeenth, where the wealth and rapid growth of the capital is seen as predatory and disruptive.[26] It is natural enough that More, a citizen and sheriff of London (as he announces on the title page of *Utopia* in 1516), should use Amaurot, a reflection of London, with its Thames-like (no-)river, as the exemplar of the Utopian nation. That Borde, born in Sussex and brought up in Oxfordshire, should do likewise is a manifestation of what Lawrence Manley dubs 'the emergence of London as a mental fact in the national

---

[25] William Caxton, *Descrypcyon of Englande [. . .] taken out of Polycronycon accordynge to the translacon of Treuisa* (1498), A1^v, D6^v.

[26] Andrew McRae, *God Speed the Plough: The Representation of Agrarian England, 1500–1600* (Cambridge: Cambridge University Press, 1996), 87; Paul Slack, *From Reformation to Improvement: Public Welfare in Early Modern England* (Oxford: Oxford University Press, 1999).

consciousness' during the sixteenth century.[27] This growing aware-
ness extends beyond the encomiastic works of writers such as
Edward Hall and John Coke identified by Manley, and the
Venetian *Relazioni*, which by 1530s were approvingly noting
London as the principal city.[28] It seeps into the state papers
surrounding the very issue of Carthusian disobedience which
dogged Borde himself. As Bedyll explains in a letter to Cromwell in
1537, it is all the more important to make an example of the
Charterhouse because 'London is the comon countrey of al
England from which is derived to al parts of this realme al good
and yll occurrent'.[29]

Borde's vision of his nation is consequently both cohesive—with
the metropolis a point of pride for both Londoner and non-
Londoner—and laudatory. The major vice of which he accuses his
compatriots is an overfondness for foreign fashions, a failing familiar from at least the late fifteenth century and the anonymous
Treatise of the Galaunt, published in 1510.[30] The woodcut accompanying Borde's prose shows the Englishman naked, save for a
skimpy loin cloth and a smart feathered hat, clutching a pair of
shears and waiting to make up the bale of material over his arm
into the latest style. This particular image endured: as John Lyly
writes in 1580, 'in drawing of an English man the paynter setteth
him downe naked, hauing in the one hande a payre of sheares, in
the other a peece of cloath', a description that resonates with Lucas
de Heere's 1570 representation of the Englishman in the Earl of
Lincoln's gallery.[31] The Englishman's 'newfangledness' is a modest
failing, however, and needs to be compared with Borde's portraits
of England's Celtic neighbours, whose description occupies the
next three chapters and who—unsurprisingly, considering their
proximity and subsequent impact on England's domestic security—

---

[27] Lawrence Manley, *Literature and Culture in Early Modern England*
(Cambridge: Cambridge University Press, 1995), 16.

[28] Lodovico Falier, *Relazione d' Inghilterra (1531)*, in Alberi (ed.), *Relazioni
degli Amabasciatori Veneti al Senato*, ii. 3–28, at 18.

[29] BL Cleopatra E. iv, 256ʳ.

[30] The printer, Wynkyn de Worde, misattributes this poem to John Lydgate.

[31] John Lyly, *Euphues' Glass for Europe*, in *Euphues and his England*, in R.
Warwick Bond (ed.), *The Complete Works of John Lyly*, 2 vols. (Oxford:
Clarendon Press, 1902–3) ii. 194; H. J. Wilmot-Buxton, *English Painters* (London:
Sampson Low, 1883), 20; cf. Edward Chamberlayne, *Angliae Notitia, or the
Present State of England* (1670), 64.

are discussed at most length and, unlike Caxton's more approbatory sketches in his *Descrypcyon*, subjected to particularly scornful scrutiny.

Without exception, Borde casts the other territories within England's dominions as backward and barbaric: the Cornish are starved almost to death and forced to drink ale which tastes like pig swill; the thieving Welsh, subsisting on a diet of roasted cheese, are lampooned for their pride in their genealogy, based in an oral tradition of nomenclature ('My name is ap Ryce, ap Dauy ap Flood / [. . .] My kindred is ap hoby, ap Ienkin, ap goffe', B4ʳ); the Irish are wild and 'naturally [. . .] testy' (C3ᵛ). The apparent lewdness, incivility, and regressive outlook of England's neighbours is further enhanced by the use of woodcuts: the Irishwoman is shown searching her man's hair for lice, while he gropes under her skirts (C2ᵛ); one Welshman is absorbed with his harp whilst another casts himself before a statue of the Virgin Mary, to whom—the doggerel explains—he believes himself related: 'I loue our Lady, for I am of hyr kynne / He that doth not loue hyr I beshrew his chynne' (B4ʳ). Unlike many of the subsequent woodcuts, which are recycled for different countries, those representing England, Wales, and Ireland are specific to them and reflect in detail the accompanying descriptions.

Scotland, meanwhile, is appropriated into England's cultural and linguistic embrace, undermining its status as an autonomous nation, whilst simultaneously elevating that of its English neighbour. Even the few admirable qualities—hardiness, strength, good looks, musicality—with which Borde endows the Scots are read as evidence of their resembling the English, for 'in these .iiii. qualytes they be mooste lyke aboue all other nacions to an Englyshe man' (D1ᵛ–D2ʳ). From the outset, Scotland is established as England's former vassal, a 'kyngdome, the kynge of the whyche hath in olde tyme come to the parliament of the kyng of England and hath be subiect to England' (D1ʳᵛ), a version of history propounded in such sources as John Hardyng's chronicles.[32] The chapter also ends with the comment that 'the scotysh tongue and the northen Englyshe be lyke of speche', a similarity emphasized by the transcription of Scottish speech immediately above, where the English 'Syr by my

---

[32] John Hardyng, *The Chronicle from the Fyrst Begynnyng of Englande* (1543), 16ᵛ.

fayth you be welcome' is met with 'Sher by my fayth but yows wel come', and 'I am a good fellow of the Scotyshe blood' with 'Ies a gewd falow of the Scotland blewd' (D2ᵛ). Unlike the Cornish, Welsh, and Irish language lessons, this one serves no instructive purpose. Instead, it renders Scots a slurred and inferior cousin of English.

Whilst the alleged 'barbarity' of England's immediate neighbours is used to highlight England's cultural superiority, the professed over-sophistication of areas such as Italy and Lombardy is deployed to portray England as the happy mean, neither too barbarous nor too decadent. Borde retaliates to the Italians' caustic maxim—'Anglia [. . .] mala gente'—by converting all other nationalities into potential proverbs. Description becomes a means of reduction, not embellishment, compressing each country's inhabitants into unthreatening national stereotypes: as drunk as a Dutchman; as poor as a Dane; as treacherous as a Lombard.[33] The effect is enhanced both by the brevity of Borde's sketches, which demand that a population be summarized on the strength of one or two dominant characteristics, and by Borde's division of each chapter into introductory doggerel and a section of authorial prose, in which Borde repeats and compounds the character traits broached in the opening verses.

It was not only the boorish reputation of the English that Borde had to dispel, however, but also that of his native tongue, still regarded as 'a base speche to other noble speeches, as Italion[,] Castylion and Frenche', even if that confession is quickly qualified by the assertion that 'the speche of Englande of late dayes is amended' (B2ʳ). Borde's concern to rectify the standing of his mother tongue needs to be put in context. From Chaucer's complaint in the fourteenth century that 'rym in Englissh hath such skarsete' until well into the sixteenth century, English was repeatedly attacked for its inelegance and lack of vocabulary.[34] This

---

[33] Some of these stereotypes (such as the drunken Fleming, or poverty-stricken Dane) also appear in the anonymous *Libel of English Policy*, in Thomas Wright (ed.), *Political Poems and Songs relating to English History, composed during the period from the accession of Edward III to that of Richard III*, 2 vols. (London, 1859–61), ii. 157–207, at 169–70, 177. However, the *Libel* (written *c.*1436) is more concerned with promoting the need for an English navy than with denigrating other nations.

[34] Geoffrey Chaucer, 'The Complaint of Venus', *The Riverside Chaucer*, ed. F. N. Robinson, 3rd edn. (Oxford: Oxford University Press, 1988), l. 80.

linguistic poverty is used by Wyatt in 1529, for example, to explain his unwillingness to translate Petrarch's 'remedy of yll fortune', because 'the labour began to seme tedious / by superfluous often rehersyng of one thyng. Which tho paruenture in the latyn shalbe la[u]dable / by plentuous diuersite of the spekyng of it [. . .] yet for lacke of such diuersyte in our tong / it shulde want a great dele of the grace'.[35] A similar dissatisfaction with the dearth of elegant English and the restrictions of its vocabulary compels Skelton's Jane Scrope to complain that 'our naturall tong is rude', 'rusty', 'cankered', and 'dull'.[36] To find adequate expression, Jane turns to 'Latyne playne and lyght' (l. 823). We should read these excuses sceptically, however. To some extent, they are used to add kudos: 'there might be paucity of words to choose from, but look how well *I*, as poet or author, manage.' We can certainly see this in Skelton's case. His complaints about the paucity of English rhymes are belied by the excess of rhyme he continually produces. His seemingly endless store of rhymes is another strategy for self-promotion, along with his ostentatious display of classical learning and frequent reiteration of his laureateship, an honour granted for his Latin writings and transferred by Skelton to his role as English poet. Wyatt's excuses need qualifying for different reasons. Wyatt was asked to translate Petrarch's 'remedye' by Catherine of Aragon. Complying with her literary request at this time—the late 1520s—as Catherine gathered allies around her, risked appearing like compliance with her resistance to the divorce. Wyatt consequently signals his own loyalties to the king without causing Catherine offence. He refuses to translate Petrarch's 'remedye', substituting Plutarch's 'Quyet of Mynde', the title of which suggests practising Stoic endurance, rather than seeking a solution (remedy) for ill fortune. Nevertheless, the fact that the woeful state of English provided Wyatt with a plausible excuse indicates the poor regard in which it was held. Similarly, Skelton's incessant need to advertise his learning reveals a degree of insecurity about the language in which he writes: the Latin peppering Skelton's poems is there, in part, to demonstrate that he is an educated man and is not writing in English through lack of choice. Borde, then, is

---

[35] Thomas Wyatt, *The Quyet of Mynde*, in *Poems*, ed. Muir and Thomson 440–63, at 440.
[36] John Skelton, 'Phyllyp Sparowe', in *Poems*, ed. Scattergood, ll. 774–9.

writing in a period that is both sensitive to the alleged inadequacies of English and equally anxious to assert its worth.

The explicitly national purpose of Borde's texts not only finds expression in self-congratulation and xenophobic gibes, therefore: throughout his works, Borde also strives to extend and refine his native tongue. Borde's attitude to English in relation to the 'learned' languages of Greek, Hebrew, and particularly Latin is crucial here. Whilst recognizing the linguistic excellence of the classical tongues, Borde is nevertheless careful in his *Introduction* that this superiority is not applied to contemporary speakers: he consequently distinguishes between the 'trew hebrew tongue' and 'the whych the Iues, doth speke now' (N4^r); between 'barbarouse' and 'trew' Latin (N4^r); between 'trewe grek' and 'such grek as the[y] do speke' (H2^{rv}). Discussion of Latin, meanwhile, merits a whole chapter to itself, in which England is portrayed, without qualification, as the natural home of learning. In a section entitled, in suitable Latinate terms, 'responcion of the englysh man', England is promoted as a refuge for the Latin tongue 'corrupty[d]' and 'abused' in its birthplace, Italy (M2^v). Borde's assertion of the decline of Latin in its homeland—besides its unstated and timely denigration of Rome—also indicates that, just as nations rise and fall, so languages improve and deteriorate. In this way, Borde opens up the possibility of refining his own vernacular. Considering the eminence of Latin during this period, it is natural enough that Borde should choose to do this by making English more like Latin, importing and Anglicizing Latin words. Where evidence of Borde's revisions exists, as in the reworked preface to the 1547 edition of the *Dyetary*, the additions and changes made significantly increase the number of Latinate words: 'sauyte' (safety) is replaced by 'conseruacyon of the health', 'called' by 'nomynate'; 'imbecyllyte', 'festynacyon & dylygence' and 'expedyent & necessary' are added.[37]

Borde's works abound with clusters of such verbal multiplications, as illustrated by the passage on milk in the *Dyetary*, which 'doth *humect and moysteth* the membres, and *mundyfye and clense* the entrayles, and doth *allueyat & mytygate* the payne of the lunges & the brest' (G4^v; my emphasis). Borde's use of doubling and

---

[37] Borde, *Dyetary* (1542), A2^{rv}; Andrew Borde, *A Compendyous Regyment or a Dyetary of helth* (1547), ♣1^v, ♣2^r. Unless otherwise stated, references are to the 1542 edition.

tripling aligns him with his near-contemporary Thomas Elyot, who also contributed to the expansion of the English language, coining words from mainly Latin sources, 'education or the bringing vp' being one of Elyot's famous examples.[38] Through use of doublings and triplings, Borde and Elyot show a recurrent concern to cultivate and augment their readers' language, their terms (as Elyot explains), 'new made [. . .] of a latine or frenche worde [. . .] declared so playnly by one mene or other [. . .], that no sentence is therby made derke or harde to be vnderstande'.[39] In doing so, both authors use doubling to fulfil the interpretive—as opposed to the polishing, or self-correcting—function recommended by Quintilian in his *Institutio Oratoria*.[40] They also perform implicitly what later sixteenth- and seventeenth-century dictionary writers, such as Henry Cockeram and Robert Cawdrey, establish as their express purpose, to quote Cawdrey in 1604: 'teaching the true writing, and vnderstanding of hard vsuall English wordes, borrowed from the Hebrew, Greeke, Latine, or French &c. With the interpretation thereof by plaine English words'.[41]

Frequently, though, Borde's coinings do not fill a lacuna in English: they act as ornaments upon it and the prose of the author who employs them, a purpose of language assimilation observed by Barbara Strang when she argues that cultural prestige and appreciation for linguistic variety are as much motivating reasons for vocabulary-building as the need to fill perceived gaps in the language.[42] As Erasmus writes in the prefatory matter of his *De copia*, 'even if we allow that there is absolutely no distinction in meaning, yet some words are more respectable than others, or more exalted' ('tum vt demus in significatu nihil omnino discriminis esse, tamen sunt alia aliis honestiora, sublimiora').[43] Borde is sensitive to such gradations of 'respectability', and his diction

[38] Thomas Elyot, *The Boke named the Gouernour* (1531), 15^v.

[39] Thomas Elyot, *Of the knowledge whiche maketh a wise man* (1533), A3^v.

[40] Quintilian, *Institutio Oratoria*, ed. and trans. H. E. Butler, 3 vols. (London: Heinemann, 1920–2), III. ix. 3. 45.

[41] Robert Cawdrey, *A Table Alphabeticall of Hard Vsuall English Words* (1604), A1^r. Cf. Henry Cockeram, *The English Dictionarie* (1623).

[42] Barbara M. H. Strang, *A History of English* (London: Methuen, 1970), 92–6, 120–31, 184–7, 250–7.

[43] Desiderius Erasmus, *De duplici copia verborum ac rerum*, ed. and trans. Betty I. Knott (Toronto: University of Toronto Press, 1978), *Collected Works of Erasmus*, xxiv. 308. Various editions of *De copia* were published from 1514 onwards with corrections and additions. The Latin text cited here is from the 1539 edition.

prioritizes this high register of what the later-sixteenth-century grammarian Edmund Coote terms 'hard' words, a preference for Latinate words that Richard Foster Jones dates 'as far back as Lydgate'.[44] Borde also uses his Latinate diction to create two registers of speech: the learned idiom of men such as himself, and 'naughty', unsophisticated language. As can be seen from the letters to Cromwell cited earlier, Borde is no less Latinate in his private than his public writings. Assured of an educated audience—rather than, in his own words, 'symple and vnlerned men' who form part of his public readership—he makes his Latinisms even more obscure: in a letter to Cromwell, 'coactyd', 'notycyon', 'synystrall', 'armipotentt', 'perprudentt', 'circumspate', and 'dyscrete' all appear within one sentence.[45] The Latinate diction acts as mutually flattering discourse: a learned man using learned language that acknowledges the learning of his addressee.

A similar differentiation is apparent in the five separate prefaces to the *Breuiary*, addressed respectively to physicians, surgeons, 'sycke men and those that be wounded' (A4ᵛ), 'reders of this boke' (B1ᵛ), and 'Lordes[,] Ladies and Gentylmen' (B2ᵛ). The language used to address surgeons and Borde's fellow physicians is not only denser than the subsequent prefaces in the frequency of Latinisms, but also in Latinisms that are notably rarer. From the opening sentence, Borde's physicians are met with a barrage of ornate loan-words, as he begs that 'egregiouse doctours and maysters of the Eximiouse and Archane Science of Phisicke of [their] Vrbanyte Exasperate nat [them]selfe againste [him] for makynge of this lytle volume' (A2ʳ). This difference in register between the 'prologe' and 'proheme' to physicians and surgeons on the one hand, and the prefatory matter addressed to lay readers on the other gains further significance when applied to the portrayal of England's neighbours in the *Introduction*. When Borde declares that the English are 'much more better in many thinges, specially in maners and manhood' (A4ᵛ), manners to a large degree mean language, and in the assessment of the Irish Pale, English even becomes semantically equated with, and a sign of, civility, where people 'be metely wel

[44] Edmund Coote, *The English Schoole-maister* (1596), A1ʳ; Jones, *Triumph of English*, 27.
[45] Andrew Borde, *The Seconde Boke of the Breuiary of helthe, named the Extrauagantes* (1547), A1ᵛ; PRO State Papers, Henry, 1/93/119.

manerd, vsyng the english tunge' (C_3^r). Whereas Borde's
Englishman never entirely loses his Latinate register during his
snippet of doggerel, the plain un-Latinate language given to his
Celtic equivalents is used to condemn them as much as the
disparaging prose which follows. Cornish speech is as corrupt as its
ale is 'dycke and smoky, and [. . .] dyn / [. . .] lyke wash, as pygges
had wrestled dryn' (B_2^r), a bitter swipe from someone who—as we
shall see—was so ostensibly concerned with his beer and meat as
Doctor Borde. 'In Cornwall is two speches,' he declares: 'the one is
naughty englyshe, and the other is Cornyshe speche' (B_2^v). The
Cornishman's English speech consequently abounds in archaisms
and dialect terms, as 'dup' (open), 'bedauer' (bedfellow), 'fyngered'
and 'afyngered' (hungry), whilst the attempt to capture a Cornish
accent phonetically (with 'dycke' for thick, 'dryn' for in, 'iche' for
'I', 'vare' for 'fare) intensifies their portrayal as ill-bred yokels,
alien to the metropolitan culture celebrated elsewhere by Borde.

Yet gradations of vocabulary do not always signal disparage-
ment. As an author dedicated to the ennobling of his mother
tongue, Borde's doublings and triplings not only introduce and
explain new terms or distinguish registers of speech: they also
display a range that English already possesses. During this period,
collections of synonyms were deemed suitably valuable gifts—
literal thesauri, or treasure troves—worthy of a nation. When
Erasmus offered *De copia*, a storehouse of Latin terms, to John
Colet in 1513, it was partly to repay a 'debt' owed 'to the English
nation' ('quantum Angliae debeam publicè'); Vives, in *De tradendis
disciplinis* (1531), talks of written precepts as 'public wealth in a
common exchequer' ('publicae opes in aerario communi').[46]
Borde's texts furnish his country, not with Latin words, but
vernacular variety. Thus in the *Dyetary* we have combinations such
as 'house or mansyon' (B_3^r), 'skowered and kept clene' (C_1^r),
'fylthe and sluttysshe' (C_2^v), all pairings comprising vocabulary of
long-familiar usage, the latter two formed from vocabulary of
Anglo-Saxon, rather than Latinate, origin. Borde flaunts the elas-
ticity and diversity of his mother tongue. The five prefatory
addresses of his *Breuiary* all sport different headings. As 'prologue',

---

[46] Erasmus, *De copia*, 4; trans. Knott, *Collected Works*, xxiv, 285; cited by
Judith H. Anderson, *Words that Matter: Linguistic Perception in Renaissance
England* (Stanford, Calif.: Stanford University Press, 1996), 38.

'proheme', 'preamble', 'preface', and 'appendex', the titles ('appendex' aside) serve to display long-established synonyms. Recurrently, Borde's coinings are not achieved by importing classical
terms, but by adapting extant vocabulary, as he stretches its meaning (as with the word 'destytuted', which comes to mean 'lacking',
rather than 'deprived or bereft of'), or pushes at grammatical
boundaries, transforming adjectives into verbs or adverbs (turning
Elyot's adjective 'anymat' into a verb, or extending 'insipient' into
the adverbial form 'insipiently').[47]

Borde even finds an 'ouerplus' of language. We have already
seen how, despite Skelton's complaints about the paucity of English
terms through the persona of Jane Scrope, his poetry employs a
surfeit of rhyme to assert the profusion of English vocabulary and
his own virtuosity within it. Borde utilizes similar excesses to the
same purpose. His prose can suddenly explode into a sequence of
internal rhymes, lingering on a point as long as the resources of
vocabulary allow, rather than as the subject demands. The fifth
chapter of the *Dyetary*, 'howe a man shulde ordre his howse', is a
case in point. Borde's argument is that it makes little sense establishing a household unless you can finish the job. The rest of this
chapter harps on that message in a cacophony of rhymes, imagin-
ing the unfortunate householder required 'nowe to ron for malt,
and by and by for salt, nowe to sende for breade, and by and by to
sende for a shepes heade':

such thyng is no prouysion, but it is a great abusyon. Thus a man shall lese
his thryfte, and be put to a shefte, his goodes shall neuer increase, and he
shall not be in rest nor peace, but euer in carcke and care, for his purse
wyll euer be bare, wherfore I do councyell euery man, to prouyde for hym
selfe as soone as he can, for yf of implementes he be destytuted, men wyll
call him lyght wytted, to set vp a great howse, and is not able to kepe man
nor mowse, wherfore let euery man loke or he lepe, for many cornes
maketh a great hepe.   (C3ᵛ)

Borde's linguistic effusion—surprising as it may be in a manual of
household management and rudimentary physic—is not simply
quaint or otiose. Rather, Borde is deliberately fashioning himself as
an author dedicated to the improvement of English. He appears to
have taken a strong interest in the production of his books, using

---

[47] Borde, *Dyetary*, <u>C3</u>ᵛ, <u>D2</u>ᵛ; BL Cleopatra E. iv, 70ʳ.

them at times to hasten the publication of other volumes.[48] This involvement seems to extend to the choice of illustrations. The woodcuts in the *Introduction* for the opening chapters discussing England's neighbours—arguably the most significant sections— endorse the pen portraits they accompany. It is therefore revealing that the two pictures selected to represent Borde, in the *Introduction* and *Breuiary*, are ones which are also used elsewhere to depict, respectively, Chaucer and Skelton, of whom the former is frequently credited as 'the first foundeur & enbelisher of ornate eloquence in englysh', whilst the latter both aligned himself with Chaucer, and was—as we have seen—an important figure for the promotion of English poetry.[49] Indeed, the portrait of Skelton that Borde appropriates in the *Introduction* depicts Skelton garlanded with laurels: whilst Skelton showed a degree of audacity in extending his laureateship from Latin learning to English poetry, as a self-crowned laureate, Borde is more presumptuous still.

Borde's choice of style—despite the fact that it is later mocked as ornate and ponderous by men such as Day—is consequently integral to his commitment to improving the reputation of England, its people, and language.[50] In his English 'of late dayes [. . .] amended', Borde finds a copiousness of words with which to match the copiousness of materials his homeland possesses, a celebration of indigenous abundance that is a key facet of Borde's patriotic programme. As will be explored in the next chapter, the sixteenth-century habit of literary stocktaking was well established by the 1540s. Borde's texts are eulogies to abundance. His *Peregrination* (an account of his travels round England) amounts (like much of William Harrison's *Description of England* in 1577) to a compilation of lists: of market towns, castles, bishops, mountains,

---

[48] See, for example, Borde, *Dyetary*, A2ᵛ; Andrew Borde, *The pryncyples of Astronomye the whiche diligently perscrutyd is in maner a pronosticacyon to the worlde* (1547), π2ᵛ.

[49] Borde, *Introduction*, D4ᵛ; id., *Breuiary*, A1ᵛ; John Skelton, *A litel boke called Colyn Cloute* (1545), D7ʳ; Geoffrey Chaucer, *The assemblie of foules* (?1540), A1ʳ; William Caxton, epilogue to Chaucer's *Consolacion of Philosophie*, in W. J. B. Critch (ed.), *Prologues and Epilogues of William Caxton*, EETS, original series, 176 (1928), 37; cf. Richard Pynson's proheme to *Canterbury Tales* (1526), cited by Jones, *Triumph of English*, 26; Skelton, 'The Garlande or Chapelet of Laurell', in Scattergood (ed.), *Poems*, ll. 386–99, 414–27.

[50] Day, *Englishe Secretarie*, 38–9.

stone bridges, rivers, forests, and parks.[51] This endeavour to enumerate the objects found within England's shores serves an explicitly national purpose. This is found in the works of Borde's near-contemporary, and fellow physician, William Turner, no less than those of their successor Harrison. From 1548 to 1568, Turner demonstrated his undeniable fervour for his native land by producing a series of ever expanding herbals. In his view, 'greate honoure' was accorded to 'our contre' by the 'numbre of soueraine & strang herbes [. . .] in Englande that were not in other nations'.[52] Turner's classifying continued unabated into the reign of Elizabeth, when in 1568 (despite recurrent illness) he promised her 'a Booke of the names and natures of fishes [. . .] within [her] Mayesties dominions / to the great delite of noble men / and profit of [her] hole Realm'.[53]

  Through passages copious in words and objects, Borde promotes England as a self-enclosed, self-sufficient island stronghold: a land of material riches, possessing 'copiousnes of woll & cloth', 'Gold, Siluer, Tin, Lead & Yron', and capable of economic, territorial, and linguistic expansion.[54] His paratactic prose, suited to accumulation, accrues praise in phrase after phrase, whilst the subtleties that Borde records in regard to material objects, such as food, become proof of his country's fertility and refinement. Lampreys are distinguished from freshwater lamprons; mature conies from young rabbits; cultivated filberts from wild hazelnuts; wardens, or baking-pears, from pears in general. In the *Introduction*, this foison of words also extends to the question of fortification, with the realm protected by a protracted list of 'noble defences, as castels, bulwarkes & blokhouses' (A4ᵛ); the abundance of synonyms advertises the alleged abundance of fortifications. Excess is a mode of writing for Borde. At times, matter itself spills out beyond the confines of Borde's pages, be it a list in the *Introduction* of England's 'portes and hauyns' too 'long to reherse'

  [51] Preserved as *The Peregrination of Doctor Boarde*, in Thomas Hearne (ed.), *Benedictus Abba Petroburgensis, de Vita et Gestis Henrici II et Ricardi I*, 2 vols. (Oxford, 1735), ii. 764–807.
  [52] William Turner, *The Names of Herbes in Greke, Latin, Englishe, Duche & Frenche* (1548), A2ᵛ.
  [53] William Turner, *The first and seconde partes of the herbal lately ouersene, corrected and enlarged with the thirde parte* (1568), *3ᵛ.
  [54] Borde, *Introduction*, A4ᵛ.

(B1^r), or the abundance of medical knowledge in the *Breuiary*, too great to be contained within one volume: the second volume, comprising this surplus information, carries the title *The Extravagantes*, literally meaning 'wandering out of bounds' (*OED* 1).

Yet even as, in the *Introduction*, Borde endeavours to portray England as a cohesive and copious island fortress that 'almost his grace hath munited, & in maner walled [. . .] rounde aboute' (A4^v), Borde's account is not descriptive, but prescriptive, shot through with apprehension, not celebration. England might be depicted— like More's Utopia—as the epitome of easily defensible self-reliance, but unlike Utopia, England is only potentially unassailable and self-sustaining: England's defences are still in the process of construction (as 'our noble prynce hath & dayly dothe make'), and corn is only adequate 'if they *wold* kepe [it] within their realme' (my emphasis).[55] Borde preaches a recurrent message of self-containment. 'I had no peere, yf to my selfe I were trewe,' his Englishman confesses (A4^r). As with the passage on corn, however, such potential is conditional, a hypothesis cut short by the statement—'bycause I am not so'—that follows. 'To father, mother, and freende, I wyl be vnkynde,' the Englishman confesses. When Borde imagines the English surviving 'although al nacions were set against them' (A4^v), it is less a boast than a moment that reveals both the anxiety beneath, and the motivation for, the passage, as it urges Borde's compatriots to stay loyal, for their own self-protection if no higher ideal. Borde's strident eulogy reflects the troubled position of England in the early 1540s. Henry VIII's break from Rome the previous decade isolated England from the Continent, still over-whelmingly loyal to Rome, and his divorce of Catherine of Aragon destroyed the alliance with Spain and the Holy Roman Emperor, Catherine's nephew, Charles V. England's diplomatic vulnerability naturally emboldened the old alliance of its ancient enemies, France and Scotland, and the early 1540s consequently saw England threatened on two fronts: the south coast and the Scottish border. When Borde sets England's self-sufficiency in a defensive light, dependent

---

[55] A Venetian ambassador to England notes a similar discrepancy between potential abundance and actual deficit in 1554. However, he attributes it to negligent agricultural practices, rather than exportation. See Giacomo Saranzo, *Relazione D'Inghilterra*, in Eugenio Alberi (ed.), *Relazioni degli Ambasciatori Veneti al Senato*, iii. 31–87, at 48.

on corn and fortifications, he draws attention to the essentials of withstanding a siege that seemed all too likely.

Borde's pen repeatedly reveals a country of ragged and vulnerable boundaries, compromised from both within and without. When Borde writes to Cromwell from Scotland in 1536, he begins by warning against 'by yend thre thowsand skottes & innumeralle other alyons' resident in England, 'which doth (specially the skottes) much harme to the kynges leege men thorowh ther ewyll wordes'.[56] As the account proceeds, the effect of these malevolent strangers becomes apparent: 'for as I wentt thorow ynglond I mett & was in company off many rurall felows ^english men^ that loue nott our gracyose kynge'. The tag 'english men' is inserted into the text as an interlinear afterthought, secondary to, and less certain than, their status as 'rurall felows', who, distanced from the political core, constitute a 'frontier society' that—according to the sixteenth-century historian Polydore Vergil—'seemethe more to be apperteining to the Scottishe territorie', closer to its supposed enemies (the Scots) than its nominal realm (England).[57] The 'Englishness' of these men is further diluted by the impetus of the passage in which they appear. The force of Borde's attack is geared at potentially hostile foreigners resident in England (an inversion of his interpretation of their presence as approbation of his native land in the public text of the *Introduction*).[58] 'Wolde to Iesu [. . .] that yow hade neuer an alyon in your realme specyally skottes for I neuer knew alyon goode to ynglonde exceppt thei knew profytt & lucre shold be to them,' Borde continues, resuming the assault with which the letter begins, as if it had never been disrupted or complicated by the incursion of his treacherous compatriots. The narrative momentum distracts the reader from the presence of these 'rurall felows' as 'english men', a status signalled only by that one interpolation. The act of reading thus threatens to include them under the label 'alyon', their nationality effectively annulled by their disloyalty.

---

[56] PRO State Papers, Henry 1/103/61.

[57] Polydore Vergil, *English History*, 2. For a discussion of characteristics of frontier societies, see Anthony Goodman, 'The Anglo-Scottish Marches in the Fifteenth Century: A Frontier Society?', in Roger A. Mason (ed.), *Scotland and England, 1286–1815* (Edinburgh: Edinburgh University Press, 1987), 18–33.

[58] 'In Englande howe manye alyons hath and doth dwell of all maner of nacyons. Let euery man iudge the cause why' (Borde, *Introduction*, E1ʳ).

Language is Borde's most basic unit for nationality and here England is far from the cohesive unit Borde would want it to be. As we have seen, Scottish and Northern English rub uncomfortably close. Despite the congratulatory gloss placed on the passage in the *Introduction* detailing the 'many sundry speeches beside englyshe' spoken within England, variety is not a cause for jubilation, but concern, as a threat to, and demonstration of the lack of, a coherent national identity. 'There be many men and women the whiche cannot speake one worde of Englyshe, but all Cornyshe,' Borde informs his readers in the section on Cornwall (B2ᵛ). As the Cornish are transformed into anthropological curiosities, unable to 'nombre aboue. xxx.' (B3ʳ), linguistic incomprehension accompanies cultural distance. The section on Cornwall lies uneasily on the margins of England, labelled an 'appendex', not fully incorporated within it, literally a piece of land which 'hangs on'. Similarly, Ireland and Wales, dealt with in separate chapters, retain identities structurally distinct from their English liege lord, despite the latter's official union with England effected by the second Act of Union in 1543.

THE POLITICS OF FOOD AND PHYSIC

In his expansion of English through borrowing and doubling, Borde stands in obvious debt to Elyot. The relationship is compounded by Elyot's publication of a medical handbook, *The Castel of helthe*, in 1539, three years before Borde's *Dyetary*, the content of which owes much to Elyot's treatise, in particular the twelve chapters detailing the qualities of over 120 different foodstuffs. Yet despite the similarity in subject matter and their mutual subscription to Galenic practices, the way in which the two authors use this shared tradition is revealingly different. For his discussion on diet, Elyot divides his potential readers into the four humoral types of melancholic, phlegmatic, choleric, and sanguine. In turn, each foodstuff is examined for its possible medical efficacy or harmfulness and, further to that, for its suitability for each of these 'complexions'. In contrast, Borde postpones the division of readers into humoral types until after the discussion on each foodstuff, providing separate, later chapters on the appropriate diet for each. For the bulk of the text, he can thus treat his readers as one cohesive body of Englishmen, all possessing an 'English' stomach. Not only are the medical effects of each ingredient played down, but (as in Borde's *Introduction*) food becomes characteristic of national groupings. The inhabitants of 'hyghalmen' enjoy eating 'the chese the whiche is full of magotes, [. . .] called there the best chese', consuming the grubs 'as fast as we do eate comfets'; 'ale for an englysshe man is a naturall drynke', to be distinguished from 'bere', which, whilst fitting for 'a dutche man', is 'to the detryment of many englysshe men', a contrast between the two beverages Elyot never makes.[59] Beef in particular is extolled by Borde as 'good meate for an Englysshe man'; Elyot is notably more tentative, observing that 'it maketh grosse bloude, and ingendreth melancoly'.[60] In the case of venison, Borde's belief in the 'national' properties of food is still more pronounced. Whereas Elyot concurs wholeheartedly with received medical opinion, declaring venison capable of 'ingendring melancoly, and makyng many feareful dreames, and dispos[ing] the bodye to a feuer', Borde overrides medical advice, stating that 'although the flesshe be dispraysed in physycke, [. . .] I am sure it is a lordes dysshe, and [. . .] good for an Englysshe man, for it doth anymate hym to be as he is: whiche is, stronge and hardy'.[61]

The attention Borde pays to food holds further, more personal resonance. When Borde informs his readers in the chapter of the *Introduction* which 'sheweth the author' that 'I am, as I am, but not as I was', the sentence rings with a defiant self-sufficiency (E1r). Despite the impression of opacity, however, the riddle is a plea for communication. Even in 1547, Borde was still keen to refute what he once 'was': a Carthusian monk. The Carthusian order was vegetarian and distinguished for its frequent fasting, a practice which, on fast days, allowed the consumption of bread and water only. Indeed, one of the ways in which, in the 1530s, Cromwell's agent Jasper Fyloll suggested that the inhabitants of the Charterhouse could be demoralized, and the identity of their order undermined, was through the introduction of 'fleshe' into their convent,

---

59 Borde, *Dyetary*, G4rv; F2rv. 'Dutche man' here refers to the inhabitants of what we now term Germany.
60 Ibid. H3r; Thomas Elyot, *The Castel of helthe* (1539), G4r.
61 Ibid. H1r; Borde, *Dyetary*, I1v.

'contrarye to theyre old ill custom'.[62] Renunciation of the order was signalled as much by diet as appearance, as when Fyloll comments that one monk 'hathe chaungid his habytt to seculer priestes clothing and eatyth fleshe'.[63] The abundant references to meat and alcohol that recur throughout all Borde's works consequently hold an added edge. We have already witnessed the enthusiasm of the post-Carthusian Borde for red meat. The production and partaking of good quality alcohol fulfil similar functions in indicating his approval of the secular lifestyle. 'Euell ale' is repeatedly used to decry regions such as Scotland and Cornwall (where the brew will 'make one kake, also to spew'), whilst in the case of Brabant provision of 'good wyne, and englyshe bere' is proof enough of it being 'a comodyous and pleasaunt countrey'.[64] Water, meanwhile, is judged 'not holsome sole by it selfe for an englysshe man'.[65]

Borde's deviation from Elyot's praise of water (as having 'preeminence aboue all other lycoures' and being responsible for the longevity of antediluvial mortals, 'duryng which tyme, men lyued eight or nyne hunderde yeres') is all the more striking in the light of the use Borde makes of Elyot's treatise at this point, following its phrasing and structure with unusual proximity.[66] It is worth comparing the two versions. Elyot's reads:

The rayne water, after the opinion of the most men, if it be receyued pure and cleane, is most subtyl and penetratiue of any other waters: the next is that, whiche issueth out of a spring in the east, and passeth swiftly among great stones or rockes: The thirde is of a cleane ryuer, whyche renneth on greate harde stones or pebles.[67]

Borde echoes Elyot:

The best water is rayne water, so be it that it be clene and purely taken. Next to it is ronnyng water, the whiche doth swyftly ronne from the Eest in to the west vpon stones or pybles. The thyrde water to be praysed, is ryuer or broke water, the which is clere[,] ronnynge on pibles and grauayl.[68]

[62] BL Cleopatra E. iv, 43ʳ.
[63] Ibid. 42ᵛ.   [64] Borde, *Introduction*, D1ᵛ, B2ʳ, E4ʳ.
[65] Borde, *Dyetary*, E4ʳ.   [66] Elyot, *Castel*, H4ᵛ–I1ʳ.
[67] Ibid. I1ʳ.   [68] Borde, *Dyetary*, E4ᵛ.

The opinions are those of Hippocrates and Galen (key sources acknowledged by both Borde and Elyot),[69] but the marked similarity in the order and wording of Borde's extract suggests it is influenced by Elyot's *Castel*, rather than a Greek original. Departing from Elyot, Borde deliberately emphasizes the enjoyment and benefits of meat and alcoholic beverages, 'pray[ing] God to sende [him venison . . .], physycke notwithstandyng', or cursing 'euyl ale-brewers and alewyues, for theyr euyl brewyng & euyl measure'.[70] In doing so, he hopes to neutralize his past. The path he chooses, itemizing native goods in an abundance of words and objects, is after all that taken by Turner, physician, botanist, and prominent Reformation polemicist, author of the ever expanding herbal discussed earlier and such antipapal tracts as *The huntynge and the fyndyng out of the Romishe fox* (1543).

The line Borde treads throughout his books is one of carefully phrased loyalty, signposting their unsubversive content and intentions. F. J. Furnivall and Thomas Fuller posit potential identities for the 'Pascall' from whom Borde dissociates himself in his *Introduction*, declaring that 'Pascall the playn dyd wryte and preach manifest thinges that were open in the face of the world to reubuke sin wyth the which matter I haue nothyng to do' (E1ᵛ). They suggest, respectively, Pope Pasquil II and John Paschal, a scholar and preacher in the reign of Edward III.[71] One obvious contender they omit is the protagonist of Elyot's *Pasquil the playne* (1533). Even as he calls upon the authority of Elyot, Borde is keen to distance himself from the disillusioned author of *Pasquil*.[72] If, as Thomas Betteridge convincingly argues, *Pasquil* was indeed 'an oppositional history of the religious changes of the 1530s', then Borde's desire to differentiate his work from Elyot's treatise becomes all the more pointed.[73] The wanderings

---

[69] Luis Garcia Ballester and Jon Arrizabalaga (eds.), *Galen and Galenism: Theory and Medical Practice from Antiquity to the European Renaissance* (Aldershot: Ashgate, 2002).

[70] Borde, *Dyetary*, I1ᵛ, F4ᵛ.

[71] Furnivall (ed.), *Boorde's Introduction*, 145; Thomas Fuller, *Worthies of England* (1662), part III, 59.

[72] Although Berthelet's first edition (1533) is anonymous, the second, also printed in 1533 (STC 7672.5), is attributed to Elyot on A1ᵛ.

[73] Thomas Betteridge, *Tudor Histories of the English Reformations, 1530–83* (Aldershot: Ashgate, 1999), 38.

Borde proceeds to describe in the *Introduction* are not those of a pasquilian malcontent, railing from the political margins, but are presented as a withdrawal into political and religious neutrality. Borde's division of the chapters of his *Introduction* into doggerel, spoken by representatives of each country, and authorial prose serves as a further shield to his purported objectivity. Potentially controversial statements (such as the impact of Protestantism on Saxony and Bohemia, G2^v–G3^r) can be placed in the mouth of one of Borde's foreigners, without revealing the opinion of the authorial persona, distanced as it is from the comment in terms of medium (being verse, not prose) and origin (the words of an un-English, 'fictional' character).

'SUCH A PROCTOUR FOR THE PAPISTS': THE CATHOLIC BORDE EXPOSED[74]

As argued above, Borde's portrait of ideal 'Englishness' is not only a tribute, and spur, to his compatriots: it is also the means by which he was busily constructing an identity with which to silence his potential critics. Some of these backbiters can be glimpsed in Borde's letters to Cromwell in the 1530s, in the form of 'certyn persons thatt owth me in mony & stuff'.[75] He explains in August 1536 that:

I do aske my dewty off them, & they callyth me appostate & all to nowght & sayth they wyll troble me, & doth slawnder me by hynd my bak off thynges that I shold do xx^{ti} yeres a gone, & trewly they can nott proue ytt nor I neuer dyd ytt / this matter ys that I shold be conuersantt with women.

In calling Borde 'appostate'—someone who renounces their religious order without legal dispensation (*OED* 2)—these men not only attempt to intimidate Borde into cancelling their debts by raising the ghost of his monastic past: they also carry that past dangerously into his present. Even after the break with Rome and dissolution of the monasteries, Henry VIII still demanded that the English religious keep their vows of celibacy. Through their accusations of apostasy and sexual misconduct, Borde's enemies nullify

---

[74] Ponet, *Apologie*, 48.   [75] PRO State Papers, Henry, 1/105/295.

his dispensation from the Carthusian order which he is so eager to advertise in his correspondence with Cromwell. In doing so, they make a monk of him again. Within his works, Borde frequently plays on the dual meaning of his surname as both 'quip' and 'table of fare', both of which conjure the image of the jovial glutton with which he seeks to disprove any allegiance to his ascetic Carthusian past.[76] His name, however, is also transformed into an edgier pun in the *Introduction*. 'Andreas parforatus est meum nomen,' he writes ($M3^r$), rendering his surname as 'parforatus': 'pierced, or bored through'.[77] Pinioned by his past, at the heart of Borde's works is a sense of imminent persecution, a further incitement to his attempted self-reinvention.

Within Borde's texts, jibes at contemporary Rome and its allegedly corrupt church act as a fittingly antipapist veneer and an easy means of combating associations with a past linked with resistance to religious reformation and the royal supremacy. 'I dyd se lytle vertue in rome, and much abhominable vyces,' Borde informs us in his *Introduction*, in the chapter which 'treateth of Italy and Rome', a coupling that yokes together Italy and papacy, tainting both with each other's vices ($H4^{rv}$). He even promises to return to these abominations in detail, declaring that 'who so wyl se more of Rome and Italy, let hym loke in the second boke, the lxvii. chapter'.[78] Rome also becomes the site of a particularly ingenious form of poisoning in chapter 362 of the *Breuiary*, where 'in Rome they wyll poison a mannes sterope, or sadle, or any other thynge' and 'if any parte of ones body do take any heat or warmnesse of the poison, the man is than poisoned' ($Mm3^r$). The most extended attack on Rome comes (tellingly enough) in the chapter on the 'Demoniacke person' in the *Extrauagantes* ($A4^v$). Here, Borde's eyewitness account of a mad woman, carried 400 miles from Germany to be cured in St Peter's, deviates into his exposure of the physical and moral decay at the heart of papal Rome, as witnessed by the 'vile case' of St Peter's crumbling fabric, and the 'Lechery & boogery, deceyt and vsury in euery corner & place' ($B2^r$). Rather than a place to exorcise devils, Rome becomes a place of devils. 'Be

---

[76] See, e.g., Borde, *Introduction*, $D1^r$, $F2^r$.

[77] 'Perforo', in Charlton T. Lewis and Charles Short (eds.), *A Latin Dictionary* (Oxford: Oxford University Press, 1879).

[78] This second book was either lost or never published.

nat these creatures possessed of the deuyl[?]' Borde enquires, referring to those so-called Christians who 'kyll [their] owne soule[s]' with vice and who, through neglect of God, 'wyl se their Cathedrall churche to lye lyke a Swynes stie' (B2^{rv}). He adds a further note of reformist resentment. Whilst '*their* Cathedral church' lies in shameful ruins, it is '*our* Peter pence' (English money gathered in the annual collection for the pope, a custom discontinued by Henry VIII) that 'was wel bestowed to the reedifienge of saint Peters church the which did no good but to noryshe sin & to mainteine warre' (B2^v; my emphasis).

The occasion on which Borde adopts this suitably antipapist stance reveals a disjunction in textual intention, however. His assault on Roman morals tactfully curtails a potentially hazardous narrative. The mad woman has been brought to Rome to be cured at a pillar 'within the precynct of S. Peters church without saint Peters chapell [. . .] to the whiche our Lorde Iesus Chryst dyd lye in him selfe vnto [sic] in Pylates hall, as the Romayns dothe saye' (B1^r). Even as he prevaricates on the veracity of the pillar's history, with the interjection 'as the Romayns dothe saye', Borde's continuation of the tale to its conclusion would necessarily first, offer decisive opinion on the potency of the very type of relic vilified and destroyed in the first wave of religious reformation, and secondly, validate the practice of driving away devils banned by the injunctions issued in July 1547, the year of the text's publication.[79] Borde withdraws from the scene before the cure can be effected, thus replacing one first-hand description (of a miracle) with another (of Roman depravity) guaranteed to be more palatable to the Edwardian regime. The confusion of the narrative at this point, however, is further signalled by Borde's sudden shift into an attack on swearing, an evil—caused by the devil—with which England is apparently afflicted. Borde thus manoeuvres his text away from the histrionic possession condemned by the Edwardian Reformation to a less contentious issue. The chapter, moreover, ends dutifully, placing the 'remedy' for swearing—and heresy—firmly in the hands of 'the kinge our soueraigne Lorde with his most honorable counsell' (B3^r). Borde's loyalty to the royal supremacy and regal jurisdiction in spiritual affairs is consequently reasserted.

Borde's texts are full of such narrative U-turns. The chapter on

---

[79] *Iniunccions geuen by the moste excellent prince, Edward the sixte* (1547), C2^v.

Navarre in the *Introduction* deviates from the habitual structure of brief, third-person descriptions of each country's people, economy, language, and coinage. Instead, Borde recounts the story of the miraculous survival of a pilgrim unjustly hanged whilst journeying to the shrine of St James in Compostella and the marvellous resurrection of a brace of chickens due to be eaten by the justice of the town (L3ʳᵛ). The legend is narrated without scepticism, credulity suddenly revoked by the incursion into the text of Borde's own persona and first-hand experience. 'I dyd se a cock and a hen ther in the churche and do tell the fable as it was tolde me not of thre or .iiii. parsons but of many,' he comments, deferring belief in the yarn, now dubbed a 'fable', on to a host of anonymous dupes (L3ᵛ). As Borde continues, declaring 'that there is not one heare nor one bone of saint Iames in spayne in compostell' (L4ʳ), his prose takes on the semblance of a good Protestant narrative, exposing the falsity of shrines and mendacity of clerics who profit from them. Nevertheless, this potentially reformist strategy is qualified by the fact that Borde heard the shrine was bogus during confession. Retelling the story, Borde attempts to distance himself from the religiosity of this occasion and the religious susceptibilities of his younger self. His actions in going to confession are, with hindsight, marked as 'illudyd' (L4ʳ). He then suggests his 'absolucion' is in exchange for medical services: the 'auncyent doctor of dyuynite' who takes confession is described as 'blear yed' and Borde chooses to 'passe ouer' whether confession was given 'to haue [his] counsell in physycke or no'. Yet this extraneous detail does little to excuse Borde's participation in 'papist' ritual and, on closer examination—for all Borde's exposure of the duplicity of Compostella—it is not the genuineness of relics he questions, but their whereabouts. St James's bones, removed by Charlemagne, lie in Toulouse, not Compostella. For Borde, they are still those of St James, and the doctor's 'blear yed' condition is actual, in need of medical attention, not—as in Reformation polemic—symbolic of spiritual blindness.[80]

Whether in homage to this saintly skeleton, or to discredit further the priests of Compostella, Borde 'therefore' travels to Toulouse, and 'by olde aucentyck wrytinges & seales' establishes

[80] For an attack on 'blynde custom', see Wilson, *Rhetorique*, 18ᵛ; cf. Borde's correspondence with Cromwell, PRO State Papers, Henry, 1/103/61.

'the premyses [of his confessor] to be of treuth': 'but thes words cannot be beleued of incipient parsons specially of some englyshe men and Skotyshe men for whan I dyd dwell in the vniuersite of orlyance [. . .] I dyd mete with .ix. Englyshe and Skotyshe parsons goyng to saynt compostell' (L4ᵛ). Borde is careful to distinguish himself from these pilgrims. The meeting is highlighted as one of chance, as he was 'casually going ouer the bredge into the town', and he depicts himself trying to dissuade them from their mission, 'aduertys[ing] them to returne home to England'. Unmoved by his advice, the pilgrims continue and, heedless of his own warnings, Borde accompanies them. The narrative that ensues provides a very different 'pilgrim's tale' to that found earlier in the benevolent comedy of St James's feathered friends, for 'in the retornyng thorow spayn for all the crafte of Physycke that I coulde do[,] they dyed all by eatynge of frutes and drynkynge of water the whych I dyd euer refrayne my selfe' (M1ʳ). Once Borde has arrived safely in Aquitaine, it is not a shrine that he kisses, but unhallowed ground, in joy of his deliverance.

By providing this revised pilgrim's tale, Borde weaves his way around the problematic issue opened up by his initial excursion into the genre, stemming the 'old-style' Roman Catholicism that threatens to disrupt his pose of conforming to the Henrician rejection of the Roman Church. Yet the central core of belief—the validity of pilgrimages to 'genuine' shrines—remains unchallenged, the subject effectively unbroached until the final chapter. In contrast to 'the cyrcuyte [. . .] of Europ' mapped out by the bulk of the *Introduction*, in the concluding chapter, the trajectory of travel is suddenly linear, as Borde traces the route, necessary timing, and organization of a pilgrimage to Jerusalem, despite the fact that pilgrimages were outlawed by the injunctions of 1538.[81] Not only is the exact path detailed (from 'Douer or Sandwhich [. . .] take shypping to Calys, from Calis let him goe to Grauelyng, to Nuporte, to Burges, to Anwarpe' and beyond), but also the optimum date for departure ('after Ester .vii. or .viii. dayes') and requirements for travel, such as making a 'banke or exchaunge of [. . .] mony [. . .] to be payd at Venis', or instructions on how and where to charter a ship (N3ʳ). The text, ending in Jerusalem, at the tomb of Christ, becomes a pilgrimage itself, standing without

81 Duffy, *Stripping of the Altars*, 407.

ironic comment; the last language lesson finishes on a prayer: 'Iesus of nazareth kyng of Iues. The son of god haue mercy on me. Amen. / Iesuch natzori melech Iuedim. Ben elohim conueni. Amen' (N4ʳ).

For all Borde's noisy refutations of his Carthusian past, manifestations of his adherence to previous religious practices seep into his texts, with sometimes surprising disregard. Borde's choice of dedicatees appears particularly unguarded. The only two books addressed to named patrons are the *Introduction* and *Dyetary*, offered respectively to 'lady Mary doughter of our souerayne lorde kyng Henry the eyght' (A1ʳ), and Thomas, Duke of Norfolk, head of the powerful Howard faction. Both dedicatees were prominent in their resistance to reformed religion, and are notable for the paucity, and (in Mary's case) the controversial nature, of books dedicated to them during the 1530s and 1540s. Mary, whose connection with Borde's *Introduction* is even flaunted on its title page, is (whilst a princess) the recipient of a mere six extant books besides Borde's own, two of which (published in 1525 and 1526) predate the religious troubles resulting from the split with Rome. Of the remaining four, three are of a distinctly religious turn: namely, a translation of St Bernard by the Austin friar Thomas Paynell, entitled *A compendious & moche fruytefull treatyse of well liuynge* (1545); Paynell's *The pithy and moost notable sayinges of al Scripture* (1550); and John Proctor's *The fal of the Late Arrian* (1549), listing reasons for doubting Christ's divinity with their accompanying refutations (also found in Christopher Marlowe's papers after his death).[82] The fourth book is Giles Duwes's *Introductorie for to lerne to rede, to pronounce and to speke Frenche Trewely*, first published in 1533. As Greg Walker has shown, this seemingly apolitical French grammar 'carries a clear and effective political agenda', as—through dialogues—it 'portrays a world of domestic harmony placed clearly in the period before the king's "Great Matter" ', and 'focuses upon a happy and well-integrated royal family: Henry, Catherine and Mary, the centre of a prosperous and contented realm'.[83]

Just as the dedications of Borde's works position him within religiously conservative circles, so too the works themselves cling to tenets of the 'old' faith. Borde's medical handbooks, instructing

[82] *STC*, ii. 253.
[83] Walker, 'Dialogue, Resistance and Accommodation', 106.

readers how to live, serve as secular equivalents to lay devotional treatises, such as Richard Whiford's *A werke for householders* (1533) or Andrew Chertsey's *The arte or crafte to lyue well and to dye well* (1505). Entitled *The boke for to learne a man to be wyse in buldyng of his howse for the helth of body & to holde queyetnes for the helth of his soule, and body,* Robert Wyer's extract of the first eight chapters of Borde's *Dyetary* (published in 1550) also draws attention to this proximity of body and soul, a concept encapsulated in the Latin word *salus*, translatable as both 'health' and 'salvation'. In Borde' eyes, health—like salvation under the Catholic scheme of good works—is something for which you need to toil, 'for sicke men & women be lyke a pece of rustye harnys the which can nat be made bright at the fyrste skourynge, but let a man continew in rubbynge and skowrynge and then the harnys wyll be bright' (B3ʳ). Towards the end of the *Dyetary*, the role of doctor even merges with that of priest. Just as the *Introduction* closes with pilgrimage and prayer, so too the *Dyetary* acquires a sudden narrative thrust. The validity of extreme unction was a point of contention throughout the 1530s.[84] Nevertheless, as the theoretical patient worsens, the *Dyetary* concludes with something akin to the last rites, and the soul of a dying man is prayed to rest (N4ʳ). The flash points of contemporary religious controversy are thus introduced in to Borde's works under the guise of medical advice, attaining the secular semantics of healthy, rather than righteous, living. 'Fre wyl', conferred by God (a concept derided as 'popishe' by John Ponet in 1555), is consequently demonstrated not through religion, but through the choice facing each reader in adopting or rejecting the modus vivendi which may 'abreuiate his lyfe by surfetynge[,] by dronkennesse, by pencifulnesse, by thought and care, by takyng the pockes with women, and many other infectious sickenesses'.[85]

In the context of Reformation England, seemingly innocent topics, such as Borde's lost diatribe against beards, acquire religious and political meaning. Its existence is only known through the reaction it elicited from a satirist, Barnes, entitled *The treatyse*

---

[84] See Diarmaid MacCulloch, *Thomas Cranmer: A Life* (New Haven: Yale University Press, 1996), 212, 277; Haigh, *English Reformations*, 132–3, 155.

[85] Ponet, *Apologie*, 84; cf. Saranzo, *Relazione*, in Alberi (ed.), *Relazioni*, iii. 71; Borde, *Breuiary*, B3ʳ.

answerynge the boke of Berdes, published by Robert Wyer in
1542. Barnes treats Borde's book as a joke, an example of the
humour Borde recommended to the Duke of Norfolk as 'one of the
chefest thynges of Physycke'.[86] Barnes therefore responds in kind,
explaining that 'wheras [Borde] was anymatyd to wryte his boke to
thende, that great men may laugh therat / I haue deuysed this
answere, to the extent, that in the readyng they myght laughe vs
bothe to scorne'.[87] The treatise is further placed in the jest-book
tradition by its attribution on the title page to 'Collyn Clowte',
persona of Skelton, who acquired the posthumous reputation of
'merie' Skelton, author of numerous jest-books.[88] Barnes traces
Borde's dislike of facial hair to a raucous evening in Montpellier,
where Borde was a medical student. After dinner at 'one Hans
smormowthes house[,] a Duche man' (A3^{v}), Borde was brought
'cupshote' to bed, where he 'vometyd' onto the friend helping him
and his own beard, wherein 'as moche as [his] berde myghte holde
vpon [his] berde remayned'. Waking next morning, and smelling
vomit in his beard, he 'fel to it a fresshe', with the result that 'when
[he] sawe [his] berde, [he] sayd that it was a shamfull thynge on any
mans face'. In Barnes's tale, Borde appears as both the genial come-
dian (promoting laughter as the best medicine) and the hapless
drunkard, the butt of the joke, the role of fool which is endorsed
by the woodcut adorning the verso of the title page, depicting a
fool in motley, cap awry, exposed rear raised heavenwards. The
tale is also positioned in the jest-book tradition by the presence of
the stereotyped 'Duche man', who fits the caricature drawn in
Borde's *Introduction*, where the 'base Doche' are distinguished for
their drunkenness and love of butter. Not only does Smormowthe
provide suitably Teutonic amounts to drink (to Borde's downfall),
his surname—*smor*, or greasy, mouth—also points to his nation's
image as butter-eaters.

The politics of beard-wearing, however, had a more potent
application, and one which Barnes's jovial riposte significantly

---

[86] Borde, *Dyetary*, A3^{r}.

[87] [Robert] Barnes, *The treatyse answerynge the boke of Berdes* (1542), A1^{v}.

[88] Anon., *A Hundred Mery Talys* (1526), in P. M. Zall (ed.), *A Hundred Mery
Talys and Other English Jestbooks of the Fifteenth and Sixteenth Centuries*
(Lincoln: University of Nebraska Press, 1963), 71–2; Anon., *Tales and quicke
answeres, very mery, and pleasant to rede* (1535), ibid. 252. This tradition culmi-
nated in the publication of *Merie Tales, Newly imprinted and made by Master
Skelton, Poet laureat*, printed by Thomas Colwell (c.1567).

suppresses. As Diarmaid MacCulloch demonstrates in relation to portraits of Cranmer, 'the significance of clerical beards as an aggressive anti-Catholic gesture was well-recognized in mid-Tudor England', a religious connotation of facial hair also found in Thomas Wilson's conjunction of writers who 'dispraise beards, or commend shauen heddes', the latter being a mark of monasticism more immediately apparent to a reader even now, over four centuries later.[89] Borde, as a clean-shaven ex-monk, obviously needed to justify his beardlessness. Barnes's efforts, published by Wyer, who printed Borde's *Dyetary*, were (I would argue) in collaboration of this end. Hidden within the *Breuiary* lies a further risqué joke. In chapter 133, which 'dothe shewe of a mannes face', Borde's text declares that 'the face may haue many impedimentes. The fyrst impediment is to se a man hauynge no berde' (P2ᵛ). His words are contradicted by the decorative capital 'F', depicting a beardless cleric, carrying the crosier borne before the bishop as a symbol of his authority. Although woodcuts are often unrelated to the text they decorate, there is at least a wry appropriateness here to the juxtaposition of text and ornament.

Despite lip service to certain aspects of English antipapalism, therefore, Borde retains many tenets of the 'old' faith. His books not only provide a means of trumpeting his national loyalty: they are also an arena in which he endeavours to craft a discourse that is both English and adhering to elements of the old-style religion, bridging the gap between retention of religious ritual and loyalty to the royal supremacy. Even as the *Introduction* is dedicated to Mary, it also memorializes Borde's connection with Cromwell, the agent of reformation. Borde's initial travels 'round about Europ', the raw material for the *Introduction*, were noted in 'a booke of euery region, counter, and prouynce, shewynge the myles, the leeges and the dystaunce from citye to cytie [. . .]. And the cyties & townes names wyth notable thynges within the precyncte or about the sayde cyties' (E1ᵛ). The expanse of 'all chrystendom' was apparently recorded. It is remembered by Borde, however, for its association with one English manor house, 'byshops waltam .viii. myle from Wynchester', the residence of his patron, who is introduced with studied casualness as 'one Thomas cromwell'. In commemorating Cromwell, the recipient of the original book, the

---

[89] MacCulloch, *Cranmer*, 361; Wilson, *Rhetorique*, 4ᵛ–5ʳ.

Introduction thus links two diametrically opposed factions: those of Cromwell and Mary. Borde can be seen attempting a form of accommodation here, trying to reconcile elements, and followers, of unreformed doctrine with loyalty to the new English regime, just as his own works adapt old genres, such as advice-books for pilgrims, to promote the new England, proudly separate from the Roman Church. Borde, that is, points to a period in English history when national identity was only just beginning to be drawn along confessional lines. As such, he reminds us that the equation between early modern Englishness and Protestantism was neither clear-cut nor inevitable.

Despite Borde's recurrent attempts to portray himself as a loyal servant of the nation—and implicit with that, supportive of his king's religious policy—his past caught up with him. Literary history remembered Borde as a joker, posthumously crediting him with a number of jest-books of dubious provenance.[90] Reformist history labelled him a papist, a label that became synonymous with traitor. By 1555, six years after his death, Borde was notable enough to be used by the Protestant Ponet as an example of 'popishe' lechery, and, despite his loud avocation of alcohol and red meat, of 'popishe' fasting, which Borde himself describes in his *Breuiary* as being banished with good works in the religious upheavals of the 1540s.[91] Borde's appearance in Ponet's text alongside the notorious Elizabeth Barton, 'the mayde of Kent' who prophesied Henry VIII's death should he marry Anne Boleyn, further suggests Borde's ill fame amongst reformist circles, and is all the more ironic considering Borde's reference to Barton in the *Introduction*, where he equates her with the heathen Mahomet for practising 'subtyll and crafty castes' (N1^v). The picture Ponet paints is of a distinctly unreformed Borde, 'a proctour for the Papists' who—despite public support for the royal supremacy— nevertheless cultivated a Roman Catholic body, fasting, shaving and, like Thomas More, chastising himself in private, as Ponet describes how Borde, 'wearinge of a shirte of heare / and hanginge

---

[90] A.B., *The Merie Tales of the Mad Men of Gotam*, ed. Stanley J. Kahrl (Evanston, Ill.: Northwestern University Press, 1965); *The first and best Part of Scoggins Iests* (1626); *A ryght pleasaunt and merye Historie, of the Mylner of Abyngton* (1576).

[91] Borde, *Breuiary*, B4^v; for Cromwellian moves against fasting, see Duffy, *Stripping of the Altars*, 405, 430.

his shroud or socking / or buriall sheet at his beds feet / and morti-fyeng his body', 'thryse in the week would drink nothinge but water'.[92] This 'Catholic' body is also associated with 'popishe' hypocrisy and sexual depravity; Borde's 'straytnes of lyfe' is a mere 'color of uirginitie' to cover the fact that this 'holy man [. . .] kept thre whores at once in his chambre at Winchester / to serue not onely himself / but also to help the virgin preests about in the contry as it was prouid / That they might with more ease & lesse payn keepe theire blessed uirginitie'. According to John Bale, Borde was subsequently incarcerated in Fleet prison, where he wrote his will on 11 April 1549. Within a fortnight, he was dead, allegedly poisoned by his own hand.[93]

Just as Borde was eventually exposed as irredeemably papist, so too his writing style became synonymous with papist error. For Wilson, writing in 1553 when associations between Protestantism, Englishness, and the plain style were beginning to be drawn, Borde's distorted syntax (characterized by the signature mark 'of phisick doctour', inverting the usual word order) was as deviant as his Catholic faith.[94] Despite the dominance of later Protestant voices, however, the history of the English Reformations and their literature, in which Borde plays a part, is not merely a Protestant narrative. It can be traced from the 1530s onwards in the abundance of texts that react to, resist, or accommodate religious and cultural changes already under way. These texts recurrently reflect the religious uncertainty of the 1530s and 1540s when—although many observations and rituals of the Roman Church had been cleared away—the world view that had accepted them had not yet been revised. As such, the story begins long before the emergence of a fully fledged Protestant nation and is as much the tale of 'unre-formed' authors such as Borde as it is of vociferously Protestant writers like Bale, Ponet, and John Foxe. To some extent, there are two Reformation narratives. On the one hand, we have that of England reacting to religious and cultural change; on the other, the

[92] Ponet, *Apologie*, 48–9; cf. William Roper, *The Lyfe of Sir Thomas More*, ed. Elsie Vaughan Hitchcock, EETS, original series, 197 (1935), 48–9, 99; Eiléan Ní Chuilleanáin, ' "Strange Ceremonies": Sacred Space and Bodily Presence in the English Reformation', in A. J. Piesse (ed.), *Sixteenth-Century Identities* (Manchester: Manchester University Press, 2000), 133–54.
[93] John Bale, *Scriptorum illustrium maioris Britanniae, Catalogus*, 2 vols. (Basle, 1557, 1559), ii, 105.   [94] Wilson, *Rhetorique*, 89[v].

story of a later Protestant nation. Borde belongs to both. He is party both to the earlier process in which we see authors such as Elyot or Duwes responding to the Henrician Reformation, and to the later process, in which Protestants like Bale surveyed their history and retrospectively felt the need to model it into some kind of order, dividing the players into reformed heroes and unreformed villains.

2

John Leland and 'the bowels of Antiquity'[1]

Not onely ded Johan Leylande collect these frutefull auncyent authors togyther, that men myghte by them inueye agaynste the false doctryne of papystes, corruptynge both the scriptures of God and the chronycles of thys realme, by execrable lyes & fables[,] but also that their wyttye workes myghte come to lyght and be spredde abroade to the whorthye fame of the land. For by them maye it wele apere, the tymes alwayes consydered, that we are no Barbarouse nacyon, as contemptuouslye the Italyane wryters doth call vs.[2]

Chapter 1 explored how Andrew Borde constructed ideas of national identity and publicized his own 'Englishness' in order to shape an acceptable persona with which to negotiate his way through late Henrician and early Edwardian England. As such, Borde is both a pertinent—and poignant—example of an author reacting directly to the first phase of the English Reformation, and a writer who demonstrates the significance of geography, language, and lifestyle (manifested through diet, clothing, and social customs) to conceptions of nationhood in mid-Tudor England. In Chapter 2, I examine how one of Borde's contemporaries, John Leland, responds to the immediate pressures placed upon English identities by the split with Rome. A bibliophile and antiquarian, Leland attempted to fashion a 'new' English history presenting England as a land with a long tradition of justified resistance to papal authority. Like Borde, Leland was also concerned to refute England's reputation as a 'Barbarouse nacyon' and to depict his country as a place of learning, literary accomplishment, and material comfort.

---

[1] Thomas Hearne, *De Rebus Britannicis Collectanea*, 6 vols. (London, 1770), i. p. lii. [2] Bale, *Laboryouse Iourney*, <u>C6ᵛ</u>–<u>C7ʳ</u>.

Stuart Piggott describes Leland as 'a topographer-antiquary whose allegiance was more to the medieval tradition than to the new learning, despite his Paris training in the Renaissance modes of thought'.³ This overstates Leland's 'medievalism', however. Leland was, like Borde, indebted to earlier genres of literature and, more especially, forms of history. Like Borde, he adapted these to the demands of his own age. Leland brought to medieval chronicles both a fashionable humanist Latin style and a historical approach which recognized the need to understand the vernacular languages of Anglo-Saxon, Welsh, and Scots; influenced by his Parisian encounters with Guillaume Budé, a collector of ancient coins, Leland also appreciated the importance of assessing evidence found in artefacts and landscapes. Leland is thus a bridging figure. For national prestige, he clung to ancient legends, such as the foundation myth of the Trojan Brutus and tales of King Arthur, but he fused the material with the new learning and new antiquarianism and formulated it to meet contemporary debates about England's status as a country that was both autonomous from Rome and worthy of international acclaim. Leland's choice of Latin as his preferred medium is both the natural product of his academic training and, as it was for his rival the historian Polydore Vergil, a means of gaining access to a European audience. Latin also allowed Leland to disprove accusations of England's backwardness, employing his versatility in Latin prose and poetry—shown, for example, through ostentatious use of different verse forms in his *Genethliacon* (1543)—to demonstrate the accomplishment of English scholars.⁴ Leland consequently illustrates the changing nature of English humanism during the second quarter of the sixteenth century and its coexistence with, rather than displacement of, earlier traditions.

Leland, who was born between 1503 and 1506, was the product of a model humanist education. After St Paul's School, he proceeded to Christ's College, Cambridge, Oxford, and finally, under some form of royal patronage, to Paris. 'A scholar of international reputation' (James Carley's description), Leland demonstrates the

³ Stuart Piggott, *Ruins in a Landscape: Essays in Antiquarianism* (Edinburgh: Edinburgh University Press, 1976), 11.
⁴ Leicester Bradner, *Musae Anglicanae: A History of Anglo-Latin Poetry, 1500–1925* (New York: Modern Language Association of America, 1940), 27.

increasingly 'domesticized' character of English humanism charted by J. K. McConica in the 'first two decades of the sixteenth century', by which time it was no longer necessary to import humanist talent from France or Italy, as it had been during the reign of Henry VII.[5] Instead, thanks to scholars such as John Colet, founder of St Paul's, English soil was producing home-grown humanists. Leland's humanism not only reflects McConica's 'domesticity' of origin, however. It also represents a shift in English humanism, whereby the international outlook of the 'More circle', to which Leland's master at St Paul's—William Lily—belonged, was being replaced by a more nationally orientated mindset, as younger scholars akin to Leland redirected their humanist learning towards furthering national esteem.[6] 'The desire to award the palm for learning to one's own country', judged by Herbert Weisenger 'a strongly motivating force' in 1580s and 1590s, consequently pre-dates the humanist-educated generation of Philip Sidney, Gabriel Harvey, and Samuel Daniel.[7] That ambition and competitive sense of national honour was no less keen forty years earlier on the part of Leland and contemporaries such as John Bale.

From Thomas Hearne onwards, readers of Leland and Bale have often drawn a sharp distinction between the two. For Hearne, where Leland 'delivered things impartially and in smooth language, so *Bale* quite contrary, and full of scurrilities'; this stylistic difference is manifested in ideological terms in the works of critics such as John Scattergood and James Simpson, who cast Bale as the 'strident', 'radical Protestant', and Leland as the 'civic and literary humanist'.[8] The other much repeated 'truism' is the chaotic nature of Leland's studies. Since Thomas Smith's description in the 1550s—cited by William Huddersford in the eighteenth century—

[5] John Leland, 'Four Poems in Praise of Erasmus by John Leland', ed. and trans. James Carley, *Erasmus in English*, 11 (1981–2), 26–7, at 27; James Kelsey McConica, *English Humanists and Reformation Politics under Henry VIII and Edward VI* (Oxford: Clarendon Press, 1965), 72.

[6] For Lily's connections with More, see Pearl Hogrefe, *The Sir Thomas More Circle* (Urbana: University of Illinois Press, 1959), 26 and passim.

[7] Herbert Weisenger, 'The Self-Awareness of the Renaissance as a Criterion of the Renaissance', *Papers of the Michigan Academy of Science, Arts and Letters*, 29 (1943), 561–67, at 565.

[8] Hearne, *Collectanea*, i. p. lvi; John Scattergood, 'John Leland's *Itinerary* and the Identity of England', in Piesse (ed.), *Sixteenth-Century Identities*, 58–74, at 62; James Simpson, 'Ageism: Leland, Bale and the Laborious Start of English Literary History, 1350–1550', *New Medieval Literatures*, 1 (1997), 213–35, at 225.

of the 'vast heap of observations, which he had thrown together
[. . .] without order, and with a hasty pen, just as they had occurred
to him', and William Harrison's complaint in the 1580s, repeated
by Hearne, that 'his annotations are such and so confounded, as no
man can (in a maner) picke out ciuil sense from them by a leafe
togither', Leland's scholarly enterprises have been criticized, in
Piggott's words, for the fact that they 'seem at no time to have been
planned with any definite idea of how he might utilise the source
material he so industriously gathered'.[9] Both conceptions of
Leland—moderate humanist or disorganized pedant—need closer
consideration. Contrary to Simpson's assertion that Leland 'writes
without any characteristically Protestant flavour at all', I would
argue that, at times, Leland shares Bale's reformist diction.[10]
Leland was, after all, author of *Antiphilarcia*, 'one of the first
works to use antiquarian knowledge as means of establishing
precedents for an independent English church' and which employs
the same techniques of selection and compilation that Henry VIII's
team of scholars used in the late 1520s and early 1530s to assem-
ble arguments from biblical and theological sources justifying his
divorce.[11] Leland's 'Newe yeares gyfte', meanwhile, is replete with
indignation against 'the vsurped autoryte of the Byshopp of Rome
and hys complyces'.[12] As Leland deplores 'the whole college of the
Romanystes, clokynge their crafty affeccyons and argumentes' and
banishing 'truthe' from 'the generall counsell' (C5^v), there is little
to divide his tone from that of the more intemperate Bale.

Bale and Leland harboured a shared ambition to give England a
literary, and reformist, history, and when Leland died with most of
his works unprinted, it was natural enough for Bale to ensure their
publication, be it with accompanying commentary, as with the
'Newe yeares gyfte', printed as *The laboroyouse Iourney* or incorporated into his own studies, as with Leland's *Commentarii de
Scriptoribus Britannicis*, which Bale drew on for his *Scriptorum*

[9] William Huddersford, *The Lives of those eminent Antiquaries John Leland,
Thomas Hearne, and Anthony à Wood*, 2 vols. (Oxford, 1772), i. 26; Hearne,
Collectanea, i. p. lv; Piggott, *Ruins*, 12.   [10] Simpson, 'Ageism', 225–6.
[11] James Carley, 'John Leland's *Cygnea Cantio*: A Neglected Tudor River Poem',
Humanistica Lovaniensa, 32 (1983), 225–41, at 232; Graham Nicholson, 'The Act
of Appeals and the English Reformation', in Claire Cross, David Loades, and J. J.
Scarisbrick (eds.), *Law and Government under the Tudors* (Cambridge: Cambridge
University Press, 1988), 19–30, at 19–22. Leland's *Antiphilarcia* is in CUL MS Ee.
v. 14.   [12] John Leland, 'Newe yeares gyfte', C5^r.

illustrium maioris Britanniae, Catalogus (1557, 1559). Moreover, to recognize the centrality of their common historical project is to restore coherence to Leland's endeavours. The longevity of Leland's reputation as an ultimately doomed scholar, frittering away his energies in obsessive piles of unusable notebooks, is in part due to a division in subsequent work on Leland between those who look at his antiquarian prose and those who study his Latin poetry. It is Leland's poetry, much of which was published during his lifetime, not his private notes or works in progress, which represents a 'finished product', however, and it should be remembered that, for his contemporaries, Leland was a poet as well as an antiquarian, with the cause of his eventual insanity attributed as much to his 'Poëtical Wit' as to his inability to undertake the ambitious projects promised in the 'Newe yeares gyfte'.[13] By looking at the whole range of his work, this chapter offers a re-evaluation of Leland's writings, arguing that they comprise a consistent scholarly programme, championing England as an autonomous 'empire' and thus responding to the mood and needs of the 1540s.

RECOVERING 'THE OLD GLORY OF YOUR RENOUMED BRITAINE'[14]

The 'renoume' (renown) of Leland's native land is a recurring concept—not just in his 'Newe yeares gyfte', but throughout his works, proving their central and common concern over a span of three decades and a variety of genres. The choice Leland makes to engage with images of England, its wealth and culture, to ensure royal favour and financial patronage testifies to the potency and necessity of such writings during this period. As argued in the Introduction, Henry's repudiation of papal authority had caused a radical break with the immediate past, at least for those—such as Leland—close to, or on the fringes of, court life. Any such rift with the past needs a supporting ideology, and it is this that Leland, amongst others, attempted to provide through recourse to the *studia humanitatis*. It was not only England's new-found autonomy that Leland needed to justify, however. As we have seen, England's reputation as a country of refinement and learning left

---

[13] Hearne, *Collectanea*, i, p. liii.   [14] Leland, 'Newe yeares gyfte', D7^v.

much to be desired in the opening decades of the sixteenth century, and it is this ignominy too that Leland seeks to redress. The 'Newe yeares gyfte', presented to Henry in 1546, illustrates the ways in which Leland hoped to fulfil these aspirations. When Leland promises Henry that 'your realme shall so wele be knowne [. . .] that the renoume therof shal geue place to the glory of no other regyon' (E4^r), the means by which he aims to accomplish this— compiling histories of Britain, British writers, and British nobility— demonstrates the centrality of history to his programme of national glorification.

Anthony D. Smith is just one among many historians and theorists of nationhood to recognize the importance of history as a key component of national identity. For all his resistance to the chronology proposed by Benedict Anderson and Ernest Gellner, however, Smith does slip into teleological modes of thinking, where the 'nation' is a mark of the modern era. Nevertheless, Leland's own position is exactly that captured in Smith's statement that 'the "past" that is to serve modern [that is, national] purposes must not only be "full", it must be well preserved—or it must be "reconstructed" '.[15] Leland's historical agendum is threefold: it is phrased as rediscovery; it is seen as a means of dignifying his native land; and it is aimed at a European, as well as domestic, audience. He seeks recognition of his country's worth in its most precise etymological terms as re-cognition, to know again: his role as historian, described in the 'Newe yeares gyfte', is to 'open this wyndow' onto the past, 'that the light shal be seane [. . .], by the space of a whole thousand yeares stopped vp' (D7^v). By recovering this 'lost' history, Leland's works will restore 'the *old* glory', not just for English eyes, but for those of Europe, as the fame of 'renoumed Britaine' will '*re*florish through the world' (D7^v; my emphasis).

Leland is conscious of the constructed nature of history, declaring that 'the Romans were as famous to future generations as either the eloquence or favourable disposition of writers wanted to make them' ('tam clari posteris erant Romani, quam scriptorum uel eloquentia, uel adfectus eos facere uoluit').[16] History is made by a

---

[15] Smith, *Ethnic Origin of Nations*, 137; Anderson, *Imagined Communities*; Ernest Gellner, *Nations and Nationalism* (Oxford: Blackwell, 1983).

[16] John Leland, *Syllabus, et interpretatio antiquarum dictionum*, appended to John Leland, *Genethliacon illustrissimi Eaduerdi Principis Cambriae, Ducis Coriniae, et Comitis Palatini* (1543), G3^r.

nation's authors, who consequently assume an important national role establishing and perpetuating their country's fame, suppressing, if necessary, the competing traditions of other races, as did the Romans in Leland's treatise on King Arthur, *Assertio Inclytissimi Arturii Regis Britanniae* (1544), translated by Richard Robinson in 1582, where 'the *Romanes* made almost all the whole worlde bond slaues: and writers which proceeded amongest them, and were there borne applyinge their mindes to the study of eloquence, made their owne exploytes euen admirable or wonderfull; but the enterprises & actes of other Nations they dyd euen so obscure and debase, that almost they made them none at all' ('Romani autem vniuersum pene orbem seruum reddiderunt, & scriptores apud eos nati, & educati sua facta vel admirabilia eloquentiae innixi studio fecerunt. Caeterorum vero facta, vel ita obscurabant, vel eleuabant, vt nulla pene facerent').[17] The act of recording is all the more significant because, on Leland's pages, it becomes territorial, staking ownership to a particular writer's work, or particular hero's deeds, on the nation's behalf. Much is added to Leland's store by his use of the term 'Britaine', through which he annexes British history to enhance what is essentially an Anglocentric vision of his native island. Where Leland's Italian contemporary Polydore Vergil carefully distinguishes between England and Britain, declaring that he writes English, not British, history, Leland has no such qualms.[18] The easy slippage between the two terms is demonstrated in Bale's commentary to the 'Newe yeares gyfte', which shares the acquisitive spirit of Leland's historical texts, as he talks of 'thys oure Englyshe or Bryttyshe nacyon' (B3ᵛ). For Bale and Leland, 'Britaine' is simply the old label for England, and 'our relme in those days called Britaine / [is] now named Englande'.[19]

As Leland declares his country 'three and four times blessed [. . .] with deeds and riches' ('terque, quaterque beatam / [. . .] opibus, rebusque'), history becomes synonymous with material wealth, a

---

[17] Richard Robinson, *The learned and true assertion of the original, life, actes, and death of Prince Arthure, king of great Brittaine* (1582), 35ᵛ; John Leland, *Assertio Inclytissimi Arturii Regis Britanniae* (1544), 34ʳ.

[18] Denys Hay, *Polydore Vergil: Renaissance Historian and Man of Letters* (Oxford: Clarendon Press, 1952), 153.

[19] John Bale, *The Vocyacyon of Johan Bale in the bishoprick of Ossorie in Irelande* (Wesel, 1553), 44; contrast Thomas Elyot's definition: 'Brytane, which doth containe Englande, Scotlande, and wales' (*Dictionary* (1538), B8ᵛ).

national hoard in need of protection.[20] Leland's defence of 'British' history, and its construction along national lines, can best be examined by turning to his *Assertio*. The work is not, as might be expected, a narrative of Arthur's life. Rather, it is an 'assertion' of both the existence of this potent national icon, and of his 'British' (read English) identity. Sydney Anglo has disputed the cultural symbolism of Arthurian legends in sixteenth-century England and the extent to which the Tudors used them to bolster their right to the throne.[21] Leland, however, is not concerned with Arthur's dynastic implications. Arthur is significant because he is a figure of international standing, 'the chiefest ornament of *Brittayne*' ('Britanniae ornamentum maximum'), choice of phrasing which captures Leland's obsession with the way in which such heroes enrich national culture.[22] History is drawn along what Robinson translates as a 'frontier' (35^v) and fought out along national lines. Facts become booty that can be pilfered by envious strangers, such as Hector Boece and Polydore Vergil, both of whom are pilloried throughout Leland's works as foreigners, 'Hector the Scot' and 'Polydore the Italian', working to undermine 'British' history for partisan ends. It is poisoned 'with *Italian* bitternesse' ('Italo [. . .] aceto') that Vergil questions the reality of Brutus, legendary founder of Britain, and Arthur.[23] Boece, meanwhile, stands accused of forgery, 'destroying' ('eruenda') evidence in the archives and 'shamelessly' ('temerè') passing off 'British' achievements as Scottish, an allegation that again shows Leland identifying Britain with England to the exclusion of Scotland.[24] Not for Leland Polydore Vergil's scrupulous explanation in his *Anglica Historia* that 'the whole countrie of Britaine' 'at this daie, as it were in dowble name, is called Englande & Scotlande'.[25]

It is not history per se that Leland seeks to protect or recover, moreover, but a specific version of history. His concepts of historical worth are shaped by the European context in, and for, which he wrote. Civility is measured along classical lines, with eloquence

[20] Leland, *Genethliacon*, A2^r.

[21] Sydney Anglo, 'The *British History* in Early Tudor Propaganda', *Bulletin of the John Rylands Library*, 44 (1961), 17–48.

[22] Robinson, *Assertion*, 1^r; Leland, *Assertio*, 1^r.

[23] Robinson, *Assertion*, 19^v; Leland, *Assertio*, 19^v.

[24] Leland, *Syllabus*, G2^r.

[25] Polydore Vergil, *English History*, 1.

deemed the height of education, and elegant language the antithesis of barbarity. The 'history' Leland professes to reclaim is consequently one that establishes the learning and literary accomplishments of his native land. His *Commentarii de Scriptoribus Britannicis*, unpublished during his lifetime, is a mammoth work, ostensibly providing a lengthy catalogue of British writers from the time of the druids to the reign of Henry VIII. The size alone (593 chapters) is intended to bear physical witness to the mass of native talent, whilst Leland's Ciceronian prose, punctuated with variations on the triplet 'learned, witty, and elegant' ('docte, argute, eleganter'), endeavours to do justice to their refined literary style.[26] Within the *Commentarii de Scriptoribus*, Trevor Ross has noted the 'energy' Leland 'expends [. . .] trying to refute other nations' claims on writers, many of them legendary, who he believes are quite properly British'.[27] It matters in the *Commentarii de Scriptoribus* that the druids originate from Britain, not France: despite the evidence of 'most authors' ('autores plerique') to the contrary, Leland prefers to follow the one exception, Julius Caesar (i. 1). Later in the work, explaining the surname of the historian Matthew Paris provides an anxious moment (ii. 269), and the necessity of defending Bede's native origins from 'Hector Boece the Scot' provokes a furious attack (i. 118). Conflation of 'Britain' and 'England' also allows Leland to maximize the reputation of native letters when, in contrast to British (Welsh) bardic traditions, English (Anglo-Saxon) learning offers little of any worth. Indeed, since the Latin *Angli* means both English and Angles, these Teutonic settlers posit considerable embarrassment for Leland. Faced with the heathen, anti-intellectual reputation of this race, as found in Geoffrey of Monmouth's *Historia Regum Britanniae*, one of Leland's main sources, Leland segregates this compound people into 'the noble race of Angles' ('nobile genere *Anglorum*', i. 134) and 'treacherous race of Saxons' ('*Saxones*, gentem perfidam', i. 71), a distinction Monmouth never draws. Barbarity is deflected onto the latter, protecting the English and Angles (the 'Angli') from accusations of incivility and ignorance.

---

[26] Leland, *Commentarii*, i. 27 and passim.
[27] Trevor Ross, 'Dissolution and the Making of the English Literary Canon: The Catalogues of Leland and Bale', *Renaissance and Reformation*, new series, 15 (1991), 57–80, at 62.

The activity of writers and scholars is continually manifested in concrete terms, made into what Leland and Bale call 'monumentes of learnynge', or seen as 'treasures' ('thesauros') which men like the fifteenth-century humanist John Tiptoft accumulate for their native land.[28] Learning, that is, assumes a tangible, commercially exchangeable, financially profitable form. In return, fame is owed ('debet') to authors not by a republic of letters, but by their compatriots: Erasmus should be commemorated by 'Germany', 'the poet Bourbon' by his homeland France, just as one day 'Britain will celebrate [Leland's own] Muses' ('cantabit Musas terra Britanna meas').[29] Leland's attitude to these scholarly assets, moreover, is essentially one of competitive mercantilism. One country's gain is another's loss, and here Leland's native authors are conscripted into the battle for national esteem. The English poets whom Leland celebrates are, he tells us in the 'Newe yeares gyfte', co-opted to expose the 'arrogance' of the 'Italianes them-selfe, that counte as the Grekes ded [. . .], all other nacyons to be barbarouse & vnlettered, sauinge their owne' (C4^r), a quotation which equates civility with literacy and literary accomplishment. Wyatt and Chaucer are consequently compared favourably with their Continental counterparts. As Leland writes in the *Commentarii de Scriptoribus*:

> *Florence* deservedly boasts of *Dante Alighieri*,
> All of *Italy*, of your metres, *Petrarch*:
> Our *England* reveres the poet *Chaucer*,
> To whom the native tongue owes its charms.

> Praedicat *Aligerum* merito *Florentia Dantem*,
> *Italia* & numeros tota, *Petrarche*, tuos:
> *Anglia Chaucerum* veneratur nostra poetam,
> Cui veneres debet patria lingua suas.

> (ii. 422)

Leland's elegies on Wyatt in 1542 follow a similar vein:

---

[28] Leland, 'Newe yeares gyfte', C7^v; John Leland, 'Instauratio bonarum liter-arum', *Principum ac illustrium aliquot & eruditorum in Anglia virorum, encomia, trophaea, genethliaca, & epithalmia*, ed. Thomas Newton (1589), 74.

[29] Leland, 'Four Poems', 26, 27; John Leland, 'Gallia Borbonium celebrat facunda poetam', in James Carley, 'John Leland in Paris: The Evidence of his Poetry', *Studies in Philology*, 83 (1986), 1–50, at 39–40. The translations of all Leland's Parisian poetry cited here are by Carley.

Beautiful Florence of Dante justly boasts,
And kingly Rome approves the excellence
Of Petrarch's songs. In his own tongue as worthy,
Our Wyatt bears the palm of eloquence.
Bella suum merito iactet florentia Dantem.
Regia Petrarchae carmina Roma probet.
His non inferior patrio sermone Viatus
Eloquii secum qui decus omne tulit.[30]

Lauded in virtually identical terms (even repeating the phrase
'merito [. . .] florentia Dantem'), the authorial characteristics of
Wyatt and Chaucer are subordinate to their role as cultural champions of 'our England'. Leland shapes them into figures of his own
making. He celebrates 'our Wyatt', for instance, as 'the Ornament
of his Country' ('ornamentum patriae'), an epithet typical of the
material worth Leland invests in literary achievement, fashioning
Wyatt into a poet with a national programme, akin to the Wyatt of
Surrey's epitaph, within whose head 'some work of fame / Was
dayly wrought to turne to Britains gaine'.[31] The image, enduring
though it is, is far from the impression made by Wyatt's poetry,
which is, on examination, the work of private spaces and defensive
self-reflexivity from which a notion of 'Britain' is notably absent.[32]
The figure of Wyatt as the cultivated, courtly, national poet—writing sonnets, *strambotti*, and epistolary satires, genres in which
Italians such as Dante, Petrarch, and Alamanni had won international acclaim—nevertheless fulfils a need on the part of Leland
and Surrey to provide a suitable example with which to counter
England's long-standing reputation as a country bereft of literary
accomplishment.

   Leland's continual endeavours to memorialize his country's
achievements bear testimony to his belief in the public purpose of

[30] John Leland, *Naeniae in mortem Thomae Viati equitis incomparabilis* (1542),
A3ᵛ; trans. Kenneth Muir (ed.), *The Life and Letters of Sir Thomas Wyatt*
(Liverpool: Liverpool University Press, 1963), app. A, 264. For Surrey's role in helping Leland publish his *Naeniae*, see Elizabeth Heale, *Wyatt, Surrey and Early Tudor
Poetry* (London: Longman, 1998), 19.
[31] Leland, *Naeniae*, A5ᵛ, in Muir (ed.), *Life and Letters*, 268; Henry Howard,
'Wyatt resteth here', in *The Poems*, Emrys Jones ed. (Oxford: Clarendon Press,
1964), ll. 7–8.
[32] The exception being 'Tagus, farewell', with its evocation of 'My kyng,
my Contry, alone for whome I lyue' (Wyatt, in *Poems*, ed. Muir and Thomson,
82.

education, an emphasis on the practical ends to which schooling should be put evident from an epistolary poem written to William Paget during Leland's student days in Paris. Leland commends the king's secretary for having 'returned to [his] native land and post' ('tu patriam repetis <praes>idiumque tuum') and applying his learning, the 'fertile knowledge of languages' ('linguarum nitida cognitione frui'), to serving his country in the political sphere.[33] Leland's commitment, even as a lifelong scholar, to the *vita activa* is characteristic of his humanist upbringing, commemorated in a poem to his one-time guardian, Thomas Myles, where Leland praises his teacher Lily, 'Under whose care diligent and gifted young British boys / Learned to speak with eloquence' (Cuius ab industri cura didicere Britanni, / Facunde pubes ingeniosa loqui').[34]

The spirit in which Leland applies the eloquence imbibed in Lily's classroom, however, is far from the cooperative internationalism of Lily's own humanist circle led by More, whose pan-European collaborations are exemplified by texts such as *Utopia*—buttressed by approbatory letters from Continental scholars, endorsing and extending More's learned joke—or by William Nucer's elegy on More's death in 1535. Here Nucer praises More precisely for his lack of national prejudice, remembering him for the favour which, unlike many, he extended beyond his own people to include the Irish, French, and Germans; nor is it a fellow Englishman, or family member, whom Nucer deems More's chief mourner, but his erudite collaborator, the Dutch-born Erasmus.[35] Admittedly More participated in a bitter exchange with the German-born humanist Brixius after the latter published on the sinking of the *Cordeliere* in a sea-battle between the French and English in 1512.[36] Yet within their protracted skirmishes in poetry and prose, More attacked his opponent not to promote England, but to berate Brixius for 'an irresponsible defection from the cause of committed New Learning' and for using his training for exactly the sort of jingoistic ends Leland himself pursues.[37] More carefully

---

[33] John Leland, 'Ad Gulielmum Pagetium', in Carley, 'Leland in Paris', 30, 32.

[34] John Leland, 'Ad Thomam Milonem', ibid. 22–3.

[35] *LP*, VIII, itm 1096.

[36] Thomas More, *The Latin Poems*, ed. Clarence H. Miller et al., *The Complete Works of St. Thomas More*, vol. iii, pt. 2 (New Haven: Yale University Press, 1984).

[37] Daniel Kinney, 'The *Antimorus* of Germanus Brixius', in More, *Latin Poems*, app. A, 472.

defuses the national potential of his critiques. Brixius is dissociated from the French, recurrently noted as 'Brixius the German' in verse headings and on title pages, and is even blamed for having diluted the glory of the French, and the French sea captain Hervé, through his historical falsifications.[38] More's disgust was also shared by Erasmus who, in a letter of 1513, 'expressed a powerful dislike for the bellicose, mendacious style of "historical" poetry in which Brixius' *Chordigera* was written'.[39]

Deploying his humanist learning for national aggrandisement, therefore, Leland was more aligned with forms of what Sam Wheelis calls 'patriotic humanism' already practised in France and Germany, than with his immediate English forebears.[40] For these 'patriotic humanists', learning was a means of asserting and acquiring national pride, as in the works of the French scholar Salmon Macrin, to whom Leland addressed an epigram in the mid-1520s, a poet whom Ian McFarlane credits as 'leader of a vigorous current' of Latin poetry with 'serious pretensions to deflate Italy's cultural supremacy'.[41] When, as Revilo Oliver explains, the bickerings between More and Brixius 'quickly became [. . .] a controversy over the antagonists' respective accomplishments as Latinists', fluency and accuracy in Latin represented evidence of scholarly integrity.[42] On the pages of writers such as Macrin, however, Latinity was more than a sign of individual academic standards: it was a means of affirming national achievement.

For 'reformed' writers, particularly in Germany, Latinity also became a measure of morality. Although Germany was not a unified nation in the political sense during the early modern period, it was frequently recognized as an ethnic entity.[43] As befits the cradle of the Reformation, what Lewis Spitz terms 'cultural nationalism' took

---

[38] More, *Latin Poems*, 219. Cf. Daniel Kinney, 'More's *Letter to Brixius*', ibid., app. C, 559.   [39] Ibid. 564.

[40] Sam Wheelis, 'Ulrich von Hutten: Representative of Patriotic Humanism', in Gerhart Hoffmeister (ed.), *The Renaissance and Reformation in Germany: An Introduction* (New York: Ungar, 1977), 111–27.

[41] John Leland, 'Laus Macrini', in Carley, 'Leland in Paris', 39; I. D. McFarlane, *A Literary History of France: Renaissance France, 1470–1589* (London: Ernest Benn, 1974), 75.

[42] Revilo P. Oliver, 'More's Latinity and the Strictures of Brixius', in More, *Latin Poems*, 22–32, at 24.

[43] See, e.g., Leland's reference to the fame Germany owes Erasmus (Leland, 'Four Poems', 26).

a particular turn in this area, coinciding with 'religious enlighten-
ment', and for early sixteenth-century scholars such as Conrad
Celtis—to whom Bale compares Leland in the *Laboryouse Iourney*
(B7ᵛ)—'antipathy towards Italian humanists was very easily transferred to Italian churchmen as well'.[44] Displaying a 'correct' Latin
style, therefore, was not only a mark of intellectual rigour: it
symbolized moral standards. The two conflicting associations of
Rome, the classical (revered) and ecclesiastical (abhorred), cohere
in the return to an allegedly 'purer', Ciceronian Latin, with the
language's intervening decay regarded as coeval with the moral
decline of the church under the 'bishops of Rome'. Here again
Leland is comparable with his German counterparts. Rome might
be, as Leland puts it in the *Commentarii de Scriptoribus*, 'the
parent of letters' ('literarum parentem'), but—as we saw with
Borde in the previous chapter—in contrast to English diligence, it
is seen to have squandered its intellectual birthright (i. 176).
Visiting Rome, Leland's Stephen Harding is horrified by the louche
behaviour he encounters, disillusionment all the more shocking
owing to the city's previous claims to scholarly achievement. It is
difficult to capture the pointed economy of Leland's phrase
'corruptissimis moribus' in translation. Not only do superlatives
sound clumsy when converted into English, but the Latin also
benefits from first, the multiple meanings of *corruptus*, which
(significantly, considering Leland's mercantilist attitude to learning) include financial and moral implications, and secondly, the
shock of the paradox created by the choice of the word *mores*,
which (besides signifying 'character' and 'behaviour') is etymolog-
ically rooted in the word for 'morals'. Rome has thus corrupted
what should be pure. Morality and language are interlinked. When
Leland's 'Britain' is represented as the natural home of learning, it
is not merely Roman eloquence it is seen to possess: it also has
superior moral claims to religious authority.

As indicated earlier, England's estrangement from Rome after
1533 placed further pressure on its 'patriotic humanists'. Leland
not only needed to establish the Latinate credentials of his native
literature: he also needed to accrue evidence of the purportedly
ancient autonomy of the English church. When the Act in Restraint

---

[44] Lewis W. Spitz, *The Religious Renaissance of the German Humanists*
(Cambridge, Mass.: Harvard University Press, 1963), 2.

of Appeals declared in 1533 that 'this realm of England is an empire, and so hath been accepted in the world', it based its claim on 'divers sundry old authentic histories and chronicles'.[45] Leland's own 'divers' and 'sundry' works similarly proclaim an historical basis for the royal supremacy. The task is the rationale behind his *Antiphilarcia* and a unifying purpose for his bibliographical and poetic writings. Bernadette Cunningham has described how Boece's *Scotorum historiae* 'depicted the Scottish people as loyal Christians never veering from the true faith'.[46] Here Leland has much more in common with his old enemy than he would allow (as indeed he does with Polydore Vergil, who was similarly perplexed by the fact that England lacked 'worthy memorial of herself', a deficit—like Leland—he strove to redress).[47] As May McKisack writes, 'the breach with Rome enhanced national self-consciousness and the desire to demonstrate the scriptural (as distinct from Romish) foundations of the land's ecclesiastical traditions'.[48] Leland consequently rewrites history, constructing a tradition of religious resistance, framing the recent break with Rome as being both consistent with established practice and a return to the purity of the primitive British church which—as late imperial Rome succumbed to pagan forces—had maintained its faith, despite the Saxon invasion.[49] The *Commentarii de Scriptoribus* even aligns 'the arrogance of *Romans*' with the 'tyranny' of the heathen Saxons ('*Romanorum* fastum vel *Saxonum* tyrannidem'), both of whom should be expelled from 'the *British* commonwealth' ('re publica *Britannorum*', i. 71). The objectionable Romans attacked in this statement are not the imperial conquerors of ancient Britain. These words are spoken at the synod of Whitby, at which the seventh-century saint Diuma objects to the overweening power of the pope in the suitably 'copious, serious, and learned' ('copiose, graviter, docte') fashion that the reader has, even by now, in the early stages of the book, come to expect from one of Leland's 'British' scholars. Continuing this tradition of resistance, within the *Commentarii de Scriptoribus*, King John is recast, as in Bale's *King*

---

[45] Elton (ed.), *Tudor Constitution*, 353.   [46] Cunningham, *Keating*, 84.

[47] Hay, *Polydore Vergil*, 153.

[48] May McKisack, *Medieval History in the Tudor Age* (Oxford: Clarendon Press, 1971), 1.

[49] For an overview of later narratives of the struggle between Anglo-Saxon paganism and the British church, see Kidd, *British Identities*, 99–122.

Johan (*c*.1538), as a national hero, celebrated for his stand against papal interference within England's jurisdication (i. 248). Elsewhere, in the notes comprising Leland's *Itinerary*, the Poyntz family is remembered primarily for challenging the authority of Rome: 'the name of Pontz is spoken of emong the names of certen noble-men that denied in Edwarde the first dayes in open parlament the request of a bisshop of Rome, that saide that though the King wold[,] they wold graunt no such request.'[50] It is the act of refusal, not what is refused, that is significant, and the detail by which Leland chooses to memorialize the family.

'PAYNTED WITH HYS NATYUE COLOURS': THE ILLUSION OF ELOQUENCE[51]

The *Commentarii de Scriptoribus* is designed to fulfil Leland's vow in the 'Newe yeares gyfte' to show Henry 'how greate a numbre of excellent godlye wyttes and wryters, learned wyth the best, as the tymes serued, hath bene in thys your regyon' (C6ᵛ). Yet signs of Britain's learned past are notably sketchy. Like Borde in the previous chapter, Leland writes from a position of embarrassment. Where, for example, Tiptoft is just one amongst a myriad of talented authors catalogued in the *Commentarii de Scriptoribus*, in the funeral oration the Italian humanist Lodovico Carbone delivered on Battista Guarino in 1460, Tiptoft (one of five Englishmen Carbone numbers among Guarino's most distinguished pupils) is all the more remarkable because he is English, 'men by nature barbarous'.[52] Leland is not without his own misgivings about his ancestors' intellectual accomplishments. He is careful, though, to frame his criticisms in the past tense. 'The English tongue was rude, its verses vile,' he comments: 'Now, skilful Wyatt, it has known your file' ('Anglica lingua fuit rudis & sine nomine rhthymus: / Nunc limam agnoscit docte Viate tuam').[53] Leland copes with the inadequacies he is forced to acknowledge by casting them in a temporal context. 'The whole of *Europe* was gripped by the

---

[50] John Leland, *Leland's Itinerary in England*, ed. Lucy Toulmin-Smith, 4 vols. (London: George Bell & Son, 1907–10), iii. 111.
[51] Leland, 'Newe yeares gyfte', E4ʳ.
[52] Cited by R. J. Mitchell, *John Tiptoft* (London: Longman, 1938), 54.
[53] Leland, *Naeniae*, A4ᵛ; trans. Muir (ed.), *Life and Letters*, 266.

darkest barbarity,' he declares in the *Commentarii de Scriptoribus* ('tota *Europa* à crassissima barbarie occupata', i. 176). Comparisons are drawn between then and now, not England and the Continent, France, or—ever lurking as the source of validation—Italy. James Simpson has written eloquently about the impact and motivation of Leland's historical 'ageism'. In contrast to the 'deadly darkenesse' of even the recent past, Leland describes his own era as a 'most flourishing time' ('hac nostra tam florenti aetate'), enjoying 'the age of / Smooth-tongued Cicero' ('facundi Ciceronis illa saecla') and 'Attic charm' ('Atticus [. . .] lepos'), able—this implies—to provide the suitably felicitous imitation of Ovid that the late fourteenth-century poet John Gower could not, inhabiting as he did 'a semi-barbarous age' ('semibarbaro saeculo').[54]

Leland's promise in his 'Newe yeares gyfte' to reveal his country 'paynted with hys natyue colours' is thus aptly phrased (E4ʳ). The choice of imagery exposes its author-painter's sleight of hand: the vaunted 'renoume' is no more authentic than that produced by the 'crafty coloured doctryne of a rowte of Romayne Byshoppes' (C1ʳ). The colours with which Leland daubs his homeland are, moreover, patently not 'natyue'. Leland shares what Spitz describes as Celtis' 'zeal' in 'searching out cultural documents of [his country's] past' and a similar lack of reserve 'in singing her praises'.[55] However, unlike his German counterpart, Leland does not celebrate the 'noble innocence' and traditions of his 'primitive' predecessors.[56] Instead he attempts to fashion his countrymen in an overtly classical tradition. The 'bonae literae' at which Leland's 'Britons' excel are those taught them by the Roman settlers: it is classical Rome, not vernacular Britain, which sets the standard and provides the models to emulate. Leland's choice of Latin as the medium in which to write consequently works in three ways: in contrast to the barbarism of ages past, it records the attributes of his compatriots for the benefit of an international, Latin-reading audience whilst simultaneously demonstrating the eloquent standards he himself attains as a representative of contemporary English learning.

---

[54] Leland, 'Newe yeares gyfte', B8ʳ; John Leland, 'Ad Richardum Hirtium', I and II, in Carley, 'Leland in Paris', 26–8; Leland, *Commentarii*, ii. 415; see Simpson, 'Ageism', 230.   [55] Spitz, *Religious Renaissance*, 84.
[56] Ibid. 85.

Further to that, it enables him to transform his native country into a classical literary landscape.

Within Leland's two most significant Latin poems, the *Genethliacon* (1543) and *Cygnea Cantio* (1545), Leland's 'Britain' is made to rival Rome in material and stylistic achievement. Both works are enthusiastic encomia of the glories of Henry's realm: the first is a fictionalized account of celebrations at the birth of Prince Edward, the long-awaited male heir; the second follows a swan down the Thames, noting en route Henry's navy and splendid palaces. These texts classicize the English, Cornish, and Welsh terrain and display the Latin learning to which Leland aspires. In the *Genethliacon*, nymphs pour from diverse counties to worship the newborn babe; dryads, naiads, and oreads come bearing gifts; and men from Bangor to Penzance honour the prince's birth with public games, a set piece in any classical epic, until the shore resounds and skies re-echo with shouts in a suitably Virgilian mode (C4^r, D3^r).[57] Leland proves an inveterate magpie of Roman culture, accumulating snippets with which to ornament his native land. The verse itself is unable to contain the proliferation of historical and literary riches he is anxious to display, necessitating the addition of accompanying prose commentaries to both his *Genethliacon* and, at still greater length, his *Cygnea Cantio*. Through liberal use of quotations from Latin and Greek, these attendant expositions flesh out a history for Leland's homeland not only as a nation worthy of literary attention, but as one that has already received it. The stress that Leland lays is, as we have seen, on the *restoration* of a national heritage.

As a student in Paris, Leland hoped to sing in 'the resounding / Strains of Horace' ('ut resono / Flacci carmine').[58] For work of national significance, however, Virgil, the imperial epicist, is the obvious pattern. Leland crams in allusions to the Latin poet, weaving the *Genethliacon* from a web of texts drawn from both the *Eclogues* and *Aeneid*. Edward is likened to a 'small Aeneas' ('paruus [. . .] Aeneas', A2^v) and greeted in the figure of the saviour of the Fourth Eclogue, with his mother, Jane Seymour, becoming the 'virgo' of that poem, greeting her son with a slight misquotation of

---

57 Cf. the funeral games, Virgil, *Aeneid* VI, in *Virgil I*, ed. and trans. H. Rushton Fairclough, rev. edn. (London: Heinemann, 1935).

58 John Leland, 'Ad Robertum Severum', in Carley, 'Leland in Paris', 35.

the Latin text: 'begin, dear boy, to recognise your mother with a smile' ('incipe chare puer risu dignoscere [sic] matrem', A4ᵛ).[59] The borrowed text, which medieval interpreters read as prophesying Christ's birth, renders Edward a new messiah, asserting England's claims to scriptural truth over Rome. Leland exploits this neo-biblical strain by making Jane Seymour a second Mary, like her New Testament counterpart noted as 'the daughter of a virgin' ('filia virginei', A2ᵛ). In his eagerness to acquire an Anglo-equivalent to Roman literature, however, Leland is not always so opportune in his choice of allusion. Rumour's appearance bringing news of Edward's birth with Virgilian 'ruinous wings' ('perniciter alas', E1ʳ), is one such moment, plucked as the reference is from *Aeneid* IV, where Rumour's tittle-tattle helps bring the love affair of Dido and Aeneas to its fatal conclusion, heaping further curses on the hero's race, and ultimately leading to the Punic Wars and the near-collapse of an emergent Roman empire.[60] As Leland applies a veneer of borrowed culture over the cracked and inadequate façade of native learning, the suitability of the quotation is of less concern than achieving the grand style.

The role of a writer is that of a craftsman, hammering unwieldy raw material into the requisite shape and beautifying it (where needed) with borrowed colours. If, as Leicester Bradner has noted, 'it was a Renaissance commonplace that poetry should instruct', then Leland's works were training his compatriots to reconceptualize their native land.[61] The next section of this chapter looks at Leland's use of topographical poetry to further this cause. Topography is a potent medium, drawing together past and present, memory and landscape. It elucidates the history inscribed in the terrain, imprinted in natural and artificial features jostling for attention in Leland's texts. The footprints ('vestigia') of time are etched in ditches and walls, or glimpsed in the deforestation of Anglesey, used by Leland as proof of its identity as the Roman 'Mona' when he argues that the dearth of trees corresponds with historical accounts in which its dense thickets were burnt as a measure against the druids.[62] The landscape spells out and legitimates the history and legends of Leland's homeland. Arthur's existence is vindicated

---

[59] Cf. Virgil, *Eclogues*, in *Virgil I*, ed. and trans. Rushton Fairclough (London: Heinemann, 1935), IV. 60: 'incipe, parve puer, risu cognoscere matrem'.

[60] Cf. Virgil, *Aeneid*, IV. 180: 'pernicibus alis'.

[61] Bradner, *Musae Anglicanae*, 27.   [62] Leland, *Syllabus*, F4ʳ, F3ᵛ.

by the mountains of Cardiganshire, where the burial mound of a giant he slew can still be seen, or by the 'bones and harneys' found by Cornish ploughmen at Dunmere 'yn token' of his last battle.[63] Yet, besides its use as historical record, topography also offers resources for depicting Leland's 'Britain' as a cohesive island nation: it is this function of topography that the next section addresses.

'TO [. . .] SE YOUR OPULENT AND AMPLE REALME':
THE ROLE OF TOPOGRAPHY[64]

Freed from the necessity of representing the physical terrain as accurately as possible on the page, topographical writing can mould its subject matter into the desired image. The pen constructs and maintains imagined boundaries, able both to appropriate and exclude. As we saw in the introduction, the Act in Restraint of Appeals had found authority in the jurisdictional limits of the realm. In the context of the act, 'limits' are not restrictive, but empowering, part of the triplet 'limits, power and authority', and Henry is given power—described in tautological terms as 'plenary, whole and entire'—of 'final determination' over 'all manner of folk resiants or subjects within this realm, in all causes, matters, debates and contentions happening to occur, insurge or begin within the limits therof, without restraint or provocation to any foreign princes or potentates'.[65] This self-sufficiency is also extended to the English church, which is self-reflexively 'sufficient and meet of itself'. As discussed in Chapter 1, that rhetoric of self-supporting confinement resonates throughout Tudor (and Stuart) depictions of the nation, and Leland—like Borde, and later Milton—recurrently depicts his homeland as an island stronghold, ample but also enclosed: 'spacious Britain encircled by the great Ocean' ('clauditur Oceano spatiosa Britannia uasto').[66]

[63] John Leland, *Leland's Itinerary in Wales*, ed. Lucy Toulmin-Smith (London: George Bell & Sons, 1906), 119; Leland, *Itinerary in England*, i. 316.
[64] Leland, 'Newe yeares gyfte', D4ᵛ.
[65] Elton (ed.), *Tudor Constitution*, 356.
[66] Leland, *Genethliacon*, B2ᵛ. Cf. John Milton, 'In quantum Novembris, Anno aetetis 17', in *Poetical Works*, ed. Douglas Bush (Oxford: Oxford University Press, 1966).

That sense of reassuring encirclement carries through into the description of inland regions. Throughout Leland's works, the building of walls becomes 'just labour' ('labore iusto'), and repairs 'worthily' ('insigniter') done.[67] The initiators of such projects assume heroic status, such as the 'virago' Aethelfleda in the *Genethliacon* (C3[r]), or Ranulph of Chester in the accompanying commentary, who 'most famously, waged a very fierce war against the Saracens, besides building heavily fortified castles in his native Cheshire from the very foundations themselves' ('hic accerrimo contra Saracenos bello se praeclarissimè gessit. Castra insuper munitissima in sua Deuania vel ab ipsis erexit fundamentis', G1[r]). Edward III—a clear role model for his Tudor namesake—is remembered as 'a very powerful prince' ('Princeps potentissimus'), lauded in the commentary to the *Cygnea Cantio* as much for his ambitions to leave behind a 'memorable building' ('aeditio [. . .] memorabili') as for his victories over the French and Scots (Q4[v]). The *Genethliacon*, meanwhile, calls on Prince Edward to turn his own hand to building, encouraging him to fulfil the prophecies of 'ancient poets' ('vatibus antiquis') and reconstruct Ranulph's shattered ramparts (E1[rv]). Manley has pointed out the significance of epic heroes, from Aeneas onwards, as builders of city walls, a motif found in Virgil's announcement that Aeneas will 'build a city [. . .] whence came the Latin race, the lords of Alba, and the walls of lofty Rome' ('conderet urbem / [. . .] genus unde Latinum / Albanique patres atque altae moenia Romae') and perpetuated in figures such as Ariosto's Ercole d'Este, who enlarged Ferrara 'con muro e fossa' ('with a wall and ditch').[68] In conjuring this epic trope, Leland employs the resources offered by native geography (Ranulph's ruins) to continue his construction of 'Britain' and the 'British' in a suitably classical literary vein.

Topography not only fills Leland's homeland with reassuring defences, it also allows him to model it into a fertile and cohesive entity. In the notes to his *Itinerary*, England and Wales are depicted as tamed and productive landscapes, as Leland habitually records the crops growing by the wayside. Every town or village is on the way to, and from, another, a legacy of intercommunication he left

---

[67] John Leland, *Cygnea Cantio* (1545), D3[r]; John Leland, *Commentarii in Cygneam Cantionem*, appended to Leland, *Cygnea Cantio* (1545), E1[r].
[68] Virgil, *Aeneid*, I. 5–7; Manley, *Literature and Culture*, 180–1.

to his successor, Harrison, whose *Description of England*, which owes much to Leland, culminates in a chapter dealing with 'our innes and thoroughfares'.[69] Leland's writing binds England and its disparate territories into one unit, emphasizing connections between the regions through which he travels. Within the *Genethliacon*, Latin lends a fortuitous lack of specificity to the means by which news of Edward's birth is spread. Latin nouns, lacking an article, give Leland's messenger a convenient vagueness. It can thus be read as *the* messenger (one man conveying the tidings to all corners of Henry's kingdom), rather than the many different messengers such dissemination would in practice require. The poetry smothers any sense of a geographically, culturally, or politically divided realm. England and Wales are fashioned into a compact body, in which Snowdonia hears the nymphs paying homage to Edward at Hampton Court (B4^v), and no acknowledgement is made of Calais's estranged position over the Channel. It becomes another harbour town, alongside Dover and other southerly ports.

The significance of cartography and its close relation, topography, as means of territorial acquisition is well substantiated within the Tudor period. It was for the benefit of map-making as a tool of warfare that Elyot, Castiglione, and Machiavelli recommended learning draughtsmanship, a practical application of penmanship exemplified in 1512 by Sebastian Cabot's commission to make a 'carde' of Guyenne to assist a planned invasion.[70] Topography proved no less useful to military offensives, as illustrated by the 'Abstract that Englishmen might knowe the realme of Scotland throughout', a topographical description—probably dating from the campaign of 1547, the success of which was ensured by such chorographical projects—in which 'knowledge' amounts to an invasion plan, with Scotland marked out in forced marches and sites of strategic importance.[71] Topography offers more than a

[69] William Harrison, *The Description of England*, ed. Georges Edelen (Ithaca, NY: Cornell University Press, 1968), 397.

[70] Elyot, *Gouernour* (1531), 25^r; Thomas Hoby, *The Book of the Courtier*, ed. Virginia Cox (London: Everyman, 1994), 87; Peter Barber, 'England I: Pageantry, Defense and Government: Maps at Court to 1550', in David Buisseret (ed.), *Monarchs, Ministers, and Maps: The Emergence of Cartography as a Tool of Government in Early Modern Europe*, (Chicago: University of Chicago Press, 1992), 26–56, at 27.   [71] BL Vespasian D. xviii, 135^v–137^v.

device for the physical accumulation of land, however. As an art that re-presents and interprets landscapes, it was a medium ideally suited to what Philip Payton calls the 'twin imperatives' of Tudor England, 'centralism and expansionism', which governments sought to achieve through 'unification, uniformity and pacification'.[72] Leland's *Genethliacon* in particular exemplifies this three-pronged policy, promoting the image of a fully integrated island nation. In contrast to Borde, who treats Wales and Cornwall as appendages to England, within Leland's works—just as there is no recognition of the physical division between England and its outposts across the Channel—so too there is no acknowledgement of social conflict with, or cultural resistance from, Wales or Cornwall.

Whilst the union of Wales and England was accomplished with seeming ease and the complicity of its elites,[73] in the early 1540s, recollection of the threat posed by Cornwall, a territory holding more in common with Brittany than it did with England, was still within living memory. In 1497, supporters of the Cornish Rising, 'the most important revolt in Henry VII's reign', had reached Blackheath, just outside London, fighting a pitched battle there on 17 June, an incident of enough significance to be used to date Hythloday's visit to England in More's *Utopia*.[74] These potentially resistant men, whom the Elizabethan Thomas Cely described as 'the roughest and most mutinous men in England', and who rebelled over the Book of Common Prayer in 1549 (six years after the publication of the *Genethliacon*), are transformed by Leland into loyal subjects.[75] Within the *Genethliacon*, men pour from the mines, the origin of discontent in 1497, singing with 'one aspect

---

[72] Philip Payton, *The Making of Modern Cornwall: Historical Experience and the Persistence of 'Difference'* (Redruth: Dyllansow Truran, 1992), 58. Cf. A. L. Rowse, *The Expansion of Elizabethan England*, rev. edn. (London: Macmillan, 1969).

[73] Williams, *Welsh Reformation*; P. R. Roberts, 'The Union with England and the Identity of "Anglican" Wales', *Transactions of the Royal Historical Society*, 5th series, 20 (1972), 49–70.

[74] John Guy, *Tudor England* (Oxford: Oxford University Press, 1988), 58; Thomas More, *Utopia*, ed. and trans. George M. Logan and Robert M. Adams (Cambridge: Cambridge University Press, 1989), 15.

[75] Cited by G. R. Lewis, *The Stannaries: A Study of the English Tin Miner* (Cambridge, Mass.: Harvard University Press, 1908), 217; Edwards, *Modern English State*, 179; Mark Stoyle, *West Britons: Cornish Identities and the Early Modern British State* (Exeter: Exeter University Press, 2002), 27, 29, 42–3.

and one voice' ('una [. . .] facies [. . .] oratio [. . .] una') in sponta-
neous praise of the new prince (D1^v). Leland describes their
wrestling, for which Cornishmen were famed, and their boat races,
set down 'according to the laws of their ancestors' ('leges [. . .]
auitas', D1^r).[76] Edward is thus used by Leland as a figure ostensibly uniting England, Wales, and Cornwall, mimicking the policy of
accommodation by which English governments attempted to
reconcile Wales and Cornwall to 'incorporation in the state and to
secure within the periphery the authority of the centre'.[77] As Prince
of Wales and Duke of Cornwall, titles noted on the book's cover,
Edward symbolizes these regions' 'unique relationship with the
Crown and [. . .] special constitutional identity', which 'created an
aura of semi-independence', a nominal sop employed by the Tudor
regime in the interests of stability and state formation.[78] The local
customs Leland describes are not used as manifestations of regional
identity, but to celebrate a national event: the birth of Prince
Edward. Leland annexes Cornish traditions in the service of Tudor
myth-making and composing a panegyric to England's future king.
They are then further wrested from their ethnic roots by their
representation within a classical form, a literary style fashioning
them into Virgilian set pieces, negating their Cornish origins and
context and replacing them with a textual, Latinate parentage.
That same desire to tame troublesome elements can also be used to
explain the otherwise puzzling appearance of Virgil's Rumour,
highlighted above. Leland remodels Dido's nemesis into a loyal
royal servant, spreading the glad tidings of Edward's birth,
harnessing—in poetic fantasy—the subversive forces of rumour
and sedition that the Henrician regime continually tried to
control.[79]

Denis Wood has written about the creative aspects of mapping,
the selectivity of material recorded, the iconic nature of signs and
names, and the culturally constructed and constructing power of
maps.[80] Topography is equally, if not more, suited to such manipulation. Within Leland's works Latin acts as a homogenizing force.

---

[76] For the fame of Cornish wrestlers, see Thomas Cromwell's letter to William
Godolphin in June 1532, asking him to send two Cornishmen, 'proper fellows for
the feat of wrestling' (*LP*, V, itm 1093).

[77] Payton, *Making of Modern Cornwall*, 43.   [78] Ibid. 47–8.

[79] See, e.g., BL Cleopatra E. iv, 213–15.

[80] Denis Wood with John Fels, *The Power of Maps* (London: Routledge, 1993).

Leland converts vernacular place names into Latin, unlike his contemporary John Major, the Scottish historian, who also wrote in Latin, but who resisted 'giv[ing] what would be almost a Latin turn to the names of our own people and places', lest 'we that were born in Scotland' 'scarcely should understand what was meant'.[81] Leland thus defamiliarizes the landscape, a use of renaming that makes additional assault on Cornish and Welsh identity. Although he claims in the commentary to the *Cygnea Cantio* to recover ancient place names and 'restore to light' ('luci resituere') their 'ancient glory' ('antiquam [. . .] gloriam', A2ʳ), Leland is in fact erasing the history encapsulated in vernacular place names by replacing them with Latin alternatives, rendering Cornwall and Wales uniform with England, to which he has applied the same technique. Moreover, whereas English towns and counties are renamed to preserve or create historic pride, the Latinate names given to Wales and Cornwall strip away memory: on the one hand, 'Troynovant' (New Troy) links London with the legend of Brutus, fabled founder of Britain, and Castrum Bellini (the Tower of London) honours Bellinus, one-time king of Britain; on the other, Marazion is arbitrarily dubbed 'Forum Iovis'; Bodmin (from Cornish for 'house of monks') is transformed into 'Bosuenna'; Chepstow, 'Noua Venta'.[82]

Leland's topographical approach also doctors the terrain, removing disruptive features. Towns and cities are safely bounded by well-maintained walls, and sprawling suburbs and urban decay—present in the private notes of his *Itinerary*—are edited out of the picture. Leland distinguishes between material appropriate for public texts and private notebooks. Within the public forum of his poetry, he suppresses any dissonant details that would jeopardize his image of a vibrant, cohesive nation. No mention is made of negative aspects captured in his *Itinerary*, such as the moribund harbour of Kidwelli or crumbling fortifications of Clun and Monmouth, celebrated in the *Genethliacon* for their 'lofty homestead' ('domus alta') and 'high towers' (turres [. . .] alta', C2ᵛ).[83]

---

[81] John Major, *The history of greater Britain*, ed. and trans. Archibald Constable, Scottish History Society, 10 (1892), p. cxxxv.

[82] Leland, *Syllabus*, E3ʳ, F2ʳ; Eilert Ekwall (ed.), *The Concise Oxford Dictionary of English Place Names*, 4th edn. (Oxford: Oxford University Press, 1960), 51; Leland, *Genethliacon*, C1ʳ.

[83] Contrast the description of these towns in Leland, *Itinerary in Wales*, 53, 46, 59.

The next section explores Leland's commitment to the public role of the author, acting within and on behalf of the commonweal, before returning to the discrepancy between private and public utterance, and the burden placed upon his topographical writings and pronouncements of English learning by the 'process of sudden ruination' resulting from the dissolution of the monasteries in the 1530s and 1540s.[84]

STRONG WITH SPLENDOUR: THE POLITICS OF DISPLAY

Throughout Leland's works, images of light indicate respect and approval. As contemporary learning is held against the shadows of ignorant ages past and 'monumentes of auncyent wryters' are 'brought from darkenesse to a lyuely lyght', Leland's chiaroscuro distinguishes his age from previous eras marred both by professed intellectual dullness and—through the reformist associations of such diction—spiritual blindness.[85] This vocabulary of approbatory luminosity is applied as much to architectural 'monuments' and fortifications as to the learned men gathered like 'lyghtes' around 'the daye starre', Henry VIII.[86] As Leland's swan glides down the Thames in the *Cygnea Cantio*, it describes Henry's various palaces with recurrent phrases of insistent brightness. The gables of Sheen 'glisten' ('coruscant', B3^v); at Westminster, the bird notes the 'great shimmering of many buildings, which now glow with their gleaming light' ('aedium nitelas / Multarum, radiant suo emicanti / Quae nunc lumine', B4^v); the palace at Greenwich 'shines' ('niteat') as the swan catalogues the 'delights of the shining garden' ('delicias nitentis horti', C3^r); Guyenne 'shines, bound on all sides with a new ditch and rampart' (radiat, nouaque fossa, / Vallo & cingitur undecunque forti', D4^v); and Henry is described in the accompanying commentary as 'the one light of architecture in his age' ('unicum huius saeculi in architectura lumen', H4^v). In a period epitomized by the competitive consumption of the Field of the Cloth of Gold in 1520, size and showiness matter, and the noun

---

[84] Margaret Aston, 'English Ruins and English History: The Dissolution and the Sense of the Past', *Journal of Warburg and Courtauld Institutes*, 36 (1973), 231–55, at 242.   [85] Leland, 'Newe Yeares Gyfte', B8^r.
[86] Ibid. D1^r.

amplitudo provides Leland with a useful play on words, through its double meaning of 'breadth' and 'distinction'. Spectacle is power. The approving adjectives tagged to virtually every town and landmark throughout Leland's poetry and prose are those indicating high public profile. *Celebre* and *notissimus* signal perceived renown, whilst Leland's use of the Latin adjective *conspicuus* ('remarkable') is informed by its primary meaning in English, which by the mid-1540s signified 'clearly visible' (*OED* 1). Conspicuousness is praiseworthy, with Richmond 'a city conspicuous [or remarkable] in fame' ('urbs famae conspicuae'), and the building recently erected at Chelsea noted as a 'conspicuous [or remarkable] palace' ('conspicuas aedes').[87] Leland is similarly concerned to make knowledge visible. As he promises Henry in the 'New yeares gyfte', 'your grace shall haue ready knowledge at the fyrst sighte of many right delectable, fruteful, and necessary pleasures, by contemplacion therof, as often as occasyon shall moue yow to the syghte of it' (D5ᵛ). The emphasis is strongly visual; knowledge is acquired through looking, and such is the pledged clarity of Leland's chorography, 'a descripcion' of Henry's realm 'in wryttinge', that 'it shall be no mastery after, for the grauer o[r] painter to make the lyke by a perfect example' (D6ᵛ).

Chapter 1 examined how ideals of defensive encirclement and material self-sufficiency were conjoined in the rhetoric of the Tudor period. Snugly held within its maritime boundaries, Leland's 'Britain' (like Borde's) is presented as being buttressed against both incursion and deprivation. Calling upon classical literary motifs of the Golden Age, Leland portrays his country as a haven blessed with self-reliant fertility of Arcadian proportions. As he writes in the *Genethliacon*, in the passage on Cornwall, this is a land where 'every race of bird' ('genus omne uolucrum') chooses to nest, and 'different types of fish play in the sea' ('uarii pisces, / [. . .] aequore [. . .] ludunt', D1ᵛ). Nature is there for the eating. Just as the fish are 'sumptuous to the palate' ('lautique palato'), so too the trees are laden with fruit and 'it is scarcely possible to count the cattle and flocks' ('armenta, gregesque / Vix numerare licet').

Yet the Saturnian picture painted in the *Genethliacon* takes a significantly different turn from that found in the first book of Ovid's *Metamorphoses*, a key source for such prelapsarian idylls.

[87] Leland, *Commentarii in Cygneam Cantionem*, L2ᵛ, N2ᵛ.

The Ovidian Golden Age is marked by its lack of warfare, and the arts of mining base metal, which enable such hostilities, lie undiscovered. 'There were no trumpets of straight, nor horns of curving brass, no swords or helmets. There was no need at all of armed men,' the Latin tells us ('non tuba derecti, non aeris cornua flexi, / non galeae, non ensis erat: sine militis usu').[88] In contrast, Leland's description of Cornwall is thick, not just with references to abundant foodstuffs willingly pressing themselves upon their potential consumers, but with minerals and metals about to be mined. It is not only sheep that are 'copious' ('copia'), but 'tin' ('stanni') and 'veins of copper and silver' ('uena [. . .] / Aeris & argenti', D1^v). The use of Saturnian tropes thus establishes Leland's homeland as a site of Latinate literary pretensions rivalling those of ancient Rome, but the application of these motifs also differentiates England from Ovid's prehistorical landscape, performing what Manley calls 'cultural *translatio*' by adapting those conventions to the specific circumstances of England and its dominions in the later reign of Henry VIII.[89] Ovid's portrait of a Golden Age is replete with moralistic nostalgia for a lost era, before human greed scarred the soil with mines and pitched man against man; Leland's is a celebration of the very material abundance that allows military strength, and looks not back, but forward, to a new age and the 'laurelled triumphs' ('laurigeri [. . .] triumphi') these 'gifts' ('dona') will bring (D1^v).

The belligerence underlying Leland's description of English resources stems directly from the situation in which Henry's realm was placed after the break from Rome, and it is no coincidence that in the *Cygnea Cantio*, it is Leland's discussion of recent religious politics that provokes an extensive list of England's coastal fortresses. Leland relates how the 'English church began to despise of Roman wages' ('ecclesia coepit Anglicana / Romanas nihili aestimare merces'), and how Henry, 'the great-spirited king, threw off the insupportable yoke with the public consent of his people' ('Rex magnanimus iugum reiecit / Non portabile publico suorum / Consensu'), thus ensuring that 'long-sought-for liberty returned' ('petita longum / Libertas rediit', D3^v). The passage is typical of

---

[88] Ovid, *Metamorphoses*, ed. and trans. Frank Justus Miller, 3rd edn., rev. G. P. Goold, *Ovid III* (London: Heinemann, 1977), i. 98–9.

[89] Manley, *Literature and Culture*, 173.

Leland's narrative of the Henrician Reformation, with autonomy from Rome portrayed as a return to ancient freedoms after a long tradition of popular resistance. There is a simultaneous insistence on two manifestations of enclosed independence: the theoretical (England's claims to autonomy) and the material (images of city walls and sea defences). The medium of Latin also glamorizes England, able to transform even an acknowledgement of weakness—that the monarch is plagued by 'dreadful wars'—into something impressive (D3^v), the phrase 'bella horrentia' alluding to the 'Martis horrentia' from the pseudo-Virgilian prologue to the *Aeneid*, endowing Henry with epic status.

Leland's concept of writing history is one of conflict, and spats with fellow historians such as Boece and Polydore Vergil are played out in metaphors of physical strife. Nevertheless, the concept of literature and history as a branch of warfare is more than a verbal motif, and it is revealing that in the preface to his translation of Leland's *Assertio*, Robinson is prompted to recall Ascham's *Toxophilus* (1545), 'the commendation of this peaceable practise of shooting which once I as a rawe scholler reade ouer' (A3^v), retrospectively placing the *Assertio* within a tradition of militant Protestant texts. *Toxophilus*, written contemporaneously with Leland's *Assertio* and his topographical poems and responding to the same diplomatic crisis, is far from Robinson's epithet 'peaceable', however. Rather, it emphasizes the way in which words and weapons were closely linked in the rhetoric of the Henrician Reformation. The royal coat of arms appearing on the title page of *Toxophilus* is displayed under a closed imperial crown, endorsing Henry's claims to imperial status. On either side of the royal escutcheon are two warlike mottoes: the left-hand tag celebrates an ideological victory already achieved, using reformist idiom aligning Rome and Babylon as it revels in Henry's rejection of the Roman Church, 'the scourge of Babylon' ('Babylonica pestis'); the right-hand one predicts a future military victory, when the 'Scotsman and Frenchman will lie broken and tamed, / Proud necks subjected to their [English] master' ('Scotus & Gallus fracti domitique iacebunt, / Subiecti Domino colla superba suo'). Underneath are printed pictures of a book carrying the word *veritas* (truth), and an archer's bow stamped with the verb *vincit* (prevails). From the start, the truth-bearing book and the conquering bow are linked together, a connection manifested in the subsequent format of the introductory pages to the work. The dedicatory letter addressed to Henry VIII ends sharpened to an arrow's point by its layout on the printed page; the table of contents is typeset to resemble a long-bow, an arrow fitted, ready to fire. Words become visual represen-tations of weapons, just as the text hopes to persuade readers to strive for proficiency in archery and learning to meet the threat posed by the enemies both of England and, in Ascham's eyes, the holy, truth-giving Bible. Both book and bow hark back to a lost, but retrievable past: the former to the primitive church, before it was corrupted with redundant ceremonies and rituals; the latter to England's victories over the French under Henry V, when English bowmen routed superior numbers of Gallic horsemen.

Within Leland's works, as in Ascham's *Toxophilus*, knowledge of letters is linked to martial success. The twin legacies of Thomas Howard, one of the few contemporaries mentioned in the commen-tary to the *Genethliacon*, are his victories against the Scots and his poet son, the Earl of Surrey, 'most accomplished in elegant litera-ture' ('elegantis literaturae planè studiosissimum', F2ᵛ). Alfred the Great is similarly remembered for the fact that 'he vanquished the Danes and was the one Maecenas of his age' ('deballauit Danos, et unicus sui saeculi Mecoenas fuit').[90] Again, the frame of reference is classical, to Maecenas, patron of Virgil and Horace, and the two activities—warfare and literary patronage—are held in syntactic equality. In Leland's eyes, poetry is as applicable to national defence as more traditional weaponry. His function as poet is more than decorative, and here choice of Latin has the pragmatic advan-tage of still being an international language, allowing Leland to reach a European, as well as domestic, audience. The *Genethliacon* was written and published in 1543, five years after Edward's birth. Despite its initial appearance as a poem of celebration, it addresses pressing problems. The date of composition was the year in which Wales was legally integrated with England through the second Act of Union, as well as being a year of mounting tension between France and England. Leland's poem is therefore timely, celebrating and prescribing cohesive national identity at a time of external threat and internal change.

Leland's subsequent publications also reflect this increasingly fraught political climate. The *Assertio*, published in 1544, celebrates

---

[90] Leland, *Commentarii in Cygneam Cantionem*, A4ᵛ.

Arthur, a national hero, who—as a leader who united the kingdom and drove ungodliness from the land (in the form of the heathen Saxons, Danes, Picts, and Scots)—had much to offer as a role model for Leland's own monarch, Henry, who banished ungodliness (in the form of what Bale termed 'laysy lubbers & popyshe bellygoddes') and claimed a place for his realm on the international stage.[91] As hostilities with France heightened, Leland continued to use poetry to engage with, and play his part in, the incipient crisis. The *Cygnea Cantio* was published in 1545, the year in which the French landed on the Isle of Wight and when the Scots were once again threatening England's northern border.[92] The text is clothed in the language of both erudition—with Henry asked to accept the book 'most learnedly' ('eruditissime')—and war, as Leland wishes that Henry 'terrify, prostrate and, best of all, conquer the French and perfidious Scots' ('Scottos genus foedifragum, & Gallos [. . .], concutias, prosternas, tandemque fortunatissimus debelles', A3ᵛ). Leland promotes poetry as a form of aggressive diplomacy; the *Cygnea Cantio* catalogues English warships and coastal defences, detailing 'the exact number of ships' ('triremiumque / Intentus numerum adnotabo iustum', C2ᵛ) and fortified harbours along the south coast in an attempt to stress the difficulty of invasion and ward off the gathering enemy. 'France, if you are wise, you will prepare to flee,' Leland warns ('Gallus, si sapitus, fugam parate', C2ᵛ). When, in the preface to the *Cygnea Cantio*, Leland promises to write 'abundantly' ('fusè'), offering something 'both pleasing and useful to his native land' ('& gratus & utilis patriae'), the verbal *copia* he produces, celebrating England's military strength, thus serves a practical purpose (A5ᵛ).

Like the 'sadde and expert men' commissioned in 1539, 'to viewe all the places alongest the secost wher any daunger of Invasion ys like to be' and 'make advises for the fortificacion therof', Leland patrols the coastal margins.[93] The description of Wales in the *Genethliacon* traces the coastline from Bristol to Chester, before proceeding to talk of the inner regions, whilst the *Cygnea Cantio* provides a roll-call of sea defences along the English Channel, as Leland paints a picture of an inviolable realm. The

[91] Bale, *Laboryouse Iourney*, A7ᵛ–A8ʳ.
[92] Carley, 'Leland's *Cygnea Cantio*', 230.
[93] BL Titus B. i. 473.

author-scholar proves active participant in political affairs in the
dual capacities of both ambassador (attempting to avert military
engagement by verbal threats and posturing) and counsellor (advising Henry how best to protect his country should hostilities ensue).
The two roles are played out within the public domain of Leland's
poetry, requiring him to undergo a series of verbal contortions in
order to present a version of England that encourages its monarch
to address strategic weak spots without undermining the impression of imperviousness created for the benefit of an international
audience. The passage on Falmouth in the commentary to the
Cygnea Cantio shows the two dynamics. On the one hand, it
lobbies for yet more building, highlighting the advantages of 'a
fortress on its peak' which 'would indeed strike great terror into
enemy ships' ('si Cragus castellum uertice portaret, terrorem &
quidem magnum, in portus ostiis nauigantibus incuteret', G3ʳ). On
the other, the request is framed within a description emphasizing
the strength of its natural fortifications, with Falmouth judged 'the
foremost port in the whole country' ('a primo totius Britanniae
portum', G3ᵛ). As the ease of entrance for friendly ships is balanced
against the difficulty posed to hostile forces, the image is reminis-
cent of More's Utopia, the epitome of impenetrable isolation,
where the island curves protectively around a harbour further
defended by the necessity of gaining access via perilously rocky
channels, negotiable only with the aid of the Utopians themselves.
Leland's poetry thus responds to the real needs of his nation at a
time of threatened invasion. As John Guy explains, 'when France
and Spain recalled their London ambassadors at the beginning of
1539', following the break with Rome, 'a concerted Catholic invasion of England on the scale of Philip II's Armada of 1588 was
feared': 'musters were held, men and armour assembled, and ships
fitted out. A general survey of coastal defences was undertaken [. .
.]. And a national network of fortifications was built [. . .,] the
largest before the Napoleonic Wars.'[94]

Critics of Leland's poetry have frequently accused him of obse-
quiousness. In Leland's panegyrics to Henry, as James Carley
observes, 'adulation is the emotion expressed, flattery is the
means'.[95] For the purposes of the *Cygnea Cantio*, the poetic voice

---

[94] Guy, *Tudor England*, 184. Cf. Fowler, *English Sea Power*.
[95] Carley, 'Leland in Paris', 4.

adopted is, after all, that of a swan, a bird under royal protection since the thirteenth century, and which Thomas Kendrick notes as an 'over-loyal bird [. . .,] a Tudor panegyrist of such exceptional ardour that thereafter he could waste very little time on scenery or buildings that did not contribute to the Tudor glory'.[96] Certainly Leland pipes the royal tune. His anti-Gallic fervour displayed in the *Cygnea Cantio* and *Bononio-Gallo Mastix* (a poem celebrating Henry's capture of Boulogne) was timely in 1545. It was quickly revoked after hostilities ceased the following year: despite his previous renunciation of poetry in the *Cygnea Cantio*, where Calliope, the epic muse, is rejected in favour of her historical sister, Leland issued the *Laudatio Pacis* in August 1546, categorized by James Hutton as a conventional occasional poem in the tradition of Continental peace poetry.[97]

Yet it is unfair to dismiss Leland as a royal sycophant. As we have seen, his conceptualization of the role of poet as ambassador and counsellor is more proactive than such a label allows, and here Bale's description of Leland's work being worthy of a 'noble citizen' shows how subjects of early modern monarchies adapted classical ideas of citizenship, and those of Italian city-states, applying them to their own constitutional circumstances. In his preface to the 'Newe yeares gyfte', Bale defines citizenship according to lines set down by Cassiodorus, the first-century rhetorician. 'By this worthye propertye (sayth Cassiodorus) is a noble citezen knowen,' Bale declares: 'he seketh the commodite, praise and aduauncement of hys countreye' (B6ʳ). This formulation of the term *citizen* not only envisages allegiance to a wider body than the city-state, it also extends it beyond its primary meaning, 'the possession of civic rights and privileges' (*OED* 1). For Bale, citizenship is shown by belonging to, and acting on behalf of, a national community. Members of monarchies such as England were thus more engaged in public affairs than the label 'subject' suggests: they were also citizens, a role that did not conflict with obedience to the sovereign, but where it was the monarch's duty to consider the advice of counsellors who were, like Leland, taking an active role on behalf of the commonweal.

[96] T. D. Kendrick, *British Antiquity* (London: Methuen, 1950), 62.

[97] James Hutton, 'John Leland's *Laudatio Pacis*', *Studies in Philology*, 58 (1961), 616–26.

'DEPOPULATING THE LIBRARIES' AND THE 'LAWFULL
OUERTHROW OF THE SODOMETROUSE ABBEYES'[98]

Like Borde toiling round the Continent in service of his king,
Leland famously trudged the byways and highways of England and
Wales, recording his travels in a series of notebooks (published
posthumously as his *Itinerary*) and in an effusive list of topographical features detailed for Henry's benefit in his 'Newe yeares gyfte',
where he boasts that:

I haue so traueled in your domynions both by the see coastes and the
myddle partes, sparynge neyther labour nor costes by the space of these .vi.
yeares past, that there is almost neyther cape nor baye, hauen, creke or
pere, ryuer or confluence of ryuers, breches, washes, lakes, meres, fenny
waters, mountaynes, valleys, mores, hethes, forestes, woodes, cities,
burges, castels, pryncypall manor places, monasteryes, and colleges, but I
haue seane them.   (D4ʳᵛ)

In a characteristic desire to grant knowledge a physical form,
Leland then proceeds to envisage this 'worlde of thynges verye
memorable' 'engraued in syluer or brasse' (D6ᵛ). Peter Barber has
discussed the symbolic purpose of such *mappa mundi*, used 'in
medieval society as an expression of history, religion, and legend,
as well as of geography'.[99] The tradition can be found in John
Rastell's *The Four Elements* (1520). Throughout that play, a map
of the world hangs at the back of the stage, symbolizing the world
of learning Humanity can acquire should he apply himself with his
fellow protagonist, Studious Desire.[100] Leland's planned
'quadrate', in contrast, shows a narrowing of focus. This is no
mappa mundi in the conventional sense, depicting the scope of the
known world. Rather, it is limited to Henry's dominions, a 'worlde
and impery' within themselves, and is presented not (as Rastell's)
as a symbol of human possibilities, but as an expression of royal
power. The 'worlde' Leland offers is one placed specifically under
Henry's ownership: 'so shall your Maiestie haue thys your worlde
and impery of Englande so sett fourthe in a quadrate table of

---

[98] Leland, *Commentarii*, i. 134; Bale, *Laboryouse Iourney*, A2ᵛ.
[99] Barber, 'England I', 26.
[100] John Rastell, *The Four Elements*, in Richard Axton (ed.), *Three Rastell Plays*
(Cambridge: Brewer, 1979). For a discussion of the *mappus mundi* as stage prop,
see pp. 6–7.

syluer,' he promises (D5^v). Leland's topographical endeavours mimic the most practical function of topography: the use of surveying from 1520s onwards in establishing and enforcing boundaries, in order that, as the county historian John Norden later wrote, 'the lord of the Manor, under whom, & in whose land you dwell, shuld know his owne'.[101] Leland uses surveyors' techniques of observation and annotation on a national scale; the lord for whom he charts his native land is the monarch.

Despite the triumphant tone, Leland's vision of this quadrate of 'syluer or brasse', necessary so that England's glories 'may be more permanent, and farther knowne' (<u>D6</u>^{v}), exposes the limitations of his belief in the powers of writing and, ultimately, his own work. The need to make knowledge visually splendid reveals the fact that books are not enough: a large, expensive artefact will always have more impact, and be more appreciated by Henry (as well as less literate onlookers), notwithstanding all Leland's plaudits of his 'learned' king. As England's propagandist, Leland is forced to construct a 'monument' of native letters founded on rapidly shifting sands. His loud praise of England's love of learning echoes over a notable silence maintained throughout his works. Bale explains in his commentary on the 'Newe yeares gyfte' how Leland was sent out 'to serche and peruse the Libraries of [Henry's] realme' (<u>B8</u>^{v}). However much Bale represents this royal initiative as 'a stodye of thynges memorable, and a regardynge of noble Antiquite', he cannot disguise that this is done during the 'vtter destruccyon' of the monasteries, which held most of the nation's collection of books, a policy authorized by Henry and which funded the very building projects (costing over half a million pounds) Leland praises so highly: expensive monuments prioritized over books indeed.[102]

The loss of learning haunts Leland's texts, although it is never discussed in direct relation to the dissolution. In 1549, Bale (safely outside Henry's reign) can 'dolourouslye lamente so greate an ouersyghte in the moste lawfull ouerthrow of the sodometerouse Abbeyes & Fryeryes, when the most worthy monumentes of this realme, so myserably peryshed in the spoyle' (A2^v). Bale also has his own agenda in drawing the attention of the book's dedicatee,

---

[101] John Norden, *The Surveiors Dialogue* (1610), 4; cf. McRae, *God Speed the Plough*, ch. 6.   [102] Guy, *Tudor England*, 184.

Edward VI, to the destruction of the previous decade, since he intends the *Laboryouse Iourney* to be a lesson, instructing Edward 'what is in your comenwelth to be followed, and what to be chefely eschewed. What causeth a realme to floryshe, and what to dymynysh the estate therof', thereby investing his role of historian with urgency and national significance (A3ᵛ). Leland, caught up in the neglectful regime he extols, can only mention the ruination in a private letter to Henry's chief minister Cromwell, in which he deplores the despoiling of the libraries he has witnessed. 'The Germans perceive our desidousness,' he warns, 'and do send daily young scholars hither that spoileth [books], and cutteth them out of libraries, returning home and putting them abroad as monuments of their own country.'¹⁰³ Leland has no faith in the durability of knowledge without the written word. Just as British history was obliterated because, unlike the Romans, the Britons lacked historians who wrote it down, so too knowledge is here shown to rely on books rather than mental retention or oral dissemination. Losing the books, England has lost the knowledge within them, and the reflective glory of that knowledge. English learning, that is, is far from 'permanent'; the only reputation that is 'farther knowne' is that of a nation that disregards its store of literature, what Bale calls 'a moste horryble infamy amonge the graue senyours of other nacyons' (B1ʳ), lamenting the fact that 'for so lytle estemynge our true Antiquytees, the proude Italyanes haue always holden vs for a Barbarouse nacyon' (C5ʳ). In works Leland intended for publication, however, such 'depopulation of the libraries' ('bibliothecae depopulatoribus'), to paraphrase the *Commentarii de Scriptoribus*, is left to barbarians like the Danish pirates devastating the monastic libraries of Lindisfarne (i. 134), not to the king who, in the *Cygnea Cantio*, 'most learnedly' ('eruditissime') receives Leland's books (A5ᵛ).

Leland thus maintains a politic silence about the destruction. Even within the 'Newe yeares gyfte', the threat posed to the libraries as a result of the dissolution is never made apparent. Leland's tone is buoyant. He talks not of loss but of 'encreases' (E1ʳ) as the contemporary situation is seen to offer enhanced possibilities, liberating knowledge from dusty monasteries. Leland

¹⁰³ Cited by Anthony à Wood, *Athenae Oxonienses*, new edn., ed. Philip Bliss, 4 vols. (London: F. C. and J. Rivington, 1813–20), i, col. 198.

displays the same belief as Bale, and later John Foxe, in printing as
a feature distinguishing their age from the previous eras of darkness
and ignorance, celebrating the 'empryntynge of such workes as laye
secretlye in corners' (C2ʳ).¹⁰⁴ In the notes for Leland's English
Itinerary, references to the dissolution are guardedly laconic. Leland
follows the official line, acknowledging with approval such details
as 'Mr Candisch', having 'turnid the monasterie [at Milwood Park]
to a goodly manor place' (i. 38). Yet these pages record a landscape
in which, as monastic land was turned to private use, 'the patterns
of land-tenure were changing radically' and where 'the country was
taking on a new identity'.¹⁰⁵ A reader does not have to be far into
Lucy Toulmin-Smith's edition of the *Itinerary* to sense the ubiquity
of the upheaval, which one Venetian ambassador describes having
left London 'deformed' ('deformata') with 'the ruins of many
churches and their monasteries, where there were once friars and
monks' ('le ruine di molte chiese colli suoi monasteri, che già erano
di frati e monache').¹⁰⁶ Leland's description of Northampton in the
English *Itinerary* exemplifies his cautious tone: 'St Andreas the late
[*monastery*] of blake monkes, stood yn the north parte of the toune
[. . .] The Gray-freres House was the beste buildid and largest house
of all the places of the freres [. . .] The Blake-Freres in the streate
where the horse market is kept ons a weke. The White-Freres House
stoode a litle above the Gray-Freres' (i. 8–9). A subtext of devasta-
tion lies beyond the understated past tenses and attention paid to
unemotive particulars: the horse market once a week; the comparative size of the friaries and quality of building; their relative
geographical positions. Leland's observations on Wales are a striking illustration of the speed of the destruction and the veil he draws
across the subject. Toulmin-Smith argues that the antiquarian probably made at least two journeys to Wales between 1536 and
1539.¹⁰⁷ Between his visits, the dissolutions took their toll. On what
must be the initial trip, Leland notes 'a priori of Blake Chanons
standing in Old Cairmardine on the river side' (51), and 'at
Chepstow a litle priori *aliquot monachorum Benedictinorum* [of a

¹⁰⁴ Cf. John Foxe, *The Acts and Monuments*, 8 vols. (London: Seeley, Burnside &
Seeley, 1843–9), iii. 718–22.
¹⁰⁵ Scattergood, 'John Leland's *Itinerary*', 71.
¹⁰⁶ Giacomo Saranzo, *Relazione d' Inghilterra*, in Eugenio Alberi (ed.), *Relazioni
degli ambasciatori veneti al Senato*, serie 1, vol iii. (Florence, 1853), 31–87, at 51.
¹⁰⁷ Leland, *Itinerary in Wales*, p. ix.

few Benedictine monks], a celle to Bermundsey at London' (50).
On his return, he notes their demise: 'the celle of a Blake Monke or
two of Bermundsey by London was lately there suppressed,' he
comments at Chepstow (43); 'Cairmardin Priori of Blak Chanons,
down,' he writes, still more sparingly (58).

Leland offers learning as an ornament of his country. Yet, for all
his brave words, he could not help but see, at first hand, the poor
esteem in which it was actually held, when all around him, as Bale
describes it, 'lybrarye bokes' were being sold off to 'grossers and
sope sellers', used as blotters, or to 'scoure [. . .] candelstyckes, &
[. . .] rubbe [. . .] bootes'.[108] Leland's own labours seem to have
gone similarly disregarded. A poem addressed to Thomas Cranmer
in 1547 shows Leland 'begging' ('implorare') for patronage.[109]
According to Thomas Smith in the 1550s, the stipend owed him
never came, and 'whether deterred by the difficulties of the
promised work, or tired and broken with immense labours,
whether perhaps oppressed with too much grief, and melancholly,
because he had not found a reward equal to his industry, and just
expectation [. . .], he suffered the loss of his senses'.[110]

Despite the respect of his peers, Leland never received the official recognition he had argued to be every scholar's right. Leland's
powerlessness in this respect is mirrored by the physical impotency
into which he fell, surrendered on 21 March 1550 by letters patent
to his brother, in whose charge, 'receiv[ing] no benefit from the
assistance of friends, or of medicines, [he] continued in this sad
state to his death, April 18, 1552'.[111] Leland's 'vast heap of observations', his unpublished works, proved a living inheritance,
however, initially passed around a significant Protestant reading
circle in the household of Mary Fitzroy, Duchess of Richmond,
which included Cheke, Bale, and Foxe.[112] According to Leland's
eighteenth-century biographer Huddersford, Cheke would have
'published [these manuscripts], had he not been hindered by the
iniquity of the times, occasioned by the untimely death of K.
Edward' (an association locating Leland and his works within a

[108] Bale, *Laboryouse Iourney*, B1ʳ.
[109] John Leland, 'Ad Thomam Cranmerum, Cantior. Archipiscop.', in
Huddersford, *Lives*, i. 23.   [110] Cited by Huddersford, ibid., i. 26.
[111] Ibid. i. 24.
[112] Ibid., i. 26; Jesse W. Harris, *John Bale: A Study in the Minor Literature of the
Reformation* (Urbana: University of Illinois Press, 1940), 37–8.

Protestant tradition).[113] Bale, meanwhile, did use Leland's works, citing his *Commentarii de Scriptoribus* in his own catalogue of writers—*Scriptorum illustrium maioris britanniae catalogus*—and publishing the 'Newe yeares gyfte' as *The laboryouse Iourney*. Later Tudors, such as Spenser and Drayton, also drew upon the potential of topographical and river poetry as 'national' forms, and William Camden, John Stow, and Harrison all recycled Leland's topographical descriptions, with Camden even accused by Ralph Brooke of pilfering the work of 'that worthy & learned Englishe Antiquarie Maister Iohn Leyland' to 'fether [his] nest' with 'borrowed plumes'.[114]

Leland's legacy, however, is greater than the predominantly antiquarian projects for which his immediate successors appreciated him. In his portrayal of the nation, Leland was very much a writer of the 1530s and 1540s, when there was an active attempt to construct a sense of, and pride in, national identity. Whilst the early decades of the sixteenth century witnessed jingoistic episodes like the flytings of Skelton or poems of Brixius, these remain reactions to specific incidents. The attacks are small-scale snipings, intended to knock down, or crow over, particular opponents. Within a generation—a generation that witnessed the split from Rome—that programme had changed. Leland's works may react to identifiable events and strive to undermine his opponents, but they also attempt to depict a realm that is rich and independent in terms of its history, culture, and religion. Leland's account of ancient and contemporary history may be skewed, but it is thick with evidence of the conscious manipulation and construction of a national identity worthy of a country that had, only ten years previously, quite arbitrarily been declared 'an empire'. Leland 'paynted' England in what would become its 'natyue colours'. The Elizabethans, with their iconography of a godly island empire, had much for which to thank him.

[113] Huddersford, *Lives*, i. 27.
[114] Spenser, *Faerie Queene*, IV. xi–xii; Michael Drayton, *Poly-olbion* (1612); William Camden, *Britannia* (1586); John Stow, *The chronicles of England* (1580); Harrison, *Description*; Ralph Brooke, *A discoverie of diuers errours* (1595), 79–80.

3

William Thomas and the Riches of the Vulgar Tongue

Wherfore seing that our nation is nolesse prompte of capacitie and quicke of memorie, than other nations be, I wolde nowe see what shulde be the cause that amongest so many thousandes of vs as haue studied the latine tongue, it almost harde to finde any good Aucthour in our owne mother tongue. Surelie if I take not my marke amisse, the faulte herof consisteth in the bringing vp of our youthe. For the childe hath no sooner learned his A.B.C, but straight waies his maister putteth the latine grammer in his hande, and so proceadeth in teaching him the latine tongue, er ever he can speake good Englishe.[1]

The first two chapters charted concerted attempts during the 1540s to model a sense of national identity reflecting England's status as an autonomous realm. As Andrew Borde and John Leland endeavoured to enhance the international reputation of their country as a land excelling in letters and learning, they followed a classical paradigm. Latin was the expected scholarly medium for Leland; Borde tried to improve the English language by making it more like Latin. For both authors, England offered linguistic and intellectual refuge for Latinate culture betrayed by its Roman homeland: 'Latyn, welcome to me,' Borde's Englishman cried in his *Introduction*.[2] The next three chapters turn from the intellectual dominance of Latin in the Henrician era to the increasing emphasis on the English tongue from the late 1540s onwards. The authors who appear in the subsequent chapters—William Thomas, Thomas Smith, and Thomas Wilson—were educated in the classics. Their works are imbued with the literature and history of the ancient world and they belong to a tradition of civic humanism, where learning is intended for use in

[1] William Thomas, *The Boke of the Sphere*, BL Egerton 837, 3[r].
[2] Borde, *Introduction*, M2[v].

the *vita activa*. Their humanism, however, is modulated by growing respect for the vulgar tongues and recognition of the need for writings in those languages. Even as Wilson and Smith continued to use Latin in their private correspondence and some of their published works, like Thomas, they synthesized their classical models with those of the European vernaculars, and of Italy in particular.

We begin this examination of a more vernacular humanism by looking at the works of William Thomas. Where Borde and Leland adapted 'medieval' traditions to suit England's situation in 1540s, in Leland's case grafting them onto the New Learning, Thomas, in contrast, turned to contemporary Italian culture to advance both himself and his nation. The influence of Italy on English learning was well established by the sixteenth century.[3] Unlike previous scholars such as John Tiptoft or poets such as Thomas Wyatt, however, Thomas was drawn neither to its academic, neo-Latin humanism, nor its verse, but to its vernacular, politically engaged prose. Among Thomas's works are the first Italian history and Italian grammar in English; a translation of a Venetian's account of his eastern travels to Tana and Persia; and a set of discourses inspired by Machiavelli.[4] Thomas's works consequently constitute early responses to currents of thought more familiar to scholars of the Elizabethan period: namely, Machiavellianism; pride in the vulgar tongue; and a dichotomous view of Italy's charms. The following chapter analyses the impact of Italy on Thomas's works in four ways. First, it examines his portrayal of the affinities between England and Italy, and his use of the latter as both an inspiration and a foil highlighting England's alleged superiority over its Continental counterpart. Secondly, it explores the influence of Italian on Thomas's enthusiasm for the vernacular. Thirdly, it looks at his adaptation of Machiavellian thought to English statecraft. Finally, it traces Thomas's appropriation of Italian bibliographical fashions in the presentation of his printed texts. The chapter begins, however, with an account of Thomas's first known work, *Peregrine, or a defence of Henry VIIIth*, and his use of this 'defence' as a means of benefiting his nation and himself.

[3] Kenneth R. Bartlett, *The English in Italy, 1525–58: A Study in Culture and Politics* (Geneva: Slatkine, 1991).

[4] William Thomas, *The Historie of Italie* (1549); id., *The Principal rules of the Italian grammer* (1550); id., *Voiages*, BL Royal 17. C. x; Thomas, Political discourses (*c.*1551), BL Vespasian D. xviii, 2^r–45^r.

THOMAS'S 'DEFENCE'

Thomas encountered Italy at first hand in 1545. Until then, he had
been a rising Oxford graduate, enjoying the patronage of Anthony
Browne, Master of the Horse, and distributing income from certain
newly dissolved nunneries.[5] W. K. Jordan attributes Thomas's
sudden removal to Italy to his 'advanced Protestant views', which
would have exposed him to attack in the mid-1540s, during the
backlash against more radical reform.[6] However, Edmond Harvell,
then English ambassador to Venice, ascribes Thomas's flight to
more worldly events, when 'reduced to ruin' by 'folly and misfortune of play', Thomas embezzled money from Browne and escaped
to Venice.[7] Thomas was apprehended by Harvell and imprisoned
briefly; after his release, he remained in Italy, probably to avoid
prosecution by Browne. It was at Bologna, following news of
Henry VIII's death in the winter of 1546–7, that Thomas composed
his earliest known work, *Peregrine, or a defence of Henry VIIIth*.
Categorized by Thomas's biographer E. R. Adair as 'a piece of
time-serving', the work deserves more attention than this dismis-
sive remark affords it.[8] As the earliest manifestation of Thomas's
commitment to a nascent Protestant nation (an allegiance for
which Thomas later died), the text is central to Thomas's works.
The means by which he advanced both self and country, moreover,
exemplify the strategies and preoccupations displayed throughout
his writing career, as he drew on Italian culture and adapted
humanist conventions to his own circumstances and those of the
regime he served.

The *Peregrine* is presented as a pre-dinner conversation in the
literary mode of More's *Utopia* or many of Erasmus' *Colloquia*,
and—like the former—purports to record an autobiographical
encounter. Into this archetypal humanist setting and genre, the
dialogue, Thomas brings a strident defence of his erstwhile
monarch—in particular, his split from Rome—and a lavish eulogy
of his country, building on the rhetoric of nationhood developed

---

[5] E. R. Adair, 'William Thomas: A Forgotten Clerk of the Privy Council', in R.
W. Seton-Watson (ed.), *Tudor Studies* (London: Longmans Green, 1924), 133–60,
at 134.
   [6] W. K. Jordan (ed.), *The Chronicle and Political Papers of King Edward VI*
(London: George Allen & Unwin, 1966), p. xx n. 3.   [7] *LP* XX. i. 515.
   [8] Adair, 'Thomas', 138.

during the preceding decades: King John is rehabilitated as a proto-Protestant martyr; Henry VIII enjoys the imperial status of 'a prince in his owne Realme'; the Roman Church is condemned through hyperbolic descriptions of 'hipochrisies / murders / ydolatries / miracles / sodomies / adulteries / fornicacions / pryde / Envye / and not seuen/butt more than .700. thousande deadly synnes'.[9]

When Thomas portrays an abundant island nation, the economic independence of which reflects and enables the jurisdictional autonomy of its sovereign, he develops familiar Henrician motifs. In response to the commercial expansion of the late 1540s, however, he modifies his predecessors' approach.[10] England's fertility is not vaunted in the context of isolated and defensive self-sufficiency found in Borde's *Introduction* or Leland's *Genethliacon*. Thomas celebrates, rather than denigrates, export trade, recognizing that it enriches, not denudes, the nation. His description of England emphasizes flourishing trade links as well as material abundance. 'Have we leather,' states Thomas: 'whereof contynually goeth out of the Realme a marvaylous quantitie / a good wytnesse of the greate abundaunce of Cattel that the countrey doth nourish'; 'leade and tynne' prove 'so abundant / that there is contynually bought and sold out of the Realme greate quantities thereof'; from 'mynes of naturall Coale' 'there is yerely sold out of the realme a greate quantitie [. . .] in duchland / flaunders & fraunce' (48ᵛ). Unlike Leland's attitude to 'monuments of learnyng', it is not the removal of goods that is detrimental, but a failure to recognize their English provenance, thus obscuring their source. Where Leland is a collector, acquiring unique and irreplaceable objects, Thomas resembles a merchant, dealing in renewable resources, anxious only that their proper origin is acknowledged. Thomas's inventory of native goods is consequently a possessive act that marks them out, from Thomas's perspective, as 'our[s]'. 'All the fyne Clothes which are called *panni di fiandra* are also English clothes / wrong named by occasion of the marte at Andwarpe in Flaunders,' he explains, reclaiming the English genesis of the cloths in question (48ʳ).

---

[9] William Thomas, *Peregrine, or a defence of Henry VIIIth* (1547), BL Vespasian D. xviii, 46ᵛ–81ʳ, at 53ᵛ, 63ᵛ–64ʳ.
[10] David Loades, *England's Maritime Empire: Seapower, Commerce and Policy, 1490–1690* (Harlow: Longman, 2000), 43, 53.

As 'fyne clothes', these *panni di fiandra* are also important as a sign of English refinement, evidence with which to counter accusations of uncouthness. England needs to rival Italy in terms of manners and sophistication as well as trade. Faced with England's reputation for ill-breeding, Thomas protests his compatriots' 'knowlege of Ciuilitie' (48^r). In Thomas's description of Ireland, as in Borde's *Introduction,* civility even becomes a mark of Englishness. According to Thomas, Ireland is 'diuided into two sundry partes' along lines of 'Ciuil liuyng', 'that is to say the English pale & the wyld Irish', where Thomas's 'wyld Irish' ('vnreasonable beastes [. . .] without knowlege of god or good maners') are noted for the 'barbarity' that, by the mid-twelfth century, 'had become, and was to remain, a cliché in describing the Irish'.[11] For Thomas, the imposition of English rule is not aggressive, 'for desyre of dominion / or for avarice of Reuenue': it is civilizing, with 'these wyld men' brought 'from Rude / beastly [/] ignorant [/] cruel & vnruly infidels / to the state of ciuil [/] reasonable / patient / humble / and well gouerned Christians' (74^v). In contrast, the Scottish—like the wild Irish, still outside English rule—remain a people 'somewhat Barbarous' (75^r).

Thomas's enthusiastic depictions of England's strength and civility are not conducted for the eyes of Italy alone. His primary target is the influential elite at the English court. Despite the language in which the purported conversation takes place and nationality of its supposed auditors, the earliest manuscripts are written in English, not Italian. The *Peregrine* was published in Italian five years later, in 1552, after Thomas's successful political rehabilitation.[12] In 1547, however, it was friends back home that he needed to win in order to effect his return to England. The title 'Peregrine' is from the Italian *peregrino* ('strange or foreign'): the 'defence of Henry VIII' grows out of, and is necessitated by, Thomas's foreignness, alienated from his native land. The word, in one manuscript version, is replaced by

[11] Thomas, *Peregrine*, BL Vespasian D. xviii, 74^r; Gillingham, 'English Invasion of Ireland', 24.
[12] William Thomas, *Il Pellegrino Inglese ne 'l quele si difende l'innocente, & la Sincera vita del pio & Religisso Re d'Inghilterra Henrico ottauo, bugiardamente caloniato da Clemente vii & da gl' altri adulatori de la Sedia antiChristiana* (Zurich, 1552). W. K. Jordan inverts the order of the English manuscript and Italian printed versions (Jordan, *Edward VI*, ii: *The Threshold of Power. The Dominarice of the Duke of Northumberland* (London: George Allen & Unwin, 1970), 416).

'pelegrine', from *pellegrino*, the Italian noun for traveller and a synonym for *peregrino* as an adjective for foreign.[13] It is the need to terminate these two undesirable states of travelling and estrangement that motivates the ensuing treatise. As a pilgrim (the medieval Latin meaning of *peregrinus*), Thomas does not journey to a saint's shrine to show his devotion; true to the spirit of the Henrician Reformation, he uses words in service of the English crown.

For the sake of Thomas's domestic readership, much stress is laid on the personal danger Thomas encounters in his role of advocate for king and country. He characterizes himself as impetuous but loyal. Barely able to contain his rage on hearing his dead king insulted, he threatens to stalk out of the assembled company (49ʳ). Later, drama is provided when one listener, angered by Thomas's outspoken attacks on the pope (vital for his defence of the English church), draws his dagger 'with [which] to have smytten [him]' (56ᵛ). Thomas's rash temperament, the very characteristic his work endeavours to excuse, thus acquires legitimacy and value (conveniently, the secondary meaning of *peregrino* is 'rare and precious'). The text is written with Thomas's previous crimes in mind: the 'defence' is not just of Henry, but also of Thomas, and the fate of the defamed recorded in the epigraph—'He that dieth wyth honeur lyueth for euer / And the defamed dead recouereth neuer'—is one that Thomas wishes to avert for himself as much as his late monarch. At the outset, he reminds his audience and potential benefactors of his unsolicited exile, whilst simultaneously stifling the circumstances of his disgrace by the obliqueness of the allusion. 'Constrayned by misfortune to Abandon the place of [his] natiuitie / and to walke at the randon of the wyde world', Thomas transforms himself from active offender into passive victim of bad luck (47ʳ). As Adair writes, the *Peregrine* 'achieved its reward'.[14] After Browne's death in May 1548, Thomas was free to return home, possibly under William Cecil's protection.[15]

Thomas thus uses a display of national and royal fervour to shape an authorial persona designed to advance his own social and national reintegration. Pietro Aretino initially seems an unlikely dedicatee for the *Peregrine*. However, as a figure with a dubious

---

[13] William Thomas, *Pelegrine*, BL Add. 33, 383.
[14] Adair, 'Thomas', 138.
[15] Jordan, *Threshold of Power*, 416.

past who engineered his entry into elite circles through his ability with the pen, Aretino provides a model for Thomas's own rehabilitation. Like Thomas, Aretino was a servant (albeit of lower social rank than Thomas) discredited for stealing from his master. At least according to his enemies, he then amassed an impressively dissolute curriculum vitae, as—amongst other things—a street singer, moneylender, mule skinner, and hangman's assistant, before publishing in 1512 a small book of verse, imitating Serafino.[16] Henceforth, he was increasingly courted by the princes of Europe, not least because refusal of patronage habitually unleashed his venomous satire. Despite his association with Pope Clement VII, from whom he received his first pension, Aretino was also ripe for an appearance in a tract defending the Henrician Reformation, thanks to his pasquinades against various members of the Roman clergy, as well as his version of the Penitential Psalms, imitated by Wyatt at the start of an English Protestant tradition of psalm sequences.[17] Further to that, Aretino was author of a satirical dialogue about gambling, *Le carte parlanti*, published in 1545, a potential allusion to the disreputable past Thomas circumvents in the *Peregrine*. The *Peregrine* consequently prefigures Thomas's subsequent texts, as he absorbs and adapts Italian culture, creating a thoroughly Anglicized product by which to profit both his country and himself.

'THE INFINITE COMMODITIES THAT GROW OF THE READYNG OF HISTORIES'[18]

In their 1990 article, ' "Studied for action" ', Anthony Grafton and Lisa Jardine reconstruct Gabriel Harvey's reading using marginal annotations and titles of acquisitions to demonstrate the 'goal-orientated' nature of reading and writing history in the sixteenth century.[19]

---

[16] *The Letters of Pietro Aretino*, trans. Thomas Caldecot Chubb (Hamden, Conn.: Archon, 1967), ch. 6.

[17] King, *English Reformation Literature*; Rivkah Zim, *English Metrical Psalms: Poetry as Praise and Prayer, 1535–1601* (Cambridge: Cambridge University Press, 1987).   [18] Thomas, *Historie*, A2r.

[19] Anthony Grafton and Lisa Jardine, ' "Studied for action": How Gabriel Harvey Read his Livy', *Past and Present*, 129 (1990), 30–78, at 30; cf. Lisa Jardine and William Sherman, 'Pragmatic Readers: Knowledge Transactions and Scholarly

Their article shows that the humanist vision of history as a written record of the experience and political knowledge necessary for the *vita activa*, endorsed by authors such as Thomas Elyot, was followed in practice as well as theory.[20] Although conducted on material annotated during the 1570s and early 1580s, Grafton and Jardine's findings are representative of humanist reading practices throughout the sixteenth century and are applicable to Thomas's *Historie of Italie*, published in 1549, the year after his return to England. Books, Harvey observed in 1580, 'shewe what should be done', and the directed nature of Thomas's *Historie*, geared to political analysis, is apparent from the outset.[21] Thomas's labours 'to publishe vnto our owne nacion in our mother tongue the dooynges of straungers' are commended to his readers for 'the infinite commodities that grow of the readyng of histories' and the 'profite thei maie gather by trauailyng therein' (A2^r). The title page establishes the work's instructive purpose as 'a boke excedyng profitable to be redde' 'because it intreateth of the astate of many and diuers common weales, how thei haue ben, & now be gouerned' (A̲1^r). Italy acts as a mirror for England, not least because of the parallels drawn between them: topographically, Italy is 'almost an ilande' (1^r); like England, it is also primarily a trading nation (2^r). As Thomas praises the liberty of conscience, learning, and 'conformitee of speeche' that the Italians enjoy (3^{rv}), therefore, they become prescriptive of what England, similarly blessed as a 'commodious' country, can attain (1^v). Readers are especially guided to the 'ciuilitee' (the quality Thomas so eagerly claims for England in his *Peregrine*), with which 'the Italian nacion [. . .] seemeth to flourisshe [. . .] moste of all other at this daie' (A2^r).

Historical study fulfils an admonitory, as well as an exhortative, function, however, and as the *Historie* proceeds, the initially glowing portrayal of Italy is quickly undermined. Italy is not seen in its role as the former *caput mundi*, nor even, despite the inclusive title, as a cohesive body (a situation that reflects the fact that, politically, Italy was not a nation during this period, but a collection of city-states

Services in Late Elizabethan England', in Anthony Fletcher and Peter Roberts (eds.), *Religion, Culture and Society in Early Modern Britain* (Cambridge: Cambridge University Press, 1994), 102–24.

[20] Elyot, *Gouernour*, 38^v–41^r.
[21] Cited by Grafton and Jardine, ' "Studied for action" ', 39.

and kingdoms). Italy is only presented as a political entity in the past tense, when Thomas relates the history of ancient Rome as 'an abridgement of the state of Italie, from the beginning vntill the Romaine empyre was vtterly diuided' (8^r), a manoeuvre placing Italy's claims to domination in a now long-gone age, and—with reformist spite—simultaneously extracting that impressive history from Rome's sole ownership. The fragmentation of a once great nation into a collection of ever vulnerable city-states acts as a further caveat to Edwardian England. Throughout the *Historie*, Thomas shows the instability of commonweals riven by internal factionalism and, still more seriously, dependent on the favour of more powerful foreign forces (the French king and Holy Roman Emperor). When Adair terms the *Historie* 'the first English guide book to Italy', he thus obscures the centrality of history to the instructive function of the work, a purpose also lost in George B. Parks's abridged edition which omits every historical section, the significance of which he further diminishes by dubbing them 'often little more than a chronology of [. . .] rulers'.[22]

Thomas paints a picture of Italian history as tumultuous as that found in Francesco Guicciardini's *Historia d'Italia*, written during the 1530s, which, once translated into English in 1579, helped consolidate Elizabethan perceptions of Italy as a violent, treacherous nation.[23] Besides offering topical political advice, therefore, the depiction of an alien country also builds English national esteem, holding up a foreign power, comparison with which will reflect favourably on England, a technique Thomas employs most obviously in his translation of Joseph Barbaro's *Voiages to Tana and Persia* in the early 1550s. Thomas uses the *Voiages* to silence those 'Englishemen' who 'wote not why they whyne' and to 'advaunce [his] cuntrey for goodnes to be one of the best partes of [the best] ixth parte [of the world]'.[24] The portrayal of England relies on the negative images of the 'evill cuntreys' Tana and Persia to throw it into positive relief (1^r). Thomas's 'better proofe' of England's preeminence is to display 'what barbarowse people arr in other regions, what wante of good foode they have, what miserable lyves

[22] Adair, 'Thomas', 135; William Thomas, *The History of Italy (1549)*, ed. George B. Parks (Ithaca, NY: Cornell University Press, 1963), p. xviii.
[23] Geoffrey Fenton, *The historie of Guicciardin, conteining the warres of Italie and other partes* (1579).
[24] Thomas, *Voiages*, BL Royal 17 C. x, 1^r, 2^r.

they leade, what servitude and subiection they endure, what
extremities of heate and colde they suffer, what superstitions they
folowe, and what a nombre of other inconveniences do hange vpon
them' (2ʳ). Likewise, in the *Historie*, Thomas's homeland lies
beyond the text as a point of comparison against which Italy
appears tawdry, or marred by the oppression of its husbandmen
(5ʳᵛ). Even its geographical description acquires a sense of licen-
tiousness. Although 'almost an ilande', unlike England depicted in
the *Peregrine* as self-containedly 'enuyroned with the Ocean sea'
(50ᵛ), Thomas's *Historie* describes Italy with 'so many [. . .] riuers,
and hauens, that it is an open lappe to receiue the trade of all countreys', a moralistic aside tempering Italy's mercantile dominance
(1ʳᵛ).

This opening slur sets the ambivalent tone of the *Historie*, which
continually qualifies the praise awarded. Scarcely a city passes
without some superlative accolade. The fort at Venice 'for
strengthe and beautie is one of the rarest thynges dooen in these
daies' (74ᵛ); Florentine conduits are 'one of the excellentest thynges
in all Europe' (138ᵛ); Andrea Doria's Genoese villa is 'the goodliest
house that any priuate man hath builded in our daies' (161ʳ).
Nevertheless, Felix Raab is misguided when he states that Thomas
'had nothing but good to report of the Italians', and the appeal of
these architectural splendours is undercut by continual reference to
the Italians' sexual incontinence in particular.[25] The Genoese figure
as versifying lovers, flirting 'openly' in church and street 'with what
wife so euer she be' (162ʳ); Florentines are remembered for their
'Sodomie in tyme past' (139ᵛ); Venice is notable for 'lewdnesse',
whore-mongering, and serial bastard-bearing, illegitimate offspring
who grow up to fill the offices of the Roman Church (84ᵛ). On the
one hand, Italy is a place of beauty to visit; on the other, a den of
iniquity to abhor and avoid—a dual vision prefiguring the oppos-
ing strands of Elizabethan representations of Italy, both on stage
and in prose works such as Richard Mulcaster's *Positions [. . .]
necessarie for the training vp of children* (1581), or Roger
Ascham's *Schoolmaster*, written in the late 1560s.

If Italian morals are under scrutiny, then it is naturally Rome—
for an English Protestant writing during the increasingly evangelical

[25] Felix Raab, *The English Face of Machiavelli: A Changing Interpretation,
1500–1700* (Toronto: University of Toronto Press, 1964), 40.

regime of Edward VI—that bears the brunt of the attack. Rome is
the site of twofold ruin: physical (shown through the imperial ruins
dominating Thomas's description of the city) and moral (depicted
by the lecherous and vainglorious transgressions of its 'bishops'
and churchmen). The city's faded splendour is seen as symbolic of
its lost status and fitting punishment for its political ambitions: 'the
iudgement of god [. . .] hath made those antiquitees to remayne as
a foule spoyle of the Romaine pride, and for a witnesse to the
worldes ende of their tyranny, ' Thomas states (22ᵛ). As a picture
of the old ruins supplants a description of Rome itself, its imperial
and ecclesiastical identities merge. The tyranny ended is not just
that of ancient Rome, but also that of its contemporary rulers: the
'bishops' themselves. For Borde, neglect of ecclesiastical property
was a sign of Rome's moral decrepitude, the imperial ruins carrying no especial significance.[26] Thomas, however, like the French
poet Joachim du Bellay (who arrived in Rome five years after
Thomas's departure), links the city's moral and physical deteriora-
tion, its papal and imperial sins.[27]

The history of Rome, meanwhile, is presented as a digression.
'Because my principal purpose tendeth to descriue the astates of
Italie,' Thomas explains, 'I neede not to vse muche circumstance,
either in mattiers of religion, or yet in writing all the liues of the
bishops of Rome' (41ᵛ). For the sake of brevity, Thomas thus
licenses a tellingly selective reading of papal history, designed to
emphasize secular ambition and unholy lusts. The thirty-three bishops before Sylvester (314–35 CE) are of little interest, since they
give little opportunity for reformist indignation. Owing to continual persecution, 'they alwaies kept theim selfes out of sight,
preachyng and ministryng secretlie without pompe[,] astate or
solemne ceremonie' (42ʳ). 'From the tyme of Silvester', however, 'as
they grewe in wealthe, so encreased theyr worldely maiestee and
ambicion'. It is therefore with Silvester that Thomas's papal history
begins, although a convenient silence is also drawn between
Syricius (389–99 CE) and Gregory II (715–31 CE), because this
period again offers little scope for scandal, 'seyng that till the time
of *Gregorie* the seconde [. . .] the Romaine bishops trauailed most

---

[26] Andrew Borde, *The Extrauagantes* appended to *Breuiary* (1547), B2ʳ.
    [27] Joachim du Bellay, *Le premier livre des Antiquitez de Rome* (Paris, 1558); id.,
Les Regrets et autres oeuvres poetiques (Paris, 1558).

in mattiers of religion [. . .] without peculier dominion' (44^r). History, as in the *Peregrine*, is used by Thomas to expose the false foundations of papal power, discrediting the validity of the '*Donacion of Constantine*', disproving St Peter's connections with the city, and (in a series of lurid papal biographies) removing Rome's claims to spiritual leadership. Even in abbreviated form, the size of the section on papal history (sixty-seven pages) exceeds that on Venetian history, the next largest at fifty-six.[28] It is, furthermore, Thomas's biographies that comprise the historical description of the city, replacing the potentially more impressive history of imperial Rome with a tapestry of papal depravity.

Thomas's treatment of contemporary Rome is similarly dominated by the desire to disclose the temporal excesses of the Roman Church. The passage on 'the present astate of Rome' is devoted solely to relating the processions witnessed 'on Christmas daie, the yere of our lord 1547' (37^v). The true Christian calendar is set against the pope's diary of festivity and ritual, with Christmas described as 'a principall feast celebrated in *Pontificalibus*', during which—as Thomas depicts it—the significance of Christ's birth is lost in a sea of cardinal red. Opulence and ceremony, 'riche clothe' and 'preciouse stones' (38^{rv}) occupy the entire six-page section, denying the city any life or purpose beyond the empty frippery of papal pomp. At the tail of the procession, Thomas introduces the clergy's 'harlottes' (39^v). A jibe at the clerics' long robes, under which they hide 'the greattest pride of the worlde', slides into an account of their private lives, another area of concealment and hypocrisy: 'for theyr ordinarie pastime is to disguise them selfes, to go laugh at the Courtisanes houses' (39^v). Even in 'shrouyng time', the season of Lenten fasting and preparation for Easter, the holiest part of year, these churchmen 'ryde maskyng about' with their whores, 'whiche is the occasion that Rome wanteth no iolie dames', a stupendous (and inflated) '.40000. harlottes mainteigned for the moste parte by the clergy and theyr followers'. Rome is displayed, in deed as well as metaphor, as the 'harlot Church' of Protestant polemic, or—as Thomas writes in the *Peregrine*—the 'whorish mother Church' (56^v).

The story of an ideologically embattled England defining itself

---

[28] Calculations from the 1st edn. (1549), printed by Thomas Berthelet, *STC*, 2nd edn. 24018.

against the papacy it had rejected was already, by 1549, common-place. In comparison with his predecessors' diatribes, however, what is strikingly absent from Thomas's critique is an attempt to appropriate England as a home for the learning disappointed by its native city. England is not promoted as a refuge for Latin culture, as it is explicitly in Borde's works, or implicitly in Leland's through his prioritization of Latin as the symbol of intellectual achievement. For Thomas, classical Rome offers no more than its debauched ecclesiastical counterpart. Even when he wanted to reach an inter-national audience, as with his defence of England and Henry VIII in *Il Pellegrino*, it was one of the vulgar tongues (Italian) that he chose, not Latin, despite a knowledge of Latin acquired through his schooling and university education and later displayed in a trans-lation of part of Livy's histories as *An Argument wherein the appa-raile of women is both reproued and defended* (1551). It was to contemporary, secular Italy that Thomas looked for inspiration, finding it in the rise of the vernacular that facilitated growth beyond the dual shadows of papal and imperial Rome.

'THE BENEFITE OF THEIR OWNE TONGUES'[29]

Thomas's second printed work, written in 1548, was the first English–Italian primer, published in 1550 as *The Principal rules of the Italian grammer* accompanied by an English–Italian word list compiled from Alberto Acharisio's *Vocabolario, Grammatica, et Orthographia de la lingua volgare* (1543) and Francesco Alunno's *Richezze della lingua volgare* (1543). In contrast to Anglo-French equivalents such as John Palsgrave's *Lesclarissement de la langue francoyce* (1530), or Giles Duwes's *Introductorie for to lerne to pronounce and speke Frenche trewly* (1533), Thomas's title makes bold claims for the Italian vernacular as a ruled language, a quality hitherto attributed only to Latin and Greek. As Adair points out, Thomas's grammar is also laid out according to 'good classical models', a format which (unlike Palsgrave's or Duwes's conversa-tional method, teaching through dialogue) again stresses, visually, the regular, logical nature of Italian.[30] A necessary by-product of

[29] Thomas, *Boke of the Sphere*, BL Egerton 837, 4ʳ.
[30] Adair, 'Thomas', 138.

this approach is that English too is shown in tabulated form as a language with its own pattern. Writing an Italian language manual thus highlights the grammatical structure of Thomas's own vernacular. English, no less than Italian or Latin, has an 'imperatiue', 'optatiue', and 'subiunctiue mode', and amongst those words that the OED credits Thomas with importing into English are the grammatical terms 'aduerbiallie' and 'adiectiuelie'.[31]

Thomas's reading for the grammar, moreover, exposed him to the similarities between the situation of his own language in the late 1540s and that facing Italian ten years earlier. As Acharisio explains, it is the dearth of vernacular in comparison with classical writings that provokes his *Vocabolario*, since 'realising that these are no less useful and necessary than those which there already were [. . .] in Latin, [he] began to wish to write a little work on Grammar, Spelling, and vocabulary' ('Conoscendo quelle non meno utili & necessarie, che già sieno state [. . .] le latine, mi misi à uoler fare una operetta di Grammatica, Orthographie, & vocaboli').[32] From Italian books Thomas learnt that the state of a language is not pre-ordained: it can be bettered through effort, and when he commends Italian in the *Principal rules* for its improved standing in relation to Latin and Greek, it is in awareness of the 'diligence, that in these tenne yeres passed' Italians have invested in their vulgar tongue (π2^v). The process is also recent, within the last decade, and as such should be added inducement to English speakers. In turning from classical languages to the example of Italian, Thomas's works strike another chord with those of du Bellay, another traveller to Italy in the middle decades of the sixteenth century, whose *Deffence et Illustration de la Langue Françoyse* appeared in 1549, the year after Thomas wrote his *Principal rules*. The Frenchman similarly battles against unquestioning reverence of Greek and Latin and holds up Italian (or rather Tuscan) as a model for his compatriots. No language is intrinsically richer than another, he insists, 'but only owing to the skill and industry of men' ('ains au seul artifice, & industrie des hommes').[33]

[31] Thomas, *Principal rules*, D2^r–D3^v, S1^v, Gg3^v.
[32] Alberto Acharisio, *Vocabolario, Grammatica, et Orthographia de la lingua volgare* (Cento, 1543), A1^v.
[33] Joachim du Bellay, *La Deffence et Illustration de la Langue Françoyse*, ed. Fernand Desonay (Geneva: Lille, 1950), A4^v.

In the *Principal rules*, the ramifications of Thomas's propaga-
tion of Acharisio's beliefs in regard to English are left unstated. It
is not until the prefatory matter of his unpublished translation of
Sacrobosco's *De Sphera* (*c.*1551) that Thomas transposes them to
an overtly English setting. Here again, his passionate arguments for
education in the vernacular stem directly from his Italian reading.
As an early example of a writer promoting education in English,
and one who—owing to the fact that these opinions are in manuscript, not print—is overlooked by Richard Foster Jones's
admirable survey of attitudes to the vernacular in early modern
England, Thomas's views are worth citing at length. Like
Acharisio, he bemoans the lack of books written in his native
tongue, 'seing that our nation is nolesse prompte of capacitie and
quicke of memorie, than other nations be, I wolde nowe see what
shulde be the cause that amongest so many thousandes of vs as
haue studied the latine tongue, it is almost harde to finde any goode
Aucthor in our owne mother tongue'.[34] What Thomas refuses to
recognize is that the inadequacy is innate or insurmountable. The
established pattern of educational practice, not a 'faulte' of the
language, is held responsible for the current paucity of English
works, 'For the childe hath no sooner learned his A.B.C, but
straight waies his maister putteth the latine grammer in his hande,
and so proceedeth in teaching him the latine tongue, er ever he can
speake good Englishe'. Time is wasted over 'Ovide, Virgill, Tullii,
Aristotle, and suche other as the maister him self dothe somtime
skarslie well vnderstande wherein the childe consumeth the flower
of his learning youth, and if he arryue ons at the writing of a pistle
in latine, than is he saufe enough, though well he can not write
halfe apistle in Englishe.' Thomas does not hesitate over pairing
'good' with 'English'. When Leland protests against slanderous
suggestions that 'there's no such thing as a good Briton' ('*Nemo
bonus Britto est*'), he defends his compatriots' ability to show
learning by writing eloquently in Latin, as he himself hopes to do.[35]
What Thomas champions less than five years later is the language
itself, a stance rare in the early 1550s and more habitually associated by scholars such as Jones with the late 1570s.[36]

34 Thomas, *Boke of the Sphere*, BL Egerton 837, 3ʳ.
35 Leland, *Commentarii*, i. 32.
36 Jones, *Triumph of English*, ch. 6, esp. p. 211.

Thomas thus taps into a Continental, rather than national, mood, where a du Bellayan 'deffence' of the mother tongue was already a point of duty. 'Whenever I could honour my homeland, I have done so willingly, even to my own burden and danger,' proclaims the anonymous author of *Il discorso intorno alla nostra lingua*, an early sixteenth-century treatise attributed to Machiavelli ('sempre che io ho potuto onorare la patria mia eziandio con mio carico et pericolo, l'ho fatto volentieri').[37] As the book evolves, that native sentiment is expressed and proven by reclaiming the poetic language of Petrarch, Boccaccio, and Dante from Italy and even Tuscany for Florence itself. The main focus is on Dante, owing to his assertion in *De volgari eloquentia*, cited by Machiavelli, 'that he had not written in Florentine, but curial language' ('non avere scritto in fiorentino ma in una lingua curiale', 186–7). 'I want to show [. . .] how his speech is Florentine through and through,' Machiavelli declares in response ('io voglio [. . .] mostrare come il suo parlare è al tutto fiorentino', 188). According to Machiavelli, Dante 'composed [*De volgari eloquentia*] to show that he had not written in Florentine to avoid honouring [Florence] in any way', depriving the city of 'the reputation with which he believed his writings had endowed her' ('per non l'onorare in alcun modo compose quell' opera, per mostrar quella lingua nella quale egli aveva scritto non esser fiorentina', 'quella riputazione la quale pareva a lui d'averle data ne' suoi scritti', 187). Dante's denial of his dialect is thus seen as revenge on the city that exiled him. For Machiavelli, Dante's treachery to his homeland is equalled and manifested by his treachery to its language, for 'it is not so strange that a man who defamed his homeland in everything, should then attack its language' ('non è pertanto maraviglia se costui che in ogni cosa accrebbe infamia all sua patria, volse ancora nella lingua', 187). Conversely, by proving Dante's poetry Florentine, Machiavelli hopes to restore his city's honour. Language, identity, and civic / national pride are intertwined, and—contrary to Leland's belief that it was a writer's works that enriched the nation—it is not Dante's poetry that is seen to benefit Florence, but

[37] Niccolò Machiavelli, *Il discorso intorno alla nostra lingua*, ed. Franco Gaeta, *Opere di Niccolò Machiavelli*, 8 vols. (Milan: Feltrinelli, 1960–5), viii, 183. For a summary of arguments against Machiavelli's authorship, and their refutation, see Pierone Luigi, 'La Paternità Machiavelliana del *Dialogo Intorno all Lingua*', *Studium*, 72 (1976), 715–20.

its demonstration of the linguistic capabilities of Florentine. Indeed, Dante's belief that his writings per se had dignified the city is undermined, and even mocked, by Machiavelli's choice of phrasing 'la quale pareva a lui' ('which seemed to him', 187).

Community is thus expressed by the boundaries of language, the depository of what Machiavelli calls 'a shared understanding' ('una comune intelligenza', 185), which defines and unites it. In Thomas's *Principal Rules*, this distinction between verbal communities is lent visual form: English authors and words are set in black letter, against italic and roman typefaces for Italian and Latin, and 'our father Chaucer'—placed without comment or apology as the equal of Boethius and Cicero—is marked as English as much by the visual appearance of his name on the page as by the possessive pronoun and familial epithet. It is Chaucer's perceived services to his native tongue, moreover, that lend him a patriarchal status akin to that granted Cicero, 'father of theyr countrey and of eloquence', in Thomas's *Vanitee of this World*.[38]

Language is seen by Thomas as the means to knowledge. Inspired by Italian, Thomas consequently recommends 'the studie of latine', not as an end in itself, but 'to drawe the worthie thinges of the same into their owne tongues'.[39] For the Welsh-speaking William Salesbury, unburdened by English anxieties over linguistic inferiority, England already has a wealth of translated material, and 'attaynement of knowledge in Gods word, and other liberall sciences' is one way in which, in 1550, he tried to persuade his Welsh compatriots to learn English.[40] The Denbighshire-born Thomas, however, possesses none of his fellow Welshman's confidence, and attempts to redress what he incredulously terms 'this wonderfull lacke' of English learning by translating Scarobosco's *De Sphera* 'to provoke them of our nation that know more than I, to put their pennes to the amendement' (4r).

Belief in the 'educational value of English' was hardly a novelty in 1552 when Thomas was writing his *Boke of the Sphere*.[41] 'We may / if we liste / bringe the lernynges and wisedomes of [Greeks and Romans] in to this realme of Englande / by the translation of

[38] William Thomas, *The Vanitee of this Worlde* (1549), B5r.
[39] Thomas, *Boke of the Sphere*, BL Egerton 837, 3r.
[40] William Salesbury, *A briefe and playne introduction, teaching how to pronounce the letters in the British tong* (1550), E1v.
[41] Cited by Jones, *Triumph of English*, 41.

their warkes,' wrote Elyot in 1531, a rallying cry (like Salesbury's) concentrating on the informative capacity of language.[42] Thomas, however, sees beyond this purely pragmatic purpose. As seen above, Italian is inspirational not just for the 'science' and 'historie' it contains, but for the 'eloquence' and 'fine poesie' it displays. Vernacular languages, that is, are not only functional; they are also literary. The language Thomas promotes is not the spoken but the written word and (above that) the poetic or elevated style. No mention of Italian phonetics appears before the nineteenth page of the *Principal rules* ($C2^r$), whilst the accompanying dictionary is an amalgam of extracts from Acharisio's and Alunno's compendia of those words 'used by our approved authors, namely Boccaccio, Dante and Petrarch' ('usate da nostri approbati autori, ciò Boccaccio, Dante et Petrarca').[43] For Thomas, then, the need for works in English is not, as in Borde's view, required by the existence of a market of readers uneducated in the classical, Hebraic, and Arabic tongues to which so much knowledge had hitherto been confined.[44] Unlike Borde, Thomas does not apologize for the necessity of using English to talk down to the masses. English is not the language of the uneducated, but a language in which to be educated. It is like well water, a pure and potable substance. Behind the homespun practicality of this metaphor (criticizing 'they who at these daies write in the latine tongue, travaile to carie water from their owne welles vnto the Sea'), lies the image of the Heliconian spring, from which poetic eloquence flows.[45]

The national value of language is underlined by the economic vocabulary with which Thomas describes it. When he presents his *Principal rules* for the 'commoditee' of 'all suche of our nacion, as are studiouse in that tong [Italian]' ($\pi 1^v$), he uses the word in the sense not only of 'conveniency' (*OED* 1a), but also 'material advantage' (*OED* 5a). Romance languages offer ready metaphors of economic and linguistic wealth: it is the 'riches' ('richezze') of the vulgar tongue, for example, that Alunno confidently celebrates in the title of his dictionary, whilst we have already seen in chapter 1 the use of *thesauri* as literal treasure houses of language.

[42] Elyot, *Gouernor*, 94^v.
[43] Francesco Alunno, *Le Richezze della lingua volgare* (Venice, 1543), A2^v.
[44] Borde, *Breuiary*, B1^v.
[45] Thomas, *Boke of the Sphere*, BL Egerton 837, 3^r.

Thomas's images of linguistic enrichment befit a nation already endowed with natural resources. Language is no less an asset than wool or beef, and is, like 'wheat', reaped only when 'corne' is sown, as Thomas explains in the preface to his *Boke of the Sphere* (3ʳ). The value of language is enforced by a second metaphorical strain—military terminology—running through that preface. On the battlefield, England's reputation is apparently assured; in the field of letters which Thomas places in parallel, intellectual renown is sadly deficient, 'for notwithstanding that in dedes of Armes our predecessours haue prevailed against infinite estraungiers, triumphing nowe in Fraunce, nowe in Spaigne, nowe in Flaunders, in Scotlande, Irelande and elsewhere', the 'lacke' of reputation in learning 'hath been the ennemye of al our glorie' (2ᵛ). The world of letters adopts the language of battle, and the dreamt-of end is 'triumphe in Civile knoledge' (3ᵛ), a state achieved by 'many estraunge Nations, through benefite of their owne tongues' (2ᵛ). Thomas, in other words, tries to invest language with the same urgency as warfare, a strategy used by Philip Sidney to promote poetry three decades later.[46]

Although Thomas's commitment to the vernacular is not marked by John Cheke's prioritization of Anglo-Saxon monosyllables, (a 'plain English campaign' running concurrently with Thomas's writing career), he shares Cheke's concern for the comprehensibility of English.[47] Like Cheke, Thomas distinguishes in the *Boke of the Sphere* between 'ynkehorne termes' and the advantage of limited borrowings, not for the sake of embellishment (as in the works of Borde or Elyot), but for the clarity of expression they can provide. Faced with the task of translating a scientific text, 'the vtteraunce wherof requireth many termes that in the doinges of our Englishe aucthors ar not to be founde', Thomas is 'constrained to phraame' new terms 'as the case hath needed' (4ᵛ). The 'Alphabete', or glossary, he supplies for his readers' 'onlie commodite' does more than guide them through these coinings. Like the word list appended to his *Principal rules*, it acts as both a dictionary in miniature, explaining words grammatically and semantically, and a thesaurus, giving alternative synonyms. 'Artificiall', for example, 'is an adiectiue when any thing is

---

[46] Sidney, *Apology*, 127.
[47] John Cheke, letter to Thomas Hoby, in Hoby, *Courtier*, 10.

wrought more than naturallie'; 'accesse, is the going vnto or cummeng vnto' (5ʳ). Displaying the verbal copiousness English already possesses and adding further to it, the 'alphabete' shares on a small scale the spirit of grander lexicographical projects in the later sixteenth and early seventeenth centuries necessary 'to render knowledge of the mother tongue independent of other languages'.[48] Nor should the need for neologisms be shameful, as it was—rhetorically at least—for Wyatt and Skelton. According to Thomas, the precedent is honourable, 'folowyng thexample of the latynes who in such case haue borowed of the Greekes in like maner as the Italians do now borowe of the latines'.[49] The process, moreover, is not one of linguistic dilution (or Cheke's 'bank-rupcy').[50] When Thomas seeks to 'draw' matter 'into [his] owne tongue', the preposition 'into' encompasses a sense of metamorphosis, as words and knowledge are transformed into something English, or given (as Thomas puts it in the *Boke of the Sphere*) 'a new voice' (4ᵛ). As Machiavelli writes in his *Discorso alla nostra lingua*, 'a national language is one that converts the vocabulary acquired from others into its own use, and is so powerful that those words acquired do not disrupt it, but that it disrupts them' ('quella lingua si chiama d' una patria, la quale convertisce i vocaboli ch'ella accattati da altri nell'uso suo, ed è sí potente che i vocaboli accattati non la disordinano ma ella disordina loro', 193). The borrower-language thus imposes its own character upon words that are not loaned, but naturalized, like the body abroad adapting to foreign climes.[51]

Thomas's works are steeped in Machiavellian ideas, terminology, and analytical techniques. Just as foreign terms should be imprinted with the mark of their host country, however, so too he stamps his adaptations of Italian culture with an English identity. A conduit for Machiavellian thought into English, Thomas transforms the works of an Italian republican to suit and serve the English monarchy in a period of minority, and to advance his own

[48] Jones, *Triumph of English*, 273.
[49] Thomas, *Boke of the Sphere*, BL Egerton 837, 4ᵛ.
[50] Cheke letter, in Hoby, *Courtier*, 10.
[51] See Thomas, *Peregrine*, BL Vespasian D. xviii, where he describes how he, 'that before time could in maner brooke no fruite', 'after [he] had been a while in Italie [. . .] fell so in loue withall, that as longe as [he] was there, [he] desyred no meate more' (2ᵛ).

career. The next section addresses the Anglicization of Machiavelli, arguably the single most important influence on Thomas as a writer and thinker, in both his use of Machiavelli as a source, and his adoption of Machiavellian dictums, such as the necessity of reacting to present circumstances, governing his own behaviour. When J. G. A. Pocock conducted his magisterial survey of Machiavelli's influence on civic humanism in seventeenth-century England and eighteenth-century North America, his interest in reactions to Machiavelli's republicanism, the Civil War, and the American Revolution means that the discussion is dominated by adaptations of the *Discorsi*, Machiavelli's commentaries on Livy.[52] It is not the republican idealist of the *Discorsi* that attracted Thomas, however, but the detached political analyst of *Il Principe*, with his 'preference for success over deservingness' and the divorce of virtue from *virtù* (political wherewithal).[53] Thomas's texts, like *Il Principe*, are 'not work[s] of ideology': they are pragmatic responses to a pressing political situation.[54]

TRANSLATING MACHIAVELLI

The debt to Machiavelli is made explicit in Thomas's *Historie*. In contrast to the sections on the histories of other city-states, that on Florence not only names its source—as 'Nicolas *Macchiauegli*, a notable learned man, and secretarie of late daies to the common wealthe'—but also singles him out as 'myne onely auctour in that behalfe' (140[r]). The account that follows adheres closely to Machiavelli's *Istorie Fiorentine*, retaining the Italian's structure and idiom, yet resisting total complicity with it. Machiavelli's reference to the Goths as 'barbarouse', for example, is qualified by Thomas's parenthetical '(as the Italians calle theim)', which defines, and thus limits, the judgmental perspective as Italian. By abbreviating and occasionally adding to the Florentine's work, Thomas consequently tailors the history of a republic by a republican for his own political milieu. Sections describing the evolution, alterations, and restitutions of Florence's republican constitution are skipped over; office holders are described as 'rulers', a term encompassing monarchs as much as republican governors. For Machiavelli, Jacamo Gabriele, in taking over the republic, is a 'tyrant': Thomas affixes no such label to him.[55] Similarly, within the *Historie*, Duke Charles, who occupied Florence in 1326, is only a 'tyranne (as they call him)' (145ᵛ). The parenthesis proves a sceptical aside. A tyrant, as Thomas defines it in the *Vanitee*, is '*he that, maketh his wil a law, and for hym selfe woorketh al*' (B8ʳ). Alexander the Great is remembered in the *Vanitee* as a tyrant, not for his ambition to conquer the world, but for his inability to realize his subsequent duty to 'rule it and gouerne it well' (B7ᵛ). Tyranny, that is, is not the sole holding of power, but the abuse of that power, shown in the *Historie* by crimes 'encreasyng daiely' (147ᵛ).

Machiavelli uses history as a tool for political analysis, and his *Discorsi* dissect Livy's portrayal of republican Rome to discover the constitution of a 'perfect commonwealth' whose example Florence can then follow.[56] In contrast, Thomas's *Historie* examines 'the astate of many and diuers common weales' (A1ʳ), not to delineate an ideal, but to reveal a myriad of antitypes in need of strong and singular rule. Thomas's adaptation of Italian history is thus moulded by the audience for whom he writes. His English readers receive an account suited to the monarchical institutions to which they are habituated; prior to that wider audience is John Dudley, Earl of Warwick, to whom he dedicated the book. The work is addressed not to a monarch, but to a nobleman on the make. Writing for an ambitious aristocrat, he excises Machiavelli's philosophical meditations on the corrupting lust for power. Where Machiavelli ponders the fact that 'the more power men have, the worse they use it and become more insolent' ('quasi sempre gli uomini, che quanto piú autorità hanno, peggio la usano e piú insolenti diventano', 188), Thomas omits such speculations and even encourages self-promotion, promising in the dedicatory epistle that readers 'first shall see, vpon what little beginnyng many great astates haue risen' (A3ʳ), a dictum as applicable to individuals as to commonweals.

Thomas's dedication of the *Historie* to Dudley, dated 20

55 Niccolò Machiavelli, *Istorie Fiorentine*, ed. Franco Gaeta, *Opere*, vii. 1.
56 Id., *I Discorsi*, ed. Sergio Bertelli, *Opere*, i, book I, ch. 2.

September 1549, was 'singularly well timed.'[57] By mid September, the imperial ambassador François van der Delft was reporting divisions within the Privy Council and, with the position of the Protector, Edward Seymour, Duke of Somerset, looking increasingly unstable in the wake of the summer's civil upheaval, the patronage of Dudley, one of the most influential members of the Privy Council, would have looked ever more desirable, especially after his triumphant return to London on 14 September, having crushed Kett's Norfolk rebellion. Within a fortnight of Thomas's dedicatory epistle, Dudley, Henry Fitzalan, Earl of Arundel, and Thomas Wriothesley, Earl of Southampton, executed a putsch of the Privy Council, ousting Seymour and his supporters.[58]

The material of the *Historie* was as well chosen as its dedicatee. Despite Dudley's alleged 'lack of intellectual sophistication', the Earl of Warwick seems to have appreciated Italian culture, funding, for example, the Italian travels of the painter-architect John Shute.[59] Further to that, the *Historie* had political appeal. As Andrew Hadfield argues, Thomas's text lays out a range of constitutional alternatives, from the near-exemplary (Venice) to the downright disastrous (Naples).[60] The Venetian form of conciliar government is treated at far greater length than the political structures of other cities, such as Naples, Florence, and Genoa; Venice's conciliar constitution is, moreover, credited by Thomas with ensuring the city's enviable domestic stability and military and economic pre-eminence. His endorsement of the benefits of conciliar government accords with the form of English governance then being promoted by Dudley and his supporters, whose patronage Thomas sought. The main justification for their coup, as found in an anonymous letter in the state papers defending their actions to readers abroad, was that Seymour was guilty of misrule because he had 'disregard[ed] the matured and strenuous charge of the noble &

---

[57] David Loades, *John Dudley, Duke of Northumberland, 1504–1553* (Oxford: Clarendon Press, 1996), 200.

[58] Dale E. Hoak, 'The King's Privy Chamber, 1547–1553', in Delloyd J. Guth and John W. McKenna (eds.), *Tudor Rule and Revolution* (Cambridge: Cambridge University Press, 1982), 87–108, at 97.

[59] Loades, *Dudley*, 200; Bartlett, *English in Italy*, 54.

[60] Andrew Hadfield, *Literature, Travel, and Colonial Writing in the English Renaissance, 1545–1625* (Oxford: Clarendon Press, 1998), 26.

honourable council'.[61] In deposing Seymour, they alleged they were restoring the proper influence of the council, for the common good.

Thomas's authorial timeliness was well rewarded. On 19 April 1550, by which date Dudley was Lord President of the Privy Council, Thomas—former exile and embezzler—was elevated to one of the clerkships, an event noted in Edward VI's journal.[62] As David Loades observes, Thomas 'was something more than a sixteenth-century stenographer' and 'in short, was a minor but not insignificant figure in the court and administration'.[63] His appointment as clerk also marked 'a very definite change [. . .] in the routine of the Privy Council office'.[64] Whereas previously, 'each clerk had been severally responsible for any or all of their duties', Thomas 'was assigned the sole care of the Privy Council Register [. . .] and relieved of "all other maner of businesse" ', with the result that 'the register from April 1550 to September 24, 1551, is written almost entirely in his hand'. All council warrants also remained invalid 'unlesse [. . .] also subscribed with the hand of the said William Thomas'.[65] Further favours followed in the forms of grants, manors in Herefordshire and Sussex, and a prebend in Kentish Town. In February 1551, Thomas's social position was consolidated by receipt of a coat of arms, and in May that year he was given a significant role supporting Dudley's embassy to France.

Thomas's publications after the *Historie* are further evidence of his astute and sustained courting of the Edwardian political elite. The *Vanitee* is dedicated in 1549 to Anne, wife of William Herbert, whose defection from Seymour to Dudley had made him a key player in the autumn coup.[66] The *Principal rules* was written for John Tamworth, relative of Archbishop Cranmer and prospective brother-in-law of both Francis Walsingham and the financial expert Walter Mildmay. The unpublished translation of Sacrobosco's *De Sphera* was dedicated to Henry Grey. All were important, or rising, figures in the Edwardian government. After

---

[61] Hastings Robinson (ed.), *Original Letters Relative to the English Reformation*, 2 vols. (Cambridge: Cambridge University Press, 1846–7), i. 728.

[62] Jordan (ed.), *Chronicle*, 25.   [63] Loades, *Dudley*, 200.

[64] Adair, 'Thomas', 140.

[65] 'The Council Book', in John Gough Nichols (ed.), *The Literary Remains of Edward VI*, 2 vols. (London: Roxburgh Club, 1857), ii. 258 n.

[66] Loades, *Dudley*, 136–7.

Dudley's coup, Walsingham became his private and public secretary; Herbert was made Earl of Pembroke; Mildmay was appointed examiner of the Mint accounts; Grey was admitted to the Privy Council and, in 1551, became Duke of Suffolk.[67]

The political resonance of Thomas's choice of dedicatees is compounded by the content of his books. Throughout his works, he engages with issues of governance. The *Vanitee* is far from the conventional *de contemptu mundi* text its title promises. The first two-thirds of the book are rooted in worldly politics. The effect of deadly sins such as greed and lust on spiritual health is of less concern than their impact on social and political reputation. Lechery is a cause of civil unrest, for 'there is no iniurie so bitter, nor none that so promptly moueth the people vnto armes', Thomas notes, citing the rape of Lucrece, which caused the overthrow of the kings of Rome ($A6^r$). Gluttony is condemned for its consumption of 'substaunce and patrimonies'; its tendency, when under its influence, 'to make vs disclose our secretes'; and the likelihood that it 'bringeth vs in sklaunder' ($A4^v$). The arguments are those of Thomas's political disquisitions in BL Vespasian D. xviii; as in his discourse on 'wheather it be expedient to varie with tyme', indifference to transient pleasures becomes, in part, a tool for secular leadership and civil defence, 'wherefore', as he writes in the *Vanitee*, 'not without cause did the citee of Sparta longe tyme withhold the eies of hir citisins farre from the delices of Asia' ($A3^r$).

The genre of 'debates on women' is similarly politicized in Thomas's *Argument*, and history is again mined for contemporary relevance. Discussing 'excesse in apparayle' is here aligned with debating 'the baseness of our coyne', which 'are the common talkes of these daies', the latter forming the topic of his first and 'most important' discourse in Vespasian D. xviii, entitled 'Touchyng the reformation of the coinage'.[68] In the *Argument*, Roman censures against lavish clothing arise from a need to redirect money and materials into defending their republic then—like the English polity in the early 1550s—financially and strategically embattled. The *Boke of the Sphere* proves no less topical. As Grafton and Jardine have shown, among the works that Harvey acquired or annotated

[67] *DNB*.
[68] William Thomas, *An Argument wherin the apparaile of women is both reproued and defended* (1551), A2^r; Jordan, *Threshold of Power*, 417.

during a politically motivated reading project in 1580 are Thomas's *Historie* and Sacrobosco's *De Sphera*, the latter a text which (along with Machiavelli's works) Philip Sidney deemed necessary for 'the trade of our lives'.[69] Wilson, meanwhile, includes cosmography in a list of the disciplines befitting a praiseworthy (that is, publicly active) man, alongside languages, law, and history.[70] Thomas's printed texts, published by Thomas Berthelet, the king's printer, consequently provide their dedicatees with politically advantageous knowledge and advice; in addition, they promote the type of decisive rule which, after the civil unrest of 1549, matched the intentions of members of the revised Privy Council for whom he wrote.

Thomas had the ability, as 'saieth *Macchiauegli* [. . .] to phrame his proceadinges unto his tyme'.[71] Edward's minority was particularly suited to Thomas's adaptations of Machiavellian thought, views which were as yet 'unhampered by the weight of secondary interpretation and standard attitudes' casting the Florentine, as in the prologue to Christopher Marlowe's *Jew of Malta* (1590), as a diabolic, anti-societal figure. Edward inhabited an atmosphere of intense and continual instruction, in which everything from religion to the selection of his childhood companions was a means of tutelage; court preachers such as Hugh Latimer or John Hooper employed their Lent sermons to instruct the boy in the rights and duties of kingship, and the company of youthful peers was provided that Edward 'should gain experience in humanity'.[72] In the early 1550s, possibly encouraged by Dudley, Thomas offered to fill a gap in the king's education, a scheme that appears 'consistent with a strategy on Dudley's part to get Edward thinking about real issues, and persuading himself that he was making a full contribution to decisions'.[73] This increased interaction on Edward's part—or at least the illusion of increased interaction—is endorsed by an entry in the king's journal on 14 August 1551 that it was 'appointed that I should come, and sit at, Council, when great

[69] Grafton and Jardine, ' "Studied for action" ', 39.
[70] Wilson, *Rhetorique* (1553), 7^v.
[71] Thomas, Political discourses, BL Vespasian D. xviii, 4^r.
[72] See Hugh Latimer, *Sermons*, ed. George Elwes Corrie, 2 vols. (Cambridge: Parker Society, 1844), i. 81–281; W.K. Jordan, *Edward VI*, i: *The Young King. The Protectorship of the Duke of Somerset* (London: George Allen & Unwin, 1968), 44.
[73] Loades, *Dudley*, 201.

matters were in debating, or when I would', and by October
Edward was attending what Dale Hoak calls 'staged' council meet-
ings, designed to 'persuade the boy of the wisdom of decisions
already taken'.[74] According to Loades, 'Thomas' apparently spon-
taneous suggestion in September [1551] that he should send
Edward weekly essays on political topics was clearly part of this
new educational strategy.'[75]

Edward's schooling, that is, was about to grow more practical.
'Imagineng [. . .] that hitherto [his] Maiestie hath more applied to
the studie of tongues than any matter of historie or of policie,'
Thomas proposes writing a series of political 'discourses [. . .] gathered out of divers aucthors'.[76] The choice of the term 'discourse'
reveals the Italian inspiration for the subsequent essays, a 'discoursing head' being one of the attributes of the Italianate Englishman
marked out by Ascham's *Schoolmaster*.[77] Although Raab argues
that ' "those discourses" turn out to be *I Discorsi*, and their "divers
authors", Machiavelli', it is more accurate to say that they owe
most to *Il Principe*, as Raab reveals when he states, on the tract
'Wheather it be expedient to vary with time', that 'altogether this
essay is an expansion [. . .] of the opinion stated by Machiavelli in
chapter twenty-five of *The Prince*'.[78] The choice of *Il Principe* as a
model over the idealistically republican *Discorsi* or nostalgically
republican *Istorie* influences the tenor of Thomas's subsequent
advice. The irreligiosity of *Il Principe* repelled Thomas's contemporaries Ascham and Reginald Pole. It provides Thomas, however,
with a pragmatic mode of discourse through which to address the
exigencies of minority rule. Like Gardiner in his Machiavellian
treatise written in 1555 to advise Philip of Spain how best to
govern England, Thomas is also careful to modulate Machiavelli's
tone. Where 'Machiavelli has a tendency to stress the novelty of his
views, and to underscore their divergence from common opinion',
Thomas and Gardiner attempt 'to present Machiavelli's views in a

---

[74] Jordan (ed.), *Chronicle*, 76; Dale Hoak, *The King's Council in the Reign of
Edward VI* (Cambridge: Cambridge University Press, 1976), 121; id.,
'Rehabilitating the Duke of Northumberland: Politics and Political Control', in
Jennifer Loach and Robert Tittler (eds.), *The Mid-Tudor Polity, c.1540–60*
(London: Macmillan, 1980), 29–51, at 43.   [75] Loades, *Dudley*, 201.
[76] BL Titus B. ii, 84[r].
[77] Roger Ascham, *The Schoolmaster*, in *The Whole Works of Roger Ascham* ed.
J. G. A. Giles, 3 vols. (London: John Russell Smith, 1864–5), i. 157.
[78] Raab, *English Face*, 42–3.

way that makes them seem as consonant with traditional or ortho-dox opinion'.[79]

Within his *Deffence*, du Bellay defines the true translator through the description of its antithesis: those writers who fail to 'penetrate to the most hidden and inner parts of the Author in question' and 'only adjust themselves to the initial appearance, and amuse themselves with the beauty of the words, losing the force of things' ('qui sans penetrer aux plus cachées, & interieures parties de l' Aucteur [. . .] s'adaptent seulement au premier Regard, & s'amusant à la beauté des Motz, perdent la force des choses', B5ʳᵛ). As Thomas adopts Machiavelli's methods and outlook, applying them to the particular circumstances of Edwardian England, he thus represents du Bellay's 'true' translation. Machiavelli's work is not regurgitated in chunks, translated verbatim; Thomas absorbs Machiavelli's habits of wary circumspection and self-conscious adaptability so thoroughly that he can embellish on those questions the Florentine gestures towards, but never pursues. Amongst Thomas's discourses, for instance, is the dilemma 'Which Princes Amitie is Best?'. The question is Machiavelli's, mooted in chapter 21 of *Il Principe*: its deployment is Thomas's own. Both authors consider what Thomas terms 'the auncientie of frendeship' and 'the nature of the Prince, whose amitie is sought' (14ᵛ). To these, Thomas adds two more points 'worthie of consideracon': namely, the 'propinquitie' and 'Religion' of the intended ally. Proximity and faith are not of immediate concern to an Italian city-state at close quarters with, and sharing the Catholicism of, its potential allies: to a Protestant nation at the edge of Europe, in striking distance of Catholic Spain and France, they most definitely are.

The age of minority also lends further edge to Thomas's modifi-cations of Machiavellian theory to English statecraft. Thomas might advise his sovereign of the need (in Machiavellian terms) 'to plaie the Foxe' (5ᵛ), but he cannot provide the other half of the Italian's infamous pairing: the complementary ability to play the lion.[80] We saw earlier how Thomas used his translation of Barbaro's *Voiages* to refute the complaints of those 'Englishemen' 'who puffed vp with wealthe, wote not why they whyne' (1ʳ) by

[79] Samuel P. Donaldson (ed.), introduction, Gardiner, *Discourse*, 17.
[80] Niccolò Machiavelli, *The Prince*, ed. and trans. Quentin Skinner and Russell Price (Cambridge: Cambridge University Press, 1988), 61. All translations from *The Prince* are from this edn.

reminding England of its privileged geographical and agricultural status. 'The Sea environeth the cuntrey, to serue vs both for carieng out of our owne habundance, and also for fetching of straunge commodities hither,' Thomas relates, whilst England's economic strength is such that trade is not pursued from necessity but 'in such sorte as [. . .] we wante nothing to serue vs for pleaser' (1ᵛ). Thomas, however, is here required to maintain an image at odds with reality. By 1551, the cloth trade, which enjoyed a boom the previous decade, slumped suddenly, as the number of cloths passed from London to Antwerp fell by over third.[81] This dip in export trade coincided with domestic crisis—rent rises, declining manufacture, inflation—leaving the national mood as one of almost 'universal discontent'.[82]

That such dissonance is not banished entirely from the introductory pages of the *Voiages* is both a reflection of the perceived change in economic climate since the *Peregrine* and a response to gradations of audience and medium. An openly published work such as Thomas's *Historie*, printed in part for the benefit of national esteem, holds no place for malcontents. The semi-public manuscript of Barbaro's *Voiages* admits them to its fringes, even as it proceeds to discredit them as whining plutocrats. Within the enforced privacy of Thomas's personal communications with his monarch, there is no call to silence or marginalize such voices and, freed from the need to propagate idyllic fictions of peace and prosperity, Thomas relegates such happy visions to an equally fictionalized past. 'Tyme was in the daies of your father of famouse memorie that this astate being dradde of all our neighbours needed not to esteeme any of them more than itself was esteemed,' he relates in his 'private opinion toochyng your Maiesties outwarde affaires'.[83] Informing Edward of his own contrary standing, his words are bleakly unequivocal. 'We arr both hated and contempned by [the princes of Europe]', Thomas informs his sovereign (34ᵛ). His idiom exposes England's decline into the state against which Machiavelli consistently warns: 'that a ruler [. . .] should avoid anything that will make him either hated or despised' ('che il

[81] Loades, *England's Maritime Empire*, 53–4.
[82] J. D. Mackie, *The Earlier Tudors, 1495–1558* (Oxford: Oxford University Press, 1994), 503.
[83] Thomas, Political discourses, BL Vespasian D. xviii, 34ᵛ.

principe pensi [. . .] di fuggire quelle cose che lo faccino odioso o contennendo').[84] Further to that, it shows a change in focus from Machiavelli's concern for the status of a ruler within a community to a concern for the status of the community itself: the fate of ruler, nation, and subject is as one. The sea no longer protectively encircles the land; rather, 'we arr [. . .] in maner environned of enemyes'. The participle 'environned' which had hitherto described England's protective insularity is reapplied to convey the very opposite: the threat posed to England from across the sea. In the treatise that follows, Thomas calls upon Edward to make a Machiavellian virtue of necessity. His 'tender yeres', a point of weakness, are to be transformed to his advantage in diplomatic overtures to the Emperor, used to portray the French king as an opportunist willing to prey on vulnerable young innocents, a version of events that is to be knowingly offered to the Emperor as a moralistic gloss for his acquisitive foreign policy.

Thomas's discourses for Edward VI are clothed in the language of secrecy. His advice on the coinage, for example, is 'sealed' and disguised, 'deliuer[ed] vnto your Maiestie as it were a thinge from the Counsaill' (28^v). 'No creature lyving is or shalbe privie either to this or to any of the rest through me,' he assures Edward: 'whiche I do keepe so secret to this ende, that your Maiestie may vtter these matters as of your owne studie: whereby it shall haue the greater creadite with your Counsaille' (29^r). If Thomas's original approach was sanctioned by Dudley, as Loades suggests, then his 'mildly conspiratorial manner' has added benefit in appealing to 'a young Tudor [who] would not respond to pressure, and would resent being lectured, but [. . .] could be led'.[85] Further to that, the emphasis on confidentiality helps place Thomas's (perhaps designedly) unconventional advice-giving within a safer, more mainstream tradition of counsel, as described in John Ponet's translation of Bernadino Ochino's *Tragoedie or Dialogue of the vniuste vsurped primacie of the Bishop of Rome*, dedicated to Edward and kept in his library.[86] According to Ochino, advice should be requested by the monarch and should remain 'secrete', which both avoids undermining regal dignity and ensures free speech on the

[84] Machiavelli, *Il Principe*, ed. Sergio Bertelli, *Opere*. i. 75; Machiavelli, *Prince*, 63.   [85] Loades, *Dudley*, 201.
[86] Nichols (ed.), *Literary Remains*, i, p. cccxxvii.

part of the counsellor.[87] Besides subscribing to the usual rhetoric of
counsel being motivated by concern for the common good, Thomas
is thus at pains to emphasize both Edward's participation in the
production of these discourses and the private nature of his advice,
which (as Ochino argues) enables honesty, unfettered by fear of
censure. 'Syns it is your highnes pleaser to haue it secret (which I
do much commende) I therfore am the bolder to enterprise the
declaracon of my fantasie,' Thomas writes.[88]

Thomas's seemingly unofficial interaction with Edward also
demonstrates the continued importance of the Privy Chamber in a
court where privacy was a mark of privilege and physical space
graded in terms of its proximity to the monarch.[89] Indeed, as John
Guy argues, Dudley's coup in 1549 'illustrated precisely how
personal Tudor monarchy remained at the death of Henry VIII [. .
.]. Politics became a struggle waged at Court for possession of the
king's body, "with both sides scrambling to position themselves
and their clients in the royal apartments, next to the king's
bedchamber, as close as possible to the king himself".'[90] Even if
Thomas never enjoyed direct contact with the king, he was nevertheless in communication with those most immediate to him, since
it is gentlemen of the privy chamber, William Fitzwilliam and
Nicholas Throckmorton, a man 'much favoured' by Edward, who
act as go-betweens.[91] The desire to exploit that efficacious sense of
intimacy with the rich and powerful provides a key to the physical
presentation of Thomas's works and the use he makes of them to
foster and display the relationships through which he procured his
social and political advancement. His texts demonstrate his proximity and usefulness to the circles of power, as when the prefatory
letter to his *Historie* homes in on the moment at which Dudley
receives this 'little trauaile', 'at my poore handes' (A3[r]). This last
section examines more closely the authorial and bibliographical
strategies Thomas used to highlight, and benefit from, his role as

---

[87] Bernadino Ochino, *A tragoedie or Dialoge of the vniuste vsurped primacie of
the Bishop of Rome*, trans. John Ponet (1549), Y2[r].

[88] BL Vespasian D. xviii, 28[v].

[89] John Murphy, 'The Illusion of Decline: The Privy Chamber, 1547–1558', in
David Starkey et al (eds.), *The English Court: From the War of the Roses to the
Civil War* (London: Longman, 1987), 119–46; Cf. Hoak, 'King's Privy Chamber'.

[90] John Guy (ed.), *The Tudor Monarchy* (London: Arnold, 1997), 90–1, citing
Hoak, 'King's Privy Chamber'.   [91] *DNB*.

author, and in the process, the continued inspiration he drew from his amalgamation of humanism and contemporary Italian culture.

Thomas's humanist forebears offer rich precedent for authorial self-fashioning or what Joseph Loewenstein terms 'self-composition'.[93] Erasmus' image, as Jardine has shown, was constructed through the scholar's skilful deployment and distribution of self-advertising works.[94] Similarly, the *Epigrammata*, which 'by its design and manufacture helped make More's name', demonstrates the potential impact of bibliographical techniques and presentation, to which Thomas was particularly attuned.[95] When Thomas manipulates his own literary resources in the interests of self-promotion, therefore, he does so within an identifiable humanist tradition, using in particular personalized manuscript copies of his works as a means of nurturing client–patron relationships. As Harold Love has pointed out, scribal publication continued alongside the printing press well into the seventeenth century, with the older form often possessing an aura of added value thanks to 'the exclusivity of the scribal medium', 'in which the values of orality—and the fact of presence—are still strongly felt'.[96] Love is here indebted to Walter Ong's argument that handwriting is more intimate than print, the former being only one remove from the immediacy of speech.[97] Whilst this model somewhat dubiously establishes 'presence' as integral to the handwritten form, denying the potential functionality and anonymity of manuscripts, it is nevertheless true that early modern writers developed and manipulated a rhetoric of 'presence'.

Certainly Erasmus celebrates the potential kudos of handwritten artefacts, engraved as they are with their authors' laborious devotion.

---

[92] Thomas, *Voiages*, BL Royal 17 C. x, 1ᵛ.

[93] Loewenstein, *Jonson*, 146.   [94] Jardine, *Erasmus*.

[95] David R. Carlson, *English Humanist Books: Writers and Patrons, Manuscripts and Print, 1475–1525* (Toronto: University of Toronto Press, 1993), 143.

[96] Harold Love, *The Culture and Commerce of Texts: Scribal Publication in Seventeenth-Century England* (Amherst: University of Massachusetts Press, 1998), 61, 142.

[97] Walter Ong, *The Presence of the Word: Some Prolegomena for Cultural and Religious History* (New Haven: Yale University Press, 1967), 114–15.

'Although I was not just busy, but swamped with work, I sent you a letter in my own hand, reckoning that this would give it added value in your eyes,' writes Erasmus to Maximilian of Burgundy ('nam licet obrutus verius quàm occupatus negociis, tamen epistolam 'αυτόγραφομ ad te miseram, quòd facile coniectarem, eam ita tibi fore chariorem').[98] When the letter fails to arrive, Maximilian is said—to Erasmus' 'great pleasure' ('voluptatem')—to be 'more upset than [. . .] if [he] had lost one of [his] most cherished posessions' ('aegrius tuleris, quàm si quid earum rerum perisset, quae tibi maxime sunt in deliciis'). Between them, the handwritten letter represents a mutually reinforcing bond of gratification. Its value is such that it is replaced, not by another letter, but by an entire book (*De recta latini graecique sermonis pronuntiatione*), and its non-delivery described as 'treachery' ('perfidia', A2ᵛ).

When Thomas presented the manuscript of Barbaro's *Voiages*, written in his own hand, to Edward VI in the early 1550s, his dedicatory epistle capitalizes on this function of the handwritten work as a symbol of zeal and affection. 'Most humbly' he asks the young king 'to accept this poore newe yeres gifte being the worke of [his] owne handes' (2ᵛ). He makes his work more than a token of expected loyalty ('the faithfull loue that I am bounde to beare vnto yow'). The coda he adds ('as through the speciall goodnes that I haue founde in yow') places him, rhetorically at least, in a more personal, reciprocal relationship with his monarch, possibly reflecting his role as Edward's unofficial political tutor by this date. The work 'of myne owne handes' is fashioned to express more than the fealty due from subject to monarch: it is designed to reflect and extend a 'speciall goodness' already enjoyed.

Whilst much work has been done on the significance of prefatory matter and the choice of dedicatee, the *mise en page* of dedicatory epistles is relatively neglected. Yet the format of these epistles—which, in accordance with the common practice of the time, preface each of Thomas's works—shows him adopting contemporary Italian fashions to recreate the immediacy of the handwritten work in his printed texts. What is unusual about Thomas's printed epistles for this period is that they strive to reproduce the conventional

---

[98] Desiderius Erasmus, *De recta latini graecique sermonis pronuntiatione [. . .] dialogus* (Paris, 1528), A2ʳ; ibid., ed. and trans. Maurice Pope, *Collected Works of Erasmus* (Toronto: University of Toronto Press, 1974–), xxvi (1985), 365.

layout of scribal letters to social superiors, with his name divorced from the body of the text and offset to the right-hand margin in a different type (italic instead of black letter), as if capturing the position and appearance of an actual signature. Whilst this format was standard in printed books by the 1570s, when Thomas was publishing, it was still unusual.[99] That he influenced the format of his prefatory letters is suggested by the fact that, of the books published by Berthelet (who printed all of his works) extant between 1530 and 1554, only, and all but one of, Thomas's are laid out in this way. The layout of his prefatory letters here imitates Italian book design—familiar from his sojourn in Italy in the later 1540s—where attempts to capture epistolary verisimilitude through *mise en page* were popular by 1544, a full decade before the trend began to be established in England.

The content of Thomas's prefatory matter complements the visual pursuit of what Wendy Wall dubs the 'literary pseudomorph', printed books designed to resemble 'hand-scrawled bits [. . .] passed among friends and acquaintances within the networks of the coterie'.[100] Wall's analysis, conducted on poetic texts after 1570, extends pseudomorphism to include any prefatorial strategy that 'calls on the text's private status as a means of emphasizing the manuscript features of the book' (244). Thomas's publications abound in such techniques, as the occasional nature of his works, written in manuscript to aristocratic and gentry demand, are paraded before his print-purchasing readers. The *Principal rules* begins with a passage entitled 'the occasion', describing the circumstances of its production and linking the work into a studiedly casual appearance in print via a network of increasingly gentrified readers. The book, compiled at the request of 'John Tamwoorth gentleman' (his status is carefully noted) is 'about two yeres after [. . .] lent [. . .] to sir Walter Mildmaie knight', who, 'thinkyng it a necessarie thyng for all suche of our nacion, as are studiouse in [Italian], caused it thus to be put in printe for their commoditee'

[99] See Cathy Shrank, ' "These fewe scribbled wordes": Representing Intimacy in Early Modern Print', in Alexandra Gillespie (ed.), *Early Tudor Manuscript and Print*, *HLQ*, special issue (2004).
[100] Wendy Wall, *The Imprint of Gender: Authorship and Publication in the English Renaissance* (Ithaca, NY: Cornell University Press, 1993), 232. Cf. Arthur Marotti, *Manuscript, Print and the English Renaissance Lyric* (Ithaca, NY: Cornell University Press, 1995), ch. 1.

(π1ᵛ). The passage smacks of Thomas's hand, thanks to the appearance of characteristic idioms, such as 'drawing out' to describe the act of translation. 'The occasion' is followed by a personal letter from Thomas to Tamworth, which retains in print the extemporaneousness of the original exchange, and even two years on, apologizes for 'these fewe scribled rules' (π2ʳ). The phrase emphasizes and continues the handwritten nature of the original text into the printed medium, whilst the letter preserves the specificity of time (3 February 1548), place (Padua), and company (of 'freends') within which the text was produced, even as it is released into the public domain and elevated in status to a work 'necessarie' for 'our nacion'. The apparent failings of the text, meanwhile, are used to establish a bond between patron and author. 'Accordyng to your request, I haue taken in hand the thyng, that I am ferre vnable to perform,' Thomas confesses: 'but because emongst freends good will suffiseth, where power wanteth [. . .] I therfore (suche as they be) doe send theim vnto you, as a token of the affection and loue that I beare you.' Production in the face of professed inadequacy becomes proof of affection, and affection a quality that excuses inadequacy, just as in the manuscript of *The Boke of the Sphere*, presented to Grey, the powerful Duke of Suffolk, Thomas draws attention to the imperfection of this 'rudely handeled' object, converting the book's donation into a sign of trust and forgiving intimacy, and displaying the 'studied carelessness' ('negligentiusculus') recommended by Erasmus in the composition of familiar letters.[101]

'The destination of a dedication,' Gérard Genette reminds us, 'is always intended for at least two addressees: the dedicatee, of course, but also the reader.'[102] It is, moreover, 'always [. . .] a matter of demonstration, ostentation, exhibition: it proclaims a relationship, whether intellectual or personal, actual or symbolic, and this proclamation is always at the service of the work' (135). In Thomas's case, the dedication is also in service of himself, presenting an author fully integrated into court life after his disgrace and exile. His final work printed within his lifetime, the

---

[101] Desiderius Erasmus, *Conficiendarum epistolarum formula* (Antwerp, 1521), A2ʳ; ibid., ed. and trans. Charles Fantazzi, *Collected Works*, xxv (1985), 258.
[102] Gérard Genette, *Paratexts: Thresholds of Interpretation*, trans. Jane E. Lewin (Cambridge: Cambridge University Press, 1997), 134–5.

Argument, was published in 1551. It finds him in 'companie of dyuers gentle men and gentle women', the importance of whom is such that their identities (Thomas's apart) are coyly concealed from the general readership (A2^r): if Thomas himself does not feel the 'stigma of print', then he at least recognizes that his superiors might, whilst his own social rise is reflected in the fact that, for the first time, his name does not appear on the title page.[103]

The manuscript origins of the *Argument* are invoked by the conceit of authorial reluctance that prefaces the work. An opening address from 'the printer to the reader' gives the circumstances of the text's production, as the result of a dispute over women's clothing arising amongst this genteel coterie. The text (originally spoken *ex tempore* by Thomas) is only committed to writing at the request of one gentlewoman, entreating that for 'frendship' he might send a copy of his oration to her (A3^v). The privy nature of the work is further underlined by its author's strictures that she 'kepe it to hir selfe'. Following the printer's address is 'the letter sent by my mayster Thomas to the gentle woman, with the translacions that she desyred' (A4^v), in which the work itself is offered 'for a witnesse of [his] good will and frendship' (A5^v). The presentation of the book thus retains in print the immediacy of its own making, resisting what Love describes as 'the ability of print to empty words of presence' as it moves through the three stages of orality, manuscript, and print.[104] A text that began as an utterance reinvents and reintensifies the intimacy of that moment by preserving it, as a sign of friendship, in scribal form, which is in turn disseminated in print, bearing additional acknowledgement (in the printer's address) of the reciprocal relationship between author and sponsor. As Berthelet writes, the lady 'trust[ed] to pacify him wel enough, though he would take [publication of the *Argument*] vnkindly' (A4^r).

Thomas's texts are consequently marked by the conservation of their geneses as private works, the flattering exclusivity of which becomes all the more attractive to both author and dedicatee by being displayed in the public arena, presenting patrons wisely appreciative of good counsel, and the author achieving the humanist ideal of acting as effective adviser to the ruling sort. The *Boke*

[103] J. W. Saunders, 'The Stigma of Print', *Essays in Criticism*, 1 (1951), 139–64.
[104] Love (paraphrasing Ong), *Culture and Commerce*, 143.

of the Sphere remains arrested at this stage in its development. Thomas clearly intended its publication in print, since he envisages a general readership, extending beyond its dedicatee to include 'the vnlearned' (4ᵛ). That it was never printed was probably due, not to a disinterested patron or lack of audience, but to the change in his circumstances after the death of Edward VI.

After the accession of Edward's Catholic sister Mary in July 1553, Thomas, who had either resigned or been dismissed from his clerkship by 31 March 1553, was relieved of his subsequent position attending the English ambassadors to the imperial court.[105] Nevertheless, he continued to draw on the mechanics of familiarity that had hitherto served him so well. According to Adair, citing the Dorset minister Thomas Hancock as one of those helped by Thomas's connections, Thomas 'seems to have utilised the intimacy which he no doubt still possessed with the officials of the Council, to warn the more active of his co-religionists that proceedings were being taken against them'.[106] His efforts on behalf of his 'co-religionists' were integral to his vision of a Protestant nation. News of Mary's intended marriage to Philip of Spain in the autumn of 1553 placed further pressure on Thomas's allegiances, which ultimately favoured what he perceived as the interests of the commonweal above the rights of the monarch: according to the testimony of Nicholas Arnold, he plotted (unsuccessfully) to assassinate Mary in order 'to delyuer hys hole natyve countrey frome so many and so greate daungers as be nowe offered'.[107]

In the aftermath of Wyatt's Rebellion in January 1554, during which he lay sick in Gloucestershire, Thomas was arrested and—after a failed suicide attempt in the Tower of London—was tried and found guilty of treason on Arnold's evidence, even though, contrary to the statutes of Edward VI (and Mary herself), Arnold, who turned Queen's evidence to save himself, was the only witness.[108] As an author, Thomas successfully capitalized on the opportunities of nation-building and his accrued experience to promote both himself and the government he supported to a potentially ruthless degree.

---

[105] Adair, 'Thomas', 147.   [106] Ibid.
[107] Testimony of Nicholas Arnold, cited ibid. Cf. David Loades, *Two Tudor Conspiracies* (Cambridge: Cambridge University Press, 1965), 69.
[108] G. R. Elton (ed.), *The Tudor Constitution: Documents and Commentary*, 2nd edn. (Cambridge: Cambridge University Press, 1982) 73; Adair, 'Thomas', 151.

When he raised the corporeal image of the commonweal in his *Peregrine*, it was to sanction judicious (or judicial) bloodletting. 'Doth the phisicien well by incision of the vaine / to draw away the bloudde that is enemy of the mans helth[?]' he asked: 'Or were it better / by suffereyng it to contynue / he shold lett the man abyde in perill of destruction of his body?' (68ᵛ). Thomas thus fell victim to a political maxim he himself endorsed. On 18 May 1554 he was dragged by sledge from the Tower to Tyburn, where he was hanged, drawn, and quartered. His head was placed over London Bridge; his remaining three quarters displayed over Cripplegate.[109] Anatomized and exposed to public view, an example of the fate befalling traitors, Thomas, the consummate self-publicist and one-time cupbearer to the power brokers of the Edwardian minority, became a commodity to proclaim and protect the new reign.

For six years between 1547 and 1553, Thomas was an author with his finger on the political and cultural pulse. The range of works produced within that relatively brief period is testimony to the breadth and prescience of his interests as historian, linguist, travel writer, and political theorist. Had Edward and his regime survived adolescence, he would probably have been granted the more prominent place in English literary, lexicographic, and political history that he undoubtedly deserves. Thomas might have been precocious, but—as Gardiner's Machiavellian treatise shows—he was not isolated in his adoption and promotion of Italian ideas. His close acquaintance with Machiavellianism, his enthusiasm for the vernacular, and his ambivalence towards Italy thus reveal often overlooked continuities between the Edwardian and Elizabethan eras.

Thomas also maintained that the English were free, in contrast to the 'seruitude' endured by the inhabitants of Tana and Persia, or Italian husbandmen.[110] The belief in English liberties and in the theory that the monarch acted for the nation, and not vice versa, underpinned his prioritization of the commonweal over its ruler. In their logical extreme, these opinions justified 'doctrines of principled resistance' and were crystallized—as they were for Ponet and Christopher Goodman—by the reign of Mary, and a conviction that her vision of a mass-taking country, allied to the Habsburg

[109] Ibid.   [110] Thomas, *Voiages*, BL Royal 17 C. x, 2ʳ; id., *Historie*, 5ᴵⱽ.

dynasty, was contrary to national well-being.[111] In detaching the interests of the monarch from those of the nation, and in aligning England's well-being with Protestantism, Thomas also pre-empts Patrick Collinson's 'acephalous republic', conceptualized in Elizabeth's reign by his now ageing contemporaries William Cecil and Thomas Smith, similarly influenced by Italian political thought, as a way of ensuring England's political and religious stability in the absence of an obvious heir.[112] It is Smith's vision of the English commonweal and the active role of its inhabitants in defining and upholding it that the next chapter explores.

[111]   David Loades, *Politics and the Nation, 1450–1660: Obedience, Resistance and Public Order* (London: Fontana Press, 1974), 248; Ponet, *Shorte treatise*; Christopher Goodman, *How Superior Powers ought to be Obeyed* (Geneva, 1558).
[112]   Patrick Collinson, 'The Monarchical Republic of Queen Elizabeth I', in Guy (ed.), *Tudor Monarchy*, 110–34.

4

Thomas Smith and the Senate of Letters

That kind of reasoning seems to me best for bolting out of the truth which is used by way of dialogue or colloquy, where reasons be made to and fro as well for the matter intended as against it.[1]

The previous chapter examined the works of William Thomas and the continuing influence of Italy on English humanism. Thomas adapted Machiavellian theory to English circumstances, looked to Italy for prototypes and antitypes of English government, and—inspired by the rise of the Italian vernacular—promoted use of the vulgar tongue. This chapter concentrates on the statesman and author Thomas Smith, who—like Thomas—began his public career during the Edwardian period, was similarly concerned with improving the status of English, and applied his learning to analysing and influencing national policy. In particular, Smith consistently used the humanist genre of dialogue to analyse, and seek solutions for, issues of national concern. As this chapter argues, this fondness for dialogue reflects both Smith's humanist education—which promoted debate as a forensic tool—and his commitment to conciliar government, the existence of which would limit monarchical power and prevent tyranny.

Academically, Smith was seen by contemporaries as the 'flower' of his generation.[2] Commended by John Leland as one of Cambridge's foremost scholars, he was appointed first Regius Professor of civil law at Cambridge in 1540; within three years, aged 30, he was vice chancellor of the university.[3] Despite his

[1] Thomas Smith, *A Discourse of the Commonweal of this Realm of England*, ed. Mary Dewar (Charlottesville: University Press of Virginia, 1969), 13.
[2] Cited in Dewar, *Smith*, 1.
[3] Leland, *Cygnea Cantio*, E1ʳ; Dewar, *Smith*, 13.

unqualified academic success, Smith nevertheless exemplifies the humanist belief that scholars should assume a public role. Like his fellow Cantabrigians, John Cheke and Roger Ascham, Smith was drawn to court, and shortly after Henry VIII's death in 1547, he left university life to enter the household of Edward Seymour, soon to become Lord Protector.[4] Smith became clerk of the Privy Council in March 1547, a month after his arrival at court. From henceforth, as author and 'intellectual in office' (and, as pertinently, out of office), Smith used his scholarship to intervene in public affairs, advising—at various times—on enclosure, Elizabeth I's marriage, and the settlement of Ireland. Smith's learning and university connections remained crucial to his political career, however. It was education that, in Smith's eyes, granted men the right to govern and advise, and it was to his own learning that Smith had repeated recourse in periods of crisis, as he attempted to use his writing as a means of influence at times when he seemed politically marginalized.

'THE TRUE BANDS OF THE COMMONWEALTH':
'OUR TONGUE, OUR LAWS, AND OUR RELIGION'[5]

As we have seen in previous chapters, the reputation of English as a learned and literary language was by no means assured in the early decades of the sixteenth century. Andrew Borde and Thomas Elyot sought to remedy its perceived lack of vocabulary through Latinate neologisms; Leland turned to Latin for his public, scholarly works (and periodically slipped into Latin in his private notes). By the early 1550s, however, it was not the language itself that Thomas found faulty, but its speakers, who lacked sufficient familiarity with their mother tongue to display its full potential. He consequently formulated no plans for improving English, other than recommending that it be placed at the centre of the school curriculum.[6] Nevertheless, Thomas was an early voice championing English in its current state. He is not part of a sudden, burgeoning pride in the vernacular, and his plea for education in

[4] Leland, *Cygnea Cantio*, 26.
[5] PRO State Papers, Elizabeth, 70/81/1654, cited in Dewar, *Smith*, 157.
[6] Thomas, *Boke of the Sphere*, BL Egerton 837, 3ʳ.

English only circulated in one manuscript copy (if indeed, it did circulate at all—the treatise being devoid of marginalia and the only tract in an otherwise blank manuscript). Even so, Thomas characterizes a continuing concern to ameliorate the lowly reputation of English, and it is this concern that Smith shared.

Thomas suggested that education which prioritized English rather than Latin would increase the sophistication of vernacular composition. Smith's voice—arguing not for educational, but linguistic reform—is more typical of contributions to the ongoing debate about English during this period, since, like many, Smith felt that English itself was still deficient. The solution he advocated was not the linguistic expansion pursued by Borde or Elyot. Rather, it entailed standardizing spelling along phonetic lines. First developed in the 1540s, these ideas were published in 1568 as *De recta et emendata linguae anglicae scriptione, dialogus* ('A dialogue on the corrected and amended writing of the English tongue'). Like his Cambridge associate, John Cheke (who began a translation of the Bible using vocabulary of Anglo-Saxon derivation), Smith expresses enthusiasm for Anglo-Saxon as a model for sixteenth-century English, commending the Anglo-Saxons because 'they wrote more correctly than we do today' ('quàm nos hodie facimus, rectiúsque scripsisse').[7] Despite his attempts to justify his phonetic principles by invoking Anglo-Saxon precedents, the standards of judgement Smith deploys, demanding rational regularity, are set by the classical tongues. Drawing on the literal meaning of the word *recta* as 'ruled' or 'regulated', Smith's choice of title announces the 'rectitude' of which English is apparently capable.

The desire to prove the systematic nature of the mother tongue was not confined to England; it epitomizes linguistic patriotism across Europe in an age when Latin and Greek set the model. Joachim du Bellay, for example, felt the same pressures in his *Deffence*, where one of the main objections he feels required to address is that the French tongue is 'barbarous and irregular' ('barbare, & irreguliere').[8] Conversely, linguistic rules—

---

[7] Thomas Smith, *De recta et emendata linguaee anglicae scriptione, dialogus* (1568), 33ʳ. An edn. is available, with parallel translation, *Sir Thomas Smith, Literary and Linguistic Works*, iii, ed. Bror Danielsson, *Stockholm Studies in English*, 56 (Stockholm: Almqvist and Wiksell, 1983). The translations of *De scriptione* are my own, but are indebted to Danielsson's edn.

[8] du Bellay, *Deffence*, B6ʳ.

predictable declensions, tenses, moods, and persons—become signs of civility. Smith similarly presents his reforms as a step in the evolution of language from a natural or barbarous condition, evoking parallels with the shift from a forager's diet of 'acorns' ('glandibus') to an agrarian one of 'grain' ('fruges', 2^v), and from 'clothes made out of dead animal skins, put together any old how' ('mortuorum animantium pellibus qualitercunque coagmentatis pro vestimentis') to 'cloth made from wool or flax, and shaped by a tailor's skill to fit every part of the body' ('pannus factus è lana, linóve, & per artificis industriam aptè, & ad omneis artus humanos convenienter formatus fuerit', 3^r). Where Smith differs from both Thomas and du Bellay is that, while they assert the regularity of Italian or French as they stand, Smith sees it as a quality that English still lacks, but can attain by following his proposals.

The influence of classical learning on Smith's linguistic theorizing is unsurprising. Smith (like all Tudor scholars) had been steeped in classical learning from his grammar school days at Saffron Walden, which modelled its curriculum on the humanist programme followed at Eton and Winchester.[9] His interest in English orthography can be traced to the early 1540s, when he was collaborating with Cheke to overhaul classical Greek pronunciation at Cambridge.[10] These reforms were defended in a letter to Stephen Gardiner in 1542, printed in 1568 by the Parisian publisher Robert Stephan alongside Smith's *De scriptione* with the complementary title *De recta et emendata linguae graecae pronuntiatione* ('On the corrected and amended pronunciation of the Greek tongue'). Smith's two texts on language reform demonstrate the adaptation of neoclassical models for Anglocentric purposes, even as—written in Latin and published by a Parisian printer—they showcase English learning for the benefit of an international readership. In his linguistic reforms (of Greek and English), Smith is indebted to Erasmus, an authority cited throughout *De pronuntiatione*. By echoing the phrasing of Erasmus' 1528 treatise, *De recta*

---

[9] *VCH (Essex)*, ii. 519.
[10] According to the preface of *De scriptione*, it was whilst 'Smithus' was 'busy with a book, [. . .] about correcting our pronunciation of Greek' that Quintus, his interlocutor, remembers finding 'some observations in [Smith's] hand, on the writing of our own language' ('Libro fueras occupatus, credo fuit vt corrigeres apud nos pronuntiationem Graecam'; 'observationes quasdam manu tua scriptas de scriptione nostrae linguae', 3^v).

latini graecique sermonis pronuntiatione, the titles of Smith's two
texts announce the intellectual origins they emulate and, like all true
emulators, seek to outdo. Erasmus had tried to establish greater oral
homogeneity amongst an international, Latin-speaking community
by reforming neoclassical orthography (the bulk of the work is
concerned with Latin, not Greek). In fighting to 'retain' Latin 'as a
written and spoken method', Erasmus aimed to foster fluid communication, and thus understanding, amongst the peoples of Europe by
providing them with a common tongue.[11] His work was pitched
against the rise of European vernaculars. Smith redirects Erasmus'
techniques of linguistic analysis. On the one hand, he pursues a sepa-
ratist agenda by promoting the use of, and pride in, a vernacular
language. On the other, in his reform of Greek pronunciation, Smith
is—unlike Gardiner and Erasmus—prepared to isolate Cambridge
academically by using a different pronunciation from the international scholarly community, even if this means that Cambridge
alumni will be unintelligible to their Continental counterparts. Being
right and enabling Cambridge students to learn Greek more easily
take precedence over compliance with common practice.

   Smith does not abandon his classical roots: rather, he sees how
these lessons can be applied to his own language and literature. For
Smith, the vernacular is not—as for Erasmus—in direct competi-
tion with the classics, but draws energy from them. Latin holds no
intrinsic worth for Smith, just as it did not for his contemporaries
Thomas and du Bellay. It is instead inspirational precisely because
it was a once rude vernacular that, like Italian, had grown elegant
through the 'skill and industry of men' ('artifice, & industrie des
hommes').[12] Quintilian, after all, once lamented the state of Latin,
encouraging the readers of his *Institutio Oratoria* to rival Greek,
then respected—as Latin was in the sixteenth century—as the
eloquent and scholarly language. 'Since we cannot be so delicate,
let us be stronger,' Quintilian wrote: 'if they beat us for subtlety, let
us prevail by weight, and if they have greater precision, let us outdo
them in fullness of expression' ('non possumus esse tam graciles:
simus fortiores. Subtilitate vincimur: valeamus pondere. Proprietas
penes illos est certior: copia vincamus').[13] Perhaps unexpectedly,
humanist knowledge of the classics can therefore be seen to

---

[11] Erasmus, *De pronuntiatione*, 350.   [12] Du Bellay, *Deffence*, A4ᵛ.
[13] Quintilian, *Institutio Oratoria*, XII. x. 36.

advance the English vernacular, just as in the second half of the
sixteenth century, it was university education in England, and the
rise of the vulgar tongue there, that inspired Welsh humanists to
invest in their own language.[14]

For Smith, amending the English tongue was not merely about
asserting its worth on an international stage, it was also about
drawing together a nation of speakers, giving them what Edmund
Spenser would later call 'the kingdome of oure owne Language'.[15]
It is symptomatic of Smith's belief in the unifying powers of
language that, when planning the subjugation of Ireland in 1565,
he identified 'our tongue, our laws, and our religion' as 'the true
bands of the commonwealth'.[16] Smith's attitude to language
reform is thus entwined with other manifestations of Englishness
and good citizenship: following the state religion and obeying the
laws of the land. It is these three discourses—of correct language,
worship, and behaviour—that underpin *De scriptione*, a text that
not only sets out Smith's plans for orthographic reform, but also
reflects his conception of the commonweal.

Both *De scriptione* and *De pronuntiatione* attack custom: the
former opposes current English orthography, which it seeks to
remodel along phonetic lines; the latter, the then standard pronunciation of classical Greek, which flattened the dipthongs. There was
a ready association between error and custom amongst many of the
Cambridge group surrounding Smith and Cheke in 1540s. In a
letter to the humanist Hubert Leodius in the early 1550s, for example, Ascham's assault on 'Usage' as justification for Greek pronunciation thus finds an added barb in his aside 'that Usage alone
produces and fosters errors even in the true religion of Christ
himself, just as a stinking sow suckles its little pig, and bites to
protect it' ('[. . .] quos errores solus usus in ipsa verissima Christi
religione producit, fovet, et tanquam sus porcellum suum in foetido
sinu amplectitur, et mordicus etiamnum defendit').[17] Despite the

---

[14] Jones, *Old British Tongue*, 34.

[15] Edmund Spenser and Gabriel Harvey, *Three proper, wittie, familiar letters*
(1580), 6.

[16] PRO State Papers, Elizabeth, 70/81/1654. This triplet is reduplicated in *De
Republica Anglorum*, with 'law' replaced by 'progenie' (Thomas Smith, *De
Republica Anglorum*, ed. Mary Dewar (Cambridge: Cambridge University Press,
1982), 61).

[17] Ascham, *Works*, i. 346; *The Letters of Roger Ascham*, ed. and trans. Maurice
Hatch and Alvin Vos (New York: Peter Lang, 1989), 149.

accusation that he was 'neutrall' in religion, Smith's works display that same connection between religious and linguistic reform.[18] In *De scriptione*, advocates of spelling reform are 'pious, 'true, wise, and learned men' ('veriis, piis, sapientibus, aut doctis'), whilst he who 'defends errors and abuses' ('errores & abusus [. . .] defendit') does so 'whether in religion, and rituals, or in forms of teaching, dressing and living' ('siue sit in religione, & ceremoniis, siue in formis docendi, vestiendi, vivendi'), offending religious, social, and intellectual standards alike (1ᵛ). Spurious letters, meanwhile, are deemed 'mendicant' ('mendicitatem', 33ᵛ), a word replete with connotations of corrupt and parasitic Catholic friars, as seen in the works of Chaucer and William Langland, both of whom were appropriated as proto-reformers by sixteenth-century editors and commentators.[19]

Ascham's vilification of custom during a discussion on reforming Greek pronunciation also acts as further reminder of the connection between religious and linguistic enquiry in Cambridge during the 1540s, where attempts to restore 'authentic' Greek pronunciation through close attention to its literature coincided with interrogation of contemporary religious practice by examining original texts, with 'the scriptural canons as our guide' ('scripturam canonicam nobis proposuimus').[20] Both projects earned the censure of the authorities: Stephen Gardiner as chancellor of the university in the first instance; Thomas Cranmer as Archbishop of Canterbury in the second. If Smith was not directly involved with the religious debates, then associates—such as Ascham—were, and his linguistic endeavours were a product of that same spirit of academic enquiry and willingness to challenge orthodoxy, as Smith himself acknowledges in *De pronuntiatione*, asking, 'shall we, who are currently asserting that miracles are unnecessary to prove the most serious doctrines of our faith, seek for miracles to settle these contests of vowels and consonants?' ('nos qui ad grauissima fidei nostrae persuasiones comprobandas, hoc tempore miracula non

[18] BL Harleian 6989, 141ʳ, cited in Dewar, *Smith*, 39. Smith's prayers written in the Tower of London in 1549 also show Calvinist convictions regarding the 'elect'. See Thomas Smith, *Certaigne Psalmes or Songues of David, translated into Englishe meter by Sir Thomas Smith, Knight, then Prisoner in the Tower of London, with other prayers and songues by him made to pas the tyme there*, BL Royal 17A xvii.
[19] See, e.g., Robert Crowley's preface to Crowley (ed.), *The vision of Pierce Plowman* (1550), and Leland, *Commentarii* ii. 422.
[20] Ascham, *Works*, i. 156; id. *Letters*, 106.

esse necessaria contendimus, ad haec vocalium & consonantium certamina decernenda, miracula conquiremus?').[21]

For scholars such as Smith, Cheke, and Ascham, the word of God was a written word, and the linguistic 'reformation' for which they call has logical religious implications. Conceived in the reformist atmosphere of Cambridge in the early 1540s, Smith's treatise on English—with its emphasis on linguistic uniformity—pre-empts the Edwardian pursuit of religious conformity. This campaign is exemplified by the production of the Book of Common Prayer in 1549, when different printers were mobilized to publish identical texts, all carrying the same preface arguing for the need to standardize religion as a 'remedy' for the current abuses, disorder, and different provincial protocol. As the preface proclaims, 'where heretofore, there hath been great diuersitie [. . .] within this realme: some folowing Salsburye vse, some Herford vse, some the vse of Bangor, some of Yorke, & some of Lincone [. . .] from henceforth, al the whole realm shall haue but one vse.'[22] Smith's *De scriptione* consequently has much in common, in terms of its programme of phonetic reform and anti-papist idiom, with Edwardian texts such as Hart's *Orthographie* designed to further the reformed, book-based worship sanctioned by the current government.[23] Significantly, both texts remained unpublished until the late 1560s, when a religious settlement had been achieved and its workability proven over the decade since its implementation in 1559. *De scriptione* is thus a reminder of continuities between the Henrician, Edwardian and early Elizabethan periods, and the re-emergence of the same ideas and 'personnel' in the different regimes.

Just as linguistic and religious reform are intimately connected, so too are language and law (the first and second of Smith's 'true bands of the commonwealth'). Language serves as a social

---

[21] Thomas Smith, *De recta et emendata linguae graecae pronuntiatione* (1568), 22ᵛ. An edn., with parallel translation, is available in *Sir Thomas Smith, Literary and Linguistic Works*, ii, ed. Bror Danielsson, *Stockholm Studies in English*, 50 (Stockholm: Almqvist and Wiksell, 1978). Translations are my own, but are indebted to Danielsson.

[22] *The boke of the common Praier and administracion of the Sacrementes and other rites and ceremonies of the Churche*, Edward Whitchurch's edn. of 4 May (1549), π2ʳ.

[23] John Hart's *Orthographie* (1569), which cites Smith as an authority, was drafted c.1551 as *The opening of the unreasonable writing of our Inglish toung*, BL Royal 17. C. vii.

contract, and those who abuse it are guilty in *De scriptione* of
'fraud', for 'an Englishman speaking English to a Frenchman who
understands English [. . .] and deceives him by some verbal trick,
will be as fraudulent as a Frenchman who deceives a Frenchman in
French' ('ita vt si Anglus Anglicè Gallo Anglicè intelligenti [. . .] &
eum decipiat, per quamque verborum imposturam, tam erit in
fraude, quam si Gallus Gallo Gallicè loquens Gallum fallat', 8ʳ).
Similarly, it is those who operate outside, and against, society and
its laws that seek to subvert language, a link between 'cant' and
illegality explored further by the Elizabethan vogue for coney-
catching pamphlets and by William Harrison's *Description of
England*, where 'the first deviser thereof was hanged by the neck,
as just reward'.[24] As Smith relates in *De scriptione*, 'we find that
among cunning hucksters, and pedlars, and that mass of rascals,
prostitutes and thieves, whom they call "*Gypsies*", a different and
distinct language is used, unknown to others and serving only
themselves and their trickery' ('inter callidos negotiatiores
conspicimus, & errones illos, qui pedariam exercent mercaturam,
atque illam colluviem nebulonum, meretricum, & furum quos
appellant *Ægiptios*, discretam, distinctámque linguam exerceri,
incognitam aliis, sibi suáeque tantùm imposturae servientem', 6ʳ).

That link between speech and society is also apparent in the
metaphors that underpin *De scriptione*. Throughout the text,
Smith shows a concern to settle sounds, to stop them 'wandering'
('vagantur', 32ʳ). On a practical level, this is driven by a desire to
standardize English, so that—like Latin and Greek—there are fixed
ways of spelling, rather than the fluid early modern system. Within
Smith's reformed alphabet, no letter represents more than sound,
and composite sounds like *sh* and *th* are indicated by single characters, drawn from the Anglo-Saxon alphabet.[25] However, the
language with which Smith describes his system brings an added
nuance to the text as it taps into a rhetoric of civil society, which
vilified vagrancy as an asocial practice where the able-bodied
shirked their responsibilities and fed off the community, rather
than contributing to it. In an extended allegory, individual letters
of the alphabet are thus converted into citizens in a commonwealth
of language, placed by Smith in a 'senate of letters' ('literarum

²⁴ Harrison, *Description*, 184.
²⁵ Smith's alphabet has 29 letters: 19 Roman; 4 Greek; 6 Anglo-Saxon.

senatu', 25^r). In this alphabetical commonwealth—as in any healthy body politic—it is crucial that each letter does its duty and performs its proper function (the senate here intriguingly encompassing all letters, not merely a patrician class). Letters, as good citizens, should therefore aver the two evils of Italian political thought: the idleness and ambition found when letters are 'superfluous' ('supervacaneum, 42^r) or usurp the position of other letters. The letter *c*, for example, is a 'monstrous' ('monstrum'), 'androgynous' ('androgyne') letter, which by 'wilful pretence drives *s* and *k* from their homes' ('per eiusmodi impostures pro suo arbitrio tam *s* quàm *k* exigat aedibus', 22^r). The idiom is that of law and government, and—besides contravening gender norms—*c* 'would be easily convicted by a just judge' ('neque dubito quin vbi sit aequus Praetor, facile C cadet causa'). *Q*, meanwhile, is 'a fraudulent intruder, unnecessarily and injuriously occupying the place of a true letter' ('supposititiam, & nulla necessiate verae literae locum iniuriosè occupantem'), deserving 'exile far away' ('longè hinc exulare', 29^r). The over-reaching *q*, 'always coming before its *u*, like a proud serving maid' ('semper pracedentem suae *u*, vt ancilla spuerba'), is also unworthy of a free language: 'the Greeks, lovers of liberty, never allowed her among them, nor did the ancient Anglo-Saxons,' Smithus—Smith's textual persona—comments approvingly ('Graeci homines vt amantes libertatis, nunquam illam sunt passi apud eos versari; sed nec vestussimi Anglosaxones', 29^v), drawing on the same discourse of Anglo-Saxon liberties found in Stephen Gardiner's *Discourse on the Coming of the English and Normans to Britain*, written for Philip of Spain in the 1550s. However, whilst Gardiner's treatise defends custom as the foundation of English freedoms, warning Philip against meddling with English law in particular—a facet of English society that is dated back to Saxon times—Smith's recourse to Anglo-Saxon is only skin-deep, wrapping innovation in a rhetoric of precedent to authorize an approach that is, in fact, a radical break from the past, a technique supporters of the English Reformation recurrently used to present religious change as a return to the pure and primitive English church.

Smith's linguistic programme was extreme, requiring a people to abandon engrained, if illogical, orthographical habits and embrace an entirely unfamiliar system. Nonetheless, he was not a lone voice. Hart, as mentioned earlier, concocted a similar method during the same period—the reign of Edward VI—and the Elizabethan scholar Gabriel Harvey assimilated and acknowledged some of Smith's orthographic principles.[26] English spelling proved as hot a topic for men such as the lexicographer William Bullokar or schoolmaster Richard Mulcaster as quantitative verse and rhyme would later in the century.[27] The parallels between the debates about spelling, diction, and verse are striking: all three are about the search for an English style of which England could be proud, and whether this entailed substituting classical practices for English traditions or wholeheartedly embracing what English already had to offer. In all three cases—rhyme, orthography, and vocabulary—custom won. It was not root and branch reform that ultimately fostered English as a national language, providing some semblance of unified experience, but religious texts such as the Book of Common Prayer, the Homilies, and the English Bible. With the backing of statutes, these were regularly read across the realm and suffused philological learning with the idioms of spoken English drawn from different regions of England, not least—in the case of the Bible—Tyndale's native Forest of Dean.

Where it was the expansive hybridity of English which eventually triumphed, thanks to texts such as Tyndale's Bible (on which the Great Bible of 1539 and subsequent translations were based), Smith's phonetic system, in contrast, is constrictive, attempting to force a wide variety of spoken Englishes into one standard model. Further to that, his new letters, capturing peculiarly 'English' sounds, mean that his reformed alphabet is suited to English alone. 'If our Welsh and the Spanish have their own peculiar sound which they express by the double *ll* [. . .,] what has that got to do with this discussion?' Smithus asks: 'we are only talking about English letters and sounds' ('et si Walli nostri & Hispani suum habent peculiarem sonum, quem exprimunt duplici ll [. . .] quid hoc ad id quod nunc est in manibus?'; 'de Anglicis tantùm literis & sonis propositum est dicere', 14ᵛ). Language reform is thus made a matter of national responsibility, and for Smithus 'any people is free to invite its learned men to correct its errors' ('liberum erit cuique genti suos,

[26] Virginia Stern, *Gabriel Harvey, his Life, Marginalia and Library* (Oxford: Clarendon Press, 1979), 215, 236.

[27] William Bullokar, *The Amendment of Orthographie for English Speech* (1580); Richard Mulcaster, *The first part of the elementarie which entreateth chefelie of the right writing of our English tung* (1582), 82 ff.

adhibitis doctis viris, errores corrigere'). Besides exposing the peculiar status of the Welsh—simultaneously dubbed 'our Welsh' and deemed outside the boundaries of English, one of Smith's 'bands of the commonwealth'—Smith's words also demonstrate his belief in an educated elite as the proper arbiters of language. Correct speaking is arrived at 'by agreement and consensus among learned men' ('pactione quadam, & consensu inter doctos', 5ᵛ). It is this emphasis on the role of the wise and learned counsellor, and of agreement arrived at through conversation, that the next section of this chapter examines.

'THE COUNSELL OF SUCH GRAVE AND
DISCREETE MEN'[28]

Mary Dewar has argued convincingly for Smith's authorship of the anonymous *Discourse of the Commonweal of this Realm of England*, a text also attributed to John Hales, who sat on the Enclosure Commission of 1548.[29] Besides circumstantial evidence (that 'W.S.', the person responsible for bringing the manuscript into print in 1581, was Smith's nephew and heir, William), there are strong similarities in style and content between the *Commonweal* and Smith's other acknowledged works. Like the majority of these, it is a dialogue and—as we shall see—displays Smith's recurrent commitment to political participation and belief in the power of counsel to influence policy. The *Commonweal* was written some time after the autumn of 1549, when Smith was at Eton, where he held the post of provost, in semi-retirement from politics after the fall of his patron, Edward Seymour, Protector Somerset. Barred from the Privy Council and alienated from court, Smith uses his writing to participate in politics. As the *Commonweal* considers causes and possible solutions for the current economic crisis, concentrating above all on enclosure, it seeks to propose a remedy for pressing political issues. Further to that, it allows us insight into Smith's belief in reasoned and informed debate as the surest method of formulating policy.

---

[28] Smith, *De Republica Anglorum*, 65.
[29] Mary Dewar, 'The Authorship of the "Discourse of the Commonweal" ', *Economic History Review*, 2nd series, 19 (1966), 388–400.

Written in the form of a dialogue and set after a meal in the garden of a prosperous provincial merchant, the *Commonweal* epitomizes civil conversation. Representatives of different sorts and occupations—a clerical doctor, knight, merchant, husbandman, and tradesman—gather to share a meal ('a pasty of venison', 15) and participate in fruitful discussion intended to help solve the contemporary socio-economic ills of inflation, urban decay, and civil unrest. The provincial setting for the dialogue extends political participation beyond the immediate environs of court and parliament, whilst the varied backgrounds of the interlocutors reflect the social depth of this participation. Smith's discourse is dominated by the social and intellectual elite (the knight and, above all, the doctor, who emerges as the most authoritative speaker). The views of the husbandman and tradesman—as well as the wealthier merchant—are represented nonetheless, and the husbandman (as witness) joins the knight in the work of the commissions then investigating enclosure. Recognition is made of the expertise of different 'sorts', each of which has the potential to contribute something unique to the commonweal. 'The gifts of wit be so divers,' the doctor states:

therefore I would not only have learned men (whose judgement I would wish to be chiefly esteemed herein) but also merchantmen, husbandmen, and artificers (which in their calling are taken wise) freely suffered, yea and provoked, to tell their advice in this matter; for some points in their feats they may disclose that the wisest in the realm could not.   (12)

Smith's doctor recurrently talks in terms of mutuality at both local and national level. 'We be not born to ourselves but partly to the use of our country, of our parents, of our kinfolk, and partly of our friends and neighbors,' he remarks, citing Cicero (16). That duty to offer oneself in public service is enforced by the preface. 'Consideration and reformation' of abuses pertains to more than 'the King's Council', although it 'does chiefly belong' to it (11). The author's involvement is consequently justified by both his position in House of Commons, 'where such things ought to be treated of', and—as importantly—by his status as 'a member of the [. . .] Commonweal'.

Within the *Discourse* there is thus a strong and consistent belief in counsel, and in the merits of wide political participation, which spreads beyond court and parliament across different social categories. As the doctor states, 'princes, though they be never so wise themselves, yea the wiser that they be, the more counsellors they will have' (11). These counsellors, moreover, should be receptive to the expertise of others 'which in their calling are taken wise' (12). Smith's knight is an admirable character—and a fit social superior—precisely because he is prepared to take advice from others, particularly the learned doctor. Smith's dialogue consequently represents a positive model of eloquence, as the doctor is shown persuading his assembled audience of the merits of his solutions for 'common and universal griefs that men complain on nowadays' (13). More usefully still, he convinces the knight, who has the political wherewithal to ensure 'his reasons [. . .] take place' (137). Yet the *Commonweal* is not a naively idealistic text. Besides the fact that its optimism is tempered by the sudden, unwanted departure of the doctor, curtailing further productive discussion, the text also acknowledges failings in the system. Matters of national interest 'ought to be treated' in the Commons, for example; the choice of the conditional mood indicates that this does not necessarily happen. The *Commonweal* also underscores the pressing need for a forum for discussion across boundaries of sorts and occupations. Within the dialogue, however, this communication is impeded by the different speakers' tendency to see things from the perspective of their social group alone. It takes the doctor to break down those perceptions; without him, the speakers would remain trapped within their own misconceptions, their ability to blame others for the current situation a barrier to necessary reform. As Andrew McRae points out, the philosophy behind the doctor's proposed solutions is also notably pragmatic.[30] Unlike *Utopia*, the *Commonweal* does not hide behind a fantastic setting and detached irony: it makes concrete suggestions for improving the lot of Edwardian England. Self-interest is not vilified as the root of all evils, as it is in Utopia, where the method by which it is eradicated (banning private ownership) offers no practical solution for early modern Europe. In the *Commonweal*, that self-seeking is harnessed to benefit the commonweal: sheep farming is not to be penalized; rather, growing arable is to be rewarded on an equal basis to induce men to cultivate corn instead of Hythloday's man-eating sheep.

---

[30] McRae, *God Speed the Plow*, 56.

That debate figures in the *Commonweal* as a means of suggesting answers to the economic malaise of the late 1540s is characteristic of Smith's belief in counsel as the proper means of policy-making and political intervention. Smith's persuasion in this matter is proven in deed as well as word. In the early 1570s, for example, whilst planning the colonization of Ireland, Smith staged a debate, where, as Harvey records in the marginalia of his copy of Livy, 'Thomas Smith junior & Sir Humphrey Gilbert [debated] for Marcellus, Thomas Smith senior and Doctor William Haddon for Fabius Maximus, before an audience at Hill Hall consisting at that very time of myself, John Wood, and several others of gentle birth'.[31] Not only does this demonstrate the pragmatic ends for which sixteenth-century humanists read their history, it also shows Smith's conviction that the key to good statecraft was free and open discussion, grounded in scholarship—a belief borne out by his plans for the colonization of the Ards Peninsula in Ireland, where the 'Comon counsell', consisting of 10 per cent of the (male) colonists, was required to consider and ratify all 'weightie affaires'.[32] This belief in debate finds natural correlation in the dialogic form that Smith continually employed and endorsed in his literary works. As the preface to the *Commonweal* states: 'that kind of reasoning seems to me best for bolting out of the truth which is used by way of dialogue or colloquy, where reasons be made to and fro as well for the matter intended as against it' (13). It is therefore noteworthy that, rewriting his *De scriptione* in the 1560s, Smith recasts it as a dialogue, albeit one in which the dialogue is rather one way, dominated by one speaker, and thus creating the illusion of debate, not actual debate. As 'Smithus' reads his treatise to Quintus because 'it is spoiled by deletions and interlineations' ('deformatus lituris & expunctionibus'), Quintus' role is not to argue, but to make comments supporting Smithus' proposals.

As Jennifer Richards argues, it is also civil conversation that Smith uses to legitimate his reformed pronunciation of Greek.[33] In

---

[31] Cited in Grafton and Jardine, ' "Studied for action" ', 40.

[32] 'Offices prescribed by Sir Thomas Smith for the Ardes', ERO D/DSh/01/7.

[33] Jennifer Richards, *Rhetoric and Courtliness in Early Modern Literature* (Cambridge: Cambridge University Press, 2003), 82. Ascham's strategies justifying the Cambridge debates about the Mass in the 1540s are similar, as he describes how 'we conferred among ourselves about what we had studied' (Ascham, *Works*, i. 256; id., *Letters*, 106).

order to refute what Richards calls Gardiner's 'autocratic style', Smith insists in *De pronuntiatione* that it is through 'common consent and counsel' ('communi [. . .] consensu & consilio') with a suitably qualified group of men—Cheke, Ponet, 'and all the others amongst us who seemed proficient in Greek' ('& omne alii, qui quicquam in lingua Graeca posse videbantur apud nos', 40ʳ)—that a new theory of pronunciation has been reached.[34] It is not just conversations with Cheke and Ponet that are used to lend weight to Smith's text, however. *De pronuntiatione* also begins by reminding Gardiner of a 'pleasurable' ('voluptatis') conversation between him and Smith 'the other day at Hampton Court' ('superiore die in Hamptona Regia', A1ʳ); the subsequent treatise then attempts to continue this exchange, again as a means of influencing policy. One of Gardiner's strategies in rebuffing Smith in his often stinging reply is to expose their lack of intimacy and the insubstantiality of this dialogue at Hampton Court, which is redefined as 'a brief conversation at a public gathering' ('breui, in congressu, colloquio').[35] Another strategy used by Gardiner is to breach expected epistolary protocol, and thus reject the bonds that Smith's letter seeks to establish, by exposing the empty rhetoric of Smith's ingratiating compliments. Gardiner holds himself aloof. Unmoved by Smith's arguments and—as importantly—unresponsive to his conversational gambits, he reiterates his former instructions against the reformed pronunciation of Greek.

De pronuntiatione, *De scriptione*, and the *Commonweal* show how Smith plays with the genre of humanist dialogue. The first sets itself up, albeit unsuccessfully, as one section of an ongoing epistolary conversation (a familiar letter being, as Erasmus puts it, 'a mutual conversation between absent friends').[36] The second is presented as a discourse arising from the companionable reading of a text, with the preamble to *De scriptione* establishing an atmosphere of *amicitia*, in which Quintus is joyfully reunited with his friend Smithus. The third combines dialogue with the familiar letter, in which the discourse is related second-hand. As the narrator in the *Commonweal* explains to his unidentified correspondent:

---

[34] Ibid.

[35] Gardiner, 'Reply to Smith', BL Royal App. 87, 34ʳ–38ʳ, at 34ʳ; trans. by Danielsson in *De recta et emandata linguae graecae pronuntiatione*, 204–14, at 204.

[36] Desiderius Erasmus, *De conscribendis epistolis*, ed. and trans. Charles Fantazzi, *Collected Works*, xxv. 20.

'I will declare unto you what communication a knight told me was between him and certain other persons of late' (13).

The *Commonweal* is also characteristic of Smith's multi-layered narratives in which opinions expressed are distanced from those of the author. That same technique of reported conversation is used in Smith's *Communicacion or Discourse of the Queenes highnes mariage*, composed *c.*1561, in which Smith relates the previous evening's debate to his neighbour 'F.W.', identified in different manuscripts as either Francis Wyatt or Francis Walsingham.[37] The text, 'one of the most widely copied tracts in Elizabethan England', was extensively circulated at court.[38] Yet even as it considers an issue of obvious contemporary interest, unlike the *Commonweal*, it also exposes and undercuts its own rhetoric. The *Communicacion*, which establishes itself in the tradition of '*Platoes Academie or Ciceroes Tusculano*', is set, like Erasmus' 'Godly Feast', in a location outside the town, a Horatian idyll of honest speech and simple behaviour.[39] Here, on an unadorned 'grene bancke' in Smith's garden (98ᵛ), four of his friends discuss the 'great matter' of the queen's marriage, a recurrent phrase that recalls another politically urgent 'matter', her father's divorce three decades earlier, an event equally pressing for the royal succession. Within the dialogue, eloquence is seemingly effective. The argument of the discourse is accumulative, and at each stage the character nicknamed 'the Godfather' is a model of receptiveness, responding favourably to each oration. The first speaker Spitewed's reasons against marriage are thus unambiguously nullified by the next speaker, Lovealien, who establishes the need for Elizabeth to marry. Homefriend, building on Lovealien's arguments in favour of marriage per se, then refutes the latter's support for a foreign match, and is left, uncontradicted, with the last word, advocating marriage with an English nobleman. Although the text never mentions him, the most likely candidate here is Robert Dudley, Earl of Leicester, whose patronage, Susan

---

[37] Identified as Wyatt in BL Add. 48, 047, 96ʳ; Walsingham in BL Add. 4, 149, 38ʳ. Smith was not familiar with Walsingham until the 1570s (Dewar, *Smith*, 181). Neither Wyatt nor Walsingham had estates in Essex (*VCH (Essex)*). All references to the *Communicacion* will be from BL Add. 48, 047, compiled by Robert Beale, who knew Smith personally (Dewar, *Smith*, 86 n.).

[38] Ibid. 4.

[39] Cf. Horace, *Satires*, ii, ed. and trans. H. Rushton Fairclough, rev. edn. (London: Heinemann, 1929), II. ii.

Doran argues, Smith was then trying to attract, after a quarrel with his former student, later patron, William Cecil.[40] Such a man, the *Communicacion* argues, would have none of a foreigner's disadvantages: not only would he be free from national flaws of drunkenness or jealousy that distinguished (respectively) Germanic and Mediterranean peoples, he would also share the queen's religion, education, and customs; nor would he risk embroiling her in expensive foreign wars.

Nevertheless, the apparent straightforwardness of this scheme is complicated by the way in which the text exposes the mechanics of rhetoric. The force of each argument lies not in its content, but in the manner in which it is presented. The narrator worries about the potential effect of his 'evill rehearsinge' and 'rudenes', which will 'weaken their arguments' and 'shame their eloquence' (98[r]); F.W. bemoans 'philosophers and Rethoricians' who 'care not what parte [they] take [. . .] and woulde make some simple men as [he] ys beleve that [. . .] the Moone is made of grene chese' (97[v]). Lovealien proves a particularly keen analyst of rhetorical constructions. 'Ye amplified great dangers[,] disquietnes[,] dissencions and exaggerated great cares and thoughtes and griefs,' he informs Spitewed (107[r]), exposing the use of amplication—a technique particularly recommended by rhetoricians for its persuasive power—to exaggerate the dangers of childbirth.[41] Further on, Lovealien reveals his opponent's use of insinuation, 'wherin [he] crepte so into vs' (107r).[42] Like a good rhetorician, Lovealien also follows—and draws attention to—the recommendations of classical authorities regarding the logical development of the argument: 'For it standeth not with order of disputacon (as to my rememberaunce *Aristotle* writethe) that I should goe about to prove *quale sit* before I have proved *quod sit*,' he tells his audience (118[r]).

By foregrounding the workings of rhetoric, Smith detaches himself as author from the manifest artifice of the orations he relates. In keeping with this policy of evasion, the identities of the speakers (if real) are concealed by their nicknames, and they themselves are

---

[40] Susan Doran, *Monarchy and Matrimony: The Courtships of Elizabeth I* (London: Routledge, 1996), 52.

[41] See, e.g., Wilson, *Rhetorique* (1553), 64[r]. Unless otherwise stated, all references to the *Rhetorique* will be from this first edn.

[42] Cf. ibid. 55[r]: 'a priuie twining, or close creeping in, to win fauour with much circumstaunce, called insinuation'.

reduced to stock types. Lovealien, for example, is akin to the monstrously hybrid 'Italionated Englishman' or 'Mongrell' tainted with 'outlandishe blood' whom F.W. critiques (97^v).[43] 'Yow love aliens and straungers so well and praise so well all Countries and Countrymen saue Englande and Englishe men that it is a pitie you were not borne some where els,' comments the Godfather in a similar vein (104^v). Lovealien bears out the accusation by smattering his speech with foreign proverbs ('la faccia d'huomo faccia da leone', 116^r) and foreign terms, such as '*Rivales* or *Candidati*' (120^r). Homefriend cuts a similarly exaggerated figure. Like those over-zealous compatriots criticized by William Salesbury for believing Welsh more 'fully replenished with eligancie, graces & eloquence' than it is, Homefriend is lampooned by the Godfather as the 'verie Idea of an olde Englishe man', who 'thought no Countrey so good[,] so plentyfull[,] so riche[,] so happie as Englande is, nor no men so faire[,] so well made[,] so bolde[,] so hardie[,] so good warriors[,] so wise and so discrete as we Englishe men be' (121^v).[44]

The *Communicacion* is further marked by the reluctance of its speakers. Each oration, except the last, is greeted by a sustained silence, as if the speakers were unwilling to enter the fray. These pauses are only interrupted by the Godfather, who is distinguished by his pronounced stammer, that 'vnethe can he bringe out a right worde', and a handicap that renders him unable to join the debate fully (104^r). Contrary to humanist ideals of heartfelt speech, hearts and tongues are strikingly misaligned.[45] 'None of vs should escape you if your tongue were as good [i.e. sharp] as your harte,' Lovealien tells the Godfather (104^v). Smith's model of truth-telling is, like that of Elyot's *Pasquil the playne*, grounded in plain speech and opposition, a primary meaning of *honestas* which—as Jennifer Richards argues—underpins sixteenth-century humanist dialogues.[46] According to Smith's *Communicacion*, honest counsellors 'dissent and tell the truth' as if the one guaranteed the other (111^r), whilst Smith himself

---

[43] Cf. Ascham's attack on the Italianate Englishman as the 'devil incarnate' in *The Schoolmaster*, in Ascham, *Works*, iii. 156. Cf. Wilson, *Rhetorique*, 86^r.

[44] Salesbury, *Briefe and playne introduction*, $E1^v$.

[45] Martin Elsky, *Authorizing Words: Speech, Writing, and Print in the English Renaissance* (Ithaca, NY: Cornell University Press, 1989), 84.

[46] Richards, *Rhetoric and Courtliness*, 75.

continually advertised his integrity by fashioning a rough and rude persona.[47] As he commented late in life: 'my fault is plainness and that I cannot dissemble enmity or pleasure.'[48] Yet within the *Communicacion*, the Godfather, the only potential participant with a tongue acerbic enough to speak 'honestly', is muted by the physical disability of his stammer.

Despite the mood of idyllic retreat established by the dialogue's garden setting, Smith's house is only on the way to the country. The speakers' withdrawal to the country is symbolically incomplete, and the shadow of the court, and its approval, hang over the discussion. Free and open speech is consequently circumscribed through fear of backing the wrong marital horse. As narrator, Smith never participates in the discussion, unlike the knight, who recounts the initial conversation to the letter-writer in the *Commonweal*. Smith's reticence is evident from the outset. 'And whose parte tooke you[?]' F. W. asks him, before forestalling the answer with the words that he is 'a foole to aske [. . .] before you tell me the matter and argument' (97ʳ); once 'matter and argument' are supplied, F.W.'s question is forgotten. In contrast to the *Commonweal*, where definitive solutions are clearly set out by the learned doctor, in the *Communicacion*, a final authoritative opinion is withheld. Smith resigns his role as judge because 'that were a presumption indeed before my prince and without commission' (135ʳ). 'I truste her highnes shortlie will geve sentence her self and not with wordes but with dedes shewe who toke the better parte,' he states, his reference to 'dedes' indicating that the choice is between the opinions of Lovealien and Homefriend, not Spitewed, who advocates the inaction of continued celibacy. Further debate is then curtailed by the convenient appearance of that night's dinner, a humanist device most famously appearing at the end of *Utopia*, where the meal distracts Morus from arguing with Hythloday and bridges the impasse reached. Structurally, the conclusion of the *Communicacion*, like entertainments such as Philip Sidney's *Lady of May* eighteen years later, requires Elizabeth's intervention. The queen, however, denied resolution. The marriage question thus imposes an open-endedness on Smith's work. Both produced by, and mimetic of frustration, its enforced inconclusiveness prefigures the sterile, postponed, or aborted unions endemic to such later

[47] Dewar, *Smith*, 115.   [48] Ibid. 57.

Elizabethan texts as Spenser's (ultimately unfinished) *Faerie Queene*.[49]

Smith's *Communicacion* was not his first foray into debating the matrimonial options of the English monarch. In 1538, Smith and Cheke were brought to court by William Butts, the king's physician, to debate before Henry the pros and cons of a foreign match. Cheke's twentieth-century biographer Paul Strope Needham argues that this discussion was not intended to influence the king's policy, but was staged to demonstrate the 'wealth of versatile learning' of which Cambridge, Butts's alma mater, was capable.[50] There are crucial differences between debating Elizabeth's and Henry's marriage, however. When Smith and Cheke performed for Henry, he already had an heir, and a boy at that. In addition, Henry was male. Marriage could be seen as a luxury, not a necessity, and its discussion, a means of diverting the court and raising the profile of Cambridge University. Elizabeth had no heir: the need to marry was therefore urgent. As a female monarch, her choice was also more circumscribed than her father's. Since women were traditionally seen as subject to their husband, a king could marry one of his noblewomen without undermining his position; a queen marrying one of her noblemen was placed in an anomalous position: as sovereign, she was superior to her consort; as wife, inferior. A Continental match brought other problems. Where the foreign marriage of an English king posed no threat (since, as husband, he would automatically take precedence), the union of an English queen and foreign prince risked rendering England a satellite power, with its monarch and foreign policy serving alien interests, as it had under Mary Tudor.

Besides hardening some factions against a foreign (and Catholic) match, Mary's reign also sparked an open debate about the rights of female rule, demonstrated by John Knox's *First Blast of the Trumpet against the Monstrous Regiment of Women* (1558) and

---

[49] See, e.g., Colin Burrow, 'Original Fictions: Metamorphoses in *The Faerie Queene*', in Charles Martindale (ed.), *Ovid Renewed: Ovidian Influences on Literature and Art from the Middle Ages to the Twentieth Century* (Cambridge: Cambridge University Press, 1988), 99–119. Cf. the lack of resolution to the marriage question in the final act of Thomas Sackville and Thomas Norton, *Gorboduc* (1561) (Jessica Winston, 'Expanding the Political Nation: *Gorboduc* at the Inns of Court and Succession Revisited', *Early Theatre*, 8 (forthcoming)).

[50] Paul Strope Needham, 'Sir John Cheke at Cambridge and at Court', unpublished dissertation (Harvard University, 1971), 141.

John Aylmer's reply, *An Harborowe for Faithfull and Trewe Subiectes* (1559). Although ostensibly a defence of female monarchy, Aylmer's *Harborowe* reads more like an apology for it, as it preaches pragmatic resignation to God's will and the current situation. 'Better [a female monarch] in England, then any where, as it shall wel appere to him that without affection, will consider the kinde of regiment,' Aylmer argues, for, 'the regiment of Englande is not a mere Monarchie [. . .] nor a meere Oligarchie, nor Democratie, but a rule mixte of all these, wherein ech one of these haue or shoulde haue like authoritie'.[51] According to Aylmer, that is, England can survive a female monarchy because—as a polity in which the different 'sorts' are given a voice—it already has in place the necessary counterbalances to monarchical ineptitude.

As texts such as Aylmer's and Knox's undermined the authority of the female monarch, they contributed to a shift in the rhetoric of counsel. Where—as we saw in Chapter 3—Ochino depicted counsel as confidential advice, requested by the monarch, to be followed or ignored, Elizabeth's ministers saw it as a means of making policy, even if the queen had other ideas. Of course, pre-Elizabethan counsellors hoped to be heard, and complained bitterly when they were not, as texts such as *Utopia* and *Pasquil the playne* indicate. What changed was the openness and forcefulness with which Elizabeth's advisers expressed their expectations of remit and influence. Francis Knollys, for example, complained to Elizabeth in 1569 that 'it was not possible for [her] "most faithful counsellors" to govern her state well unless she could find it in herself "resolutely [to] follow their opinions in weighty affairs" '.[52] As John Guy points out, Knollys here formulates (in a 'less tactful' manner) opinions and frustrations expressed by Cecil, Elizabeth's principal minister, ten years earlier. For both men, counsellors shape policy, not the queen. Smith thought likewise, stating in *De Republica Anglorum* that female rule is tolerable only if 'such personages never do lacke the counsell of such grave and discreete men as be able to supplie all other defaultes' (65). Female rule is thus likened to minority: both the female monarch and child king

---

[51] John Aylmer, *An Harborowe for Faithfull and Trewe Subiectes, agaynst the late blowne Blaste, concerninge the Gouernment of Wemen* (Strasburg, 1559), H2ᵛ–H3ʳ.

[52] John Guy, 'Tudor Monarchy and its Critiques', in Guy (ed.), *Tudor Monarchy*, 78–109, at 95.

need a body of sagacious mentors to make decisions for them, although at least with Edward—as we saw in Chapter 3—there was a pretence of his involvement in the decision-making process. In a letter to Cecil in 1563, Smith even compresses the two states of minority and femininity, reducing the queen to a child, able to be 'used' as 'children are used, when they have gotten a piece of gold or silver, or peradventure, a knife' and, shown 'some fair printed paper, or some pretty apple [. . .,] lets fall the one to reach at the other'.[53]

Written in reaction to often pressing events, in order—as Smith saw it—to benefit the commonweal, Smith's works habitually contain a note of resistance and unwillingness to be seduced into an uncompromised rhetoric of monarchical adulation. When, in the marriage discourse, F.W. states that 'for vs that are subiectes, dewty compellethe to loue honour and obeye her, to take her parte whatsoeuer it shal please her highnes to doe in that case. But yet I can not chuse but wishe otherwise' (97ᵛ), his words indicate a difference between the expected public endorsement of monarchical policy, and the privately held (but potentially pertinent) opinion. Smith's *Communicacion* also highlights the monarch's duty to the commonweal. Lovealien, for example, embarks on an oration in the persona of England, a technique recommended for its emotive impact in rhetorical manuals such as Thomas Wilson's *Arte of Rhetorique*.[54] Within this speech, England reminds Elizabeth of the debt she 'owe[s]' her country 'to bringe forthe yonge babes' (115ʳ). To remain childless and unwed, is the implication, is to fail in sovereign 'dewtie' (115ʳ). This is not, of course, radical thinking. Smith and the interlocutors of his dialogues might see themselves as wiser than the queen: there is no suggestion that they would seek to overthrow her. Nevertheless, Smith's faith in the counsel of learned men over what he saw as the whims of an albeit highly educated woman inevitably affected his attitude towards monarchy in general. It is Smith's promotion of a limited monarchy and depiction of a 'subiectes dewty' in Smith's most famous text, *De Republica Anglorum*, that the next part of the chapter explores.

---

[53] *LP*, foreign series (1563), itm 561.   [54] Wilson, *Rhetorique*, 63ᵛ.

'THE MANER OF GOVERNEMENT OR POLICIE'[55]

'The most high and absolute power of the realme of Englande, is in the Parliament,' Smith writes in his *De Republica Anglorum* (78). This 'much-quoted statement' is highlighted by Dewar as a sentence 'beloved of historians' when examining the constitutional nature of both Smith's text and early modern England.[56] Dominated by events of the seventeenth century, however, such enquiries, searching for the causes of the Civil War, have focused on the relationship between crown and parliament and the two chapters about the English parliament at the start of Book II. Parliament, Elton points out, includes the monarch, and as Dewar argues, 'there is indeed nothing in Smith's account of Parliament which would have offended even Elizabeth's sharp sense of the Crown's authority'.[57] What has generally passed without comment is the equivocal nature of the first sixteen chapters with which Smith opens Book I. These chapters, preceding the main bulk of the text (which concentrates on the English polity), act as a theoretical introduction to alternative types of government. Far from endorsing monarchy in its purest and most absolute state, this opening section offers substitutes for, or limitations on, monarchy—such as that of conciliar government—besides those potentially provided by parliament.

The contentious nature of Smith's *De Republica Anglorum* seems to have been noted by the editor of the first printed edition, published posthumously in 1583. Dewar's painstaking editorial work, collating different manuscripts, has greatly eased comparison between these and the printed text, revealing systematic alterations to manuscript sources. The cautious approach of the 1583 editor, who consistently works to moderate controversial comments, extends to the tricky problem of resistance theory, a key dilemma of Renaissance political thought.[58] The second chapter of Book I addresses the question of 'What is just or lawe in everie

---

[55] Smith, *De Republica Anglorum*, 49.   [56] Ibid. 4.
[57] G. R. Elton, 'Parliament in the Sixteenth Century: Functions and Fortunes', *Historical Journal*, 22 (1979), 255–78, at 258; Smith, *De Republica Anglorum*, 5.
[58] See, e.g., William Tyndale, *The Obedience of a Christian Man* (1528); Thomas Starkey, *A Dialogue between Reginald Pole and Thomas Lupset*, ed. Kathleen M. Burton (London: Chatto & Windus, 1948); Allen, *History*, pt. II, ch. 2; Skinner, *Foundations*, ii.

common wealth or government' (49). Here the manuscripts analyse rightful resistance through the scenario of the 'just man' who 'for his just and true meaninge [. . .] would amend that which is amisse, and helpe the common wealth' (50). The initial statement that if this is 'contrarie to the Lawe [. . .] he be by the lawe justly condemned', is soon qualified, however, by the addition 'if he be to be accompted justly condemned who is condemned for doing contrarie to the lawe and ordinance of that part which doth commaunde'. The integrity of those in power is undermined, the implication being that laws which protect the interests of the ruling part are not necessarily just. In the printed edition, that tentative prizing apart of law and justice is curtailed:

The just man may *offend (notwithstanding his just and true meaning) when he* would amend that which is amisse, and helpe the common wealth, and doe good unto it. For in asmuch as he attempteth to doe contrarie to the Lawe which is already put, *he therefore by the lawe is justly to be condemned, because his doing is* contrarie to the lawe and ordinance of that part which doth commaunde.

The added or amended words (signalled by italics) and the clarified syntax present an unambiguous message negating the right of resistance raised in the manuscript sources.

In the passage on rightful resistance, the 1583 editor resolves linguistic ambiguities in such a way that the text is made to endorse monarchical power. Structurally, the opening sections of *De Republica Anglorum* impede further imposition of such 'clarifications', however. The chain of thought in these initial chapters is not straightforward; it continually digresses and contradicts, or revises, previous statements. Smith begins by following the traditional Aristotelian pattern, familiar from Elyot's *Gouernour*, of classifying political systems as monarchies, aristocracies, or democracies, according to who holds power. Unlike Elyot, who critiques Athenian democracy for its instability and tendency to banish or slay 'the beste citezins', Smith does not draw judgement on any of the three prototypes.[59] Each comes with its negative counterpart of tyranny, oligarchy, and anarchy (50–1). This simple model is then shown to be inadequate as Smith asserts that 'seldome or never shall you finde any common wealthe or governement which is

---

[59] Elyot, *Gouernour*, 6ᵛ.

absolutely and sincerely made of the one above named, but always mixed with an other' (52).

Six chapters on, this statement is further complicated by the introduction of an evolutionary model, which moves from this 'mixte' system back towards the 'absolute' and 'sincere' typology rejected earlier. Monarchy, aristocracy, and democracy are now presented as a sequential pattern moving from monarchy via aristocracy to democracy. England, as a monarchy, is consequently only in the initial stages of its political development. This potentially radical statement is tempered by its introduction through metaphor, or pseudo-legend, whereby each generation is associated with a different political process: the monarchical grandfather; the aristocratic uncles; the democratic cousins. Nevertheless, the passage sheds light on Smith's attitude to both political change and monarchy. Movement from one form of government to another results from the dissatisfaction of the governed with their lot as subjects. Aristocracy emerges because, after the first king's death, his 'sonnes [. . .] and brethren among themselves' did not have 'reverence to any, nor confidence of wisedome in any one of them' (60); the final stage, democracy, is brought about by the 'merites of education', which result in 'so many arising and such equalitie among them, [that] it was not possible that they should be content to be governed by a fewe' (62). There is, in other words, no hint of a God-given, natural-born right to rule. Rather, social change leads inevitably and 'natural[ly]' to political change, and once again, there is no special regard for those polities which function as monarchies. The choice of constitution is entirely pragmatic, selected to ensure the smoothest running of the body politic, just as 'a garment' is made to 'fyt to a man's bodie or a shoe [. . .] a man's foot' (63).

For Smith (as for many humanists), 'rulers were meant to serve fairly obvious, rational, intelligible, utilitarian ends', and kingship did not fulfil 'some inscrutable and divine purpose too mysterious for ordinary man to understand'.[60] Throughout *De Republica Anglorum*, there is consequently a marked indifference to the pomp and ceremony of monarchy. There are even signs of scepticism about the foundations of monarchical authority. Considering the

---

[60] Geoffrey Morris, *Political Thought in England: Tyndale to Hooker* (Oxford: Oxford University Press, 1953), 21.

etymology of the word *king* from the Anglo-Saxon *cyning*, Smith ponders the derivation of the latter: 'whether it cometh of *cen* or *ken* which betokeneth to know and understand, or *kan* or *kon* which betokeneth to be able or to have power, I can not tell' (56). In the one case, the title is a reflection of wisdom; in the other, simply of the fact of rule, regardless of ability. It is this awareness of the monarch's potential fallibility that leads Smith to stress the role of counsel.

Smith's belief in the benefits of counsel is not limited to a period of female or minority rule. As we saw earlier, it was 'common consent and counsel' in *De pronuntiatione* that was used to authorize reformed Greek pronunciation and challenge Gardiner's autocratic rule, which overrode what Smith terms 'freedom of speech' ('libertatem sonandi', 26^v) and undermined the liberties proper to scholars as 'citizens of the university' ('in Academia Ciues', 25^v). Countering Smith's arguments in his reply, Gardiner is consequently careful to undermine Smith's rhetoric of counsel by describing the reformers' actions as 'the presumptuous behaviour of private individuals' ('priuatorum temeritati').[61] The political— no less than the academic—commonwealth needs free and open debate amongst its citizens to resist the 'tyranny' that, as history teaches, inevitably results from absolute power. It is therefore congruent with this commitment to balancing power that Smith elaborates in *De Republica Anglorum* on the metaphor of the body politic, explaining the concept of the mixed constitution through recourse to humoral theory. Just as 'the governements of common wealthes be thus divided', so too 'wise men have divided for understandinges sake and fantasied iiii. simple bodies which they call elementes [. . .], and in a mans bodie foure complexions or temperatures, as cholericke, sanguine, phlegmatique, and melancolique' (52). In the same way in which the human body cannot be comprised of 'one utterly perfect' complexion 'without mixation', so too with commonwealths. If we take this metaphor to its logical conclusion, a mixed constitution is not only more probable; as Aylmer argued in the *Harborowe*, its varied composition is also the source of its health, which is ensured by achieving and maintaining balance between the different humours (H3^r). Within monarchy,

<hr/>

[61] Gardiner, 'Reply to Smith', BL Royal App. 87, 35^r; trans. by Danielsson in *De recta et emendata linguae graecae pronuntiatione*, 207.

therefore, there is room and need for a 'mixte' government which relies on the magistracy of Smith's 'grave and discreete men' to 'supplie all other defaultes' of their sovereign (65). This need is all the greater, but not unique, under a female monarch.

Smith's depiction of the 'mixte' monarchy goes further than advocating an aristocracy of politic counsellors. One telling revision to the 1583 edition comes in chapter 9, when dealing with the source of royal authority. According to the manuscripts, the monarch 'helde of God and hymself, his people and sword, the crowne' (56). The printed version revises this, substituting the words 'held of God to himselfe, and by his sword his people and crowne'. The people, rather than helping the king hold the crown, are now held by that king along with his crown through the power of the sword. The mutual responsibility of monarch and people, found in the manuscripts but negated in the printed edition, is reflected in Smith's definition of commonwealth, which is based on popular volition. 'A common wealth'—in Smith's terminology—is 'a society or common doing of a multitude of free men collected together and united by common accord and covenauntes among themselves, for the conservation of themselves aswell in peace as in warre' (57).[62] Without that long-term commitment to mutual benefit, the commonwealth cannot exist, 'for properly an host of men is not called a common wealth but abusive, because that they are collected for a time and for a fact'. Neither does it exist when its members are devoid of any voice or ability to exercise self-interest, for:

if one man had as some of the old Romanes had [. . .] v. thousande or x. thousande bondmen whome he ruled well, though they dwelled all in one citie, or were distributed into diverse villages, yet that were no common wealth: for the bondman hath no communion with his master, the wealth of the Lord is onely sought for, not the profit of the slave or bondman.

Liberty—coexistent with monarchy—thus underpins the very existence of the English commonwealth.

Smith's belief in political participation, found within the *Commonweal*, is displayed within *De Republica Anglorum* by both Smith's endorsement of the need for counsel and his account of the

---

[62] Cf. 'when many cities, boroughs and villages were by their common and mutuall consent for their conservation ruled by that one and first father of them all, it was called a nation or kingdome' (Smith, *De Republica Anglorum*, 59).

English polity, which details the workings of various legal and executive bodies, staffed by a body of publicly and politically engaged Englishmen. *De Republica Anglorum* also shares with the *Commonweal* a similar message of political engagement at all social levels. In 1563, the year before Smith began compiling his *De Republica Anglorum*, Lawrence Humphrey published *The Nobles, or of Nobility*. Humphrey's book, the subtitle of which covers 'the original nature, dutyes, high and Christian institucion therof', promotes the traditional view of the nobility as the rightful 'piller and staye of all commen weales' (A3^r). Aimed, like Elyot's *Gouernour*, at the nobility, it endeavours to impress upon aristocratic parents the necessity of educating their children, lest they lose their time-established place in government. Smith's work, in contrast, fails to strike this reactionary note. Drawing on a draft of William Harrison's description 'Of degrees of People in the Commonwealth of England', which appeared in the 1577 edition of Holinshed's *Chronicles*, Smith initially categorizes 'Gentlemen' as 'those whom their blood and race doth make noble and knowne' (70). However, 'they be made good cheape in England', and the definition is amended to include 'whosoever studieth the lawes of the realme, who studieth in the universities, who professeth liberall sciences, and to be shorte, who can live idly and without manuall labour, and will beare the port, charge and countenance of a gentleman' (71–2). Gentility does not run in the blood: it is a state that can be achieved by education or financial independence. As Keith Wrightson describes, by the later sixteenth century, 'the distinguishing mark of the gentleman became the possession not only of wealth and leisure but also of the breeding and personal virtues necessary for government': 'gentlemen were defined as governors, and true gentility as the quality and capacity to govern'.[63] The sixteenth century also saw a 'marked numerical expansion' in the class of ' "mere" gentlemen', Smith (son of a 'struggling', small-time Cambridgeshire sheep farmer) among them.[64] It was to education—which Smith finds responsible for the shift from aristocracy to democracy in chapter fourteen of his *De*

[63] Keith Wrightson, 'Estates, Degrees and Sorts: Changing Perceptions of Society in Tudor and Stuart England', in Penelope J. Corfield (ed.), *Language, History and Class* (Oxford: Blackwell, 1991), 30–52, at 38.

[64] Ibid. 39; Dewar, *Smith*, 2.

Republica Anglorum—that Smith owed his social rise. The workings of Smith's res publica are thus shown adapting to historical necessity and the conditions encountered during his own political career. Even the position of the 'fourth sort of men which doe not rule' and, unlike the yeomen class, 'have no voice nor authoritie in our common wealth', is subjected to immediate revision: 'and yet they be not altogether neglected. For in cities and corporate townes for default of yeomen, they are faine to make their enquests of such manner of people,' Smith concedes (76–7). In villages, meanwhile, 'they be commonly made Churchwardens, alecunners, and manie times Constables, which office toucheth more the common wealth, and at the first was not imployed uppon such lowe and base persons'.

Smith's pragmatic attention to the historical moment is used to distinguish *De Republica Anglorum* from previous examples of commonwealth literature. The polity described is 'not in that sort as *Plato* made, [. . .] nor as *Syr Thomas More* his *Utopia* feigned' (144). Rather, it is placed specifically 'as Englande standeth and is governed at this day the xxviii of March *Anno* 1565'. Where *Utopia* claims on its frontispiece to investigate 'the best state of the common wealth' ('De Optimo Reipublicae Statu'), any intimation of excellence is omitted from Smith's title. It is simply the 'maner of governement or policie' of England that it announces (49). The description of England that follows does not, as Harrison's, branch out into geographical, historical, and linguistic topoi. It remains closely focused on the institutions of government and the active role of Englishmen within them: a commonwealth neither impinging on royal authority, nor challenging social hierarchies, but nevertheless one which 'that staunch republican Machiavelli— equally no democrat—would have recognized [as . . .] a species of republic'.[65] It is here again worth commenting on the choice of title. While the English subtitle refers to a monarchy ('realme') of England, the Latin conversely delineates a *Republica Anglorum*: a commonwealth of Englishmen (women do not figure in Smith's political scheme, with the regrettable exception of female monarchs). Yet Smith's title does not conceal a discrepancy: it indicates the function of English government in practice. England was a monarchy, and yet the monarchical system allowed—and even

65 Collinson, 'Monarchical Republic', 114.

relied on—a measure of devolved power, which enabled men to perform their civic duty in the public domain, serving as magistrates, alderman, jurymen, down to Smith's aleconners and church wardens.[66] As Patrick Collinson argues, 'by defining England as a realm, Smith was not denying its political status as a commonwealth, even as a kind of republic, a term not yet incompatible with monarchy'.[67]

An awareness, and acceptance, of change permeates *De Republica Anglorum*, from Smith's revised opinions on gentlemen and 'the fourth sort of men' to his reflections on the evolution of commonwealths, where 'mutations and changes of fashions of governement of common wealthes be naturall, and do not alwayes come of ambition or malice' (62). Even the unswervingness desirable in the law (the legitimating force for every 'forme of governement') can only ever be approximate, and 'the right rule' is 'whereby [. . .] he [is] to be reckoned to make his worke straightest who goeth neerest to the straightnesse of yt' (49). The pragmatics of rule, and the need to adapt to the varying circumstances of government, are of more import than absolutism and ideology. Such flexibility has an added resonance in the context of Elizabethan England, where—besides the perceived undesirability of a female monarch—the practitioners of government were increasingly faced with the likelihood of a dramatic 'mutation' in government, and the prospect of a (temporarily) monarchless country should the heirless Elizabeth die without naming her successor. In a lecture fittingly called after Smith's *De Republica Anglorum*, Collinson argues that 'with the stream of Tudor blood running dry' Elizabethan statesmen—such as Cecil, Smith's former pupil—were quite capable of conceptualizing England as a sovereign state: 'an acephalous commonwealth in which the great offices of state and the institutions of consultation and government, council and

---

[66] See Phil Withington, *The Politics of Commonwealth: Citizens and Freemen in Early Modern England* (Cambridge: Cambridge University Press, 2005).

[67] Collinson, '*De Republica Anglorum*', 17. Francis Bacon provides an early example (1626) of defining *republic*—in contradistinction to *monarchy*—as a polity in which power rests in the elected representatives of the people. Bacon writes, 'it may be, in civil states, a republic is a better policy than a kingdom' (cited by *OED*, 'republic', 2a). The use of *republic* as a synonym for *commonweal* (a term including monarchy) continued well into the 17th cent., however (e.g. H.G., *Scanderbeg Redivivus*, 1684: 'The Republick might be highly endangered by an Inter-Regnum', cited by *OED*, 'republic', 1).

parliament, would continue in being, as if there were no hiatus'.[68] Smith's detailed analysis in *De Republica Anglorum* of the workings of an English commonwealth that focuses, not on the monarch, but on institutions such as the law courts is thus consistent with the Elizabethan interest in 'conservative republicanism' that—as Stephen Alford has shown—dates back to the 1560s.[69] While such conservative republicanism does not seek to depose the monarch, it does grant the country sovereignty, seeing it as an immortal body in whose name, and on whose behalf, government is conducted.

Placing *De Republica Anglorum* in the context of these anxieties about the continuance of the English commonwealth is also to position it within an ongoing, and urgent, dialogue about government. Towards the end of the final chapter, Smith addresses the reader:

> So that whether I writ true or not, it is easie to be seene with eies (as a man would say) and felt with handes. Wherfore this being as a project or table of a common wealth truly laid before you, not fained by putting a case: let us compare it with common wealthes, which be at this day in *esse*, or doe remaine discribed in true histories, especially in such pointes wherein the one differeth from the other, to see who hath taken the righter, truer, and more commodious way to governe the people aswell in warre as in peace. (144)

Dewar interprets this as indicating that Smith intended his book on the English polity to be the first part in a multi-volumed work.[70] In contrast, I would argue that Smith is here following the humanist pattern—as found in *Utopia*—of opening out a work at its end to encourage ongoing discussion. The end of a book does not signal the end of debate: it is there to prompt further conversation that (ideally) will lead to action. It is precisely this sort of self-examination and reflection—in which comparative study leads to knowledge of the 'best' or most 'commodious' form of government—in which counsellors should be involved. The discursive ending to *De Republica Anglorum* is thus entirely consistent with Smith's

---

⁶⁸ Collinson, '*De Republica Anglorum*', 18–19.
⁶⁹ Stephen Alford, 'Reassessing William Cecil in the 1560s', in Guy (ed.), *Tudor Monarchy*, 233–52, at 247; cf. Alford, *The Early Elizabethan Polity: William Cecil and the British Succession Crisis, 1558–1569* (Cambridge: Cambridge University Press, 1998).   ⁷⁰ Dewar, *Smith*, 161.

commitment in his other works to dialogue as an instrument of policy.

'BY REASON OF OUR GREAT FAMILIARITEE': SMITH AND HIS READERS[71]

It is a paradox that Smith, advocate of wide political participation, was predominantly a manuscript writer, a form that necessarily limits readership: in the case of the *Commonweal*, he restricts this to an audience of two, 'between us two to be weighed only and considered and not to be published abroad' (12–13). Of all Smith's works, only *A Letter sent by I.B. gentleman* (1571) was printed close to the time of its inception. *De scriptione* and *De pronuntiatione* were published in 1568, over two decades after their composition; the *Commonweal* and *De Republica Anglorum* were published posthumously (in 1581 and 1583 respectively); the *Communicacion*, Smith's penitential psalms, and the treatise on the wages of a Roman foot soldier remained in manuscript throughout the early modern period.[72] This last section seeks to explain Smith's restrictive publishing policy by arguing that Smith's works were disseminated in a format designed to suit their target audience.

Despite its anonymity, the *Letter* is—as Dewar argues—almost certainly Smith's work, not least because he was immediately accused of being the author by the Privy Council.[73] Its form, a reported dialogue, is akin to that of the *Commonweal* and *Communicacion*, and as a dialogue retold in a letter, it is particularly close to the former. Like Spenser's *View*, which concentrates on a later stage in the Irish colonial project, the conversation in the *Letter* occurs between someone newly returned from Ireland (supposedly Smith's son) and a greenhorn, whose misconceptions are gradually corrected. Within the discourse, as in Spenser's *View*, the more experienced speaker lays out a plan for the subjugation of—in the case of the *Letter*—not the whole of Ireland, but the Ards Peninsula, a process of colonization that is seen as part of

---

[71] Thomas Smith, *A Letter sent by I.B. gentleman* (1571), A2ʳ.
[72] Smith's *Certaigne Psalmes* (BL Royal 17A. xvii) is now published in his *Literary and Linguistic Works*, i, ed. Danielsson.
[73] Dewar, *Smith*, 159.

God's plan for his English nation. 'I iudge surely, that God did make apte and prepare this nation for such a purpose,' 'Smith' declares, describing how Ireland offers opportunities to relieve a growing English population and excess of landless younger sons: 'let vs therefore vse the persuasions which *Moses* vsed to *Israel*, [. . .] and tell them they shall goe to possess a lande that floweth with milke and honey' (D1^r).

The Ards Peninsula is held up as a place of Utopian possibility. 'How say you now, haue I not set forth to you another *Eutopia*?' 'Smith' asks, amending the ambiguous spelling of Utopia (Ou-topia, No Place) to Eu-topia, Good Place (E1^r). Even the geography has fortuitous Utopian resonances. Jutting into the sea, the peninsula is—like Utopia—protected to some extent from the troublesome and polluting mainland. Where Utopus, the first king, physically isolates the peninsula of Abraxas by cutting a channel through the connecting landmass, Smith is forced to content himself with fortifying a five-mile stretch, 'that straight once kept and defended, all the reste of the Countrie must of necessitie become quiet and safe' (C1^v). There is a crucial difference between More's *Utopia* and Smith's Irish project, however. Like More, Smith recognizes that self-interest is an unavoidable part of human nature. 'Men are more moved by peculiar gaine: than of respecte they haue to common profite,' he writes (C4^v). Unlike More, he does not despair: as in the *Commonweal*, he capitalizes on it. The revenue from the frontier lands is to be given to the soldiers who defend it, motivating them to do their job effectively.

The *Letter* is presented in the language of *amicitia*. The discourse contained in I.B.'s letter sent 'unto his very friend and master' (A1^r) and 'so singuler freende', R.C. (A2^r), is itself the product of 'great familiaritee' between I.B. and the younger Thomas Smith, the alleged interlocutor. The *Letter*, however, targets a far wider audience, both as a defence of Smith senior, who (I.B. indicates) fears he is being 'defaced' in his absence in France (A2^v), and as a form of gathering support for a project that, as Smith's correspondence reveals, was in danger of stalling.[74] The discourse is therefore followed by a direct appeal for volunteers to accompany the younger Smith to Ireland and participate in the colonization of the Ards, also published as a

[74] Dewar, *Smith*, 159.

separate broadsheet entitled *The offer and order given furthe by Sir Thomas Smythe knighte, and Thomas Smyth his sonne, vnto such as be willing to accompanie the sayd Thomas Smyth the sonne to his voyage for the inhabiting some partes of the North of Irelande.*[75] The printer Henry Binneman's shop here becomes part of the recruitment plan, as interested readers are invited to 'resorte into Pauls churchyard to the signe of the Sun' in order to inspect the 'Letters Patents' and 'Indentures of Couenauntes' legitimating the enterprise (H2^r).

Smith needed print to access a wide, general audience for his Irish *Letter* in order to attract personnel and financial support for his Ards campaign, and the *Letter* has been credited as 'the first direct printed publicity in England for any business venture'.[76] Similarly, it is clear why Smith's penitential psalms and 'other prayers' should have circulated in their chosen medium, what seems to have been—unlike the much copied *Communicacion*—a single manuscript copy. This series of psalm translations, prayers, and psalm-inspired poems was written during Smith's imprisonment in the Tower in 1549 in the aftermath of Dudley's coup and the fall of Protector Somerset, Smith's patron. Despite the harsh assessment of their twentieth-century editor, Bror Danielsson, these poetic experiments in various forms of versification and metre are not without merit. At times, there are even hints of affinities with Thomas Wyatt, particularly in the two 'other' psalms (Smith's own compositions, rather than translations). Drawing on psalmic idiom, the first paints a picture of court corruption akin to that found in Wyatt's third epistolary satire, 'A spending hand', in which wrongdoing is cynically presented as the way to get ahead in a world where, as Smith describes, 'the wicked flaterer speedith best' (35). The second reflects the fickleness of courtly favour and lurking death memorably described in Wyatt's translation of Martial's epigram, 'Stand whoso list upon the slipper top', where—in Smith's words—even in the courtier's moment of triumph 'yet maie the ax, stand next the dore' (37).

[75] Ibid. 157. Dewar mentions one surviving copy of this broadsheet, in possession of the Society of Antiquaries. She does not indicate that surviving copies are also appended to the *Letter*.
[76] D. B. Quinn, 'Sir Thomas Smith and the Beginnings of English Colonial Theory', *Proceedings of the American Philosophical Society*, 89 (1945), 543–60, at 551.

The adaptations Smith makes to his biblical translations transform the Psalms into a personal expression of fear and resentment. The Psalms of David are—as Surrey shows—a perfect vehicle for prison writing, with their references to enforced enclosure in cramped and dark conditions; their vehement calls for retribution; the ever present terror of predatory enemies; and their protestations against slander, erroneous judgement, and a treacherous friend. To compound these (in)felicitous parallels with his own position in 1549, Smith also manipulates the tenses of his translations. Where, for example, Psalm 142 in the Book of Common Prayer (1549) reads 'I cryed unto the Lord with my voyce' (translating the Vulgate 'Voce mea ad dominum clamaui'), Smith's version follows the incorrect translation of the Great Bible and renders the line in an ongoing present: 'To thee o Lorde I crie and call, and my voice I do exalte' (18).[77] Similarly, whereas the biblical David thanks the Lord because he 'hast not delyuered me ouer into the handes of the ennemye' but 'hast set [his] fete in a large rowme' ('non conclusisti me in manu inimici statuisti in loco spacioso pedes meos'), Smith writes in the future tense: 'Thou wilt not shit me in myn enimies hand, but keepe me as a charge / And set my feete where they shall stand, abrode again at large' (21).[78] This psalmist (unlike the biblical one) still awaits liberation.

Smith's translation of the Psalms thus accentuates the parallels with his own situation. Where David is as much in search of spiritual as bodily freedom, Smith's psalmist focuses on physical liberation, recurrently choosing to translate the ambiguous Latin *anima* as 'life', not 'soul'. Smith's 'keepe thou my lief both sure and fast' (20) contrasts with the biblical 'kepe my soul' ('custodi animam meam'),[79] whilst Smith replaces the biblical request to 'bryng my soule out of prieson' ('Educ de carcere a[n]i[m]am meam') with 'Of prison, o Lord, bring my bodie out' (18).[80] A number of Smith's free translations arise from the need to fill his hexameters. Nevertheless, it is significant how he chooses to do this, taking the opportunity of extra words to depict his own position. It is consequently not

[77] *Quincuplex Psalterium Gallicum. Rhomamum. Hebraicum. Vetus. Conciliatum*, facsimile de l'edition de 1513 (Geneva: Librairie Droz, 1979), 222v, henceforth referred to 'Vulgate Psalms'; *The Byble in Englyshe* (1539) (also known as 'The Great Bible'), 231v.   [78] Vulgate Psalms, 44; *Byble*, 191ᵛ.
[79] Vulgate Psalms, 124; *Byble*, 202ᵛ.
[80] Vulgate Psalms, 223ʳ; *Byble*, 213ᵛ.

merely an 'unjust word' ('verbum iniquum') about which Smith's psalmist complains.[81] Rather, he follows the Great Bible by referring to 'a wicked sentence thei haue giuen', placing the affliction in a distinctly legalistic framework (23).[82] Smith's additions even blame someone's slander for his current incarceration: the 'craftie deceitfull tongue, that furste hath brought me hither' (19).

Rivkah Zim has described how Smith's 'other psalmes' do 'not function as a vehicle for the expression of personal devotion'. Rather, they reveal 'a devout man articulating personal reactions to his situation'.[83] The same could be said of his biblical translations. Yet the Psalms and 'other poems' are not private meditations. Their posturing is for benefit of other eyes. Great stress is placed on the psalmist's innocence, his unjust imprisonment, and persecution as the victim of slander. Smith's prayers and collects, whilst continuing his campaign on behalf of those, such as himself, 'wrongfully sclaundered and oppressed by false witnesses' (32), judiciously include a prayer for the realm, which—as in the Irish *Letter*— comments on the special relationship between God and the English nation: 'This realme, o Lord, shuld be and is a chosen Realme to thee' (33). That the work should be for more than Smith's eyes alone is indicated by the appearance of the manuscript. This is no private, scribbled memo. It is a presentation document, in writing remarkably neat and well spaced for Smith's habitually cramped hand, with a title page laying out the circumstances of the poems' production: *Certaigne Psalmes or Songues of David translated into Englishe meter, by Sir Thomas Smith, Knight, then Prisoner in the Tower of London, with other prayers and songues by him made to pas the tyme there. 1549.* Nevertheless, the transparently autobiographical nature of these poems and prayers—and particularly his jibe at the ennoblement of Dudley and his supporters, 'this day made new Duke, Marques, Earle, or Baron' (37)—renders a restricted manuscript audience highly desirable.

The attention to the time and place of composition found on the title page of *Certaigne Psalmes* is typical of Smith. I have already noted the peculiarly exact date for *De Republica Anglorum* (28 March 1565). When *De pronuntiatione* is eventually printed in

[81] Vulgate Psalms, 63[r].
[82] *Byble*, 194[r].
[83] Rivkah Zim, *English Metrical Psalms*, 78.

1568, care is taken to preserve its original form and it is still presented as a letter to now dead Gardiner, with the original dating and location: Cambridge, 12 Aug 1542 (48ᵛ). *De scriptione*, meanwhile, not only refers back to the 1540s and the first draft, produced during the controversy about Greek pronunciation; it also makes a point of recording the occasion of its major revision, two years previously, a period that is in turn memorialized by reference to a specific date eighteen months earlier:

> When I was in France as the Queen's ambassador with other ambassadors of kings and commonwealths, at the hot baths of Bourbon l'Archambault, a year and nine months after the treaty with the king of France at Troyes [11 April 1564] at the time when the French king by his edict cleared the head of the French navy [. . .] from the suspicion of having murdered the Duke of Guise.

> Cùm in Gallia cum caeteris legatis Regum, & rerum publicarum pro nostra Regina legatus agebam ad calida Balnea Burbonis Archembaldici, anno & novem mensibus post icta cum Francorum Rege foedera Trecensia, eo tempore quo Gallorum Rex per suum edictum suspicione Guisianae caedis liberavit Praefectum Galliae maritimum [. . .].   (4ʳ)

Even as these linguistic texts belatedly emerge from manuscript, therefore, they can be seen attempting to retain the more intimate groupings within which, and for which, they were produced. These traces of the 'coterie' are all the more important to preserve—as we saw in Chapter 3—as the texts are released to a larger audience of anonymous strangers, and it is telling these same strains are apparent in the printed Irish *Letter*, with its repeated emphasis on *amicitia* in a text seeking wide circulation.

Smith's works demonstrate his recurrent use of humanist learning to address the particular circumstances of Edwardian or Elizabethan England and attempt to influence current policy, 'giving counsell for the better administration thereof'.[84] Even the seemingly arcane subject matter of Smith's tract on the wages of a Roman foot soldier 'reveals a grasp of monetary and coinage problems in his own as well as the ancient world', whilst—on a more personal level—*Certaigne Psalmes* advocates his innocence in a particular moment of crisis.[85] It is consequently clear that Smith chose to circulate his work in the medium—manuscript or print—

---

[84] Smith, *De Republica Anglorum*, 144.   [85] Dewar, *Smith*, 4.

that fitted most closely with the intended audience of his work. That only the *Letter* is made immediately accessible to a wider public would also indicate that when advising on policy—the express aim of all his works—Smith was concerned to address those in power, the exception being the Irish *Letter*, which, for once, needed public interest. The majority of his works therefore circulated in manuscript among statesman like Cecil: certainly in Smith's last years—when forced to retire from public life by what proved to be a fatal illness (probably throat cancer)—he wrote to Cecil asking him to return some of these works.[86] Smith's habitual recourse to his books and learned but politically engaged treatises in times of enforced inactivity (be it political exile after 1549, when the *Commonweal* was produced, or *De Republica Anglorum*, compiled during a slow-moving embassy in France) also demonstrates his commitment to the public use of scholarship. If he could not be involved in person, then at least his works could play a part. In form and content, Smith's humanist learning was closely engaged with, and tried to solve, problems facing the English polity. As such, it shows a narrowing of focus from More's Continental and often abstracted humanism consistent with Smith's conciliar vision of 'grave and discreete men' striving for 'the commonweal of this realm of England'.

[86] BL Harleian 6992, itm 20, cited in Dewar, *Smith*, 188.

5

Thomas Wilson and the Limits of English Rhetoric

If the worthines of eloquence may moue vs, what worthier thing can there be, then with a word to winne cities and whole countries? [. . .] Boldly then may I aduenture [. . .] that no man oughte to be withoute it, whiche either shall beare rule ouer manye, or muste haue to do wyth the matters of a Realme.[1]

The preceding two chapters have explored the ways in which William Thomas and Thomas Smith translated Italian and classical learning to Edwardian and Elizabethan England. This chapter turns to the works of Thomas Wilson, another 'vernacular' humanist who, after editing one early work—a collection of Latin and Greek elegies on the sons of Katharine Brandon, dowager Duchess of Suffolk—applied his classical learning to the promotion of native eloquence.[2] Throughout his career, Wilson's path intertwined with that of Smith. During the 1540s, they were both prominent Cambridge scholars and associates of John Cheke, with whom they shared a commitment to reforming the English language. Under Elizabeth I, in 1571, they led the interrogation of Thomas Howard, Duke of Norfolk, and his servants in the aftermath of Howard's plot to marry Mary Queen of Scots. During that period, they established a lasting friendship, Smith's thanks to Wilson for letters written 'so fully and clearly' demonstrating both affection and a mutual belief in lucid prose style.[3] Both men were also (by 1558) civil lawyers, and were similarly dedicated to the

---

[1] Wilson, *Rhetorique*, A1ᵛ.

[2] Thomas Wilson, *Vita et Obitus Duorum Fratrum Suffolciensium, Henrici et Caroli Brandoni* (1551). Wilson also contributed a Latin epigram to *De obitu doctissimi et sanctissimi theologi Martini Buceri*, edited by John Cheke (1551).

[3] Cited in Dewar, *Smith*, 135.

public, and national, application of their learning. Nevertheless, where Smith's works promote a participatory view of governance, Wilson's adopt a sternly authoritarian tone.

Wilson looks at people and finds little that is admirable, writing in the early 1570s that 'men be worldely, selfe louers, geuen for the most parte to euil, full of hypocrisie, & dissimulation, & very loth to do good, when they see no profite folowe, and vnwyllynge to be such, as they are bounde and commaunded to bee'.[4] His works consequently seek to unify the nation by establishing standards of thought and behaviour. In the process, Wilson promoted the rhetor as an authoritarian figure, and rhetoric as a means of instilling obedience in a restive population. This top-down view—in which rhetoric is primarily intended for those in government—is complemented by Wilson's growing dissatisfaction with the philosophy and terminology of 'commonweal'. Wilson is increasingly drawn towards vocabulary of the 'state', which focuses on how the commonweal is governed rather than commonweal itself.[5] The second half of the chapter addresses the inevitable disappointment of Wilson's apparent confidence in eloquence as a tool of government. It examines how Wilson's regulatory overstructure is undercut by the survival, within his works, of the Lucianic heritage of writers such as More, with their playful ability to see both sides of a question and articulate scepticism about the efficacy of humanist ideals and learning in the business of government in practice.

'TO PERSWADE WITH REASON, ALL MEN TO SOCIETYE'[6]

In 1553 Wilson published *The Arte of Rhetorique*, a text—modelled on manuals of classical rhetoric—designed to teach English eloquence by explaining rhetorical terms and strategies, and providing examples of their use or abuse. Barnabe Barnes later credited the book with 'redress[ing] / Our English barbarism'.[7] The accolade cannot be ascribed to sycophancy: Wilson was twelve

---

[4] Thomas Wilson, *A discourse vppon vsurye* (1572), 204[r].
[5] *OED* 28a.   [6] Wilson, *Rhetorique*, A3[v].
[7] Barnabe Barnes, prefatory sonnet in Gabriel Harvey, *Pierces Superogation or a New Praise of an Old Ass* (1593), ***3[v].

years dead by the time of its inscription (1593), and his *Rhetorique* had seen no fewer than seven editions, rendering it 'one of the most successful sixteenth-century books of its kind in England'.[8] It was still an authority in 1619, sixty-six years after its first publication, when Milton's friend Alexander Gill cited its strictures against inkhorn terms.[9] Twentieth-century critics have attributed the text with shaping the five-part schema traditional to English rhetorical thought, and held up its author as the first English writer to strive at 'sustaining connections between prose and speech, on the one hand, and between prose and the faculty of thought, on the other'.[10]

Despite the attention applied to the *Rhetorique*, however, the work should be seen as a companion to Wilson's more neglected treatise, *The Rule of Reason*, a handbook on logic, published two years previously in 1551. Together, the *Rhetorique* and *Reason* stand as a diptych of reason and rhetoric, where:

> Rhetorique at large paintes wel the cause,
> And makes that seme right gay,
> Whiche Logique spake but at a worde.[11]

For this close coupling of logic and rhetoric, and the texts of the *Rhetorique* and *Reason* themselves, Wilson is indebted to classical authors, including Cicero and Quintilian, whose *Institutio Oratoria* provides a major source for the *Rhetorique*, and for whom logical argument was necessary for oratory.[12] That link between logic and rhetoric is also reflected in the order in which the books were produced. The *Reason* was written with the encouragement of its printer, Richard Grafton;[13] the *Rhetorique*, at the

---

[8] Peter E. Medine, *Thomas Wilson* (Boston: Twayne, 1986), 55.

[9] Alexander Gill, *Logonomia Anglica* (1619), B3[r]. Gill taught at St Paul's when Milton was a pupil, but was never Milton's master.

[10] Quentin Skinner, *Reason and Rhetoric in the Philosophy of Hobbes* (Cambridge: Cambridge University Press, 1996), 53; Janel M. Mueller, *The Native Tongue and the Word: Developments in English Prose Style, 1380–1580* (Chicago: University of Chicago Press, 1984), 350.

[11] Thomas Wilson, *The Rule of Reason* (1551), B2[r].

[12] Quintilian, *Institutio Oratoria*, I. x. 37; other key sources are Cicero's *De Inventione* and the apocryphal *Ad Herennium* (Thomas O. Sloane, *Donne, Milton, and the End of Humanist Rhetoric* (Berkeley: University of California Press, 1985), 305 n). Cf. William Howell, *Logic and Rhetoric in England, 1500–1700* (Princeton: Princeton University Press, 1956), 12–31, 98–110.

[13] Wilson, *Reason*, A4[r]; Howell, *Logic and Rhetoric*, 13.

instigation of another, more important patron, John Dudley, Earl of Warwick (son of William Thomas's patron, John Dudley, Duke of Northumberland) in direct response to the earlier book. As Wilson reminds Dudley, 'It pleased you [. . .] earnestlye to wyshe that ye myghte one daye see the Preceptes of Rhetorique sette forthe by me in Englyshe, as I hadde erste done the Rules of Logique' (A2ʳ).

Reason and rhetoric might appear an orthodox academic pair; nevertheless, their treatment at Wilson's hand is highly politicized. Like William Thomas, Wilson translates his sources. On his pages, classical learning is not merely rendered into English; it is 'brought across' (*trans-latum*) and relocated in an English context. The *Rhetorique* and *Reason*, conceived at the height of the Edwardian Reformation by a man who belonged to Cheke's circle of Cambridge reformers, are products of an overtly antipapist mood. Illustrative examples teaching the parts of logic, for example, allude to key doctrinal controversies: the legality of married priests; justification by faith alone; an English Bible; papal authority; divine presence in the sacrament; worshipping images and saints; purgatory and masses for the dead.[14] Wilson habitually frames his explanations of logic and rhetoric in antipapist terms and seizes every opportunity for ridiculing the papacy, as in the following passage from the *Rhetorique* explaining the necessity of relevance. 'Would not a man thinke him mad that hauyng an earnest errand from London to Douer, would take it the next way to ride first into Northfolke, next into Essex, & last into Kent?' Wilson asks: 'And yet assuredly many an vnlearned & witlesse man hath straied in his talke much farther a great deale, yea truely as farre, as hence to Rome gates' (48ʳ). 'Errand'—from the Latin *errare* (to err or stray)—assumes its gerund form, becoming a wandering into wrong-headedness represented simply by the word 'Rome'. The implications of this equation between Englishness, straight-thinking, and Protestantism are still more explicit within the *Reason*, where to be English is to be logical and see through the fug of papist paraphernalia. 'For we Englyshe men knowe,' Wilson declares, '(not only by heare say, but also by good experience) that custome is the mother, and the sucke geuer vnto all error' (T5ʳ). If 'we Englyshe men knowe' to reject the erroneous tyranny of

---

¹⁴ Wilson, *Reason*, O2ᵛ; <u>I6ᵛ</u>; <u>L8ʳ</u>; Q3ᵛ; R2ᵛ–R3ʳ; S2ᵛ; T2ʳᵛ; T4ᵛ.

custom—a word which within both the *Rhetorique* and *Reason*
holds strongly papist connotations—then to accept it becomes
evidence of un-Englishness.[15] The all-encompassing term 'we
Englyshe men' renders subscription to reformed religious opinions
as much a requirement of citizenship as adherence to the laws of
the land, and it is significant that Wilson's misguided wanderer
heads first into Norfolk, cradle of Kett's 1549 rebellion.

That these texts brought charges of heresy on their author is
proof enough of their controversial nature. After fleeing England in
the reign of Mary, Wilson settled in Italy, first in relatively tolerant
Padua, where he met his old Cambridge associates Cheke and
Thomas Hoby. In 1556, however, Wilson moved to Rome, probably for financial reasons after the death of his patron (and possible
pupil), the Catholic Edward Courtenay, removed a regular source
of income.[16] At Rome, Wilson acted as advocate in a suit over a
contested marriage involving Agnes Woodhall, ward of the
Brandons, his former patrons. This employment gained Wilson the
enmity of Mary's ambassador, Edward Carne, and a series of royal
summons back to England, which Wilson ignored.[17] Wilson's time
in Rome coincided with the escalation of Paul IV's campaign
against heretical books, which doubled the number of authors
listed in the 1554 Index of forbidden books and in particular
increased the prohibition of vernacular literature.[18] Possibly as
denounced by Cardinal Pole, Wilson was arrested in Rome in
1558. Charged with heresy on the basis of 'this booke of
Rhetorique, and the Logike also', he was convicted and imprisoned, in the inquisitorial prison on Via di Ripetta.[19] Wilson alludes
to these events in the prologue to the 1560 edition of the
Rhetorique in which he states his refusal to amend the book or
become involved in its republication, declaring, with a liturgical-

[15] For negative connotations of *custom*, see Lawrence Manley, *Convention:
1500–1750* (Cambridge, Mass.: Harvard University Press, 1980), 67–90.
[16] Medine, *Wilson*, 19. Wilson also delivered Courtenay's funeral oration (in
Latin) (John Strype (ed.), *Ecclesiastical Memorials, relating chiefly to religion, and
the reformation of it*, 3 vols. (Oxford: Clarendon Press, 1822), iii, pt. 2, 420–7).
[17] *Calendar of State Papers, Foreign Series, of the Reign of Mary, 1553–1558*
(London: Public Record Office, 1861), itms 685, 686, 692, 765, 786, 791, 810.
[18] Paul F. Grendler, *The Roman Inquisition and the Venetian Press, 1540–1605*
(Princeton: Princeton University Press, 1977), 116.
[19] Thomas Wilson, *The Arte of Rhetorique* (1560), A4ʳᵛ. Unless otherwise stated,
all references are to the first edn. (1553).

style triplet, 'I will none of this booke from henceforthe [. . .]. As it was, so it is, and so be it still hereafter for me' (A5ʳᵛ).[20]

Wilson's rejection of his text is not as clear-cut as he claims: he took the trouble to add the new prologue, relating his experience of the Pauline Inquisition, and at least two pages of material on humour, including a number of characteristically anticlerical jokes. The force of Wilson's prologue, however, lies in this performance of seeming renunciation. The *Rhetorique* is republished ostensibly unaltered: Wilson thus signals his triumph, and that of his country, over popery. Despite the threat of burning endured during his incarceration in Rome, Wilson shows he has recanted neither his faith nor one word of his work. He refuses to change any aspect of his book, whether by moderating its virulent antipapism, re-addressing the dedicatory epistle (now its previous dedicatee, Dudley, is dead), or updating references to the late 'king' (Edward) by substituting the word 'queen'. Wilson's purported willingness to stand by his words is politicized by the narrative context within which it appears. 'I was ware as I could be, not to vtter any thing for myne owne harme, for feare I should come in their daunger,' he writes of his experience in prison: 'For then either should I haue died, or els haue denied, bothe openlie & shamefullie, the knowen truthe of Christ and his Gospell' (A5ʳ). Triumph lies in keeping the faith, unlike Wilson's former mentor, Cheke, whose prominence as a Protestant figurehead led to his capture, imprisonment, and forced recantation in 1556.[21]

Within the revised *Rhetorique*, Wilson does not defend his works by answering the accusation of heresy. Rather, he argues their legitimacy on the grounds of England's jurisdictional independence, a right on which legislation effecting the break with Rome was founded.[22] 'A straunge matter,' Wilson ponders, 'that thinges doen in Englande seuen yeres before [. . .] should afterwardes be laied to a mannes charge in Roome' (A4ᵛ). In his view, his works, 'doen in Englande', are only liable for judgement within England. As Andrew Hadfield shows, Wilson equates the experiences of self and nation.[23] 'GOD be praised,' he writes in the 1560

---

[20] Cf. the Blessing, 'As it was in the beginning, is now, and evershalbe' (*Boke of the common Praier*, A1ʳ and passim).

[21] John Strype, *The Life of the Learned Sir John Cheke* (Oxford, 1821), 110–12.

[22] See Elton (ed.), *Tudor Constitution*, 354–6.

[23] Hadfield, *Literature, Politics and National Identity*, 112.

Rhetorique, 'and thankes be giuen to him onely, that not onelie hath deliuered me, out of the Lions mouth: but also hath brought Englande, my deare Countrie, out of great thraldome, and forrein bondage' (A6ʳ). Wilson's Englishman is, like himself, Protestant, and religion a defining factor that spreads beyond the church doors and informs his ideal of a self-regulating island nation. As a handbook on logic, laying down paradigms of true and false reasoning allowing little leeway in thought, the *Reason* proves the perfect vehicle for imparting this ideal. Wilson's logical system is predicated on adherence to Protestant beliefs. False arguments are consequently demonstrated by ridiculing the Roman Church for its alleged prioritization of custom over scripture: 'the Gospel is beleued, for the churche sake,' writes Wilson: 'Ergo the Churche is of more aucthoritee' (I3ᵛ). The context requires readers to acknowledge this statement 'nothyng true' (I3ʳ): should they insist the church has more authority than the Bible, they cannot understand a logical system that categorizes such beliefs as 'false argument'. The book thus shapes its readers into a 'right'-thinking (Protestant) entity differentiated from 'wrong'-thinking (papist) Others.

Wayne Rebhorn contrasts Wilson's willingness to play the fool with Castiglione's admonitions against clowning, distinguishing between the Italian's promotion of the self-contained and controlled 'classical body' and what Rebhorn sees as Wilson's barely suppressed relish for the grotesque and ridiculous.[24] The *Rhetorique* can suddenly blossom with material familiar from a vernacular jest-book tradition: the lascivious priest, cuckolded husband, and sexually voracious wife, or the countryman misusing complex words. Nevertheless, Wilson is not helplessly fascinated by the grotesque, the result, according to Rebhorn, of his 'ambiguous social class'.[25] On the one hand, Wilson's social status is far from 'ambiguous': his elevation, through education, from yeoman roots in Lincolnshire, was commonplace in the period. On the other, laughter is didactic, with a reforming edge, and among those mocked by Wilson is an 'old grandame' confused about the role of the Virgin Mary, whom she thinks takes precedence over Christ.[26]

---

[24] Wayne A. Rebhorn, 'Baldesar Castiglione, Thomas Wilson and the Courtly Body of Renaissance Rhetoric', *Rhetorica*, 11 (1993), 241–74.
[25] Ibid. 241.   [26] Wilson, *Rhetorique* (1560), 73ʳᵛ.

As 'erroneous' beliefs are ridiculed, laughter coheres those in on the joke against the mocked outsider. Where Laurent Joubert's 1579 treatise, *Traite du Ris*, portrays laughter as a social mechanism, instituted by God 'because man is meant to be a sociable, politic and gracious animal, and should live and converse pleasantly and kindly with others' ('d'autant qu'il convenoit à l'homme d'etre animal sociable, politic & gracieus, afin quel l'vn vequit & conversat avecques l'autre plaisammant & beninemant, Dieu luy ha ordonné le Ris'), Wilson follows classical rhetoricians, such as Quintilian, in endowing laughter with a social role, not for facilitating harmonious communication, but for vocalizing the contemptibility of the derided Other.[27] 'The occasion of laughter, and the meane that maketh vs merie [. . .] is the fondnes, the filthines, the deformitee, and all suche euill behauior, as we se to bee in other,' Wilson writes.[28] The butts of Wilson's jokes are consequently those who display vices worthy of scorn: pretentiousness, foolishness, greed, ignorance, hypocrisy, religious delusion.

As Albert Schmidt states, 'like all Renaissance writers Wilson approached scholarship for didactic purposes, and the goal that he established for himself was less to teach Englishmen logic and rhetoric than to teach citizenship'.[29] The citizenship Wilson imparted was designed, as we have seen, to create a national body of 'right thinkers' fashioned according to the religious and political beliefs of the Edwardian regime. For humanists such as Wilson, moreover, 'right-thinking' was achieved through 'right-speaking', a theory encapsulated in the humanist doctrine that 'at least ideally, good societies produce good speakers, as good speakers produce good societies'.[30] Wilson's vision of a unified, obedient nation thus rests on the reformation of English speech, a concern he shared with others of the Cambridge-educated, Protestant-inclined group centred on Cheke and including Smith and Hoby. Where Smith focused on standardizing orthography, his fellow reformers tended to concentrate on vocabulary. In doing so, they led a dual campaign. On the one hand, following Cheke's famous dictum that 'our own tung shold be written cleane and pure, unmixt and

---

[27] Laurent Joubert, *Traite du Ris* (Paris, 1579), 232.
[28] Wilson, *Rhetorique*, 74ᵛ.
[29] Albert J. Schmidt, 'Thomas Wilson and the Tudor Commonwealth: An Essay in Civic Humanism', *HLQ* 23 (1960), 49–60, at 50.
[30] Elsky, *Authorizing Words*, 84.

unmangeled with borowing of other tunges', they attacked what was seen as the polluting effect of foreign words; on the other, their endeavours to standardize English prioritized their own educated idiom, working against regional dialect.[31]

For these reformers, importation of non-English words caused two problems: first, language overburdened with foreign neologisms threatens to drive apart, not bring together, the national community by hindering communication, particularly for the less educated, accentuating social difference. The solution proposed in Wilson's *Rhetorique* is linguistic extradition, that 'we must of necessitee, banishe al suche affected Rhetorique and vse altogether one maner of language' (87^r). When the lexicographer Robert Cawdrey set about combating misunderstandings introduced by 'hard' English words fifty years after the first publication of the *Rhetorique*, he cited Wilson's opinions on this matter verbatim and at length, albeit without acknowledgement.[32] Yet even as Cawdrey purports, in words borrowed from Wilson, to 'banish all affected Rhetorique', he does not seek to exile 'alien' words. Rather he provides his readers with a dictionary as a means by which these foreign terms can become familiar, a mark of both widened social access to 'higher' linguistic registers and a shift away from anxiety about the 'pollution' of English. Where, in the 1540s, Andrew Borde used 'difficult', Latinate words to flatter an educated elite, and in the 1550s Wilson sought to remove them, the dictionary writers of the late sixteenth and early seventeenth centuries were concerned to explain and 'democratize' them.

Despite frequent misreadings, however, neither Cheke nor any of his supporters advocate blanket avoidance of borrowings. Hoby's translation of Castiglione's *Il Cortegiano*—completed at Padua in the company of Cheke and Wilson between 1554 and 1555—is far from purist;[33] Cheke acknowledges the need to fill lexical lacunae in the language 'as being unperfight she must' (10); Wilson approves their use where necessary 'to set furthe our meanyng'.[34] Such words, though, should be supplied, to quote Cheke's letter to Hoby, from 'old denisoned words', familiar and rendered English through long usage. Such words are permissible

---

[31] John Cheke, letter to Thomas Hoby, in Hoby, *Courtier*, 10–11, at 10.
[32] Cawdrey, *Table Alphabeticall*, A3^r. Cf. Wilson, *Rhetorique*, 86^r–88^r.
[33] Hoby, *Courtier*, pp. viii, 377, n. 14.   [34] Wilson, *Rhetorique*, 87^v.

because they do not breach Wilson's ruling principle that language should be comprehensible, 'plain for all men to perceiue'.[35] Yet none of these linguistic commentators can suggest how, or when, neologisms become 'denisoned' (and, hence, acceptable). The difficulty is illustrated by Wilson's anecdote about a poor man denied help with his rent because he asks for 'contrary Bishoppes' and 'reuiues', not 'contribucion' and 'relief'.[36] As Paula Blank points out, the man's language and poverty are directly related.[37] Nevertheless, neither *contribution* nor *relief* are recent or unnecessary borrowings: according to the *OED*, both were in circulation from the end of the fourteenth century.

The territorial terms in which the Cheke circle call loanwords 'denisons', or threaten to 'banish' them, highlight their second objection to foreign neologisms: the risk they posed to national identity. In Wilson's *Rhetorique*, Englishmen returning from abroad contaminate their native tongue and 'like as thei loue to go in forrein apparell, so thei wil pouder their talke with ouersea language' (86[r]). Wilson's French-talking Englishmen and 'Angleschi Italiani'—Englishmen grotesquely mutating into Italians—display a tongue as un-English and effeminate ('pouder[ed]' like women's faces) as their exotic garb. Their language is physically 'outlandish', not of England's shores. This unnaturalness is compounded by recourse to emotive familial imagery: 'I dare swere this, if some of their mothers were aliue, thei were not able to tell, what thei say,' Wilson complains. This fear of foreign contagion is accentuated by comparison with Castiglione's *Cortegiano*, which shares the English reformers' interest in the vernacular and the moralistic terms in which 'correct' and 'incorrect' language is described. The man who strays from the right use of language, for example, is compared by Castiglione's Frederico to 'he that walketh in the darke without lyght, and therefore many times strayeth from the right waye' ('come chi camina per le tenebre senza lume e però spesso erra la strada').[38] Although this simile shares the spatial disorientation of Wilson's 'outlandish' meanderings, it lacks the geographical dislocation inherent in Wilson's turn of phrase. Light and shade make

35 Ibid. 88[r].   36 Ibid. 87[v].
37 Blank, *Broken English*, 42.
38 Castiglione, *Cortegiano*, 68; trans. Hoby, *Courtier*, 60.

no reference to territorial boundaries, and Castiglione's 'wrong-speaking' is not haunted by the threat of foreignness that troubles Wilson and Cheke.

Castiglione's attitude to dialect is also revealingly different. Castiglione defends his right 'in writing [to take] the wholl and pure woord of [his] owne Countrey, then the corrupt and mangled of an other' ('Io scrivendo ho usato [. . .] l'integro e sincero della patria mia che 'l corrotto e guasto della aliena').[39] 'Countrey' here means native region, not Italy: Castiglione is championing the place of his Lombard dialect within the Italian vernacular against Florentine (then the dominant literary tongue) and those Italians who speak nothing but 'il Petrarca e 'l Boccaccio'. Through Lodovico da Canossa (Hoby's Count Lewis), one of the more authoritative protagonists, Castiglione argues for an Italian language that employs 'gorgeous and fine woordes out of every parte of Italye' ('parole splendide ed eleganti d'ogni parte della Italia').[40] His pleas mirror the composite nature of Italian identity, comprised of numerous city-states and principalities. In contrast, the reforms suggested by Wilson and Cheke reflect their pursuit of national uniformity: that they might 'vse altogether one maner of language'.[41]

In the interests of uniformity, English speech, like government, is to be centralized. The standards of 'civility' and proper speech approved by Wilson are those of London and the South-East: 'London', where 'the people [are] more ciuill, and [. . .] for the moste parte more wise', is preferred over 'Lincolne', principal town of Wilson's native county.[42] In the 1390s, at the beginning of the ascendancy of south-eastern dialect and the move towards modern English, Chaucer dubbed his king the 'lord of this langage'; Wilson similarly places language under royal authority as the 'kynges English'.[43] The first citation given by the *OED* for the term 'the king's English' is over forty years after Wilson's *Rhetorique*, in Shakespeare's *Merry Wives of Windsor*, a play in which characters tellingly seek to exclude foreigners (including Welshmen who make 'fritters of English') from, and by, use of what they judge 'good

---

[39] Castiglione, *Cortegiano*, 27; trans. Hoby, *Courtier*, 16.
[40] Castiglione, *Cortegiano*, 73; trans. Hoby, *Courtier*, 66.
[41] Wilson, *Rhetorique*, 87[r].   [42] Ibid. 7[v].
[43] Geoffrey Chaucer, *A Treatise on the Astrolabe*, ed. Larry D. Benson, in *Riverside Chaucer*, 662; Wilson, *Rhetorique*, 86[r].

English'.[44] Where Falstaff and friends utilize their perceptions of standard language to humiliate outsiders, however, Wilson (in an era of only nascent concepts of 'good English') attacks internal division and the unnaturalness of jargon, which holds the potential to drive communities and even families apart. Social subsets, incomprehensible to others, remain locked in their own linguistic systems, providing Wilson with a Babel tower of non-communication. The lawyer 'wil store his stomack with the pratyng of Pedlers'; the auditor 'makyng his accompt and rekenyng, cometh in with sise sould, and cater denere, for vi.s. iiii.d'; the courtier gabbles 'nothyng but Chaucer', while 'Poeticall Clerkes' speak 'nothyng but quaint prouerbes', 'delityng muche in their awne darkenesse, especially, when none can tell what thei dooe saie'.[45]

In comedies throughout the late Elizabethan and Jacobean periods, pretentiously otiose speech was consistently used as a source of fun.[46] When it comes to accents, it is stage foreigners—not English provincials—who are used for an easy laugh, like the fake Dutchman, Hans Meulter, in *The Shoemaker's Holiday*, or the Irishman Bryan in *2 Honest Whore*, brought on as an excuse to say 'shit' (for 'sit').[47] Similarly, in *Henry V*, accent does not distinguish Englishmen from Englishmen, but from the Scots, Irish, and Welsh, and serves as a demonstration of the union possible within Britain and Ireland, as Gower, Jamy, Macmorris, and Fluellen join in brave and loyal service of the English crown. For late fifteenth- and earlier sixteenth-century writers, diversity of dialect and accent within England is a cause of comment and concern. As Caxton wrote in 1498, 'hit seemeth a grete wonder that Englyshmen haue so grete dyuersyte in theyr own langage in sowne & in spekynge of it'.[48] Caxton further comments on the lack of understanding between 'northern & southern', and on the 'sharpe' and 'unshappe' language of 'the Northumbres & specially at Yorke [. . .] that we southern men may vnneth vnderstande'. For Edwardian writers,

---

[44] William Shakespeare, *The Merry Wives of Windsor*, in *Oxford Shakespeare* v. v. 136, 129.   [45] Wilson, *Rhetorique*, 86ʳᵛ.
[46] See, e.g., William Shakespeare, *Love's Labours Lost*, in *Oxford Shakespeare*, ɪv. ii; Thomas Heywood, *A Woman Killed with Kindness*, in Kathleen McCluskie and David Bevington (eds.), *Plays on Women* (Manchester: Manchester University Press, 1999), ɪ. ii.
[47] Thomas Dekker, *The Second Part of the Honest Whore* (London: Nick Hern Books, 1998), scene i.   [48] Caxton, *Descrypcyon of Englande*, C3ʳᵛ.

such as Wilson, writing in the wake of the Western Rising and Kett's Norfolk Rebellion in 1549, there was a pressing need to counter these internal divisions. These two serious rebellions, to which Wilson repeatedly refers in his *Rhetorique*, prompted a flurry of obedience tracts, including Cheke's *Hurte of Sedicion* (1549). Wilson's *Rhetorique* can be seen as part of this obedience literature, warning that loyalty to linguistic factions—vocational or regional—overrides greater social impulses towards comprehensibility, and threatens to counteract the 'familiar humanist claim that savage men were first rendered into civilised communities by the power of eloquence'.[49]

Wilson's concern for clarity consequently extends beyond those passages in which he attacks 'ynkehorn termes': it underlies the entire book. Rhetoric is the linchpin on which civil society rests, Wilson explains in his preface, recycling Cicero's *De Inventione*, 1. ii. 2–3. It is therefore crucial that the rhetor be understood. Incomprehensibility undermines social stability and the divisiveness of dialect, and local loyalties, haunts Wilson's works. Linguistic order reflects social order, and 'correct' speech mirrors 'correct' thinking and behaviour, hence his objections to Borde's inverted syntax which proves as aberrant as Borde's adherence to 'papist' rituals: 'Some [. . .] not contented with a playne and easye composition, but seke to sette wordes they can not tell howe, and therefore one not likynge to be called and by printe published Doctoure of Phisike, would nedes be named of Phisike Doctour,' complains Wilson.[50] In Wilson's eyes, social hierarchy is preserved by linguistic hierarchies, for 'who is so folyshe as to saye the counsayle and the kynge, but rather the Kinge and his counsayle, the father and the sonne, and not contrary.'[51] Likewise, men should be as liable to be 'charge[d] for counterfeiting the kynges English' as for forging the king's coin, a comparison that aligns control of language with control of the coinage, one of the marks of sovereignty defined by the sixteenth-century French political theorist Jean Bodin.[52] The 'Northern man', who 'barkes out his English [. . .] with I say, and thou lad' thus disrupts more than linguistic

[49] Dominic Baker-Smith, *More's Utopia* (London: HarperCollins, 1991), 49.
[50] Wilson, *Rhetorique*, 89ᵛ.   [51] Ibid. 89ʳ.
[52] Ibid. 86ʳ. Jean Bodin, *On Sovereignty: Four Chapters from the Six Books of the Commonwealth*, ed. Julian H. Franklin (Cambridge: Cambridge University Press, 1992).

uniformity: he cuts against cultural, social, and legal stability, and it is the Northumbrian men of 'Tindale, and Riddesdale', with their clan culture and 'introverted regional loyalties', who show the greatest propensity for crime, for which they 'may the soner be suspected'.[53]

In Wilson's *Rhetorique*, eloquence is an instrument of control, necessary to 'perswade with reason, all men to societye' (A3^v). It is also a confidence trick necessary for social cohesion, dissipating the self-interest that would end in fragmentation, 'for what manne [. . .] would not rather loke to rule like a lord, then to lyue lyke an vnderlynge: if by reason he were not perswaded that it behoueth euerye man to lyue in his owne vocation, and not to seke anye hygher rowme, then whereunto he was at the first appoynted?'(A4^r). Like God bestowing the powers of utterance on a Calvinist elite ('these appoynted of God'), Wilson is consequently selective of the recipients of his gift of eloquence. Leonard Cox dedicated *The arte or crafte of rhetoryke* (1524) to Hugh Faryngdon, Abbot of Reading and patron of the school where Cox taught and for which the work was intended as a textbook; Richard Sherry offered his *Treatise of schemes & tropes* (1550) to Thomas Brooke, probably the fellow writer and translator of Calvin. Wilson, in contrast, aims (as he does in all his works) at the circles of high politics and presents the *Rhetorique* to John Dudley, Earl of Warwick and Master of the Horse (the third officer of the royal household), with the words that 'no man oughte to be with-oute [rhetoric], whiche either shall beare rule ouer manye, or muste haue to do wyth matters of a Realme' (A1^v).[54] Unlike Cox's book, Wilson's is not intended for the edification of English schoolboys. It is a tool for its governing elite. 'Consideringe [. . .] your Lordshyps hyghe estate, & worthy callyng', Wilson chooses 'to ioyne the perfection of Eloquente vtteraunce' with 'the gyfte of good reason and vnderstandynge' that Dudley apparently already possesses (A1^v). As in the prefatory fable, reason and persuasive

---

[53] Mervyn James, *Society, Politics and Culture: Studies in Early Modern England* (Cambridge: Cambridge University Press, 1986), 95–8; Wilson, *Rhetorique*, 50^r.

[54] The *Reason* is dedicated to Edward VI; *Vita et Obitus* to the influential Duchess of Suffolk; *The three orations of Demosthenes* (1570) to William Cecil; *A discourse vppon vsurye* (1572) to Robert Dudley, Earl of Leicester. Wilson's dedicatees (like Sherry's) are further distinguished by their reforming tendencies, and it is their vein of religious and nationally minded politics that Wilson fosters.

speech are attributes pertaining to a ruling class. Nevertheless, there is an inherent tension between the elite audience at whom the work is directed and the fact that this is a printed book, available to any literate person who can afford or borrow it.[55]

The authoritarian role of rhetoric propounded in Wilson's preface is borne out by the exempla, illustrating its appropriate application, that follow the treatise itself. The use to which Wilson puts language is not 'courtly' in the sense of *courtier* intended in the *Arte of English Poesie* (1586), but of the law courts, for Wilson, the seat of government in action. Despite the swing away from judicial oration that Brian Vickers finds characteristic of Renaissance rhetoric, legal issues and instances dominate Wilson's work.[56] Rhetoric is seen as a combative art, with the orator defending someone against another before a judgmental audience. 'It is wisedome to consider the tyme, the place, the man for whom we speake, the man against whom we speake [. . .], and the iudges before whom we speake,' Wilson establishes at the opening of the *Rhetorique*, introducing rhetoric in general, before its division into its demonstrative, deliberative, and judicial parts (5^r). Legal issues also leak into the account of both demonstrative and deliberative rhetoric. The former is exemplified by an oration 'in commendacion of Iustice' (13^v–16^r); the latter is demonstrated, over ten pages, by the question of how 'to aduise one, to studye the lawes of Englande', a debate which concludes with a passionate declaration of the necessity of the law for maintaining national and personal well-being (17^r–21^v). The apparatus signalling the voice of the guiding narrator, suggesting how points might best be framed, falls away, leaving the message not as a piece of role-play, but of the text itself. 'Take awaie the lawe, and take awaie our lifes,' it cries: 'for nothyng mainteineth our wealthe, our health, & the sauegard of our bodies, but the lawe of a Realme, wherby the wicked are condempned, and the godly are defended' (21^v).

For Wilson, law and government are necessary to quell latent anarchy, and justice is manifested when 'lawes take force' (83^v). As he writes in the *Reason*, which lays similar stress on legal control,

[55] Probably about 17d., estimated using figures provided in H. S. Bennett, *English Books and Readers, 1475–1557* (Cambridge: Cambridge University Press, 1952), 229–34.
[56] Brian Vickers, *Classical Rhetoric in English Poetry* (London: Macmillan, 1970), 68–73.

'unquiet people, rebelles, disobedient people, are the cause why magistrates are ordeyned' (N8ᵛ). It is not an unbroken civil peace that we see, but the necessities of punishment resulting from its disruption, as when the definition of a magistrate hangs on the fact that 'euerie politicall Magistrate ought to kepe vnder disobedient persones, with corporall punishement'.⁵⁷ In the preface to the *Rhetorique*, Wilson presents rhetoric to his nation's leaders as a weapon suitable for territorial aggression. The story with which he begins the dedicatory epistle demonstrates the power of words 'to winne cities & whole countries' as Cineas, a 'noble Oratour [. . .] throughe the eloquence of his tongue, wanne more Cityes vnto [Pyrrhus, his master], then euer [Pyrrhus] him selfe shoulde els haue bene able by force to subdue' (A1ʳ). Yet throughout the work, it is not foreign cities that we see subjugated by rhetoric, but the native, disobedient subject.

Wilson's focus on the need for governors to regulate their subjects is highlighted when the *Reason* and *Rhetorique* are compared with Elyot's *Boke named the Gouernour*, a significant predecessor in the genre of 'manuals for magistrates'. Like Wilson, Elyot addresses a future ruling elite, a magistracy of 'inferiour gouernours' (13ᵛ), and through their works, both writers hope to help achieve domestic stability. Elyot's opening chapters lend his authority figures a paternalistic gloss as officials that exist for 'the only preseruation of other theyr inferiours' (5ʳ). He preaches self-regulation, shown in his long digression on self-control learnt through the analogy of the dance (74ʳ–94ᵛ) and the necessary reflections of magistrates on adopting office (101ᵛ–106ʳ). Wilson, in contrast, concentrates on the regulation of the masses. Where Elyot's work, although no less politicized, fosters the internal cultivation of an ideal magistrate, Wilson's concerns the external manifestations of government in practice. Elyot's 'multitude' remains Horace's abstracted 'Monstre with many heedes', an image also employed by Wilson.⁵⁸ Wilson's pages, however, are also breached by the 'monstre's' continual incursion in human form, as the rebels of recent history—'Iacke Straw' and 'Capitayne Kete'—or through fictional cases of 'abhorred murder', which are nevertheless presented as real and infamous events, such as 'the knowledge of a

---

⁵⁷ Wilson, *Reason*, G5ʳ.
⁵⁸ Elyot, *Gouernour*, 6ᵛ; Wilson, *Rhetorique*, 6ᵛ.

notable and mooste haynous offence, committed by a Souldiour' used to demonstrate a judicial oration.[59]

As self-appointed spokesperson for the political elite, Wilson demonstrates the regulatory office of rhetoric. Even as the *Rhetorique* teaches and exposes the 'tricks' of rhetoric, it employs those same tricks to preach love of, and loyalty to, king and country. Wilson goes further than simple exhortation; he also attempts to coerce readers into 'correct' opinions. One trope used for this purpose is paradiastole, or the art of renaming. Quentin Skinner highlights the 'habitual hostility' of English Renaissance poets and moralists to this trope. 'Drawing directly' on classical authorities such as Socrates, Thucydides, and Plutarch, they warn against the suitability of paradiastole to the 'fickleness' of the multitude 'and above all to their disposition to confuse the language of vice and virtue to suit their own purposes'.[60] Within the *Rhetorique*, however, that power of redescription is reclaimed for the governing classes. Definitions are rewritten to suit the authoritative/ authorial pen, as in the case of 'communes or equalitee', the legal nature of which, narrowed to the question of enclosure rights, is reduced on Wilson's pages to reactionary disobedience, 'when the people by long time haue a ground [. . .] the whiche some of them will kepe still, for custome sake, and not suffer it to be fensed, and so turned to pasture, though thei mighte gain ten tymes the value' (19^r). Repeated stress on the derogatory word 'custome' (a bias quickly acquired within the text by its continual association with papist ceremonies) adds further censure. Opposition to enclosure is recategorized as irrational and unjustifiable obstinacy, since 'such stubburnesse in kepyng of Commons for custome sake, is not standyng with Iustice, because it is holden against all right'. Adherence to unreasonable custom (here associated with resistance to enclosures, one motive for Kett's rebellion in 1549) thus becomes a sign of disloyal, un-English behaviour.

As rhetoric metamorphoses from the seemingly benign personification at the opening of the *Reason*, where she gaily paints the

---

[59] Wilson, *Rhetorique*, 68^r, 50^v. The fictionality of this latter example is evident from the hyperbolically uncivil nature of the soldier, brought up among the 'rude and uncivil' Northumbrian reivers, yet displaying a propensity for French lace and velvet (Cathy Shrank, 'Civil Tongues: Language, Law and Reformation', in Jennifer Richards (ed.), *Early Modern Civil Discourses* (Houndmills: Palgrave, 2003), 19–34.
[60] Skinner, *Reason and Rhetoric*, 172–80.

words of her sibling logic, into the authoritarian rhetor, so too the concept of commonweal is phased out of the picture. In comparison with previous English *artes rhetorica* and Wilson's own *Reason*, the *Rhetorique* is notably reticent in expressing commitment to a wider public good, even in its introductory sections (the usual site for such altruistic protestations). Cox uses his preface to declare his intention to render rhetoric 'more comen', and hence 'better';[61] Sherry's advertises his intention to raise national pride by proving that 'schemes & fygures [. . .] verely come no sildomer in the writing and speaking of eloquente englishmen, then either of the Grecians or Latins';[62] in the preface to the *Reason*, Wilson adopts the humanistic pose of undertaking a work made 'commune to all', not in pursuit of personal glory or enamoured of his own capabilities, but 'because no Englishman vntill now hath gone through with this enterprise' (A4ᵛ). He desires solely to act 'but as a spurre or a whet stone, to sharpe the pennes of someother, that they may polishe, and perfect, that I haue rudely, & grossely entered'. The task is shouldered in an air of egalitarianism, both in the author's posturing as one among equals, and in the intended recipients of his work: through the *Reason*, logic will become 'a free denisen' in England, accessible to all.

In contrast, in the *Rhetorique*, such protestations of national purpose are confined to the Latin poems prefacing the work, poems rendered less inclusive by their medium (Latin), and two of which were cut after the first edition. Even there, rhetoric is not offered as a means of increasing England's honour, but that of its monarch, to whom Robert Hilermius offers 'this work, which will give fame to your deeds through the ages, and bear your name to the stars' ('Hoc opus, hoc uestrum est, uobis per secula famam / Quod dabit, & vestrum nomen ad astra feret', π2ʳ). The exclusivity of the glory proffered in the prefatory matter is borne out by the main text. It is only in the penultimate paragraph, after more than 200 pages, that we find even a hint that proficiency in rhetoric might be a means of bolstering the nation's pride or reputation. 'As we ought to haue good regarde for the vtteraunce of our wordes,' Wilson decrees, 'so we ought to take heede that our gesture be comely, the whiche bothe beyng wel obserued, shal encrease fame and gette estimacion vniuersally' (118ᵛ).

---

[61] Leonard Cox, *The arte or crafte of Rhetoryke* (1524), A3ʳ.
[62] Richard Sherry, *A treatise of schemes & tropes* (1550), A7ʳ.

His phrasing, though, is tellingly vague, and actual mention of the nation is evaded. Fame is not offered indeterminately to the wider commonweal, but to the individual reader alone. The failure to equate effective speech and national prestige is all the more glaring in the light of Wilson's debts to Quintilian, whose *Institutio* is underwritten by such a premise, and where (as we saw in Chapter 4) the reputed failings of Latin in comparison to Greek were an added spur to investment in the Latin tongue.[63]

The exclusionary bent of Wilson's approach to government is highlighted by the terms he uses to describe the body politic. Just as the veneer of communality extant in the prefatory matter of the *Reason* is stripped away in the *Rhetorique*, so too there is a change in constitutional vocabulary. In the *Reason*, the standard term describing the English polity is 'commune weale', defined as being 'deuided into the state of people whiche beare rule, & also into that powre where the beste, and wisest haue the gouernaunce, and thirdly into ones hande which alone beareth the stroke and is chief magistrate' (E2^r). In contrast, in Wilson's *Three orations of Demosthenes* (1570), 'commune weale' appears once only in thirty quarto-sized pages of vernacular prefatory material, in comparison with 'countrie' (twenty-nine times); 'land', as in 'native land' (twice); 'realme' (once); and 'nation' (once). A new term, 'state', occurs seven times, employed by Wilson to mean 'the body politic as organized for supreme civil rule and government', a usage for which Thomas Starkey's *Dialogue between Reginald Pole and Thomas Lupset* (*c*.1534) provides the first *OED* citation (29a). Wilson's use of the word clusters around two passages translated from Sophocles' *Antigone* and Livy's *History of the Roman Republic*. In neither of the original texts is there any linguistic prompt suggesting the translation 'state', which is how Wilson renders 'πόλισ' (city), 'χθονὸσ' (native country), and ''ορθης' (a metaphorical description of the polity as a 'ship');[64] 'integras res' (entire thing) and 'ipsam urbem' (the city itself).[65] As Skinner has

---

[63] Quintilian, *Institutio Oratoria*, XII. x. 36.

[64] Sophocles, *Antigone*, ed. and trans. Hugh Lloyd-Jones (London: Heinemann, 1994), ll. 178/187/190. Lloyd-Jones translates them as 'city', 'citizens', and 'the ship on which we sail'.

[65] Livy, *The History of the Roman Republic*, ed. and trans. Evan T. Sage, rev. edn. (London: Heinemann, 1936), XXXI. vii. 10. Sage translates them as 'resources' and 'the gates [of Rome]'.

argued, however, the Italian form of the word, *lo stato*, was being used with increasing frequency in Italian political thought of the period (and above all by Machiavelli) to refer to 'the presence of particular regimes or systems of government'.[66]

Wilson's familiarity with Italian political thought, and Machiavelli in particular, is suggested not only by his time in Italy between 1553 and 1558, but also by his association (through the dedication of the *Rhetorique*) to the circle around Dudley, patron of that early Machiavellian, William Thomas. Wilson's Machiavellian interests, and those of the Dudleys, are further indicated in his dedicatory epistle to Robert Dudley in *A discourse vppon vsurye*, written concurrently with the *Orations*, although unpublished until 1572. Here Wilson comments on Dudley's interest in 'the Italian good & sounde wryters, to knowe and to vnderstande the best vsed gouernement' (¶¶1ʳ), an allusion to the diagnostic intention behind Machiavelli's *Discorsi*. The Florentine's influence resonates through the dedicatory epistle, as Wilson espouses the doctrine of political necessity, with Elizabeth 'enforced much against her nature, to vse the sworde, a thing so needefull when gentle meanes wil not serue, that without so doing no state coulde stande, nor man could lyue'(¶¶1ᵛ). 'Such hath thys world ben, is, and wilbee euer,' he continues, 'that Princes upon cause must doe, & in reason are bound to do that whiche they would not of themselues doe, yf it were not for very necessity, to auoyde a greater inconuenience.' The Machiavellian traces resident in the key words 'cause', 'reason', and 'necessity' are compounded by Wilson's concluding assertion that when 'clemencie will not serue, [Princes] maye vse the contrary', the argument of chapter 17 of *Il Principe*.

The entry of the term 'state' into Wilson's vocabulary after 1553 gives him the linguistic ability to express distinctions, latent in his earlier works, between institutions of government and the entities they govern. Differentiation between 'commonweal' and 'state', and who is entitled to represent them, extends into the *Vsurye*, Wilson's last published work. There, 'publique order and aucthoritye' stem 'from the prince and state', not 'the prince and *his*

---

[66] Quentin Skinner, 'The State', in Terence Ball et al. (eds.), *Political Innovation and Conceptual Change* (Cambridge: Cambridge University Press, 1989), 90–113, at 98.

[e]state' (123^v), and 'affaires of the state' (57^v) are the remit of governors, magistrates, and ambassadors, a use of the term which shows the semantic shift of the word *state* from 'estate' or 'standing' towards a synonym for government. Within the *Vsurye*, 'common weale', in contrast, is habitually passive, a body unto which good or ill can be done. 'Regarde alwayes must bee had to the common weale, that no harme doe come therunto, by anye vnlawful dealynges,' declares Wilson's preacher in the *Vsurye*, adding that, 'the common weale smarteth by suche vnlawfull dealinges' (191^r).

To move away from expressions of 'commonweal' is not to negate political participation, however, and if Wilson's use of the term 'state' focuses power on a body of educated advisers, ministers, and ambassadors, then he placed himself firmly within this governing elite. His eagerness to engage in 'affaires of state' is demonstrated by his *Orations*, an English translation of Demosthenes' speeches urging his fellow Athenians to take military action against Philip of Macedon. The work is presented so that Wilson's compatriots without Greek might 'learne' the 'lessons' of Demosthenes 'well ynough': 'I haue taken paynes in him for their onely sakes,' Wilson declares (∗∗2^r). The humanistic gloss of a project popularizing the classics is tempered, however, by the underlying aim of Wilson's work. The *Orations* is designed to instigate armed engagement, a use of Demosthenes prefigured in Edward Walshe's *The office and duety in fightyng for our countrey* (1545), in which Walshe stresses the desirability of translating Demosthenes to foster martial enthusiasm.[67] Wilson, like Demosthenes, intends eloquence to lead to action; if all goes well, his words will, as in the prefatory poems, stir English weapons (π2^v). The text, dedicated to Cheke's former Cambridge pupil, William Cecil, secretary of state, promotes English intervention on behalf of the Protestant Dutch in their wars of independence against Spain, a revolt which began in 1567 and continued until the Treaty of Münster in 1648.[68] The topicality of the *Orations* is made explicit at the tail-end of the prefatory matter, immediately

[67] Edward Walshe, *The office and duety in fightyng for our countrey* (1545), B7^r. What Walshe means by 'our countrey' is intriguing, since he was writing as a Protestant settler in Ireland.

[68] Blair Worden, *The Sound of Virtue: Philip Sidney's Arcadia and Elizabethan Politics* (New Haven: Yale University Press, 1996), 28 n.

before the reader embarks on the main text. 'My meaning was,' Wilson explains, 'that euery good subiect according to the leuell of his witte, should compare the time past with the time present, and euer when he heareth Athens, or the Athenians, to remember Englande and Englishmen' (B1ᵛ). Wilson's militaristic Protestantism and desire to help the Dutch link him with Philip Sidney (almost thirty years his junior), whose attempts to endow poetry with national purpose, as Blair Worden argues, mirror Wilson's promotion of rhetoric as an essential national art.[69] Evidence of direct contact between Sidney and Wilson is scant, limited to a period at Kenilworth in 1566 and a joint audience with Don John in Louvain in 1577, when Wilson was ambassador to the Low Countries.[70] Nevertheless, it is probable that their acquaintance was more extensive. Wilson, as the dedication to the *Vsurye* shows, was part of the circle around Sidney's uncle, Robert Dudley, Earl of Leicester, in the early 1570s, and ideologically, besides their 'forward' Protestantism, Sidney and Wilson shared a belief that 'the liberty of speech' enabling 'plain', 'bold' counsel was 'essential to political health'.[71]

Wilson's *Orations* capitalizes on the inbuilt immediacy of an oration, appealing as it does to its audience with direct second-person pronouns, and gathering them into a collective first-person 'us' to set against a third-person enemy. Marginalia provide a further resource in Wilson's authorial armoury, and is repeatedly used to highlight pertinent themes. 'Better offende than defende,' Wilson notes (8). 'Better to annoy by offence than to stand as defence, and to begin warre, than to withstand warre,' he warns less than a page later (9). His marginalia habitually adopt the pithy tones of proverbial wisdom, proverbs commended in the *Rhetorique* for their ability to 'helpe Amplification' (66ʳ). 'The painefull man bearith away the garlande,' he comments in the *Orations* (17); 'when flatterers beares rule, all things comes to naught [*sic*]' (28). Elsewhere in the work, marginalia emphasize parallels between England and Athens. The latter lies vulnerable to

[69] For Wilson's further thoughts on foreign policy, see Albert J. Schmidt, 'A Treatise on England's Perils, 1578', *Archiv für Reformationsgeschichte*, 46 (1955), 243–9, a transcription of an unpublished treatise by Wilson from Elizabethan state papers in the PRO.

[70] Duncan-Jones, *Sidney*, 34; Worden, *Sound of Virtue*, 161 n.

[71] Ibid. 147.

a man who 'hateth euen [its] verie religion' (86). The remark, used
by Demosthenes as a rhetorical flourish, is transformed by the gloss
into a leading point drawing obvious resonance from the threat
posed to Protestant England by Catholic Spain. The message of the
orations established on the title page is not merely relevant, but
urgent: they are 'most nedefull to be redde in these daungerouse
dayes'. In failing to help the Olynthians, the Athenians gave Philip
the military advantage that eventually allowed their own subjugation. In neglecting to help the Dutch in their revolt against their
Spanish overlords, England—according to this historical model—
risks doing likewise.

As Philip of Spain maps neatly onto Philip of Macedon, and as
Athens is translated into England and the Olynthians (threatened
by Philip) into the beleaguered Dutch, so Wilson becomes the
English Demosthenes, even highlighting his adoption of the Greek's
characteristically sparse, plain-spoken style. Worried that 'it may
be thought that I doe speake ouer bare Englysh', he insists that, 'I
had rather follow his veyne, the whych was to speake simply and
plainly to the common peoples vnderstanding, than to ouer-
flouryshe wyth superfluous speach' (*4ᵛ). Clarity is Wilson's
watchword and where he deems it necessary 'for the more playne
vnderstanding' of the *Orations*, he inserts 'a sentence, or halfe a
sentence in the small Italicke letter' (**1ᵛ). These authorial additions can be divided into three categories: explanation (for example, 'twentie poundes *weight of siluer*', 41); verbal expansion,
fleshing out Demosthenes' abrupt style through redundant phrases
such as '*as it weare*' or '*(sayth one)*' (4, 8); and emotional amplification, as when Wilson replaces the Greek adverb 'ἐκεῖ' (there),
indicating the region within which the Athenians would fight, with
the alarmist phrase '*at your owne dores*' (8). A paragraph later,
'position' ('πραγμάτων') is expanded into the sequence '*for vs to
bee bearded by oure enimyes, and brested by them euen at oure
owne doores*' (9), an image which again emphasizes the terror of
warfare intruding into domestic spaces and is designed to raise the
reader's indignation.[72] Over the course of translation, it is this kind
of emotional amplification that dominates. Seemingly explanatory
additions can also carry emotive weight, however, as when Philip's

[72] Demosthenes, *Olynthiacs*, ed. and trans. J. H. Vince (London: Heinemann,
1930), 27.

attack on 'Arymbas *his Vncle*' shows his willingness to violate even familial bonds (5). Wilson's interpolations, that is, prove far from neutral.

From the title page onwards, the *Orations* addresses those 'that loue their Countries libertie'. Demosthenes' patriotism is recurrently vaunted, and in a passage describing public duty, love of your country stands next to godliness, just above obedience. Sympathetic treatment of compatriots comes 'last of all': as Wilson writes, 'Let euerye man haue thys before hys eyes, first to honour God [. . .]: next to loue the naturall Countrie where he is borne, aboue all worldly thyngs: thirdly to obey the Magistrate that is in authoritie: and last of all, [. . .] to doe to others, as they woulde haue others, doe to them' (✱✱2^r). For would-be governors, office-holding becomes proof of native love; those that shirk their duty— 'the state to saue by lore most wyse'—labelled 'of wicked men, most wicked' (A2^r). Yet Demosthenes, initially deemed 'the strong bulwarke, and mighty defence of his most deare natiue Countrie' (A2^r), is by the end of Wilson's work tainted by accusations of corruption, or at least poor judgement, for accepting gifts and money from an intimate of Alexander the Great (133). In the climactic conclusion to the *Orations*, it is not patriots that are manifest, but their antithesis: 'wicked betrayers of their naturall soyle and Countrie, who after a sort plucke out their owne bowelles' (145). Love of your native land is seen as integral to the self, rooted within the entrails. Here, however, it is signalled only by its absence, in a description that reeks of hanging, drawing, and quartering, prescribed punishment for treason.

'AN EASIE MATTER IT IS, TO TELL A TALE':
THE SURVIVAL OF THE LUCIANIC TRADITION[73]

Wilson is required to confess Demosthenes' alleged corruption because he includes a biographical section on his orator-hero. This decision also forces acknowledgement of the failure of Demosthenes' rhetoric and exposes a divided purpose that threatens to split the work from within. Wilson the scholar struggles against Wilson the propagandist. With its abundance of critical

---

[73] Wilson, *Vsurye*, 202^v.

apparatus, the *Orations* remains caught between its author's desire to provide an accurately edited text in the tradition of Continental humanist translations, and his wish to produce a polemical treatise calling for involvement in the Dutch wars. The former aim betrays and undoes the second, as the immediate impact of contemporary politics is diluted by the mass of academic detail. Attempts to doctor the text by emotive additions are undercut by the translator's scrupulousness in italicizing these interpolations. In addition, at the heart of the *Orations* lurks a recognition of the futility of rhetoric in practice: an admission that Demosthenes' words will not be heard by the statesmen to whom Wilson issues his warnings about Philip of Spain. The parallel offered by Athens threatens to run a little too neatly. As Wilson informs his readers, Demosthenes' words failed to rally his countrymen in time to save first the Olynthians and ultimately their own city-state.

That sense of fracture between aim and outcome can be traced to Wilson's early texts. In championing rhetoric, they reveal its two undesirable aspects: futility and abuse. The *Rhetorique* can even be seen to facilitate the abuse of eloquence by reducing it to a set of rules. Philosophical discussions about the ethics of rhetoric found in Wilson's classical sources (mainly Cicero and Quintilian) are given no space within the utilitarian framework of the manual, which leaves bald the constructed nature of eloquent speech. As Wilson writes, 'in mouyng affections, and stirryng the iudges to be greued, the report must be suche and the offence made so hainouse, that the like hath not been seene heretofore' (72^v). Such hyperbolic reactions are not presented as inherent to the material, but accomplished ('made') by the mechanics of rhetoric he teaches. Concern about 'thentent' of rhetoric seemingly ceases with the achievement of the desired verbal impact; what matters is how words 'appere': 'we encrease our cause by heapyng of wordes & sentences together [. . .], to thentent that our talke might appere more vehement,' he explains (70^v). By teaching eloquence as a series of easily imitated tropes, Wilson risks emulating the demise and abuse of rhetoric in Cicero's fable about the civilizing powers of eloquence, to which the preface of the *Rhetorique* alludes. As those Tudor readers familiar with *De Inventione* would know, Cicero's narrative continues past the point at which Wilson stops, recounting how ' a certain agreeableness of manner—a depraved imitation of virtue— acquired the power of eloquence' ('postquam vero commoditas

quaedam, prava virtutis imitatrix [. . .] dicendi copiam').[74] What
Cicero neglects to mention is that, in addition, eloquence is not
always successful: orators can fail to convince. The inadequacies of
rhetoric are implicit in Wilson's portrayal in the *Rhetorique* of a
society continually threatened by anarchic forces and are spelled
out explicitly in the autobiographical prologue, relating his imprisonment in Rome, inserted in the 1560 edition before the preface
and reordered Latin poems. In that edition, the fable on eloquence
is thus preceded by a true tale in which the protagonist is reduced
to defensive silence, saved from impending execution, not by
rhetoric, but by the anarchic mob and grace of God.[75]

The cracks opening in Wilson's earlier works are forced further
apart in, and by, his last published work, the *Vsurye*, a dialogue
examining the reasons for and against lending money at interest, a
practice on which England's growing international trade increasingly depended. That the only twentieth-century edition treats it
purely as an economic treatise (supplying 157 pages of detailed
socio-economic background by means of introduction) should not
blind us to the purposefully ambiguous nature of a work that prob-
lematizes Wilson's previous endorsement of logic and rhetoric.[76]
That is not to say that the issue of usury is of no account. Wilson
displayed a long-standing interest in the topic. 'No Christian is an
vsurer,' he notes in the *Reason* in 1551 (G2^r). The *Vsurye* is also
dedicated to John Jewel, Bishop of Salisbury, a well-known opponent of usurers, and 'the thoroughly traditional arguments [. . .]
put in the mouths of Master Preacher and the Civilian' were recycled in Wilson's parliamentary speeches against liberalizing usury
laws in 1571.[77] Nevertheless, the economy of Wilson's text is such

---

74 Cicero, *De Inventione*, I. ii. 3.
75 For a contemporary (anonymous) account of this riot, see L'Archivio Segreto
della Vaticana, Misc. Arm. II. 29, 275^r-284^r, which describes how books and
papers found in the prison were burnt, probably to guarantee prisoners amnesty.
Finding details of Wilson's imprisonment and trial among the Vatican papers is thus
unlikely, particularly as the archive relating to the Pauline Inquisition suffered
further depredation after its removal to Paris by Napoleon (Adriano Prosperi, 'Una
esperienza di ricerca nell' archivio del sant' uffizio', *Belfagor*, 53 (1998), 309–45).
76 Thomas Wilson, *A Discourse upon Usury*, ed. R. H. Tawney (London: G. Bell,
1925).
77 Norman Jones, *God and the Moneylenders: Usury and Law in Early Modern
England* (Oxford: Blackwell, 1986), 25. Cf. Simonds D'Ewes, *A Compleat Journal
of the Notes, Speeches and Debates, Both of the House of Lords and House of
Commons, throughout the whole Reign of Queen Elizabeth* (1693), 171–4, 179.

that in the process of producing a detailed analysis of sixteenth-century monetary practice, it also examines the effectiveness of rhetoric and logic for making and implementing policy. Wilson does this in three main ways: first, through his generic choice of dialogue; secondly, by showing how rhetoric can operate without ethical content; and thirdly, by revealing the failure of rhetoric as a tool of persuasion and socio-economic reform.

Wilson's *Vsurye* is not a controlled dialogue in the tradition of Ascham's *Toxophilus*, where one dominant didactic voice dictates reason to his less informed interlocutor. It is a polyvocal text in the mode of what Virginia Cox terms ' "true" dialogues': 'dialogues which are genuinely dialectical' as opposed to ' "false" ones', which are 'monologues in disguise'.[78] The *Vsurye* depicts a debate between a common lawyer, doctor of civil law, preacher, and merchant. Each follows a rhetorical model drawn from Wilson's early works to express their divergent opinions about usury. The preacher consequently obeys the advice of the *Rhetorique* that 'al Preachers shoulde take their begynnyng vpon the occasion of suche matter as is there written', beginning two out of his three speeches with a text he then expounds 'declaryng why and wherfore and vpon what consideracion suche wordes were in those daies so spoken' (58ᵛ). Even the merchant provides a 'type' for rhetorical speech by producing its mirror image: a disordered garble of questions, which enlightens none, and riles the civilian, breaching all three fundamental laws 'required of an Orator' set down in the *Rhetorique*, namely 'To teache. To delight. And to perswade' (1ᵛ). However, it is through the two lawyers—professional word-smiths—that Wilson puts most pressure on the ideal of rhetoric.

The amorality of the common lawyer (henceforth called the 'lawyer') is established in the preamble to the discussion, where he is singled out as 'not muche better than a pettye fogger' (¶¶7ʳ), defined in the *OED* as 'a legal practitioner of inferior status, [. . .] especially [. . .] one who employs mean, sharp, cavilling practices'. His integrity is then further undermined by his unashamed decla-ration that he loves the merchant for his wealth (10ʳ). Yet it is the lawyer who, following the precepts of Wilson's *Rhetorique*,

---

[78] Virginia Cox, *The Renaissance Dialogue: Literary Dialogue in its Social and Political Contexts, Castiglione to Galileo* (Cambridge: Cambridge University Press, 1992), 2.

produces a perfect example of a 'legall oration' in which moderate usury receives a spirited defence. From his opening 'insinuacion' to his conclusion (a model in amplification), the lawyer selects strategies designed to win over an initially hostile audience. 'Insinuacion', recommended by the *Rhetorique* 'if the cause be lothsome', functions by requesting the audience 'not streightly to geue iudgement, but with mercie to mitigate, all rigor of the Lawe' (55^r). The lawyer accordingly begins by highlighting the impractical stringency of divine law, which rules against usury. 'What man euer lyued, that did, or was able to perfourme this law?' he demands: 'none surely, sauyng Christe onely' (40^r). His rhetorical question presumes agreement with the answer he provides. With the workability of divine law against usury negated, the lawyer has a clear field in which to propose the more lenient alternatives he favours.

The lawyer's use of amplification is similarly well chosen and executed. As the rhetorical figure which most 'beautifieth' an oration, amplification is particularly suited to conclusions, 'augmentyng and vehemently enlarging that, whiche before was in fewe wordes spoken, to set the Iudge or hearers in a heate'.[79] In his summing up (53^r–54^r), the lawyer focuses on two heart-rending cases: a widow with six infants, left destitute when legalized usury would have provided a living, and a loyal servant abandoned at his master's death, forced to beg and thieve to avoid starvation, eventually ending on the gallows. This conclusion abounds in methods of amplification recommended in the *Rhetorique* (64^r), as the lawyer 'extenuate[s] and make[s] lesse, great faultes' that 'other faultes might seeme the greatest' and concentrates on 'mouyng [the] affections' of his audience through the emotive nature of these cautionary tales, which wreak disaster upon once upright citizens. Despite—or because of—his amorality, the lawyer is also at pains in his conclusion, as Quintilian urges, to establish his ethos, presenting his oration as the product of 'learninge & [. . .] conscience' (55^v), a final rhetorical flourish designed, as the *Rhetorique* explains, to 'get fauour for our awne sakes' (56^v).[80]

The lawyer's speech can thus be seen as an extreme reading of the *Rhetorique*, with the main body of the oration split into two

---

79 Wilson, *Rhetorique*, 69^r, 71^v.
80 Quintilian, *Institutio Oratoria*, III. viii. 12–13.

sections. The first is arranged according to the six parts of 'the state
legall' described in the *Rhetorique*; the second is modelled on the
seven 'places of confirmacion' for 'the state Iuridiciall' set down in
the same volume.[81] The lawyer recurrently adopts the argumenta-
tive strategies detailed in that book. 'Away with this precisenes on
godes name,' he cries (44ᵛ), mimicking the *Rhetorique*'s suggestion
of 'takyng GOD to witnesse' (57ᵛ). Elsewhere, he reinterprets the
scriptures in a fashion not unlike that demonstrated in the
Rhetorique, where Wilson observes that 'the mind of the lawe
maker muste rather be obserued, then the bare wordes taken
onely', providing examples of texts in need of such metaphorical
readings, in which 'there is no suche meanyng, as the bare wordes
vttered seme to yelde' (52ᵛ–53ʳ). Amongst them is the lesson 'go,
and sell all that thou hast, and geue it to the poore', interpreted as
a maxim which 'declares we should be liberal, and glad to part
with our gooddes to the poore and neady'. The lawyer argues likewise, echoing the *Rhetorique*'s repeated phrase 'bare words', when
he states that 'in Saint Matthew, Christ forbiddethe his disciples to
cary gold or siluer about them, or anye maner of coin [. . .] in al
whiche speches, I trust you wil grant an interpretacion, ouer and
besydes the bare letter' (50ʳ). The lawyer's performance thus highlights the fact that rhetorical prowess need not be accompanied by
ethics, evidence that runs contrary to the declaration with which
Wilson concluded his *Rhetorique*, that 'the good will not speake
euill, and the wicked can not speake well' (119ʳ). Further to that,
the rhetorical techniques on which the lawyer relies are those
taught by Wilson himself.

The civilian proves no more reliable. For both lawyers, rhetoric
is a set of rules learnt to put either side of the case. Both, for example, use the seven places of confirmation, described in the
Rhetorique, but to argue the opposite: the lawyer defends limited
usury; the civilian insists all usury is wrong.[82] The civilian presents
his speech as detached, in sentiment and vigour, from his own
opinion, and any vehemence mere rhetorical gloss. 'You shall
rather heare what I haue read & gathered of others then knowe

[81] For the lawyer's use of the state legal and places of confirmation, see Cathy
Shrank, 'English Humanism and National Identity, 1530–1570', unpublished Ph.D.
dissertation (University of Cambridge, 2000), 162–3.
[82] For the civilian's use of places of confirmation, see ibid. 167.

mine opinion directly,' he warns, 'although I may seeme to shew some heat, as occasion shal serue' (83ᵛ). Where the lawyer concentrates on 'mouyng affections' and follows the advice of the *Rhetorique*, the civilian—eager to convey an impression of 'methode or order' (84ʳ)—is indebted to techniques of logical argument imparted by Wilson's *Reason*. With the various 'parte[s]' of his 'diuision' laid before his audience, the civilian begins by defining usury according to the 'eight waies' of examining an issue set out in the *Reason* (E6ʳ).[83] He then moves into the main substance of his oration with a display of suitably concise 'proposicions', 'suche sentences, as might bee full of pithe, and contein in them the substance of muche matter', and the verbal trope on which logical argument relies.[84] 'Where no charitye is, ther is no vertue,' the civilian states, for example: 'but in the vsurers harte there is no charitie: therefore the vsurer is voide of vertue' (88ʳᵛ). For all his skilful deployment of logic and rhetoric, however, the civilian offers no solution, postponing his opinion about 'what is expedient to bee donne' until 'farther conference, & priuate debating' (84ᵛ). The preacher, moreover, remains unconvinced by his fine words. 'You, master Ciuilian, although you haue saide muche and very well [. . .] yet I doubt of your constant abiding, in the very practise and truethe of this cause,' he declares, discounting the civilian's attack on usury: 'for I feare me, you wyl beare with gloses, and winke at these worldly and politike deuises' (181ᵛ). The civilian's rhetoric ultimately holds no more truth than that deployed by the 'pettye-fogger' lawyer (¶¶6ʳ).

The protagonists remain locked into their own systems of logic and rhetoric, talking at cross purposes like the babble of courtiers, poets, auditors, and lawyers found in Wilson's *Rhetorique* (83ʳᵛ), each incomprehensible to the other. Each speaker in the *Vsurye*—except the merchant in his disorderly bluster—manipulates the same texts (Augustine, Ezechiel chapter 18, Justinian, and the statutes of Henry VII, Henry VIII, and Edward VI) to their own ends. The lawyer talks of 'conscience' (55ᵛ) no less than the preacher and appropriates the latter's call for 'charitie' (41ʳ) to support his own theory that only excessive interest constitutes usury. The interlocutors hear what they want to hear. The

[83] For the civilian's use of the eight ways of examining an issue, see ibid. 166.
[84] Wilson, *Rhetorique*, 61ʳ.

merchant, the principal usurer and therefore the prime target of the debate, dozes, unaffected by the arguments around him, 'greet[ing their] good talke with a nodde' and 'thereby the better digest[ing his] dinner' (157ᵛ). Two incidents during the preamble to the main discussion highlight the lack of true communication. First, during the meal, the preacher sits silently and 'lifting his eies often to heaven seemed to sitt in some mislykinge wyth the world': 'notwythstanding, hee was remembred by the merchaunt, master Lawier, and others to be merye as they were' (3ʳ). Secondly, comes the exchange in which the preacher (still unprompted) gives the cause for his moroseness. 'It is very certayne as I take it, the worlde is almoste at an ende,' he declares. 'What is the matter, syr? belyke you are wearye of the world[?]' asks the merchant, only able to comprehend the remark in his own earthbound terms. 'No, not weary of the world, but I thinke him angry with the worlde,' the lawyer interjects, again thinking in individual, not general, terms, but also in the conflictual sense on which his profession is founded (3ʳᵛ).

When it occurs, therefore, the characters' sudden renunciation of usury has the miraculous hallmarks of Wilson's liberation in Rome: the work of neither logic nor rhetoric, but of God, dubbed a 'conuersion' by the preacher (201ʳ). Their state of redemption is nevertheless portrayed as tellingly fragile. The merchant can only 'trust' he is 'a new man' (199ᵛ), whilst the lawyer further undermines the neat outcome by recalling that all, including the preacher, are compromised by the fact they have enjoyed the hospitality of a known usurer. 'And now will I saye, thys is the best dinner that euer I came at in al my life,' he concludes: 'And I pray god it may be so vnto you, master merchaunt, that are the chiefe of this feast, and haue been after a sorte the cause of this disputacion' (199ʳ). The lawyer's words highlight the parallels between their situation and that related in one of the civilian's 'iest[s]', which again undercuts the preacher, worker of this so-called miracle, and indicts the merchant at whom the discourse is directed. The civilian relates how 'a certayne famous preacher [. . .] not many yeres past at Paules crosse' used his sermon to lambaste usury (140ᵛ). Like the preacher of the *Vsurye*, the Paul's Cross preacher is invited to dinner, where he is thanked by his host (the greatest usurer in London) for having spoken so vehemently against the practice. Queried by another guest over the hypocrisy of this statement, the host replies, 'I do thanke him, & thanke hym agayne, for [. . .] the fewer vsurers that hee can make, the more shalbee my gayne' (141^r). The impassioned rhetoric of the Paul's Cross preacher has had no impact and is consequently reduced to 'a fewe woordes of hys trolling tong'. The situation, moreover, echoes that of the preamble to the discussion, where the lawyer sets a precedent for the ineffectuality of rhetoric, however heated, informing the preacher that, 'in all your sermons [. . .] you rattle so greatly against this offence, that you shake the bloode of some, tyll they blushe as redde as their cloakes, and manye do scratche throughe your bitter speache, where it ytcheth not' (11^r); he, however, remains unconvinced: 'for I feare mee you cannot iudge so well by diuinitie what this offence ys, as the common lawyers can do'.

The twin arts of logic and rhetoric, promoted by Wilson earlier in his career as tools of government, are thus depicted in a state of failure: manipulated, abused, or ineffectual. As such, the book anticipates its own inability to influence the economic debate (a potential reason for its delayed publication).[85] In 1571, parliament legislated on the question of usury. The remit of debate was not its abolition, but 'merely [. . .] the respective merits of ten per cent and eight per cent [interest]'.[86] The futility of the purportedly persuasive arts is underscored by the 1572 epilogue to the *Vsurye*, which exposes the fictionality of the dialogue: 'I have made but onely a rehersall of an assemblie, whiche I will not sweare to bee trew neyther, for all the goodes in Englande,' Wilson states (202^v). The convenient conversion at the end of the *Vsurye* is confuted, for 'an easie matter it is, to tell a tale, or to make a tale of any man, or of any matter eyther to or fro' (203^r). As author, it is simple to bend events to your will; as an orator, less so. Despairing of the ability of any 'tongue' or 'penne' to 'expresse at ful, the eui[l] of this world', Wilson declares instead his choice of artifice over reportage. 'I haue concluded of these men, as I woulde it were [. . .], and so al thyngs after much talke are lapped vp as you see,' he recounts, before further subverting the 'ioyful ende' he has provided. 'What yf I sayde, that these merchaunts and lawyers, notwithstanding their solempne vowes, will not be so good, as they

[85] Another explanation is Wilson's part interrogating Thomas Howard, Duke of Norfolk, and his servants in summer 1571, a considerable call on Wilson's time and energy.   [86] Wilson, *Usury*, ed. Tawney 171.

seeme to have made promyse vpon this last agrement?' he asks: 'I
thinke yf I layd a good round wager of mony vpon this matter
[. . .] there be thousands in England, that woulde bee my halfe'
(204^r).

   Gone is the cosy island status celebrated in the dedicatory poems
of the *Rhetorique* and *Reason*, with their abundance of emphatic,
self-reflexive pronouns delineating boundaries of Englishness and
rights of possession. Instead, that idealized self-sufficiency is placed
firmly in the past, shattered by what the civilian portrays as the
self-seeking merchant classes. 'Then was no fraude vsed,' remi-
nisces the civilian: 'yea in those dayes, merchauntes were beneficiall
to the prince, profitable to theire countrie' (149^v). National
communities have been replaced with international trading cartels,
for 'synce [that] tyme [. . .] seynge great gayne before theire eyes by
thexchange [. . . merchants] entered into a fraternitye to haue the
exchange amongst themeselues'. The civilian here echoes Wilson's
preface, which advocates national self-reliance: 'to whose suffi-
cience, if mans gredy appetite, could aunswere, and yelde themselues content, with the blessed frute of this lyttle paradise of
Englande, one man shoulde haue little cause to borrowe of an
other' (¶8^{rv}). The past is viewed nostalgically as a haven for justice,
as Wilson harks back to 'the olde lawes of England' (¶8^r) and
requests another Thomas Cromwell (¶6^v).

   Love of your country might be a social bond, recommended in
the *Rhetorique* for its ability to win over an audience and gain their
attention (56^r), but it proves easily unstuck. During the meal at the
start of the *Vsurye*, conversation 'was specially the honor of
England, al which speache was soothed almoste by euerye body, &
gloriously extolled for that present' (2^v). The topic resurfaces after
dinner, and initially provides agreement, as the merchant and his
guests praise the liberty, godliness, and hospitality of the English.
'Englishe subiects lyue in merueylous exemption and liberty, in
comparison of other nations,' declares the preacher (7^r), tapping
into sixteenth-century perceptions about the relative freedom
enjoyed by the English, found, for example, in the works of Smith
and Thomas.[87] 'As they liue in great freedome, so they liue most
godlye,' the lawyer rejoins. 'Do you not see how vacabonds are
whypped, and whoremongers carted, whyche is not vsed in other

---

[87] Smith, *De Republica Anglorum*, 56–7; Thomas, *Historie*, 5^{rv}.

countreys,' the merchant interjects approvingly: 'yea, and hospital-
itie better maintayned in England, then in anye place els in
Chrystendome' (7^{rv}). However, it is only 'for that present' that
'almoste [. . .] euerye body' joins in this self-congratulation: soon
after, the preacher denies his compatriots' religiosity, lawfulness,
and hospitality, and further attacks them for intemperance of
speech and diet. Usury, moreover, is a 'caterpiller' devouring the
commonweal from within (96^{v}), destroying the amity tying society
together, a 'linkage of usury with the inversion of the proper social
order' characteristic of sixteenth-century attacks on moneylend-
ing.[88] 'Whether these men be profitable, or tollerable to a common
weale, or no, I reporte me to you,' asserts the preacher, deploring
usurers who 'destroye and deuour up, not only whole families, but
also whole countreys, and bring all folke to beggerie, that haue to
do wyth them' (37^{r}).

The disillusionment of the *Vsurye* is heightened by comparison
with Smith's *Commonweal*. Both 'discourses', set after a meal in a
merchant's garden, seek to remedy current economic ills. Yet, in
contrast to Wilson's text, not only does the 1549 *Commonweal*
contain an authoritative speaker (the doctor) to whom the other
speakers listen, it is also offered in the belief that 'the state of the
Common-weal [may be] reformed again'.[89] Any promise of
improvement contained in Wilson's text, which laments socio-
economic grievances arising from similar manifestations of short-
sighted, self-centred opportunism, remains dependent on
near-hopeless prayer. 'And yet shal not I wishe and praye that al
thinges may bee wel, although it bee almost impossible, to haue
perfection and soundenes of lyfe in all men, and amongest all
states?' Wilson confesses: 'Which god graunte, for the merites of
Christ hys sonne, our onely mediator and sauiour. Amen' (204^{v}).

This vision of a malfunctioning nation, however, is not confined
to Wilson's last published work. As discussed above, governance in
the *Rhetorique* and *Reason* all too often appears in its breach and
their folios are bespattered with bloody insurrections, and within
the *Rhetorique*, the potential (and current) abuse of rhetoric is
evident, as with 'ambiguitee', for which 'lawyers lacke no cases, to
fil this parte full of examples. For, rather then faile, thei will make
doubtes often tymes, where no doubt should be at all' (53^{r}). The

---

[88] Jones, *God and the Moneylenders*, 45.   [89] Smith, *Commonweal*, 10.

Orations, meanwhile, depicts a city-state in its fading glory. The unheeding audience Demosthenes and Wilson address comprises their own compatriots, who remain as uninterested in their impending doom as those castigated in Wilson's *Rhetorique* for neglecting archery.[90] 'Our nature is so fonde that we knowe not the necessitie of a thyng, til wee fynde some lack of the same,' Wilson complains: 'bowes are not estemed as they haue bene here emong vs Englishmen, but if we were ones well beaten by our enemies wee shoulde soone knowe the wante, and with feelyng the smarte lament muche our folie' (21ᵛ).

For Peter Medine, Wilson's experiences in Rome form a watershed, signalling the end of his humanist outlook. As Medine laments, Wilson, 'who had begun his career seeking to promote his country's welfare not with force but with humanist tracts on logic and rhetoric', became 'one of the crown's most vigorous interrogators'.[91] I would argue for greater continuity between the two 'halves' of Wilson's career. The *Rhetorique* and *Reason* are permeated with instances of the very 'force' Medine regrets, whilst Wilson's later works are riven with doubts and scepticism (present in embryonic form in his earlier texts) found in the humanist writings of More and Erasmus. Indeed, Wilson's *Vsurye* can be seen as a response to More's *Utopia*, a work that Wilson (like More, a senior practising lawyer) respects as an authority, praising 'sir Thomas More for his Eutopia' alongside Lucian for 'the excellencie of his inuencion'.[92] There are echoes of More's masterpiece in the apparatus preceding Wilson's main text, relying as it does on an epistolary preamble, initiated by the discovery of a letter pertaining to the *Vsurye* 'founde in the studie of [. . .] Ihon late bishop of Salisburye, within certeine monthes after his forsaking this earthly dwellynge' (A3ʳ). As this letter passes into Wilson's hands via those of John Garbrand, author of one of the prefatory poems, and into the readers' knowledge, it becomes (like the letters in *Utopia*) a vehicle for establishing a supportive coterie of like-minded scholars.

The *Vsurye* also shares the playful ambiguity of More's work. Like More, Wilson exploits the technique of 'narrative metalepsis'

---

[90] Cf. Roger Ascham, *Toxophilus*, in Ascham, *Works*, i. 89.
[91] Medine, *Wilson*, 28.
[92] Wilson, *Rhetorique*, 106ʳ. Cf. id., *Reason*, U5ʳ.

in which 'characters' from one fictional or factual narrative intrude into another, disrupting the readers' sense of fictional boundaries.[93] The title page of the *Vsurye* announces the author as 'Thomas Wilson, doctour of the Ciuill lawes, one of the Masters of her maiesties honorable courte of requestes'. As we have seen, a doctor of civil law also features as one of the protagonists in the dialogue, and although the civilian is not the narrator, at times their voices merge, as when the civilian interrupts his speech to enquire whether his audience is bored: 'hereupon I [the narrator] wished bothe hym and all others, not to geeue occasion, & then men woulde speake the lesse againste vsurie' (134^v). The narrator continues, execrating usury. During the ensuing passage, his voice is replaced by the civilian's. Lacking a speech marker, the exact point at which this occurs remains unclear. The direct speech of the narrator ('Wilson', doctor of civil law) fades into that of a fictional character, another civilian.

As the *Vsurye* mimics *Utopia*'s disorientating tendency to mix fact and fiction, it draws further, teasing parallels with that earlier text. Like *Utopia* (and Plato's *Republic*), the *Vsurye* is set in a busy port (London to More's Antwerp and Plato's Piraeus) and the encounter similarly follows a religious service (in Plato's case, a religious festival). As in *Utopia*, Wilson's initial section is conducted over a communal meal, providing scope for social satire in the comic pen portraits of the gloomy preacher, 'his head hammeryng vpon another steethy' (2^v), the self-satisfied lawyer who 'amongest all others at that table, had most talke, as he that thought himselfe moste woorthye' (2^v), the impetuous young apprentice giving 'longer eare then hys young head coulde well endure' (13^v), and the materially minded merchant inviting admiration of his well-appointed home (3^r). The quarrel between the two lawyers (14^r–17^r) postpones the main discussion no less than that between More's monk and 'wit' at Cardinal Morton's table, whilst a further nod to *Utopia* comes in the image of England devoured now, not just by Hythloday's sheep, but by sheep and usurers: 'by these twoe idle occupacions, great vsurye and manye flockes of sheepe and heardes of beastes, this noble Countrey is made in a maner a forest, and brought to greate ruyn and decay,' complains the civilian (97^r). Further to that, Wilson's *Vsurye* replicates the same concerns with

---

93 Genette, *Narrative Discourse*, 234–6.

problems of giving counsel (that it is ignored) discussed by Hythloday in *Utopia*, Book I.

Wilson's allusions to his literary predecessor not only position his own work within a humanist heritage: they also grant it additional satirical bite. Dominic Baker-Smith argues that a critique of *avaritia* and the destruction of *caritas* is central to *Utopia*.[94] Wilson inherits his fellow lawyer's concerns, and the evils of engrossing and forestalling, which Hythloday attacks, are transferred by Wilson from enclosure to usury.[95] By displaying them in a text that advertises its own debt to that work, Wilson once again underlines the potential futility of rhetoric. The use of dialogue to criticize the perpetuation of social ills does not just point pessimistically to their continued existence: it questions the efficacy of the genre as a mode of social criticism and instrument of change. Despite More's satire, avarice remains and charitable love continues to be eroded.

Utopia provides a further, biographical parallel to Wilson's *Vsurye*. For both authors, their most elusive texts were their last fictive publications. More continued to publish, but only religious polemics; Wilson translated George Buchanan's *De Maria Scotorum Regina*, 'a pamphlet designed to discredit Mary Stuart', at the time of the Norfolk Plot, adding approximately a hundred pages of material.[96] As Medine bemoans, Wilson (like More) became a man who subscribed to official violence. His willingness to 'resort to the rack when he thought the occasion warranted' is seen by Medine as a betrayal of his humanism.[97] Yet Wilson's commitment to maintaining order through authoritarian measures was not without personal cost, as revealed in letters written during the lengthy interrogations of Thomas Howard and his servants in 1571. The process weighed heavily on Wilson and Smith, his fellow interrogator. Wilson, spending long hours in the Tower pursuing the investigation, talks of having 'made [him]self volontarelie a prysoner to doe her Ma[jes]tie true and faithful seruice'.[98] The

94 Baker-Smith, *More's Utopia*, 207.
95 David M. Bevington, 'The Dialogue in *Utopia*: Two Sides to the Question', *Studies in Philology*, 58 (1961), 496–509, at 503.
96 Tita French Baumlin, 'Thomas Wilson', in *Dictionary of Literary Biography*, ccxxxvi: *British Rhetoricians and Logicians, 1500–1600*, ed. Edward A. Malone (Detroit: Bruccoli Clark Layman, 2001), 282–307, at 302.
97 Medine, *Wilson*, 28.   98 BL Caligula C. 3, 275ʳ.

correspondence of Smith and Wilson also records their objections to the rack, which Cecil, anxious for results, instructed them to use. 'Though we be importune to crave Revocation from this unpleasant and painefull Toile, I pray you be not angry with us,' writes Smith on his and Wilson's behalf: 'we have gotten so mych as at this Tyme is like to be had; yet Tomorrow do we intend to bring a Couple of them to the Rack, not in eny Hope to get any thyng worthy [by] Payne or Feare, but because it is so earnestly commanded unto us.'[99] The task of judgement is not welcomed. 'I wold not wish to be one of Homer's Gods, if I thought I should be Minos, Aeacus or Rhadamanthas,' notes Smith, but 'rather [. . .] one of the least Umbrae in Campis Elysis'.[100]

Wilson's acceptance of force when necessary for conserving domestic peace and the safety of the monarch is not a refutation, but a natural culmination of his understanding of the humanist tradition. Throughout his career, Wilson applied his learning to promoting and protecting a nation-state which, for him, depended on strong, central government. His attack on opponents of enclosure in the *Rhetorique* (19^r), for example, seemingly contradicts his castigation in the *Vsurye* of the 'idle' occupation of sheep farming, where it is aligned with the detrimental practice of usury (97^r). However, owing to its association with Kett's 1549 rebellion, resistance to enclosure had very different connotations in the early 1550s from in the 1570s and the context of parliamentary usury debates. This apparent volte-face is consequently wholly consistent with Wilson's prioritization of obedience over fellowship, an opinion also reflected in his explanation of civic duty in the *Orations*, where love of one's country and loyalty to the monarch stand next to godliness and are more necessary than respectful treatment of others. The aim of Wilson's works was to equip his nation's governors, a class he had joined, and, as he argues in the *Orations*, 'no man can be a good Magistrate, that will not as deadlye hate, as hee deeply loueth' (130).

---

[99] Samuel Haynes (ed.), *Collections of State Papers Relating to Affairs in the Reigns of Henry VIII, Edward VI, Mary and Elizabeth, 1542–1580, left by William Cecil, Lord Burghley*, 2 vols. (1740), ii. 95.

[100] On arriving in the Underworld, the fate of the dead (the *umbrae*, or shades) was decided by Minos, Aeacus, and Rhadamanthas: the blessed entered the Elysian Fields; criminals and other wrongdoers were incarcerated and tortured in Tartarus.

6

'Workshops of the New Poetry': *The Shepheardes Calender* and *Old Arcadia*[1]

As virtue is the most excellent resting place for all worldly learning to make his end of, so Poetry, being the most familiar to teach it, [. . .] is the most excellent workman.[2]

These were rather the discoursing sort of men than the active.[3]

As diverse as the authors covered in this book are, they are bound together by a sustained interest in England as a nation. They all use their learning for national ends and see themselves, as writers, having a national role, as propagandists, counsellors, linguists improving the national tongue, or historians uncovering a glorious past and recording an even more glorious present. For them, literary and intellectual life is not contemplative. Rather, it is actively engaged in public affairs. In particular, they are conscious of the need to assert their country's worth and redress its 'barbarous' reputation. Even Leland, whose posthumous reputation paints him as an obsessive pedant scrabbling fruitlessly in the dust of monastic libraries, was committed to what he saw as a national project, restoring to light the 'old glory' of his 'renoumed' homeland.[4]

With the exception of Leland, who sought to demonstrate English capabilities in Latin letters, these writers were all concerned

---

[1] John Buxton, *Sir Philip Sidney and the English Renaissance* (London: Macmillan, 1964), 112.   [2] Sidney, *Apology*, 115.
[3] Philip Sidney, *The Countess of Pembroke's Arcadia (The Old Arcadia)*, ed. Katherine Duncan-Jones (Oxford: Oxford University Press, 1999), 285.
[4] Leland, 'Newe yeares gyfte', D7ͬ.

to refine and amend the English tongue: to fashion a national language, be it Borde's programme of linguistic expansion through the importation of Latinate terms, or Smith's linguistic standardization, in which Latin and Greek again provide the models. Similarly, even as these authors promoted an idea of English nationhood, the models to which they looked were those of the Continent, and Italy above all. As such, their writing shows the fusion of classical, Continental, and vernacular cultures, and the continued influence of Latin in an age in which English was establishing itself as a literary language. The period this book covers also marks the emergence of England, at least officially, as a Protestant country. The writers studied here were involved in that process, from Borde, whose adherence to ceremony reminds us of the incompleteness of the Henrician Reformation, to Wilson, who stridently aligns Protestantism and 'right thinking'. Finally, these writers are also linked by their shared awareness of the book as a material object, the form of which shapes the meaning and reception of their work, and their own authorial image.

This concluding chapter explores these themes in an Elizabethan context by examining Edmund Spenser's *Shepheardes Calender* (1579) and Philip Sidney's *Old Arcadia* (c.1580), both of which were written—in part—in reaction to the Anjou crisis, when Elizabeth I vascillated over marriage to François of Valois, Duke of Anjou, youngest son of Catherine de Medici, French Queen Mother.[5] Both texts show their authors reflecting on contemporary politics and the efficacy of the humanist belief in dialogue, as well as contributing directly to the development of a national literary style and canon.

'VNCOVTHE, VNKISTE': PAST AND PRESENT IN THE
SHEPHEARDES CALENDER[6]

The *Shepheardes Calender* was the first major undertaking of the man who would become the Elizabethan imperial poet with the publication of his English epic, the *Faerie Queene*, in two instalments

---

[5] Valois became Duke of Anjou in 1576; prior to that he had gone by the title Duke of Alençon.

[6] Edmund Spenser, *The Shepheardes Calender* (1579), ¶2^r.

in 1590 and 1596. The *Shepheardes Calender* is an important work—and one which usefully illustrates a continuity of tradition between the later Elizabethan period and the earlier years of the century—because it is both forward- and backward-looking. On the one hand, the work is positioned at the beginning of a more obviously 'literary' period of English writing, in which English was unapologetically accepted as a literary language. On the other, as I will be arguing, its form, content, and motivation are indebted to an English tradition emerging from the writings of the mid-sixteenth century.

Spenser's concern within the *Shepheardes Calender* to establish English as a literary language with an honourable literary tradition is a natural culmination of the linguistic endeavours of earlier generations of English authors. Despite its apparently confident announcement of the 'new' English poetry, in its consciousness of its own novelty the *Shepheardes Calender* is closer to mid-Tudor writing than that of subsequent decades, when authors generally felt less need to justify their choice of English as a language in which to write. Further to that, the *Shepheardes Calender* also continues the earlier sixteenth-century commitment to a humanist tradition of public service (together with an awareness of the failings of such ideals), the belief in writing as a means of political intervention, and displays the increasing correlation between Englishness and Protestantism. Like earlier Tudor writers, Spenser uses the *Shepheardes Calender* to address issues of immediate concern to England as a nation, in this case—like John Stubbes's *Discoverie of a Gaping Gulph* (1579)—to participate in the debate surrounding the possible marriage of Elizabeth and Anjou. The writings of Spenser and Stubbes show the extent of political participation in early modern England, a feature of the political landscape already explored in relation to previous generations of writers. Neither Stubbes nor Spenser are aristocrats or high-ranking statesmen, but both feel they have a right to hold, and publicly express, opinions on state affairs and whom Elizabeth should, or should not, marry (which, despite the attempts of parliament in 1566 and 1576, she saw as a matter on which she alone should decide). Voicing their views is not seen as disloyal—Stubbes famously cried 'God save the Queen' as he lost his hand in punishment for writing the *Gaping Gulph*—but is based on a belief that the monarch should act above all for the good of the country, an identification of land and monarch placing obligations, as much as honours, on the sovereign.[7]

Whilst much has been written about the influence of medieval literature on the *Shepheardes Calender*, with the exception of its allusions to the *Mirror for Magistrates*, rather less attention has been paid to its affinity with mid-sixteenth-century writing. Owing to the influence of humanism on the articulation of national identity and belief in the public role of the author during the sixteenth century, it is often difficult to ascertain direct influence between generations of writers. The ideas humanist-educated Elizabethan writers express may be drawn from their earlier sixteenth-century counterparts, quoting Quintilian and Cicero, or they may be drawn from classical sources themselves. Nevertheless, it can safely be said that the *Shepheardes Calender* was produced within a milieu showing a continuity of tradition between the high Elizabethan period and the previous decades of the sixteenth century, not least because of Spenser's connection with the talented Cambridge scholar Gabriel Harvey.

Harvey's posthumous reputation as an object of derision, and the 'officiousness' of which he often stands accused by modern critics, owe much to the vicious caricature of the scholarly pedant painted by Thomas Nashe in *Have with you to Saffron-walden* (1596).[8] Yet despite the recurrent embarrassment of modern scholars about Spenser's friendship with the man worsted by Nashe, Harvey's influence on Spenser during this period was crucial. Senior to Spenser in academic terms, in the late 1570s, Harvey looked set for a distinguished career, sharing Spenser's hopes of court preferment and the humanist belief that learning was the proper means of exerting 'politico-moral influence'.[9] Whilst the images of Spenser and Harvey propounded in their *Three proper, and wittie, familiar letters* (1580) are obviously staged, the publication nevertheless shows the two men posing as sounding boards for each other's ideas and literary endeavours. Harvey's involvement with the *Shepheardes Calender*, revealed in the *Familiar*

---

[7] Lloyd E. Berry (ed.), *John Stubbs' Gaping Gulf with Letters and Other Relevant Documents* (Charlottesville: University Press of Virginia, 1968), p. xxxvi.

[8] For the perpetuation of the caricatured Harvey, see, e.g., S. K. Heninger, *Sidney and Spenser: The Poet as Maker* (University Park: Pennsylvania State University Press, 1989), 1, 6, where Harvey's name is linked with the terms 'officious' and 'officiousness'.   [9] Stern, *Harvey*, 16.

letters, where we see him advising on publication and supplying the subtitle ('conteyning twelue Æglogues proportionable to the twelue monethes'), is substantiated by the printed text of the *Shepheardes Calender*, which is permeated by Harvey's presence. He appears as the shepherd 'Hobbinol' (as the September gloss confirms); as a recurrent name in E.K.'s glosses; and as the addressee of the opening epistle, a position which Ruth Luborsky argues raises him to the position of 'co-dedicatee' with Sidney, a scholarly counterpart to the aristocratic patron.[10] Further to that, Harvey is a likely candidate for the enigmatic E.K., whose glosses are an integral part of the work.[11]

During the period in which the *Shepheardes Calender* was written, Spenser was thus in regular communication with Harvey, exchanging—amongst other things—tips on reading. Not only were the shelves of Harvey's library stocked with the works of authors studied in this book, his annotations also demonstrate that he absorbed and admired them, judging them suitable works for those participating in the *vita activa*. Thomas's *Historie* is deemed to provide 'most pregnant Instructions for the affaires of the World' and 'Excellent Histories, & notable Discourses for everie politician, pragmatician, negotiatour, or anie skilful man'.[12] Wilson's *Reason* and *Rhetorique* are 'the dailie bred of owr common pleaders', with the latter judged one of Harvey's 'best for the art of jesting', alongside 'Tullie, Quintilian, [and] the Courtier in Italian'; Wilson's *Vsurye* is likewise judged 'fine and pleasant'.[13] Harvey marks his appreciation of Smith's *De scriptione* in the *Familiar letters*, and—according to the *Shepheardes Calender*— lent E.K. a manuscript of *De Republica Anglorum*.[14] In turn, Spenser sent Harvey *Scoggins Jests*, posthumously attributed to Borde, along with other jest-books and the enjoinder to read them or 'forfeit' his 'Lucian in fower volumes', requiring Harvey to complement his classical study with knowledge of a thriving vernacular tradition.[15]

---

[10] Ruth Samson Luborksy, 'Allusive Presentation in *The Shepheardes Calender*', *Spenser Studies*, 1 (1980), 29–67, at 40–1.

[11] Other candidates include Edward Kirke, a little-known fellow of Gonville and Caius College, Cambridge, and Spenser himself.   [12] Stern, *Harvey*, 237.

[13] Ibid. 239.

[14] Ibid. 236. Harvey's possession of *De Republica Anglorum* is indicated in Spenser, *Shepheardes Calender*, 2ᵛ.   [15] Cited by Stern, *Harvey*, 228.

That Leland is the only author for whom there is no direct
record is unsurprising, since the majority of his works remained in
manuscript. It is likely, though, that Harvey would have knowledge
of Leland's writing through his patron Thomas Smith (born, like
Harvey, in Saffron Walden), whose acquaintance with Leland's
works is attested by his comments about Leland's notes—that 'vast
heap of observations'—which, after Leland's death, passed into the
possession of John Cheke, Smith's former Cambridge colleague.[16]
Harvey's personal ties to Smith also position him firmly within an
English humanist tradition. We have already noted Harvey's presence at Smith's staged debate at Hill Hall in Chapter 4.[17] Smith
also advised Harvey on his legal studies, employed his sister in his
household, and bequeathed some of his manuscripts to him, whilst
Harvey's own 'pragmatic humanism' identified by Anthony
Grafton and Lisa Jardine surely owes much to the influence of
Smith's practical approach to governance.[18] Harvey and, through
Harvey, Spenser are thus linked into the English writing of the
previous decades of the sixteenth century. These connections are
further compounded by their association with the circle around
Robert Dudley, Earl of Leicester—dedicatee of Wilson's *Vsurye*
and son of the dedicatee of Thomas's *Historie*—at whose London
house Spenser was resident by the summer of 1579.[19]

The *Shepheardes Calender* is therefore rooted in the works of
the previous generations. Whilst the influence of the pragmatic
Smith might weigh most heavily on Harvey, it is nevertheless the
neoclassical Leland with whom Spenser has most in common as a
national writer. Not only do Leland's mythopoeic representations
of the English landscape in printed texts such as the *Cygnea Cantio*
and *Genethliacon* prefigure Spenser's recurrent celebration of the
Thames and its tributaries, out of all the writers studied here,
Leland is the only one who attempts to prove English accomplishments not merely by asserting their potential, but by demonstrating

---

[16] Smith also seems to have exchanged books with William Harrison, whose
Description of England owes much to Leland's *Itinerary* (Smith, *De Republica
Anglorum*, app. 3).

[17] See Grafton and Jardine, ' "Studied for Action" ', 40.

[18] BL Sloane 93, Gabriel Harvey's letter book, 85ʳ–89ʳ, 91ʳ–92ʳ, 92ᵛ–93ʳ; Stern,
Harvey, 38; Anthony Grafton and Lisa Jardine, *From Humanism to the Humanities*
(Cambridge, Mass.: Harvard University Press, 1986), 50. Harvey also published a
long Latin elegy on Smith, *Gabriel Harveii Valdinatis Smithus vel Musarum
Lachrymae* (1577).   [19] Worden, *Sound of Virtue*, 63.

them in poetry.[20] Where Leland strove to show his country's prowess in Latin verse, so Spenser sets out to flaunt the richness of poetry in the vulgar tongue. In the *Shepheardes Calender*, as in Leland's Latin poems, it is Virgil—rather than Cicero—who provides the most immediate model, and in Spenser's poetic vision of the nation—as in Leland's—the monarch plays a central role.[21]

Like Leland, Spenser also seeks to recover a native literary tradition. Even as the publication of the *Shepheardes Calender* announces the arrival of the 'new poete', the work is grounded in the past, a retrospective gaze reflected in the visual appearance of the text. By 1579, the choice of black letter for the main body of the work is deliberately old-fashioned for a work which consciously seeks to set a new agenda, and benchmark, for English writing, and which—despite its 'popular' look—is making strong claims for its literary and learned status.[22] When North's Plutarch—almost 1,200 pages long—was published by Thomas Vautrollier and John Wight that same year, for example, it was printed in roman and italic type, placing the work in line with Continental humanist translations and showing that London-based printers had the resources to produce large, high status books in roman type (type that became the norm for printing higher status texts by the 1580s). The antiquated look of the *Shepheardes Calender* is further enhanced both by the inconsistent use of decorative initial letters, protruding into the margin—imitating manuscript and earlier printed books—and by the crude woodcuts, a mode of illustration then being supplanted in high status texts by copperplate engraving, particularly on the Continent.[23]

The design of the *Shepheardes Calender* is not merely intended to appear old-fashioned or 'popular', however. As we saw in Chapter 3, the choice of typeface had national connotations. When

[20] Spenser, *Faerie Queene*, IV. xi; id., *Shepheardes Calender*, 26ᵛ–27ʳ. In the *Shepheardes Calender*, it is Morrell, the ambitious pastor, neglectful of his flock, who delivers the eulogy on Thames and Medway.
[21] See Leland, *Cygnea Cantio*, where Henry VIII's palaces are the main topographical features celebrated, providing the organizing structure for the poem.
[22] That Spenser planned the visual effect of his book is likely from the fact that the publisher, Hugh Singleton, did not publish any other extant illustrated book. See Ruth Samson Luborsky, 'The Illustrations to *The Shepheardes Calender*', *Spenser Studies*, 2 (1981), 3–53.
[23] Luborsky, 'Allusive Presentation', 54, 30; Carl J. Rasmussen, '*A Theatre for Worldlings* as a Protestant Poetics', *Spenser Studies*, 1 (1980), 1–28, at 4.

Erasmus comments that to 'write a speech of Cicero's in Gothic letters' is to render 'even Cicero [. . .] uneducated and barbarous' ('vel Ciceronis orationem scribe literis Gotticis, soloecam dices ac barbaram'), his words indicate the way in which the choice of type drains Cicero of his Roman civility, tainting his works with the rudeness associated with northern climes.[24] In the *Shepheardes Calender*, Spenser is unembarrassed by the 'uncivil' associations of his chosen typeface. Rather, he uses it to create an English style, an association between type and nation that occurs in texts such as John Hart's *Orthographie* (1569) or Thomas's *Rules of Italian Grammar* (1550), where Latin words are given in roman type, romance languages in italic, English in black letter. The outdated visual effect of the *Shepheardes Calender* is complemented by Spenser's choice of language which harks back to Chaucer, celebrated in the prefatory matter as 'the Loadestarre of our Language' (¶2ʳ), and imitated in the course of the poem by the use of archaic forms such as the *y* prefix; obsolete words like 'gryde', meaning pierced (3ᵛ); and unfamiliar spellings, such as 'youngth' for 'youth' (4ʳ). As Spenser carves out 'a kingdom of our own language', he thus endows it with a preordained heritage, based as it is on the language of Chaucer, the fourteenth-century poet recurrently lauded as the 'father of our English tongue'.[25]

The decision to write an unfamiliar English plays a crucial role in launching the new poet. As Harvey and Spenser's *Familiar letters* show, establishing a national language was the first step in achieving a national poetic style. That Spenser's poetic language should be—or at least appear—so indebted to Middle English was by no means inevitable, however.[26] Indeed, the ruminations on language within the *Familiar letters* reveal the conflicting impulses governing the pursuit of a national poetic language and style. Harvey himself practised a form of 'niu writing', omitting unpronounced letters, such as the *g* in 'might' (which he habitually spelt 'miht').[27] Within

[24] Erasmus, *De pronuntiatione*, 21ᵛ; ed. and trans. Maurice Pope, *Collected Works*, xxvi (1985), 390.

[25] See Crowley (ed.), *Vision of Pierce Plowman*, preface; Leland, *Commentarii*, ii. 421.

[26] For a critique of the exaggeration of Spenser's use of archaism, see Willy Maley, 'Spenser's Language: Writing in the Ruins of English', in Andrew Hadfield (ed.), *The Cambridge Companion to Spenser* (Cambridge: Cambridge University Press, 2001), 161–79, at 166.

[27] See BL Sloane 93, Gabriel Harvey's letter book.

the *Familiar letters*, Harvey declares the most 'regular and iustifi-
able direction, eyther for the assured, and infallible Certaintie of
our English Artificall Prosodye' or 'to bring our Language into
Arte' is 'first of all vniuersally to agree vpon *one and the same
Orthographie*'.[28] Not only does Harvey here support the principles
of standardization expounded by Smith and Hart, whose books he
owned and annotated, he even cites '*Sir Thomas Smithes* [work] in
that respect', judging it, if not 'the most perfit', then 'surely [. . .]
very good' (52). Like their predecessors, Spenser and Harvey are
torn between classical and vernacular models. On the one hand,
they strive to write quantitative verse and—in Harvey's case—
endorse the concept of fixed orthography. On the other, they are
keen to assert the worth of their own tongue and question the
wisdom of overturning established customs.

Even at the height of the discussion about quantitative metre, in
which he himself dabbled (claiming to be the father of the English
hexameter), Harvey's discomfort is made apparent, however, and
within the *Familiar letters*, he protests against distorting the
rhythms of English speech. 'In good sooth, and by the faith I beare
to the Muses,' he declares, 'you shall neuer haue my subscription
or consent (though you should charge me wyth the authoritie of
fiue hundreth Maister *Drants*,) to make your Carpēnter our
Carpēnter, or an inche longer, or bigger than God & his English
people haue made him' (52). Just as Smith described individual
letters as 'citizens', so Harvey treats words as inhabitants of a
commonwealth of language. The unnatural speech patterns
imposed by quantitative verse are deemed an assault upon their
liberty and an attempt 'against all order of Lawe, and in despite of
Custom, forcibly [to] vsurpe and tyrannise vppon a quiet companye of words'. As Harvey talks in terms of the 'several Priviledges
in Libertes' that this 'quiet companye' has 'so farre beyonde the
memorie of man [. . .] peacably enioyed', he evokes the discourse
of ancient English liberties found in texts such as Smith's *De scriptione* and *A Discourse on the Coming of the English and Normans*,
written by Smith's unlikely ally, Stephen Gardiner, as a means of
warning Philip of Spain against overriding English law.[29] Custom

---

[28] Spenser and Harvey, *Familiar letters*, 32. Text printed italic here appears in
roman type—opposed to black letter—in the original.
[29] Smith, *De scriptione*, 33ʳ. For the friendship of Smith and Gardiner, see
Dewar, *Smith*, 18, 75–7.

is no longer synonymous with papist ritual, as it had been in the
works of Wilson and, at other times, Smith.[30] Rather, it is equated
with law and the protection of English liberties.[31]

Ultimately, custom wins. For his published texts, Harvey's
'unusual but quite logical phonetic spelling' is thrown over in
favour of the more normative, but illogical, unreformed orthography.[32] Spenser rejects quantitative metre in favour of English
rhyme and eschews the purified English championed by the previous generation of linguistic reformers, with their tendency—from
Cheke to Hart—to call for the purging of romance words in favour
of Anglo-Saxon terms.[33] The *Shepheardes Calender* might regret
the 'disherit[ing]' of 'good and naturall English words' in similar
financial and sartorial terms to those employed by Cheke in 1557
or Smith in the 1540s, and protest, in a suitably vernacular phrase,
against the 'gallimaufray or hodgepodge' that has been made of
English, 'patched vp [. . .] with peces & rags of other languages'
(¶2ᵛ). Nevertheless, Spenser's is a far more eclectic English than
that promoted by the likes of Cheke. Seemingly based on Middle
English, it draws on the language of a period which saw both the
fusion of Anglo-Saxon and Norman French, and the demise of
inflected Old English in favour of a looser, less regulated grammatical system.[34] Spenser's English, unlike Wilson's, also includes
dialect terms, embracing words from the regions of England, as
well as Irish.[35] In particular, as Douglas Brooks-Davies points out,
northern terms are used, not to signal incivility, as in Wilson's
Rhetorique, but to celebrate the *honestas*, or plainness, of the
Shepheardes Calender's more reformist figures.[36] Where Wilson
wanted to unite a nation of English speakers by banishing regional
terms and providing them with 'one maner of language', Spenser is

---

[30] Wilson, *Reason*, T5ʳ; Smith, *De scriptione*, 1ᵛ.

[31] Harvey did express concern about the eclipse of civil law by common law elsewhere, in a letter to Thomas Smith, c.1574 (BL Sloane 93, 88ᵛ).

[32] Stern, *Harvey*, 144.

[33] John Cheke, letter to Hoby in Hoby, *Courtier*, 7; Smith, *De scriptione*, 33ʳ;
John Hart, *A Methode or comfortable beginning for all vnlearned whereby they
may bee taught to read English* (1570), A3ʳ.

[34] Barbara A. Fennell, *A History of English: A Sociolinguistic Approach* (Oxford:
Blackwell, 2001).

[35] e.g., 'greet' (northern English), in 'April'; 'Kerne' (Irish), in 'July'. See Maley,
'Spenser's Language', 165.

[36] Wilson, *Rhetorique*, 50ʳ; Edmund Spenser, *Selected Shorter Poems*, ed.
Douglas Brooks-Davies (London: Longman, 1995), 38.

eager to encompass a range of different Englishes and the language of England's Irish territories. Like Castiglione, Spenser chooses 'woordes out of euery part' ('parole [. . .] d'ogni parte').[37]

Visually and linguistically, then, there is a sustained and deliberate attempt within the *Shepheardes Calender* to create a vernacular style. Through use of old-fashioned printing techniques, diction, and orthography, Spenser celebrates an English literary aesthetic rooted in history and spreading across its geographical dominions. Like his predecessors, however, Spenser's vision of English letters does not reject the classical or Continental: it merges them with the vernacular. The woodcuts might be noticeably crude, far below the standard of which English craftsmen were then capable.[38] Nevertheless, their rough-hewn quality disguises a sophisticated subtlety. Specially commissioned for the *Shepheardes Calender*, these apparently inferior illustrations 'quote' other pastoral woodcuts from Scots, French, and Latin literature, including Alexander Barclay's *Egloges* (*c.*1515), Guillaume Marot's 'Le premier eclogue des bucoliques de Virgile' (reprinted 1571), and Sebastian Brant's edition of Virgil's *Opera* (1502).[39] Within the *Shepheardes Calender*, Spenser depicts a community of shepherds who gather in different eclogues and discuss each other's songs and lives. Yet this community is not limited to Spenser's text: it is picked from, and brings together, a Western literary tradition. Tityrus and Menalcas are taken from Virgil's Latin *Eclogues*; Piers / Pierce and Diggon Davie, from William Langland's *Piers Plowman* and its sixteenth-century reincarnations in the works of Crowley and Churchyard; Colin, both from Skelton's satirical personae, Colin Clout, and Marot's French pastorals (which also feature Thenot). As E.K. explains, the allusiveness of 'our new Poete' is proof of his learning, for 'how could it be, [. . .] but that walking in the sonne although for other cause he walked, yet needes he mought be sunburnt; and hauing the sound of those auncient Poetes still ringing in his eares, he mought needes in singing hit out some of theyr tunes' (¶2^r).

Chaucer's identification as Tityrus (Virgil's own persona in his eclogues) in E.K.'s epistle to Harvey is symptomatic of Spenser's

---

[37] Baldassare Castiglione, *Il libro del Cortegiano*, ed. Ettore Bonora (Milan: Mursia, 1972), 73; trans. by Hoby, *Courtier*, 68.

[38] Luborsky, 'Illustrations', 10.

[39] Ead., 'Allusive Presentation', 55, 42.

relationship with this literary tradition (¶2^r). Spenser is heir of both Chaucer and Virgil: Spenser writes eclogues in a Virgilian mode, but in pseudo-Chaucerian language, beginning and ending with a Chaucerian address to his 'little booke' (¶1^v).[40] Further to that, Spenser also becomes like Virgil himself. In looking back to centuries-old writer as model (Chaucer), Spenser imitates Virgil, harking back to Theocritus, 'whose *edyllia* were already two centuries old and were written in an obscure literary language something like rustic Doric Greek'.[41] Richard Helgerson has written about the novelty of Spenser modelling himself on a classical author.[42] There are, however, earlier English precedents for this, albeit on a more limited scale. Wilson, for example, fashions himself as the English Demosthenes in his *Orations*; Smith presents himself as the English Cicero in *De scriptione*, addressing an English Quintus, the name of Cicero's brother and interlocutor of *De divinatione* and *De legibus*.[43] They might not announce their self-identification with the great names of classical literature quite so loudly, or prominently, as Spenser. Nevertheless, imitation here extends beyond localized allusions, such as those found in Leland's Latin poems, with their reworkings of Virgilian phrases. Smith and Wilson adopt more than borrowed lines; they emulate Cicero and Demosthenes in their role as authors. The seeming confidence with which they do so is tempered, however, by an awareness of the audacity, and unfamiliarity of, their claims that English authors can rival the ancients. Smith's most Ciceronian moment therefore comes in the *De scriptione*, written in Latin, not English; where Demosthenes' brusque Greek style would pass without comment, Wilson is required to justify his own choice of plain English. Spenser's promotion of the new English poetry, and of himself as the English Virgil, is thus marked by a familiar anxiety about the status of English as a poetic or scholarly language. Bravado mingles with a need to show his learning, to prove—like Skelton—that

---

[40] Cf. 'Goe lyttle *Calender*', Spenser, *Shepheardes Calender*, 52^r, and 'Go, litel bok', Geoffrey Chaucer, *Troilus and Criseyde*, in *Riverside Chaucer*, 5. 1786.

[41] Bruce R. Smith, 'On Reading *The Shepheardes Calender*', *Spenser Studies*, 1 (1980), 69–93, at 73.

[42] Richard Helgerson, *Self-Crowned Laureates: Spenser, Jonson, Milton* (Berkeley: University of California Press, 1983), 1–3.

[43] Richards, *Rhetoric and Courtliness*, 84; 'Quintus Tullius Cicero', *The Oxford Classical Dictionary* (Oxford: Clarendon Press, 1949), 191.

writing in the vernacular is a choice, not a necessity. Each eclogue closes with an enigmatic Latin emblem and the text displays an excess of learning, from the allusive woodcuts to E.K.'s glosses, which—like the prose commentaries appended to Leland's Latin poems—allow further space to flesh out the scholarship (or pseudo-scholarship) on which the eclogues rest.[44]

Spenser's defensive championing of English as a literary language is both the result of the previous decades, in which writers from Borde to Smith asserted, and strove for, a refined and 'amended' tongue, and his immediate experience as a pupil at Merchant Taylors in the 1560s, where Spenser would have benefited from the enthusiasm of its headmaster, Richard Mulcaster, for the vernacular, not in the standardized form sought by Smith, but with all its current quirks and oddities. For Mulcaster, English had acquired the excellence found 'in the Greeke tung [. . .] when *Demosthenes* liued' and 'in the Latin tung [. . .] when *Tullie* liued, and those of that age': 'such a period in the English tung I take this to be in our daies, for both the pen and the speche'.[45] Although these words were printed in 1582, after the *Shepheardes Calender* had made a bid for English as a literary language, Mulcaster's confidence in English was demonstrated throughout his years at Merchant Taylors. Where in the 1530s and 1540s, Cheke used double translation as a means of encouraging Cambridge students to examine their English style, as well as their Latin, Mulcaster went further still.[46] English composition was not, as it was for Cheke, a side-product of Latin tuition: rather, composition in English poetry was innovatively included on the Merchant Taylors' curriculum in its own right, and the immediate fruits of Mulcaster's tutelage can be found in the works of his former pupils who, beside Spenser, included the writer Thomas Lodge, the playwright Thomas Kyd, and seven of the translators of the 1611 Bible.[47]

---

44 E.K. is, at times, misleading, the humour of some of his glosses depending on the recognition of erroneous information, such as the false etymology of 'elf' and 'goblin' from Guelph and Ghibelline in 'June' (25r), an aside that allows for the introduction of anti-Italian and antipapist feeling (a habitual feature of the glosses).
45 Richard Mulcaster, *First Part of the Elementarie*, 75.
46 Needham, 'Sir John Cheke, i. 122.
47 Richard L. De Molen, *Richard Mulcaster (c.1531–1611) and Educational Reform in the Renaissance* (Nieuwkoop: De Graaf, 1991), p. xxiv.; Richard Mulcaster, *Positions concerning the training up of children*, ed. William Barker (Toronto: University of Toronto Press, 1994), p. lxvi.

At Merchant Taylors, Spenser would also have imbibed Mulcaster's stress, in true humanist style, on education as a means to public service. According to Mulcaster, the ultimate role of the student, and those 'which ar of the vniuersitie', is that they might 'serue abrode in publik functions of the common weal'.[48] 'Education,' he wrote elsewhere, is 'the bringing vp of one, not to liue alone, but amongest others [. . .] whereby he shall be best able to execute those doings in life, which the state of his calling shall employ him vnto [. . .] according to the direction of his countrie whereunto he is borne, & oweth his whole seruice.'[49] Yet even as Spenser puts his writing to public use in the *Shepheardes Calender* by launching himself as the 'new' national poet and intervening in national affairs, he is at pains to preserve his existence within a male circle of private communication and advice-giving, a conservation of the initial circumstances of production that was a trope of the works of Smith and Thomas. The January gloss, for example, reconstructs a network of book-lending, as E.K. refers to Smith's *De Republica Anglorum* ('his booke of gouerment'), 'whereof I haue a perfect copie in wryting, lent me by his kinseman, and my verye singular good freend, M. Garbiel Haruey' (2^v). The June gloss, meanwhile, advertises E.K.'s knowledge of the poet's 'priuate affayres (as I haue bene pardy of himselfe informed)', and Harvey's role as Spenser's mentor, 'priuately' counselling him (in the persona of Hobbinol) on his preferment (24^v–25^r). The publication of the *Familiar letters* a year later further presents the *Shepheardes Calender* as a product of a scholarly and literary coterie. Many of the letters passed between Spenser and Harvey are concerned with the question of a national poetic style in general, and the publication of the *Shepheardes Calender* in particular. Their letters tie together court and university circles: Sidney and Edward Dyer on the one hand; Harvey on the other, with the ghosts of former scholars and statesmen, Smith and Roger Ascham, hovering in the background.

Richard McCabe has described how, by the sixteenth century, 'despite its escapist potential, literary pastoral had long been

---

[48] Mulcaster, *Elementarie*, ¶2^v.
[49] Richard Mulcaster, *Positions wherin those primitiue circumstances be examined, which are necessarie for the training vp of children* (1581), 185.

recognised as a controversial mode, politically as well as other-wise'.[50] Virgil's first eclogue, for example, engages with issues of dispossession and exile, contemporary evils faced by supporters of the losing side(s) in the civil unrest that led to Octavius' elevation as Augustus, Emperor of Rome. The Virgilian background to the *Shepheardes Calender*, which places the text within a tradition of complaint, is underscored by Spenser's imitation of Sackville's Induction from the *Mirror for Magistrates* in the January eclogue, with its evocation of the desolate pastoral landscape, scoured by the winter's 'blustring blastes', its 'gladsom groves [. . .] ouerthrowen / [. . .] and euery blome downe blowen'.[51] The steril-ity and disorder of Spenser's pastoral landscape, with its 'naked trees', clad in 'ysicles', not 'bloosmes' (1^v), mirrors both Colin's state of unrequited, fruitless love (his 'heart' similarly dominated by the winter's 'rage') and—thanks to the 'Mirror' tradition to which the text belongs—the state of the realm whose monarch is distracted by other affairs, namely, the French match. Spenser's shepherds do not simply represent the clergy, the shepherds of men who appear in 'May' and 'July': they also symbolize secular lead-ers and magistrates, an identification endorsed by E.K.'s allusion to Smith's etymology of 'couthe' in *De Republica Anglorum*. As McCabe notes, immediately preceding this discussion is a passage in which tyrants are denounced because they are 'not shepheardes as they ought to be, but rather robbers and devourers of the people'.[52] Throughout the *Shepheardes Calender*, the impact of neglectful shepherds on their flocks is made consistently apparent. In 'January', for example, Colin's 'feeble flock, whose fleece is rough and rent' bears witness to its 'ill gouernement' by a master 'ouercome with care' (1^v–2^r); in the aftermath of Dido's death in 'November', 'the feeble flocks in field refuse their former foode', while the 'Wolues' (Roman Catholic priests) 'chase the wandring sheep / Now she is gon that safely did hem keepe' (46^r).[53]

[50] Richard A. McCabe, ' "Little booke: thy selfe present": Spenser's Politics of Presentation', in Howard Erskine-Hill and Richard A. McCabe (eds.), *Presenting Poetry: Composition, Publication, Reception* (Cambridge: Cambridge University Press, 1995), 15–40, at 17.

[51] Lily B. Campbell (ed.), *The Mirror for Magistrates* (Cambridge: Cambridge University Press, 1938), 298.

[52] McCabe, ' "Little booke" ', 24–5; Smith, *De Republica Anglorum*, 55.

[53] For the papist connotations of 'error' and 'wandering', see Wilson, *Rhetorique*, 48^r.

E.K.'s use of *De Republica Anglorum* as a source for the etymology of *couthe* also points to the ambivalent nature of the *Shepheardes Calender*. The section of *De Republica Anglorum* to which E.K.'s note directs readers is Smith's examination of the derivation of the word *king*, which—as we saw in Chapter 4— opens up the possibility that monarchs rule because they can, not because they are gifted.[54] Even as he seemingly sets out to mythologize her, Spenser—like Smith—refuses to be dazzled by Elizabeth. Indeed, Patrick Collinson even talks of Spenser's 'barely suppressed republicanism', arguing that—when read against Erasmus' *Adagia*—the lament for Algrin (Grindal) in 'July' critiques the tyrannical behaviour of monarchs, who are 'cruelly rapacious rather than truly courageous' and, in destroying wise counsellors, 'myopic rather than "eagle-eyed" '.[55] Spenser recurrently uses Aesopian beast fable to warn (like Smith's *De Republica Anglorum*) of the need for limitations on monarchical power. Elizabeth placed herself in the role of mother to her realm, picking up on the idiom of Isiah 49: 23: 'And Kings shall be thy nursing fathers, and Queens shall be thy nurses.' As Elizabeth told the House of Commons in 1563: 'I assure you all that, after my death you may have many stepdames, yet shall you never have a more natural mother than I mean to be unto you all.'[56] Yet within the *Shepheardes Calender*, and in the May eclogue in particular, mothers prove fatal to their young, be it the goat of Piers' fable, who fails to arm her kid against the predatory papist fox, or the 'Apes folish care' (17ᵛ), a reference to the ape who kills 'her whelp, / Through clasping hard'.[57] The eclogue critiques the mother-monarch who stifles her subjects' liberties or who unwittingly leaves them prey to practitioners of the Roman faith (a fate equated with death in both the case of the kid and Dido, subject of the November elegy). Certainly Spenser's text reveals the harsher side of Elizabeth-Diana, the reference to 'Latonaes seede' (13ʳ) during the paean to Elizabeth in 'April' reminding the reader of the slaughter of Niobe's children by Apollo and Diana, Diana being a

[54] Smith, *De Republica Anglorum*, 56.
[55] Collinson, 'Monarchical Republic', 133 n. 42.
[56] Elizabeth I, *Collected Works*, ed. Leah Marcus et al. (Chicago: University of Chicago Press, 2000).
[57] Geoffrey Whitney, *A Choice of Emblems* (1586), 188. Cited by Brooks-Davies, in *Spenser: Selected Shorter Poems*, 86 n.

favoured image adopted by Elizabeth.[58] The poem's sustained reference to the 'plowman' tradition (through interlocutors such as Piers and Diggon Davey and the epilogue's reference to 'the Pilgrim that the Ploughman playde awhyle', 52ʳ) also takes on added resonance in the late autumn of 1579, thanks to the words of William Page, whose right hand was cut off for distributing Stubbes's *Gaping Gulph*. As he put his hand on the block, Page—a Londoner—claimed that 'this hand did I put to the plow and got my living by it many years'.[59]

The advertisement of Spenser and Harvey's much valued connections with the Sidney circle, and Sidney's appearance as dedicatee on the title page of the *Shepheardes Calender*, also place the text, and these writers, in the midst of the political controversy over Elizabeth's possible marriage to Anjou. In 1579, Sidney wrote to the queen unambiguously attacking the match, a letter which—although ostensibly intended for the queen's eyes alone— nevertheless gained wide circulation.[60] Spenser's choice of printer, Hugh Singleton, compounds the contemporary relevance, and controversial nature, of the *Shepheardes Calender*. Singleton was by no means the obvious choice of printer for an illustrated work. Henry Binneman, Harvey's publisher and publisher of Spenser's translation of Jan van der Noot's *A Theatre for Worldlings* in 1569, was a much more likely candidate. Not only was he already associated with Harvey and Spenser, he also had experience of printing heavily-illustrated works like Holinshed's *Chronicles* (1577), which, with its skilful cutting, attention to proportion, and use of cross-hatching to create depth, is visually of far higher quality than the woodcuts in the *Shepheardes Calender*.[61] If the selection of Singleton as printer does not make aesthetic sense, it does, however, hold political resonance. Only a month before the publication of the *Shepheardes Calender*, Singleton had almost lost his right hand as punishment for publishing Stubbes's *Gaping Gulph*. Singleton won a last minute pardon and saved his hand. Nevertheless, the choice of Singleton as printer, and Sidney as

[58] Ovid, *Metamorphoses*, vi. 165–381.
[59] Berry (ed.), *John Stubbs'* Gaping Gulf, p. xxxvi.
[60] Philip Sidney, *A Letter written to Queen Elizabeth touching her marriage with Monsieur*, in *The Miscellaneous Prose of Sir Philip Sidney*, ed. Katherine Duncan-Jones and Jan van Dorsten (Oxford: Clarendon Press, 1973), 33–59.
[61] Luborsky, 'Illustrations', 8, 10.

dedicatee, indicates the political nature of Spenser's work. It might be subtler than Stubbes's open attack, but its pages side with Stubbes and Sidney in protesting against the dangers of the French marriage.

The *Shepheardes Calender* is crammed with jibes against the match. Aesop's fable of the fox and lion is adapted in the February gloss to make its resonance with the current situation more apparent, as the fox is replaced by an ape, a reference to Anjou's representative, Simier, nicknamed by Elizabeth her 'singe', or ape (8ʳ). Likewise, the March emblem warns against gall spelt 'Gaule' (10ʳ), and the May gloss reminds the reader of the Massacre of St Bartholomew's Day in 1572 (22ʳᵛ), the unfortunate outcome of another marriage between a French Catholic and foreign Protestant prince. The campaign against the marriage is not simply conducted at the level of covert asides undermining the French. As Ralph Sadler writes, 'it is easier for subjects to oppose a Prince by applause than by armies'.[62] The April eclogue consequently plays an important role in Spenser's campaign, as it 'celebrates Elizabeth's virginity at the very moment she seemed most determined to abandon it' and thus 'seeks to imprison her in her own image'.[63] Further ironies are apparent in 'April'. As this fourth eclogue strikes, like Virgil's fourth eclogue, a more triumphant note, it must be remembered that Virgil's poem (like Leland's *Genethliacon*, which drew on the Latin text) celebrates the birth of a child, the future hope of the nation. Spenser's, in contrast, lauds an ageing, childless queen and seeks to prolong her virginal state, removing any hope of a child. Elizabeth's personification as 'Elisa' meanwhile—far from being the result of Colin's rusticity, as E.K. claims (14ᵛ)—links the English queen with Dido, also known as Elissa, another queen who met an unfortunate end after falling for a stranger come to her shores in *Aeneid* IV. Spenser further twists the story. When Dido reappears in the November eclogue, Colin's elegy envisages her walking in '*Elisian* fieldes so free' (47ʳ), unlike Virgil's embittered Dido amongst the wraiths of abandoned lovers in the myrtle woods in the Fields of Mourning.[64]

Opposition to the French match was based not merely on fears

---

[62] Cited by McCabe, ' "Little booke" ', 23.   [63] Ibid. 23.
[64] Virgil, *Aeneid*, ed. and trans. H. Rushton Fairclough, rev. edn. (London: Heinemann, 1935), vi. 450–3.

of Elizabeth's (and England's) subordination to a foreign husband. The marriage was also seen by its opponents as a threat to England's identity as an autonomous Protestant nation. Anxieties about a foreign, Catholic husband were obviously fuelled by memories of Philip's perceived hold over his wife, Mary Tudor. Yet the association between Englishness and 'right-thinking' Protestantism—whilst undoubtedly strengthened by the Marian regime—nevertheless predates it, at least among a committed minority. As Spenser rewrites the Catholic *Kalendar of Shepherds*, first translated from the French in 1506, as an English, Protestant *Calender*, he therefore compounds the equation of Englishness and Protestantism, and of Catholicism and the foreign, that can be traced at least as far back as the early 1550s and Wilson's *Reason*. Spenser's attack on the French match is thus shored up by characteristic assaults on Catholicism, found, for example, in the May fable, in which— tapping into reformist rhetoric against mendicancy, familiar from Smith's *De scriptione*—the papist fox deludes the unprotected kid with the contents of his pedlar's sack, described by E.K. as 'the reliques and ragges of popish superstition' (22^r).

Despite its political nature, however, the *Shepheardes Calender* is an elusive text (necessarily so, in the wake of the controversy over the *Gaping Gulph*). The introduction to the February eclogue, for example, makes a disingenuous statement about the ensuing poem's clarity and simplicity, declaring it 'rather morall and generall, then bent to any secrete or particular purpose' (3^r). The meaning of fable of the oak and briar that follows is at best opaque. The felling of the 'goodly Oake' at the behest of the 'bragging brere' (5^r) has been read as an attack on corruption and envy at the Elizabethan court, where sympathies lie with the oak, unjustly destroyed, to the ultimate detriment of the pastoral or courtly landscape.[65] Yet, with the upstart briar loyally 'dyed' in the Tudor colours of 'Lilly white, and Cremsin redde' (5^r), it is not clear where our sympathies should lie. Further to that, the fable carries ambiguous religious connotations, in which the oak, 'often crost with the priestes crewe, / And often hallowed with holy water dewe' (6^v), could refer either to the Druidic religion, often seen as a precursor to Christianity and therefore evidence of British

[65] Ronald R. Bond, 'Supplantation in the Elizabethan Court: The Theme of Spenser's February Eclogue', *Spenser Studies*, 2 (1981), 55–65.

prescience in religious matters, or to Catholicism justly over-
thrown, thanks to an allegorical Reformation tradition in which, in
the words of Luke 3: 9, those trees 'which bringeth not forth good
fruit' are 'hewn down, and cast into the fire'.[66]
The dialogic tenor of the work adds to Spenser's elusiveness.
Spenser's text is filled with 'the conflict of competing voices', from
the shepherds' continual debates to E.K.'s idiosyncratic glossing,
with its tendency to contradict the mood of the poetic text, as in
'April', where the hostility to the Arthurian tradition expressed in
the gloss is at odds with the approbatory tenor of the eclogue
itself.[67] Yet the discussions between the characters fail to live up to
what Annabel Patterson has described as the *Shepheardes
Calender*'s ideal of communication between different social groups
(if true, this ideal resonates with Smith's belief in wide political
debate).[68] Characters in the *Shepheardes Calender* might converse
with each other; they rarely listen, however, and are seldom
converted to their opponent's viewpoint. Eloquence is ineffectual,
particularly in the 'moral' eclogues of February, May, July, and
October, when arguably resolution is all the more pressing. As
Patrick Cullen and Louis Montrose point out, the debates in the
'moral eclogues' are between limited perspectives.[69] This seeming
dissatisfaction with dialogue, and the efficacy of eloquence (also
found in the dialogues of Smith and Wilson), goes beyond the
Virgilian tendency 'to conclude eclogues on a note of suspended
differences'.[70] This recurrent lack of clear resolution questions the
potency of poetry. Like Sidney, Spenser attributes the role and
qualities of eloquence to poetry, an art aligned with music through
the powerfully persuasive figures of Orpheus and Amphion,
charming beasts and raising city walls with their music, an allegorical manifestation of the civilizing effects of eloquence propounded
by Cicero and—following him—Wilson.[71] Yet within the

---

[66] See Brooks-Davies (ed.), *Spenser: Selected Shorter Poems*, 45 n.

[67] McCabe, ' "Little boke" ', 17.

[68] Annabel Patterson, *Reading between the Lines* (London: Routledge, 1993), 50.

[69] Cited by Louis A. Montrose, 'Interpreting Spenser's February Eclogue: Some
Contexts and Implications', *Spenser Studies*, 2 (1981), 67–74, at 71. Montrose is
here referring to Patrick Cullen, *Spenser, Marvell, and the Renaissance Pastoral*
(Cambridge, Mass.: Harvard University Press, 1970), 32–3.

[70] Paul Alpers, *What is Pastoral?* (Chicago: University of Chicago Press, 1996),
178.

[71] Sidney, *Apology*, 96; Wilson, *Rhetorique*, A3ʳᵛ; Cicero, *De Inventione*, I. ii. 2.

Shepheardes Calender, poetry palpably fails to advance its practitioners. Colin's songs fail to woo Rosalind; Cuddy is left without patronage; the reference to Orpheus' 'Musick and Poetry' recovering Eurydice from the underworld (42ᵛ) is undermined by the ultimate futility of his quest, as Eurydice slips away from him, his poetry/music powerless to stop her turning back and breaking the condition on which she had been released from Hades. The same anxieties about eloquence that we saw in relation to Smith and Wilson resurface here in regard to poetry: on the one hand, it can fail to move its audience; on the other, it can be too successful. As Piers comments in 'October', it is within the capacity of the poet 'to entice' 'trayned willes' (40ᵛ). While he here approves of the poet's ability to 'restraine / The lust of lawlesse youth with good aduice', or 'pricke them forth with pleasance of thy vaine', he nevertheless points to the dangerously seductive powers of poetry and, beyond that, eloquence. Even as Spenser freights poetry with a humanist's fervour for participating in the commonweal and influencing policy, he nevertheless displays an equally characteristic humanistic scepticism—familiar from More's *Utopia*—about the potential futility of such interventions. It is this tension between public duty and the pursuit of eloquence in Sidney's *Old Arcadia* that the final section of this chapter explores.

'SLACKING OF THE MAIN CAREER': ELOQUENCE AND DUTY IN THE *OLD ARCADIA*[72]

Like Spenser, and men such as Wilson and Smith, Sidney was educated to serve the state. His father, Henry Sidney, sent Philip to Shrewsbury School, then under the 'imaginative and innovatory' headmaster Thomas Ashton, and located within the jurisdiction managed by Henry as Lord President of the Welsh Marches.[73] At Shrewsbury, as it had been for Spenser at Merchant Taylors, the onus was very much on public service: in the words of F. J. Levy, 'Ashton's object was not to mould scholars—though the scholarship of his pupils was excellent—but to produce statesmen.'[74] From childhood, through university at Oxford and a Continental

---

[72] Sidney, *Old Arcadia*, 12.   [73] Duncan-Jones, *Courtier Poet*, 26.
[74] F. J. Levy, 'Philip Sidney Reconsidered', *ELR* 2 (1972), 5–28, at 7.

'Grand Tour', Sidney was groomed for government. Family and friends regarded Sidney with 'great expectation'; intimate acquaintances, such as the Huguenot humanist Hubert Languet, praised the learning pursued by Sidney for its usefulness to his future political life; in turn, Sidney expressed similar sentiments about the education of his brother, Robert.[75]

Sidney's education, with its Continental travels, also linked him into a network of humanists with a particular religious and political bent. His circle of friends and acquaintances numbered Languet, Philippe Duplessis-Mornay (author of *Vindiciae, contra tyrannos*, 1579), and Daniel Rogers, friend of the Scottish Protestant and humanist, George Buchanan, author of *De Iure Regni* (1579), whose pamphlet against Mary Queen of Scots was translated by Wilson, and who was praised in Sidney's *Apology* as a 'piercing wit'.[76] These men shared what Blair Worden terms 'forward' Protestantism and, further to that, the belief—expressed in *Vindiciae* and *De Iure Regni*—that a prince should assist the rebellious subjects of another prince if they are being oppressed on account of religion, or if their prince is a tyrant.[77] Such arguments are based on the assumption that the commonweal should take precedence over the desires of the monarch, who is there to serve the interests of people and country, and not vice versa. In *De Iure Regni* and *Vindiciae*, Buchanan and Duplessis-Mornay were also reacting to the persecution of Protestants in, respectively, Scotland, and France and the Netherlands, a cause also dear to Sidney, and for which he died at Zutphen. A link is consequently forged between Protestantism, true faith, and political liberty on the one hand, and Catholicism, superstition, and tyranny on the other.[78]

It is this equation of Protestantism and political liberty and emphasis on the monarch's duty to the country that we find underpinning Sidney's *Letter to Queen Elizabeth touching her marriage with Monsieur*, written in protest against Elizabeth's projected

[75] Philip Sidney, *Astrophil and Stella*, in *Sir Philip Sidney: A Selection of his Finest Poems*, ed. Katherine Duncan-Jones (Oxford: Oxford University Press, 1994), sonnet 21; Philip Sidney, letter to Robert Sidney, in *The Prose Works of Sir Philip Sidney*, ed. Albert Feuillerat, 4 vols. (Cambridge: Cambridge University Press, 1962), iii. 132.

[76] Worden, *Sound of Virtue*, 51; Sidney, *Apology*, 131.

[77] Worden, *Sound of Virtue*, 48, 282; William Dinsmore Briggs, 'Political Ideas in Sidney's *Arcadia*', *Studies in Philology*, 28 (1931), 137–61, at 143.

[78] Worden, *Sound of Virtue*, 59.

marriage to Anjou in summer 1579, probably at the instigation of his uncle, Robert Dudley, Earl of Leicester, and either his father or Francis Walsingham.[79] The *Letter* is predicated on the belief that Elizabeth should do what is best for her people and preserve the status quo by rejecting Anjou. As Greville wrote in his biography of Sidney, Sidney feared that the French match would 'metamorphose [. . .] our moderate form of monarchy into a precipitate absoluteness'.[80] England is thus seen by Sidney as the type of mixed state and limited monarchy described—or prescribed—in Smith's *De Republica Anglorum*.[81] In turn, Sidney subscribes to the myth of 'ancient' English liberties, with the English people endowed with 'native freedom', in contrast to French peasants subjected to excessive taxes and lacking a political voice.[82] Although the *Letter* arises from the same concerns as the *Gaping Gulph* and shares 'common ground' with it, Sidney's text proved much more tactful than Stubbes's forceful pamphlet.[83] Not only was it a private letter, rather than a print publication, it also—like Spenser's use of Elisa in the *Shepheardes Calender*—employed flattery, instead of overt criticism, to attempt to fix Elizabeth in the virginal image she had so long cultivated: standing alone, the *Letter* asserts, is Elizabeth's strength and glory.[84]

Elizabeth's response to the *Letter* is unknown. Numerous biographers explain Sidney's withdrawal from court in 1580 as a direct consequence of royal anger at Sidney's presumptuous intervention in the matter of her marriage. Yet, as Katherine Duncan-Jones argues, this contradicts the account given by Sidney's earliest biographer and closest friend, Fulke Greville, who explicitly states that Sidney 'kept his access to Her Majesty as before'.[85] Whatever the cause—and a quarrel with the Earl of Oxford and financial problems are two

---

[79] Worden argues for Dudley and Henry Sidney (*Sound of Virtue*, 42); Duncan-Jones for Dudley and Walsingham (Sidney, *Miscellaneous Prose*, 35).

[80] Fulke Greville, *A Dedication to Sir Philip Sidney*, in *Prose Works of Fulke Greville, Lord Brooke*, ed. John Gouws (Oxford: Clarendon Press, 1986), 32.

[81] Ernest William Talbert, *The Problem of Order: Elizabethan Political Commonplaces and an Example of Shakespeare's Art* (Chapel Hill: University of North Carolina Press, 1962), 105. Talbert also acknowledges the influence of Ponet and Hooker on Sidney's belief in the mixed state.

[82] Greville, *Dedication*, 32.

[83] Duncan-Jones, *Courtier Poet*, 162. Cf. Richard Lanham, 'Sidney: The Ornament of his Age', *Southern Review* (1967), 319–40, at 327.

[84] Sidney, *Miscellaneous Prose*, 45.

[85] Greville, *Dedication*, 38; Duncan-Jones, *Courtier Poet*, 163.

other plausible reasons for Sidney's absence from court—in the aftermath of the Anjou crisis, Sidney found himself at his sister Mary's literary-minded household, Wilton, a centre for poetry and patronage, and it was here, in spring and early summer 1580, that Sidney seems to have worked most intensively on the *Old Arcadia*.[86]

The *Old Arcadia* cannot, as Andrew Weiner argues, be read as a *roman-à-clef*.[87] Nevertheless, it arises from and reflects anxieties over the Anjou match, and other Elizabethan political crises, including the execution of Mary Queen of Scots and the dearth of an obvious successor to the ageing Elizabeth. Sidney's romance is politically engaged. Like the Arcadian shepherds and Spenser in the *Shepheardes Calender*, Sidney makes use of 'hidden forms' to 'utter such matters as otherwise were not fit for their delivery', employing a range of stylistic devices as a means of opening up debate, encouraging sceptical readings.[88] The extensive use of brackets in the 1590 printed edition of the *New Arcadia* and manuscript versions of the *Old*—far surpassing any other Elizabethan prose work—appears to be authorial.[89] Far from being digressive, Sidney's use of parenthesis is integral to his rhetorical strategy, as in the opening pages, where Basilius' concern to arm his frontiers is undermined by the parenthetical comment '(for that only way he thought a foreign prince might endanger his crown)' (6). Brackets were conventionally employed within the early modern period to mark *sententiae*, possibly—John Lennard proposes—to signal 'a first reservation of judgement' from this 'overt form of moral commentary', which clearly does not fit the use of brackets in either of Sidney's two *Arcadia*.[90] Rather, the punctuation both enables what Maurice Evans calls 'a running commentary' on the detail being related, and draws readers' eyes to that running commentary, effectively highlighting it.[91] In this case, readers are alerted to Basilius' lack of political acumen and error in thinking

[86] Sidney, *Miscellaneous Prose*, 35; cf. Worden, *Sound of Virtue*, pp. 43, xxi.

[87] Andrew D. Weiner, *Sir Philip Sidney and the Poetics of Protestantism: A Study of Contexts* (Minneapolis: University of Minnesota Press, 1978), 26.

[88] Sidney, *Old Arcadia*, 50.

[89] Philip Sidney, *The Countess of Pembroke's Arcadia (The New Arcadia)*, ed. Maurice Evans (Harmondsworth: Penguin, 1977), 49.

[90] John Lennard, *But I Digress: The Exploitation of Parentheses in English Printed Verse* (Oxford: Clarendon Press, 1991), 23–36, at 32.

[91] Sidney, *New Arcadia*, 49.

that invasion is the sole means by which a foreign power can gain
hold over another: for an English reader of Sidney's political
persuasion in the early 1580s, the threat to English sovereignty
posed by a foreign match would have immediately sprung to mind.
The presence of the Anjou crisis behind this comment is further
strengthened by the speech in which Philanax—the wise and loyal
counsellor—advises Basilius to 'let [his] subjects have [him] in their
eyes' (7), an almost exact quotation from the conclusion of the
Letter to Queen Elizabeth.[92] Although the 'uncertain' course
which Basilius embarks upon is retirement, and not—as in
Elizabeth's case—a potential French marriage, by Book Two, to his
subjects' great alarm, Basilius—no less than Elizabeth—seems to
have fallen sway to foreign influences, in the form of Pyrocles,
disguised as an Amazon. As W. Gordon Zeevald points out, the
Arcadians rebel at 'the prospect of a stranger's possessing their
secrets, draining the treasury, conquering the country without
opposition': the very fears of the anti-French party in 1579.[93]

The chaos caused when leaders follow their own desires is a
recurrent theme of the *Old Arcadia*. Their failure to consider the
commonweal makes these rulers tyrants, not true monarchs, since
by contemporary definition, a tryant is '*he that maketh his wil a
law, and for hym selfe woorketh al*'.[94] Basilius, then—for all his
foolishness and ineffectuality—is literally a tyrant, threatening the
social order of Arcadia by withdrawing to the countryside on a
whim, and then—more dangerously still—becoming thrall to the
foreign Cleophila (Pyrocles). Likewise, Erona's passion for the
unworthy Antiphilus and Otanes' ardour for Erona bring both her
and her country into danger. Love and lust are thus destructive and
antisocial forces in the *Old Arcadia*, surely no coincidence in the
work of an author who believed that—in undertaking a foreign
match—his queen risked disrupting the nation's security and stability. Within the *Old Arcadia* private desires are represented as inim-
ical to the public good. Before the book begins, Musidorus and
Pyrocles tour the Mediterranean, ministers of avenging justice, the
same form of intervention in foreign affairs recommended by the

[92] See Sidney, *Old Arcadia*, 369 n. 7.
[93] W. Gordon Zeevald, 'The Uprising of the Commons in Sidney's *Arcadia*',
Modern Language Notes, 48 (1933), 209–17, at 216.
[94] Thomas, *Vanitee of this Worlde* (1549), B8ʳ. Cf. Worden, *Sound of Virtue*,
211–12.

Vindiciae, and for which Sidney lobbied in the case of the Netherlands. The obsessive attachments Musidorus and Pyrocles form to Basilius' daughters on arrival in Arcadia, however, distract them from this life of public service. Their consequent introspection is epitomized through Pyrocles' narcissism as he changes his name—and his self—into a mirror image of the girl he adores, reflecting her name in his, and her sex in his Amazonian disguise. 'As for my name,' he tells Musidorus, 'it shall be Cleophila, turning Philoclea to myself, as my mind is wholly turned and transformed into her' (17). Musidorus, meanwhile, becomes less than himself, diminishing his social status, and curtailing his name, as the shepherd Dorus. Nor is the princes' dallying a harmless holiday romance. Lingering in Arcadia, they endanger the life of Erona, who—held captive by Artaxia—is due to be burned at the stake unless the princes return within the year. Further to that, their success in seducing Pamela and Philoclea also causes social disruption, with the princesses disgraced and they themselves facing a death sentence for the suspected murder of Basilius. It is no coincidence, then, that the most political poem in the *Old Arcadia*—'As I my little flock on Ister bank'—occurs at a wedding. The curmudgeonly Geron berates Philisides for singing such a seemingly inappropriate song, but Geron's criticism is invalid on two counts: first, it is motivated by personal revenge (for Philisides bettering him in a previous eclogue); secondly, within the *Old Arcadia*, love is not the 'matter for joyful melody' that Geron would have it be (225). The upheaval caused by passion is political: it is not families that are torn apart by love, but kingdoms.

It is worth looking further at 'Ister Bank'. The poem, Worden argues, stands out. Not only is it unique within Sidney's works for its use of archaisms, including a tantalizing use of the rare archaism *couth*, which as we saw in relation to the *Shepheardes Calender* was associated with subscription to the idea of a limited monarchy; it also commemorates Languet, the only 'real' person to be named within the *Old Arcadia*, who allegedly taught Philisides the song.[95] Languet's known endorsement of the need to resist tyranny (through his association with *Vindiciae*, which was originally attributed to either him or—more accurately—his close friend Duplessis-Mornay) makes him an appropriate source for this beast-fable,

95 Ibid. 266–7.

which relates how Man became tyrant over the animals.[96] The poem also illustrates Sidney's unawed, and even sceptical, view of kingship. Like Smith, who influenced Sidney's belief in the need for limitations on monarchical power, Sidney is unimpressed by the trappings of monarchy.[97] Monarchical power, moreover, is not innate to the body of the monarch, but is invested in the monarch by the people. In 'Ister Bank', Man is created king at the instigation of the community of beasts; his rhetoric of fellowship—exposed by Sidney/Philisides—then further beguiles them: 'Not in his sayings "I", but "we"; / As if he meant his lordship common be' (224). Within the allegory, Man represents monarchs *in genera*; when Jove describes leaders, he talks in general terms. There is no division into good and bad, just one category of 'rulers', all of whom 'will think all things made them to please, / And soon forget the swink due to their hire' (223), and all of whom are thus to be treated with considerable caution. The use of the terms *swink* and *hire* also point to the reciprocity of the arrangement: rulers owe labour in return for the position granted them. Nor is the position of this Man-monarch unassailable (rulers are, after all, on 'hire', a word that implies 'temporary use', *OED* 1). The animal-subjects, towards the end of the fable, are given two options: passive suffering, or armed resistance: 'in patience bide your hell, / Or know your strengths, and then you shall do well' (225). The poem's commemoration of Languet, however, must surely signal that armed resistance is a justified and justifiable course of action.

The attitude to kingship displayed in 'Ister Bank' epitomizes that of the *Old Arcadia*. Royalty, under this scheme, is derived not from God, but from territory and people. As William Dinsmore Briggs argues, for Sidney, 'the state of being a king has no *intrinsic* virtue; it is defined by and confined to the laws and customs of a particular country, and is, indeed, artificial and derivative.'[98] Musidorus and Pyrocles' attempt to claim their royal status exempts them from Arcadian laws is consequently invalidated by Euarchus, the voice of reason and good government (349). Here, it is not the Anjou crisis that the *Old Arcadia* evokes, but the parliamentary debates surrounding the execution of Mary Stuart, where—as Worden shows—Wilson, the subject of the previous chapter, was

---

[96] Worden, *Sound of Virtue*, 54.
[97] Talbert, *Problem of Order*, 105.
[98] Briggs, 'Political Ideas', 158.

just one of those who declared that, outside her own kingdom, the Queen of Scots was no monarch, but a 'private person'.[99] Although this statement has an obvious pragmatic purpose—designed to enable Mary's execution by removing her protective royal status— it nevertheless demonstrates the less than reverential attitude to monarchy per se that could be held by the most loyal subjects. Indeed, a healthy monarchy needs politically active citizens; without them, as Sidney writes, 'monarchal governments' risk 'great dissipations', such as Arcadia faces on the supposed death of Basilius, 'for now their prince and guide had left them, they had not experience to rule, and had not whom to obey. Public matters had ever been privately governed, so that they had no lively taste what was good for themselves [. . .]' (277). Here, Sidney's nightmarish vision of a leaderless state on the point of anarchy aligns the *Old Arcadia* still more closely with the 'conservative republicanism' of thinkers such as Smith and Cecil, who planned for the potential constitutional crisis should Elizabeth die without naming an heir.[100]

Kingship on Sidney's pages is not sacred, and monarchs are not treated with awe. Basilius, whose name is a transliteration of the ancient Greek for 'leader' or 'king' and who—despite his title of 'duke'—thus acts as an archetype of kingship, is a figure of ridicule. His judgement is poor, his eyesight poorer, as he unwittingly falls in love with a man (whose disguise tellingly fails to fool his wife, Gynecia). The *Old Arcadia* lacks the occasional sarcasm present in the *New Arcadia* in comments like 'she was a queen and therefore beautiful' (159); nevertheless there is a form of vengeful triumph— akin to that identified by Louis Montrose in relation to the obsession of Shakespeare's fairy queen with a braying ass in *A Midsummer Night's Dream*—in having a ruler make such a fool of himself for lust.[101] The *Old Arcadia*—like the *Shepheardes Calender*—is under no illusions about the foibles of monarchs, or about the dangers of the potential vacuum left by the imminent death of England's own ageing queen. Like the *Shepheardes*

---

[99] Worden, *Sound of Virtue*, 180–1.
[100] Stephen Alford, 'Reassessing William Cecil in the 1560s', 247.
[101] Louis Montrose, 'A Kingdom of Shadows', in David L. Smith et al. (eds.), *The Theatrical City: Culture, Theatre and Politics in London* (Cambridge: Cambridge University Press, 1995), 70–86; William Shakespeare, *A Midsummer Night's Dream*, in *Oxford Shakespeare*.

Calender, it is also riddled with anxiety about the power of eloquence and poetry. As Hanna Gray argues, 'the pursuit of eloquence' was 'the identifying characteristic of Renaissance humanism' and 'the bond which united humanists, no matter how far separated in outlook or in tone': humanists 'believed [. . .] that men could be moulded most effectively, and perhaps only, through the art of eloquence'.[102] Yet within the pastoral landscapes created by these two humanistically trained Tudors, eloquence is going strikingly awry. If, as G. K. Hunter asserts, 'the history of English Humanism can be seen as an exercise in the myth of the political effectiveness of learning', then—by this stage—the emphasis is on myth in the sense of 'misconception' or fiction (*OED*, 2a).[103]

Debate is central to the *Old Arcadia*, which is structured around a series of rhetorical set pieces, from the deliberative orations of Philanax, and Pyrocles and Musidorus in Book I, to the forensic oratory of Book V, and the frequent poetic debates staged in the eclogues.[104] From the outset, however, as in the *Shepheardes Calender*, these debates prove inconclusive and rhetoric, ineffectual. The first, between Philanax and Basilius, ends with 'epigrammatic symmetry'.[105] 'The reeds stand with yielding,' asserts Basilius; 'And so they are but reeds, most worthy prince,' replies Philanax: 'but the rocks stand still and are rocks' (8). Neat as this sounds, this is not conclusive; to compound the failure of Philanax's rhetoric, we then see Basilius sticking to the course of (in)action—retirement—from which Philanax attempted to dissuade him. The failure of this first debate sets the predominant pattern for debates throughout the work. Later in Book I, Musidorus fails to persuade Pyrocles back to virtuous action: his words having had no impact, Musidorus then helps Pyrocles disguise himself, in contrast to the *New Arcadia*, where Musidorus comes across Pyrocles already dressed as an Amazon. When the narrator describes the indecision following Basilius' 'death', his

---

[102] Hanna H. Gray, 'Renaissance Humanism: The Pursuit of Eloquence', in Paul Oskar Kristellar and Philip P. Weiner (eds.), *Renaissance Essays* (Rochester, NY: University of Rochester Press, 1968), 199–216, at 200, 202.
[103] G. K. Hunter, *John Lyly: The Humanist as Courtier* (London: Routledge & Kegan Paul, 1962), 15.
[104] See Walter Davis, 'Narrative Methods in Sidney's *Old Arcadia*', *SEL* 18 (1978), 103–23, at 105.
[105] Richard C. McCoy, *Sir Philip Sidney: Rebellion in Arcadia* (Hassocks: Harvester Press, 1979), 42.

comment that 'these were rather the discoursing sort of men than the active' (278) demonstrates the gulf between talk and action: words should—as the *Apology* preaches—lead to 'virtuous action' (104), but throughout the *Old Arcadia*, they fail to do so. Instead, words—designedly or inadvertently—confuse their hearers. Basilius' over-promotion of Dametas, for example, shows the age-old difficulties of differentiating rudeness from plain-speaking, and the dangers of *paradiastole* or redescription (the tool of courtly deception), as the 'flattering courtier' transforms the herdsman Dametas' ignorance and bluntness into simplicity and integrity (28).[106]

Even where rhetoric appears successful, as when Pyrocles (as Cleophila) subdues the rebellion in Book II, on closer examination, his speech is palliative, not remedial. The crowd is placated, but the Amazon's words are a mere honeyed gloss: nothing is done to remove the reason for the Arcadians' rebellion, namely Basilius' abdication and his apparent enthralment to the very woman who subdues them. The scepticism about eloquence latent in this episode can be seen more clearly in the *New Arcadia*, where Pyrocles' successful subjugation of the mob through oratory is immediately followed by an account of the origins of rebellion, fomented by Clinias through a perverted rhetoric, 'a slidingness of language' (387) that represents the degradation of true eloquence into 'a certain agreeableness of manner' or 'depraved imitation of virtue' charted in Cicero's *De Inventione* ('commoditas quaedam, prava virtutis imitatrix', I. ii. 3). The inadequacies of language are also highlighted in the *Old Arcadia* by the comparative effectiveness in Arcadia of visual stimuli, with the rebels initially silenced by Pyrocles' (Cleophila's) 'outward graces' and 'goodliness of her shape' (113). Similarly, it is Philoclea's portrait that inspires Pyrocles' devotion to her, as Musidorus sardonically points out, declaring it 'a very white and red virtue which you pick out by the sight of a picture' (21). Sidney's prose here resonates with Leland's 'Newe yeares gyfte', where Leland's doubt in the power of words alone is revealed by his assertion that his account of England should be 'sett fourth in a quadrate table of syluer' in order that the 'delectable, frutefull, and necessary pleasures' he describes be more immediately apparent to his monarch (D5ᵛ). Musidorus' reference

---

[106] See Skinner, *Reason and Rhetoric*, 172–80.

to 'the orator' who 'by his eloquence [. . .] persuades nobody' (25)
thus becomes emblematic of the depiction of rhetoric throughout
the *Old Arcadia*.

For Sidney, poetry represents the apogee of rhetoric; his *Apology*
transfers to 'virtue-breeding' poesy the moral force with which
Wilson had endowed rhetoric (141). Yet for all Sidney's edgy confidence in the *Apology*, in Arcadia even poetry, as in the *Shepheardes
Calender*, seems to have little impact. Plangus needs to summarize
his song beforehand 'for the better understanding' (59); Philisides'
'Ister Bank'—the most political, and therefore presumably most
crucial, piece in the book—offers no clear message. Rather, 'according to the nature of diverse ears, diverse judgements straight
followed' (225). Of these 'diverse judgements', moreover, only a
small proportion seem to be concerned with deciphering 'the strange-
ness of the tale', others being absorbed with 'praising his voice' or the
'pastoral style'. If—as Sidney's *Apology* asserts—poetry is the most
alluring way of instilling virtue in its readers and listeners, then the
poets and orators of the *Old Arcadia* are not hitting the mark.

As Duncan-Jones comments, 'there is no doubt, according to
theory, that eloquence should [. . .] be used for heroic or political
purposes; but in the bulk of Sidney's poetry it is not'.[107] In the *Old
Arcadia*, just as the ruling elite are being distracted from their public
duties by love and lust, so too eloquence is being used, above all (as
it is by Astrophil in Sidney's *Astrophil and Stella*) for seductive
purposes. The princes use tales to woo their beloveds, and the
number of poems embedded in each book (as opposed to those in the
eclogues) increases as their courtship accelerates, reaching a peak in
Book III, in which Musidorus and Pyrocles finally succeed in respectively eloping or sleeping with their chosen princess. Indeed, the last
poem in that book is an unashamedly erotic blazon of Philoclea's
body, a poetic striptease substituted for the actual undressing and
caressing we are invited to imagine, as the narrator, 'beginning now
to envy Argus's thousand eyes, and Briareus's hundred hands', leaves
Pyrocles 'in so happy a plight' (211). In contrast, as the narrative
takes a more serious turn in the subsequent books, the eloquent arts
are shown to be conspicuously ineffectual or inappropriate, just

[107] Katherine Duncan-Jones, 'Philip Sidney's Toys', in Dennis Kay (ed.), *Sir Philip
Sidney: An Anthology of Modern Criticism* (Oxford: Clarendon Press, 1987),
61–80, at 68.

when they are most necessary. As the leaderless (acephalous) Arcadia crumbles into chaos and is forced to call upon a foreign power for help—the very fate that Basilius (and England) hoped to avoid—the eclogues show the versifying shepherds detached from the political sphere: 'finding no place for them[selves] in these garboils, [. . . they] retired themselves from among the clamorous multitude' (284). At the moment of political crisis—the presumed death of Basilius—the nation's natural poets offer no help: they withdraw to admire the view from the 'western side of hill whose prospect extended it so far as they might well discern many of Arcadia's beauties'. Significantly, it is in this set of eclogues that Philisides, Sidney's alter ego, chooses to describe the way in which—distracted, of course, by love—he has failed to meet the expectations of public service for which his humanist education had trained him (290). Philisides, a man groomed for political action, sits by, singing of unrequited love, while his chosen homeland disintegrates.

In its disillusionment with poetry and rhetoric, the *Old Arcadia* strikes yet another chord with the *Shepheardes Calender*. Both works are influenced by similar authors—including Virgil and Chaucer, their pastoral landscapes even inhabited by characters of the same name, such as the Virgilian Menalcas—and both successfully merge classical, Continental, and vernacular sources to create an English literary mode and style.[108] The *Old Arcadia* is, for example, indebted to a third-century Greek romance by Heliodorus, a medieval French book of chivalry (*Amadis de Gaul*), an early sixteenth-century pastoral (Sannazaro's *Arcadia*), and a later-sixteenth-century Spanish romance (de Montemayor's *Diana*).[109] The end product, though, is English, steeped in the concerns of the political nation. The book, moreover, acts as 'a compendium of literary types', containing lyric, eclogues, dialogues, orations, romance, pastoral, satire, heroic literature, and near-tragedy, exemplifying the literary modes that can be expressed in the English tongue.[110] Nor does Sidney display the

[108] For the influence of Chaucer, and particularly *Troilus and Criseyde*, on the *Old Arcadia*, see Margaret Doria, 'The Providential Plot of the *Old Arcadia*', in Kay (ed.), *Philip Sidney*, 83–102.

[109] A. C. Hamilton, 'Sidney's *Arcadia* as Prose Fiction: Its Relation to its Sources', *ELR* 2 (1972), 29–60, at 30.

[110] Robert W. Parker, 'Terentian Studies and Sidney's Original *Arcadia*', *ELR* 2 (1972), 61–78, at 63.

familiar anxiety, or embarrassment, over the semantic resources of
English. When he uses the same two rhymes (of dark and light)
throughout a poem, it is almost in defiance of former complaints
about the paucity of English rhyme.[111] Yet even as Sidney champions English as a literary language, he is much less bullish than
Spenser. The *Shepheardes Calender* carries a prologue asserting the
literary potential of English; the *Old Arcadia* demonstrates it
through the abundance of metrical forms employed in its pages—
quantitative verse, English madrigals, and Italian forms such as
terza rima, ottava rima, the sestina, and sonnet—and through the
assured flexibility of the complex prose style, with its subordinate
clauses, far removed from the parataxis that characterizes much
medieval and earlier sixteenth-century prose.[112]

For all the apparent similarities between the *Old Arcadia* and
Shepheardes Calender—their shared origins in the Anjou crisis;
their pastoral setting; their anxieties about rhetoric; their hybrid
origins; even their use of the rare archaism *couth*—it must be
remembered that Sidney is a different type of writer from Spenser,
and his prose romance has a different purpose and is intended for
a different audience. Sidney's work was not initially destined for
print or for other than a coterie audience; there is no need, therefore, for Sidney—as there is for Spenser—to use his work to mould
an authorial identity for public consumption. So too where the
Shepheardes Calender tries to intervene (subtly) in the political
debate surrounding the Anjou match, the *Old Arcadia* takes a
different course. Sidney's romance is—as Worden puts it—not just
a 'meditation on politics, but is a substitute for them'.[113] Sidney
writes the *Old Arcadia* because he is not at court, because he is—
like Philisides and Astrophil—frittering away the 'great expectation' of his education. Writing, for Spenser, is a means of
participating in the political domain, as the name of his alter ego
indicates, Colin Clout being the satirical persona who railed
against church corruption in Skelton's poem of that name. For
Sidney—eschewing print—writing is a manifestation, and result, of
retirement from public life, just as singing and playing the shepherd
is for his alter ego, Philisides. There are consequently tensions

---

[111] Sidney, *Old Arcadia*, 158; cf. id., *Astrophil and Stella*, sonnet 89.
[112] For a discussion of poetic forms in the *Old Arcadia*, see Buxton, *Philip Sidney*,
101–30.   [113] Worden, *Sound of Virtue*, 65.

within the *Old Arcadia* that run deeper than the familiar humanist anxiety over rhetoric. Within its pages, Helgerson argues, civic humanism and courtly romance come into conflict.[114] Lingering in Arcadia, Pyrocles and Musidorus might flag in their commitment to public service, but the generic thrust of the piece encourages us—as readers of romance—to desire what they desire: the successful pursuit of their lady loves and the dereliction of public duty that this requires. Romantic success, moreover, means marriage, even if this places the Arcadian throne—which Pamela stands to inherit, and with the fate of which we have been encouraged to concern ourselves—in the hands of a foreign prince, the outcome feared for England should Elizabeth marry Anjou. The inevitable narrative outcome of romance thus contradicts Sidney's politics.

The divided impulses of Sidney's *Old Arcadia*, and what he completed of the *New*, are reflected in Greville's eulogy to his friend, the *Dedication to*, or *Life of*, *Sir Philip Sidney*, in which Greville continually revises his assessment of Sidney's intentions in writing in general, and the *Arcadia*s in particular. Initially, the didactic elements of Sidney's work are emphasized and attention drawn to:

his intent and scope [. . .] to turn the barren precepts into pregnant images of life, and in them, first on the monarch's part, lively to represent the growth, state and declination of princes, change of government and laws [. . .] with all other errors or alterations in public affairs; then again, in the subject's case, the state of favour, disfavour, prosperity, adversity, [. . .] travell and all other moods of private fortunes or misfortunes. (10)

Yet, this educational—and hence public-spirited—motivation is soon qualified with Greville's insistence on the private audience and light-hearted end for which the writings were produced, 'scribbled rather as pamphlets for entertaining of time and friends [. . .]'. Greville then veers back towards the 'public' Sidney with his belief in the instructive and beneficial force of what Sidney calls 'poetry' (a definition that in Sidney's *Apology* embraces 'non-factual' prose), with the assertion that 'the truth is, his end was not writing even while he wrote, nor his knowledge moulded for tables and schools, but both his wit and understanding bent upon his desire to

[114] Richard Helgerson, *The Elizabethan Prodigals* (Berkeley: University of California Press, 1976), 41.

make himself and others, not in words or opinion, but in life and action, great and good' (12).[115] Sidney's *Old Arcadia* and his attitude to writing are thus tinged with an ambivalence about the role of writer absent from Spenser's *Shepheardes Calender*; writing, for Sidney, smacks of shirking his proper, political vocation, even as his works address pressing political issues—an ambivalence that endures in Greville's posthumous reflections.

CONCLUSION

This concluding chapter has attempted to draw together the themes of the book and illustrate how two indisputably canonical Elizabethan authors are grounded in an earlier sixteenth-century heritage. Rooted in contemporary affairs, the *Old Arcadia* and *Shepheardes Calender* are characteristic of sixteenth-century English writing in their topicality (England and English affairs always lying at their core) and their cultivation of a native style through the fusion of vernacular, Continental, and classical strains. This grafting of cultures was performed with varying degrees of confidence through the period, from the often abashed Borde, overcompensating with his enthusiastic, convoluted, and Latinate proclamations of what English, and the English, should achieve, to Sidney, whose accomplished English style is left to speak for itself. The story being told in this book is, in part, about the changing perceptions of the English language. We should be wary of reading this uncritically as a straight chronological development from embarrassment to quiet pride, however; Borde quite correctly locates riches in the vulgar tongue extant in his own lifetime, and whilst Sidney might not loudly pronounce his linguistic and literary proficiency, his contemporary Spenser does, and Sidney's own stylistic acrobatics are not unselfconscious or conducted in unawareness of the barbarity of which the English language still stood accused in the late 1570s and early 1580s. There is, for example, a point to be proved in his *Apology*, written shortly after the *Old Arcadia*, *c*.1581/2, which, whilst confessing to the neglect and paucity of English literature to date, is structured as a perfect classical oration and executed in an elegant and witty English prose style.

[115] See Sidney, *Apology*, 103.

The gradual emergence of English as a literary language over this period is indebted to the Tudor authors who brought their classical learning and knowledge of Continental writing and trends to the vernacular. English, and Englishness, did not develop in isolation from Europe. When Tudor writers tried to shape a sense of pride in their language, history, and nation, it was not done merely with an eye to encouraging their compatriots, but also to emulate and impress their Continental neighbours and rivals. Nor did these writers reject a Latinate tradition. All were moulded by it, even Borde, the least humanistic among the batch of authors. The others, from Leland to Sidney, work within humanist genres: the epigram, history, familiar letter, rhetorical manual, eclogue, and above all, the dialogue. Equally important is the humanist doctrine of public duty. All these writers advocate service of the nation and the public, political role of the writer/poet (even Sidney, as he agonizes over his vocation). At the same time, however, many of their works also display the futility of such purpose, as rhetoric fails to convince its audience, advice goes unheeded, and the poet or author remains unrewarded: Borde's itinerary is lost; Leland goes unpaid; Wilson exposes the inadequacies of dialogue as a form of persuasion; Spenser and Sidney's poetic personae sing from marginal locations. Subscription to a humanist project of education and public duty coexists with an awareness of the potential perversion, or impotency, of learning in practice: a consciousness that gives these works a dark backdrop of mismatched rhetoric and antisocial impulses.

This same disquiet about the success of humanism is central to much later Elizabethan literature. Shakespeare's earliest tragedy, *Titus Andronicus*, for example, can be read as a critique of a humanistic faith in rhetoric and improving literature. Eloquence is reduced to Marcus' redundant Ovidian verbosity as his niece Lavinia stands raped and bleeding before him, while all poetry has taught Chiron and Demetrius is that—to prevent discovery—they need to outdo Tereus, who defiled and maimed Philomel, and remove their victim's hands as well as her tongue. The Elizabethan reaction against Ciceronian humanism can, in part, be attributed to the socio-economic conditions of the 1580s and 1590s, when university-educated men recurrently found few opportunities for the public service for which their education had trained them and led them to expect. As early as 1581, Mulcaster called for limits on numbers receiving more than rudimentary learning (sufficient 'for *religion* sake, and their necessarie *affaires*') lest too many be left 'gaping for preferment'.[116] His fears were realized, and Helgerson describes how the increase in university education 'quickly saturated the offices of the state with men trained in good letters, leaving few openings for those who came behind'.[117] In the works of men such as Nashe, learning thus becomes something to fritter away, as in the pornographic Ovidian parody, *The Choise of Valentines*, a text that, like the *Shepheardes Calender*, combines classical learning and a vernacular Chaucerianism. Nonetheless, even as the writers of the 1580s and 1590s react to the economic climate in which they discovered themselves, the articulation of their dissatisfaction has deeper literary roots and a longer literary legacy than those occasioned by the poor employment prospects of late Elizabethan England. The awareness of the negative aspects of the persuasive powers of rhetoric—its failure or abuse—is integral to humanist thinking, and can be traced at least as far back as Cicero's *De Inventione*, a core humanist text. When later Elizabethans interrogate the interrelation of words and virtuous action, or parody the earnestness of humanist learning, they are merely embellishing on the scepticism inherent in humanism and which underlies the writings of the mid-sixteenth century.

Whilst at first glance much mid-sixteenth-century writing might appear dry to modern tastes, or even 'drab', what C. S. Lewis terms the 'ascent' of English literature is thus not as 'unpredictable' as he suggests.[118] The linguistic, stylistic, and intellectual foundations of Lewis's 'golden age' were laid by previous generations of writers concerned to redress England's reputation for barbarity and ignorance. These writers invested in the English language, and their synthesis of Continental, classical, and vernacular models was to be a mark of the most accomplished Elizabethan writers, including Shakespeare and Nashe. Like the later Elizabethans, these Tudor predecessors focused on, and contributed to, the idea of the nation, in the service of which their learning should ideally be employed, and prescribed and described an island nation that was geographically contained in potentially favoured economic circumstances

[116] Mulcaster, *Positions*, 138.
[117] Helgerson, *Elizabethan Prodigals*, 23.
[118] *English Literature in the Sixteenth Century*, 1.

and united in language and loyalty: a myth of insularity that has exercised a lasting hold over the English imagination. Further to that, these earlier Tudors consistently promoted the role of the learned author as a wise and politic counsellor, ideals that are undercut by an awareness of their possible inversion. In the process, there was also an increasing identification between Englishness and Protestantism. Yet even as these authors sought to distinguish themselves from both Roman and Continental traditions, they were themselves caught between admiration and revulsion. The preoccupation of Elizabethan writers in the 1580s and 1590s with public service, national and linguistic identity, and a seductive but dangerous Continent are thus grounded in a rhetorical tradition emerging from the previous decades of the sixteenth century. When embarking on his own tour of recent English literary history in the 1590s, Thomas Nashe's 'page' or 'appendix' begins with English chronicle and the reign of Henry VIII in a quest that occurs predominantly on the Continent.[119] In undertaking a similar survey of Englishness and the English literary Renaissance, we should follow the example of Harvey's *bête noire*, Nashe, and do likewise.

[119] Jonathan Bate, 'The Elizabethans in Italy', in Jean-Pierre Maquerlot and Michèle Willems (eds.), *Travel and Drama in Shakespeare's Time* (Cambridge: Cambridge University Press, 1996), 55–74, at 70; Thomas Nashe, *The Unfortunate Traveller*, in *The Works of Thomas Nashe*, ed. R. B. McKerrow, 5 vols. (London: Bullen, 1903–10), ii. 210.

Bibliography

PRIMARY SOURCES IN MANUSCRIPT

L'Archivio Segreto della Vaticana, Misc. Arm. II. 29, 275^r–284^r: anon., 'Alcuni cose, occorse à Roma nella sede uacante di Paolo IV' (1559).

BL Add. 4, 149: Thomas Smith, *Dialogue touchinge Quene Elizabeths mariage* (c.1561).

BL Add. 33,383: William Thomas, *Pelegrine* (1547).

BL Add. 48,047: Thomas Smith, *A Communicacion or Discourse of the Queenes highnes mariage* (c.1561). Also know as the 'Yelverton MS'.

BL Caligula C. 3: state papers.

BL Cleopatra E. iv: records of the Reformation.

BL Egerton 837: William Thomas, *The Boke of the Sphere* (c.1551).

BL Harleian 6989: state papers (including material relating to Thomas Smith).

BL Harleian 6992: state papers (including material relating to Thomas Smith).

BL Royal App. 87: Stephen Gardiner's reply to Thomas Smith, regarding Greek pronunciation (1542).

BL Royal 17A. xvii: Thomas Smith, *Certaigne Psalmes or Songues of David translated into Englishe meter by Sir Thomas Smith, Knight, then Prisoner in the Tower of London, with other prayers and songues by him made to pas the tyme there* (1549).

BL Royal 17. C. vii: John Hart, *The opening of the unreasonable writing of our Inglish toung* (1551): published as Hart, *Orthographie* (see below).

BL Royal 17. C. x: William Thomas, *Jos. Barbaros Voiages to Tana and Persia* (c.1551).

BL Sloane 93: Gabriel Harvey's letter book.

BL Titus B. i: state papers.

BL Titus B. ii: William Thomas, political discourses (c.1551).

BL Vespasian D. xviii: state papers; William Thomas, political discourses (c.1551); William Thomas, *Peregrine, or a defence of Henry VIIIth* (1547).

CUL MS Ee. v. 14: John Leland, *Antiphilarcia*.

ERO D/DSh/01/7: 'Offices prescribed by Sir Thomas Smith for the Ardes'.

PRO State Papers, Henry, 1/84/87; 1/93/119; 1/96/43; 1/103/61; 1/105/795 correspondence of Andrew Borde (1534–6).

PRO State Papers, Elizabeth, 70/81/1654: includes material by Smith on Ireland.

PRO State Papers, 27 Henry VIII c. 63: legislation for Ireland (1537).

PRIMARY SOURCES IN PRINT

Unless otherwise stated, place of publication for books printed 1450–1800 is London.

A.B., *The first and best Part of Scoggins Iests* (1626).

—— *The Merie Tales of the Mad Men of Gotam*, ed. Stanley J. Kahrl (Evanston, Ill.: Northwestern University Press, 1965).

—— *A ryght pleasaunt and mery Historie, of the Mylner of Abyngton* (1576).

ACHARISIO, ALBERTO, *Vocabolario, Grammatica, et Orthographia de la lingua volgare* (Cento, 1543).

ALUNNO, FRANCESCO, *Le Richezze della lingua volgare* (Venice, 1543).

ANON., *Informacon for pylgrymes vnto the Holy Londe*, ed. George Henry Freely (London: William Nicol, 1824), E2ᵛ, E3ʳᵛ.

ARETINO, PIETRO, *The Letters of Pietro Aretino*, trans., Thomas Caldecot Chubb (Hamden, Conn.: Archon, 1967).

ASCHAM, ROGER, *The Letters of Roger Ascham*, ed. and trans. Maurice Hatch and Alvin Vos (New York: Peter Lang, 1989).

—— *Toxophilus* (1545).

—— *The Whole Works of Roger Ascham*, ed. J. G. A. Giles, 3 vols. (London: John Russell Smith, 1864–5).

AYLMER, JOHN, *An Harborowe for Faithfull and Trewe Subiectes, agaynst the late blowne Blaste, concerninge the Gouernement of Wemen* (Strasburg, 1559).

BALE, JOHN, *King Johan*, ed. Peter Happé, *Four Morality Plays* (Harmondsworth: Penguin, 1979).

—— *The laboryouse Iourney & serche of Iohan Leylande, for Englandes Antiquities* (1549).

—— *Scriptorum illustrium maioris Britanniae, Catalogus*, 2 vols. (Basle, 1557, 1559).

—— *The Vocyacyon of Iohan Bale in the bishoprick of Ossorie in Irelande* (Wesel, 1553).

BARNES, [ROBERT], *The treatyse answerynge the boke of Berdes* (1542).

BELLAY, JOACHIM DU, *La Deffence et Illustration de la Langue Françoyse*, ed. Fernand Desonay (Geneva: Lille, 1950).

—— *Le premier livre des Antiquitez de Rome* (Paris, 1558).

—— *Les Regrets et autres oeuvres poetiques* (Paris, 1558).

BERRY, LLOYD E. (ed.), *John Stubbs' Gaping Gulf with Letters and Other Relevant Documents* (Charlottesville: University Press of Virginia, 1968).

BODIN, JEAN, *On Sovereignty: Four Chapters from the Six Books of the Commonwealth*, ed. Julian H. Franklin (Cambridge: Cambridge University Press, 1992).

BOECE, HECTOR, *The Hystory and Croniklis of Scotland*, trans. John Bellenden (Edinburgh, 1536).

The boke of the common Praier and administracion of the Sacramentes and other rites and ceremonies of the Churche (1549).

BORDE, ANDREW, *The boke for to learne a man to be wyse in buldyng of his howse for the helth of body & to holde queyetnes for the helth of his soule, and body* (1540).

—— *The Breuiary of Helthe, for all maner of sycknesses and diseases the whiche may be in man, or woman* (1547).

—— *A Compendyous Regyment or a Dyetary of Helth* (1542).

—— *A Compendyous Regyment or a Dyetary of helth* (1547).

—— *The fyrst boke of the Introduction of Knowledge* (c.1549).

—— *The pryncyples of Astronomye the whiche diligently perscrutyd is in maner a pronosticacyon to the worlde* (1547).

—— *The Seconde Boke of the Breuiary of helthe, named the Extrauagantes* (1547).

BROOKE, RALPH, *A discoverie of diuers errours* (1595).

BULLOKAR, WILLIAM, *The Amendment of Orthographie for English Speech* (1580).

The Byble in Englyshe (1539) ('The Great Bible').

Calendar of State Papers, Domestic Series, of the Reigns of Edward VI, Mary, Elizabeth and James I, 1547–1625, 13 vols. (London: Public Record Office, 1856–1892).

Calendar of State Papers, Foreign Series, of the Reign of Mary, 1553–1558 (London: Public Record Office, 1861).

CAMDEN, WILLIAM, *Britannia* (1586).

CAMPBELL, LILY B. (ed.), *The Mirror for Magistrates* (Cambridge: Cambridge University Press, 1938).

CASTIGLIONE, BALDASSARE, *Il libro del Cortegiano*, ed. Ettore Bonora (Milan: Mursia, 1972).

CAWDREY, ROBERT, *A Table Alphabeticall of Hard Vsuall English Words* (1604).

CAXTON, WILLIAM, *The descrypcyon of Englande [. . .] taken out of Polycronycon accordynge to the translacon of Treuisa* (1498).

—— *Dialogues in French and English*, ed. Henry Bradley, EETS, extra series, 79 (1900).

—— *Prologues and Epilogues of William Caxton*, ed. W. J. B. Critch, EETS, original series, 176 (1928).

CHAMBERLAYNE, EDWARD, *Angliae Notitia, or the Present State of England* (1670).

CHAUCER, GEOFFREY, *The assemblie of foules* (?1540).

—— *The Riverside Chaucer*, ed. F. N. Robinson, 3rd edn. (Oxford: Oxford University Press, 1988).

CHEKE, JOHN (ed.), *De obitu doctissimi et sanctissimi theologi Martini Buceri* (1551).

CICERO, *De Inventione*, ed. and trans. H. M. Hubbell (London: Heinemann, 1949).

COCKERAM, HENRY, *The English Dictionarie* (1623).

COLWELL, THOMAS, *Merie Tales, Newly imprinted and made by Master Skelton, Poet laureat* (c.1567).

COOTE, EDMUND, *The English Schoole-maister* (1596).

COX, LEONARD, *The arte or crafte of rhetoryke* (1524).

CROWLEY, ROBERT, *The Select Works*, ed. J. M. Cowper, EETS, extra series, 15 (1872).

—— (ed.), *The vision of Pierce Plowman* (1550).

DAY, ANGEL, *An Englishe Secretarie* (1586).

DEKKER, THOMAS, *The Second Part of the Honest Whore* (London: Nick Hern Books, 1998).

—— *The Shoemaker's Holiday*, ed. Anthony Parr, 2nd edn. (London: A. & C. Black, 1990).

Demosthenes, *Olynthiacs*, ed. and trans. J. H. Vince (London: Heinemann, 1930).

DRAYTON, MICHAEL, *Poly-olbion* (1612).

DUWES, GILES, *Introductorie for to lerne to pronounce and speke Frenche trewly* (1533).

ELIZABETH I, *Collected Works*, ed. Leah Marcus, Janel M. Mueller, and Mary Beth Rose (Chicago: University of Chicago Press, 2000).

ELTON, G. R. (ed.), The Tudor Constitution: Documents and Commentary, 2nd edn. (Cambridge: Cambridge University Press, 1982).

ELYOT, THOMAS, *The Boke named the Gouernour* (1531).

—— *The castel of helthe* (1539).

—— *Dictionary* (1538).

—— *Of the knowledge whiche maketh a wise man* (1533).

—— *Pasquil the playne* (1533).

ERASMUS, DESIDERIUS, *Conficiendarum epistolarum formula* (Antwerp, 1521).

—— *Conficiendarum epistolarum formula*, ed. and trans. Charles Fantazzi, *Collected Works of Erasmus* (Toronto: University of Toronto Press, 1974–), xxv (1985).

—— *De conscribendis epistolis*, ed. and trans. Charles Fantazzi, *Collected Works*, xxv (1985).

ERASMUS, DESIDERIUS, *De duplici copia verborum ac rerum*, ed. and trans. Betty I. Knott, *Collected Works*, xxiv (1978).

—— *De recta latini graecique sermonis pronuntiatione [. . .] dialogus* (Paris, 1528).

—— *De recta latini graecique sermonis pronuntiatione [. . .] dialogus*, ed. and trans. Maurice Pope, *Collected Works*, xxvi (1985).

EWES, SIMONDS D', *A Compleat Journal of the Notes, Speeches and Debates, Both of the House of Lords and House of Commons, throughout the whole Reign of Queen Elizabeth* (1693).

FENTON, GEOFFREY, *The historie of Guiccardin, conteining the warres of Italie and other partes* (1579).

FOXE, JOHN, *The Acts and Monuments*, 8 vols. (London: Seeley, Burnside & Seeley, 1843–9).

FULLER, THOMAS, *Worthies of England* (1662).

FULWOOD, WILLIAM, *The Enimie of Idlenesse* (1571).

FURNIVALL, F. J. (ed.), *Andrew Boorde's Introduction and Dyetary with Barnes in the Defence of the Berde*, EETS, extra series, 10 (1870).

GARDINER, STEPHEN, *A Discourse on the Coming of the English and Normans to Britain*, in Peter Samuel Donaldson (ed. and trans.), *A Machiavellian Treatise by Stephen Gardiner* (Cambridge: Cambridge University Press, 1975).

GEOFFREY OF MONMOUTH, *The History of the Kings of Britain*, ed. and trans. Lewis Thorpe (Harmondsworth: Penguin, 1966).

GILL, ALEXANDER, *Logonomia Anglica* (1619).

GOODMAN, CHRISTOPHER, *How Superior Powers ought to be Obeyed* (Geneva, 1558).

GREVILLE, FULKE, *A Dedication to Sir Philip Sidney*, in *Prose Works of Fulke Greville, Lord Brooke*, ed. John Gouws (Oxford: Clarendon Press, 1986).

HALL, EDWARD, *The union of the two noble families of Lancaster and York* (1550).

HARDYNG, JOHN, *The Chronicle from the Fyrst Begynnyng of Englande* (1543).

HARRISON, WILLIAM, *The Description of England*, ed. George Edelen (Ithaca, NY: Cornell University Press, 1968).

HART, JOHN, *A Methode or comfortable beginning for all vnlearned whereby they may bee taught to read English* (1570).

—— *An Orthographie conteyning the due order and reason howe to write or paint thimage of a mannes voice, most like to life or nature* (1569).

HARVEY, GABRIEL, *Gabriel Harveii Valdinatis Smithus vel Musarum Lachrymae* (1577).

—— *Pierces Superogation or a New Praise of an Old Ass* (1593).

HAYNES, SAMUEL (ed.), *Collections of State Papers Relating to the Affairs of in the Reigns of Henry VIII, Edward VI, Mary and Elizabeth, [. . .] left by William Cecil, Lord Burghley*, 2 vols. (1740).

HEARNE, THOMAS (ed.), *Benedictus Abba Petroburgensis, de Vita et Gestis Henrici II et Ricardi I*, 2 vols. (Oxford, 1735).

—— *De Rebus Britannicis Collectanea*, 6 vols, (1770).

HENRY VIII, *Adsertio VII. Sacram. adv. Luth.* (1521).

HEYWOOD, THOMAS, *A Woman Killed with Kindness*, in Kathleen McCluskie and David Bevington (eds.), *Plays on Women* (Manchester: Manchester University Press, 1999).

HOBY, THOMAS, *The Book of the Courtier*, ed. Virginia Cox (London: Everyman, 1994).

HORACE, *Satires*, ed. and trans. H. Rushton Fairclough, rev. edn. (London: Heinemann, 1929).

HOWARD, HENRY, *The Poems*, ed. Emrys Jones (Oxford: Clarendon Press, 1964).

HUDDERSFORD, WILLIAM, *The Lives of those eminent Antiquaries John Leland, Thomas Hearne, and Anthony à Wood*, 2 vols. (Oxford, 1772), i.

HUMPHREY, LAWRENCE, *The Nobles, or of Nobility* (1563).

Informacon for pylgrymes vnto the holy londe, ed. George Henry Freely (London: William Nicol, 1824).

Iniunccions geuen by the moste excellent prince, Edward the sixte (1547).

JORDAN, W. K. (ed.), *The Chronicle and Political Papers of King Edward VI* (London; George Allen & Unwin, 1966).

JOUBERT, LAURENT, *Traite du Ris* (Paris, 1579).

KNOX, JOHN, *First Blast of the Trumpet against the Monstrous Regiment of Women* (Geneva, 1558).

LATIMER, HUGH, *Sermons*, ed. George Elwes Corrie, 2 vols. (Cambridge: Parker Society, 1844).

LELAND, JOHN, *Assertio Inclytissimi Arturii Regis Britanniae* (1544).

—— *Bononio-Gallo Mastix* (1545).

—— *Commentarii de Scriptoribus Britannicis*, ed. Anthony Hall, 2 vols. (Oxford, 1709).

—— *Commentarii in Cygneam Cantionem* (1545), appended to Leland, *Cygnea Cantio*.

—— *Cygnea Cantio* (1545).

—— 'Four poems in praise of Erasmus by John Leland', ed. and trans. James Carley, *Erasmus in English*, 11 (1981–2), 26–7.

—— *Genethliacon illustrissimi Eaduerdi Principis Cambriae, Ducis Coriniae, et Comitis Palatini* (1543).

—— *Laudatio Pacis* (1546).

LELAND, JOHN, *Leland's Itinerary in England*, ed. Lucy Toulmin-Smith, 4 vols. (London: George Bell & Son, 1907–10).

—— *Leland's Itinerary in Wales*, ed. Lucy Toulmin-Smith (London: George Bell & Son, 1906).

—— *Naeniae in mortem Thomae Viati equitis incomparabilis* (1542).

—— 'A newe yeares gyfte', in John Bale, *The laboryouse Iourney & serche of Iohan Leylande, for Englandes Antiquities* (1549).

—— *Principum ac illustrium aliquot & eruditorum in Anglia virorum, encomia, trophaea, genethliaca, & epithalmia*, ed. Thomas Newton (1589).

—— *Syllabus, et interpretatio antiquarum dictionum* (1543), appended to Leland, *Genethliacon*.

Letters and Papers, Foreign and Domestic, of the reign of Henry VIII, 1509–1547, ed. J. S. Brewer, 21 vols. (London: Public Record Office, 1862–1932).

LIVY, *The History of the Roman Republic*, ed. and trans. Evan T. Sage, rev. edn. (London: Heinemann, 1936).

LYLY, JOHN, *Euphues' Glass for Europe*, in *Euphues and his England*, in R. Warwick Bond (ed.), *The Complete Works of John Lyly*, 2 vols. (Oxford: Clarendon, 1902), ii. 191–216.

MACHIAVELLI, NICCOLÒ, *I Discorsi*, ed. Sergio Bertelli, *Opere di Niccolò Machiavelli*, 8 vols. (Milan: Biblioteca di classici italiani, 1960–5) i (1960).

—— *Il discorso intorno alla nostra lingua*, ed. Franco Gaeta, *Opere*, viii (1965).

—— *Istorie Fiorentine*, ed. Franco Gaeta, *Opere*, vii (1962).

—— *The Prince*, ed. and trans. Quentin Skinner and Russell Price (Cambridge: Cambridge University Press, 1988).

—— *Il Principe*, ed. Sergio Bertelli, *Opere*, i (1960).

MAJOR, JOHN, *The history of greater Britain*, ed. and trans. Archibald Constable, Scottish History Society, 10 (1892).

MARLOWE, CHRISTOPHER, *Jew of Malta*, ed. Mark Thornton Burnett, *The Complete Plays* (Everyman, 1999).

MICHELI, GIOVANNI, *Relazioni d'Inghilterra*, in Eugenio Alberi (ed.), *Relazioni degli amabasciatori veneti al Senato*, serie 1, vol. ii (Florence, 1840), 291–380.

MILTON, JOHN, *Poetical Works*, ed. Douglas Bush (Oxford: Oxford University Press, 1966).

MORE, THOMAS, *The Latin Poems*, ed. Clarence H. Miller, Leicester Bradner, Charles A. Lynch, and Revilo P. Oliver, *The Complete Works of St. Thomas More*, vol. iii, pt. 2 (New Haven: Yale University Press, 1984).

—— 'Letter to Oxford University', ed. Daniel Kinney, *Complete Works*, xv (1986).

—— *Utopia*, ed. and trans. George M. Logan and Robert M. Adams (Cambridge: Cambridge University Press, 1989).

MULCASTER, RICHARD, *The first part of the elementarie which entreateth chefelie of the right writing of our English tung* (1582).

—— *Positions wherein those primitive circumstances be examined, which are necessarie for the training vp of children* (1581).

—— *Positions concerning the training up of children*, ed. William Barker (Toronto: University of Toronto Press, 1994).

NASHE, THOMAS, *The Works of Thomas Nashe*, ed. R. B. McKerrow, 5 vols. (London: Bullen, 1903–10).

NICHOLS, JOHN GOUGH (ed.), *The Literary Remains of Edward VI*, 2 vols. (London: Roxburgh Club, 1857).

NORDEN, JOHN, *The Surveiors Dialogue* (1610).

OCHINO, BERNADINO, *A tragoedie or Dialoge of the vniuste vsurped primacie of the Bishop of Rome*, trans. John Ponet (1549).

OVID, *Metamorphoses*, ed. and trans. Frank Justus Miller, 3rd edn., rev. G. P. Goold, *Ovid III* (London: Heinemann, 1977).

PALSGRAVE, JOHN, *Lesclarissement de la langue francoyce* (1530).

PONET, JOHN, *An Apologie fully aunsweringe by Scriptures and aunceant Doctors/a blasphemous Book gatherid by D. Steph. Gardiner* (Strasburg, 1556).

—— *A shorte treatise of politicke power* (Strasburg, 1556).

PUTTENHAM, GEORGE, *The Arte of Englishe Poesie*, ed. Gladys Doidge Willcock and Alice Walker (Cambridge: Cambridge University Press, 1936).

Quincuplex Psalterium Gallicum. Rhomamum. Hebraicum. Vetus. Conciliatum, facsimile de l'édition de 1513 (Geneva: Librairie Droz, 1979) ('Vulgate Psalms').

QUINTILIAN, *Institutio Oratoria*, ed. and trans. H. E. Butler, 3 vols. (London: Heinemann, 1920–2).

RASTELL, JOHN, *The Four Elements*, in Richard Axton (ed.), *Three Rastell Plays* (Cambridge: Brewer, 1979).

ROBINSON, HASTINGS (ed.), *Original Letters Relative to the English Reformation*, 2 vols. (Cambridge: Cambridge University Press, 1846–7).

ROBINSON, RICHARD, *The learned and true assertion of the original, life, actes, and death of Prince Arthure, king of great Brittaine* (1582).

ROPER, WILLIAM, *The Lyfe of Sir Thomas More*, ed. Elsie Vaughan Hitchcock, EETS, original series, 197 (1935).

RYMER, THOMAS, *Foedora* (1704–35), 20 vols, xiv.

SALESBURY, WILLIAM, *A briefe and playne introduction, teaching how to pronounce the letters in the British tong* (1550).

—— *A Dictionary in Englyshe & Welshe moche necessary to all suche Welshemen as wil spedly learne the englyshe tongue thought vnto the kynges maiestie very mete to be sette forthe to the vse of his graces subiectes in Wales: wherevnto is prefixed a litel treatyse of the englyshe pronunciation of the letters* (1547).

SARANZO, GIACOMO, *Relazione d' Inghilterra*, in Eugenio Alberi (ed.), *Relazioni degli ambasciatori veneti al Senato*, serie 1, vol. iii (Florence, 1853), 31–87.

SCHMIDT, ALBERT J., 'A Treatise on England's Perils, 1578', *Archiv für Reformationsgeschichte*, 46 (1955), 243–9.

SHAKESPEARE, WILLIAM, *The Oxford Shakespeare*, ed. Stanley Wells and Gary Taylor (Oxford: Clarendon Press, 1988).

SHERRY, RICHARD, *A treatise of schemes & tropes* (1550).

SIDNEY, PHILIP, *An Apology for Poetry*, ed. Geoffrey Shepherd (Manchester: Manchester University Press, 1973).

—— *Astrophil and Stella*, in *Sir Philip Sidney: A Selection of his Finest Poems* ed. Katherine Duncan-Jones (Oxford: Oxford University Press, 1994).

—— *The Countess of Pembroke's Arcadia (The New Arcadia)*, ed. Maurice Evans (Harmondsworth: Penguin, 1977).

—— *The Countess of Pembroke's Arcadia (The Old Arcadia)*, ed. Katherine Duncan-Jones (Oxford: Oxford University Press, 1999).

—— *The Miscellaneous Prose of Sir Philip Sidney*, ed. Katherine Duncan-Jones and Jan van Dorsten (Oxford: Clarendon Press, 1973).

—— *The Prose Works of Sir Philip Sidney*, ed. Albert Feuillerat, 4 vols. (Cambridge: Cambridge University Press, 1962).

SKELTON, JOHN, *The Complete English Poems*, ed. John Scattergood (Harmondsworth: Penguin, 1983).

—— *A litel boke called Colyn Cloute* (1545).

—— *Why cam ye not to courte* (1545).

SMITH, THOMAS, *Certaigne Psalmes or Songues of David, translated into Englishe meter*, in *Sir Thomas Smith, Literary and Linguistic Works*, i, ed. Bror Danielsson, *Stockholm Studies in English*, 12 (Stockholm: Almqvist and Wiksell, 1963).

—— *A Discourse of the Commonweal of this Realm of England*, ed. Mary Dewar (Charlottesville: University Press of Virginia, 1969).

—— *De recta et emendata linguae anglicae scriptione, dialogus*, in *Sir Thomas Smith, Literary and Linguistic Works*, iii, ed. Bror Danielsson, *Stockholm Studies in English*, 56 (Stockholm: Almqvist and Wiksell, 1983).

—— *De recta et emendata linguae graecae pronuntiatione*, in *Sir Thomas Smith, Literary and Linguistic Works*, ii, ed. Bror Danielsson, *Stockholm Studies in English*, 50 (Stockholm: Almqvist and Wiksell, 1978).

—— *De Republica Anglorum*, ed. Mary Dewar (Cambridge: Cambridge University Press, 1982).

—— *A Letter sent by I.B. gentleman* (1571).

SOPHOCLES, *Antigone*, ed. and trans. Hugh Lloyd-Jones (London: Heinemann, 1994).

SPENSER, EDMUND, *The Faerie Queene*, ed. A. C. Hamilton (London: Longman, 1977).

—— *Selected Shorter Poems*, ed. Douglas Brooks-Davies (London: Longman, 1995).

—— *The Shepheardes Calender* (1579).

—— *A View of the State of Ireland*, ed. Andrew Hadfield and Willy Maley (Oxford: Blackwell, 1997).

—— and GABRIEL HARVEY, *Three proper, and wittie, familiar letters* (1580).

STARKEY, THOMAS, *A Dialogue between Reginald Pole and Thomas Lupset*, ed. Kathleen M. Burton (London: Chatto & Windus, 1948).

STOW, JOHN, *The chronicles of England* (1580).

STRYPE, JOHN (ed.), *Ecclesiastical Memorials, relating chiefly to religion, and the reformation of it*, 3 vols. (Oxford: Clarendon Press, 1822), iii.

—— *The Life of the Learned Sir John Cheke* (Oxford: Clarendon Press, 1821).

THOMAS, WILLIAM, *An Argument wherin the apparaile of women is both reproued and defended* (1551).

—— *The Historie of Italie* (1549).

—— *The History of Italy (1549)*, ed. George B. Parks (Ithaca, NY: Cornell University Press, 1963).

—— *Il Pellegrino Inglese ne 'l quele si difende l'innocente, & la Sincera vita del pio & Religisso Re d'Inghilterra Henrico ottauo, bugiardamente caloniato da Clemente vii & da gl' altri adulatori de la Sedia antiChristiana* (Zurich, 1552).

—— *The Principal rules of the Italian grammer* (1550).

—— *The Vanitee of this Worlde* (1549).

The Treatise of the Galaunt (1510).

TURNER, WILLIAM, *The first and seconde partes of the herbal lately ouersene, corrected and enlarged with the thirde parte* (1568).

—— *The huntynge and the fyndyng out of the Romishe fox* (1543).

—— *The Names of Herbes in Greke, Latin, Englishe, Duche & Frenche* (1548).

TYNDALE, WILLIAM, *The Obedience of a Christian Man* (1528).

VERGIL, POLYDORE, *Polydore Vergil's English History, from an early translation*, ed. Henry Ellis (London: Camden Society, 1846).

VIRGIL, *Eclogues, Georgics, Aeneid I–VI*, in *Virgil I*, ed. and trans. H. Rushton Fairclough, rev. edn. (London: Heinemann, 1935).

—— *Aeneid*, ed. and trans. H. Rushton Fairclough, rev. edn. (London: Heinemann, 1935).

Bibliography

WALSHE, EDWARD, *The office and duety in fightyng for our countrey* (1545).
WHITNEY, GEOFFREY, *A Choice of Emblems* (1586).
WILSON, THOMAS, *The Arte of Rhetorique* (1553).
—— *The Arte of Rhetorique* (1560).
—— *A discourse vppon Vsurye* (1572).
—— *A Discourse upon Usury*, ed. R. H. Tawney (London: G. Bell, 1925).
—— *The Rule of Reason* (1551).
—— *The three orations of Demosthenes chiefe orator among the Grecians, in fauour of the Olythians [. . .] with those his fower orations titled expressely & by name against king Philip of Macedonie* (1570).
—— 'A treatise on England's perils, 1578', ed. Albert J. Schmidt, *Archiv für Reformationsgeschichte*, 46 (1955), 243–9.
—— *Vita et Obitus Duorum Fratrum Suffolciensium, Henrici et Caroli Brandoni* (1551).
WOOD, ANTHONY À, *Athenae Oxoniensis*, new edn., ed. Philip Bliss, 4 vols. (London: F. C. and J. Rivington, 1813–20).
WRIGHT, THOMAS (ed.), *Political Poems and Songs relating to English History, composed during the period from the accession of Edward III to that of Richard III*, 2 vols. (London: Public Records Office, 1859–61), ii.
WYATT, THOMAS, *Collected Poems of Sir Thomas Wyatt*, ed. Kenneth Muir and Patricia Thomson (Liverpool: Liverpool University Press, 1969).
ZALL, P. M. (ed.), *A Hundred Mery Talys and Other English Jestbooks of the Fifteenth and Sixteenth Centuries* (Lincoln: University of Nebraska Press, 1963).

SECONDARY SOURCES

ADAIR, E. R., 'William Thomas: A Forgotten Clerk of the Privy Council', in R. W. Seton-Watson (ed.), *Tudor Studies* (London: Longmans Green, 1924), 133–60.
ALFORD, STEPHEN, *The Early Elizabethan Polity: William Cecil and the British Succession Crisis, 1558–1569* (Cambridge: Cambridge University Press, 1998).
—— 'Reassessing William Cecil in the 1560s', in Guy (ed.), *Tudor Monarchy*, 233–52.
ALLEN, J. W., *A History of Political Thought in the Sixteenth Century* (London: Methuen, 1928).
ALPERS, PAUL, *What is Pastoral?* (Chicago: University of Chicago Press, 1996).
ANDERSON, BENEDICT, *Imagined Communities: Reflections on the Origin and Spread of Nationalism*, rev. edn. (London: Verso, 1991).

ANDERSON, JUDITH H., *Words that Matter: Linguistic Perception in Renaissance England* (Stanford, Calif.: Stanford University Press, 1996).

ANGLO, SYDNEY, 'The *British History* in Early Tudor Propaganda', *Bulletin of the John Rylands Library*, 44 (1961), 17–48.

ASTON, MARGARET, 'English Ruins and English History: The Dissolution and the Sense of the Past', *Journal of Warburg and Courtauld Institutes*, 36 (1973), 231–55.

BAKER-SMITH, DOMINIC, *More's Utopia* (London: HarperCollins, 1991).

BALLESTER, LUIS GARCIA, and JON ARRIZABALAGA (eds.), *Galen and Galenism: Theory and Medical Practice from Antiquity to the European Renaissance* (Aldershot: Ashgate, 2002).

BARBER, PETER, 'England I: Pageantry, Defense and Government: Maps at Court to 1550', in David Buisseret (ed.), *Monarchs, Ministers and Maps: The Emergence of Cartography as a Tool of Government in Early Modern Europe* (Chicago: University of Chicago Press, 1992), 26–56.

BARTLETT, KENNETH A., *The English in Italy, 1525–58: A Study in Culture and Politics* (Geneva: Slatkine, 1991).

BATE, JONATHAN, 'The Elizabethans in Italy', in Jean-Pierre Maquerlot and Michèle Willems (eds.), *Travel and Drama in Shakespeare's Time* (Cambridge: Cambridge University Press, 1996), 55–74.

BAUMLIN, TITA FRENCH, 'Thomas Wilson', in *Dictionary of Literary Biography*, ccxxxvi: *British Rhetoricians and Logicians, 1500–1600*, ed. Edward A. Malone (Detroit: Bruccoli Clark Layman, 2001), 282–307.

BENNETT, H. S., *English Books and Readers, 1475–1557* (Cambridge: Cambridge University Press, 1952).

BETTERIDGE, THOMAS, *Tudor Histories of the English Reformations, 1530–83* (Aldershot: Ashgate, 1999).

BEVINGTON, DAVID M., 'The Dialogue in *Utopia*: Two Sides to the Question', *Studies in Philology*, 58 (1961), 496–509.

BINNS, JAMES W., *Intellectual Culture in Elizabethan and Jacobean England: The Latin Writings of the Age* (Leeds: Francis Cairns, 1990).

BLANK, PAULA, *Broken English: Dialects and the Politics of Language in Renaissance Writings* (London: Routledge, 1996).

BOND, RONALD R., 'Supplantation in the Elizabethan Court: The Theme of Spenser's February Eclogue', *Spenser Studies*, 2 (1981), 55–65.

BRADDICK, MICHAEL J., *State Formation in Early Modern England, c.1550–1700* (Cambridge: Cambridge University Press, 2000).

BRADNER, LEICESTER, *Musae Anglicanae: A History of Anglo-Latin Poetry, 1500–1925* (New York: Modern Language Association of America, 1940).

BRADSHAW, BRENDAN, ANDREW HADFIELD, and WILLY MALEY (eds.), *Representing Ireland: Literature and the Origins of Conflict, 1534–1660* (Cambridge: Cambridge University Press, 1993).

BREUILLY, JOHN, *Nationalism and the State*, 2nd edn. (Manchester: Manchester University Press, 1993).

BRIGGS, WILLIAM DINSMORE, 'Political Ideas in Sidney's *Arcadia*', *Studies in Philology*, 28 (1931), 137–61.

BURROW, COLIN, 'Original Fictions: Metamorphoses in *The Faerie Queene*', in Charles Martindale (ed.), *Ovid Renewed: Ovidian Influences on Literature and Art from the Middle Ages to the Twentieth Century* (Cambridge: Cambridge University Press, 1988), 99–119.

BUXTON, JOHN, *Sir Philip Sidney and the English Renaissance* (London: Macmillan, 1964).

CALHOUN, CRAIG, *Nationalism* (Buckingham: Open University Press, 1997).

CARLEY, JAMES, 'John Leland in Paris: The Evidence of his Poetry', *Studies in Philology*, 83 (1986), 1–50.

—— 'John Leland's *Cygnea Cantio*: A Neglected Tudor River Poem', *Humanistica Lovaniensa*, 32 (1983), 225–41.

CARLSON, DAVID R., *English Humanist Books: Writers and Patrons, Manuscripts and Print, 1475–1525* (Toronto: University of Toronto Press 1993).

COLLINSON, PATRICK, *The Birthpangs of Protestant England: Religious and Cultural Change in the Sixteenth and Seventeenth Centuries* (Basingstoke: Macmillan, 1988).

—— 'The Monarchical Republic of Queen Elizabeth I', in Guy (ed.), *Tudor Monarchy*, 110–34.

—— '*De Republica Anglorum*: or History with the Politics Put Back', in id., *Elizabethan Essays* (London: Hambledon Press, 1994), 1–30.

COX, VIRGINIA, *The Renaissance Dialogue: Literary Dialogue in its Social and Political Contexts, Castiglione to Galileo* (Cambridge: Cambridge University Press, 1992).

CULLEN, PATRICK, *Spenser, Marvell, and the Renaissance Pastoral* (Cambridge, Mass.: Harvard University Press, 1970).

CUNNINGHAM, BERNADETTE, *The World of Geoffrey Keating: History, Myth and Religion in Seventeenth-Century Ireland* (Dublin: Four Courts Press, 2000).

DAVIES, GERALD S., *The Charterhouse in London* (London: John Murray, 1921).

DAVIS, WALTER, 'Narrative Methods in Sidney's *Old Arcadia*', *SEL* 18 (1978), 103–23.

DEWAR, MARY, 'The Authorship of the "Discourse of the Commonweal" ', *Economic History Review*, 2nd series, 19 (1966), 388–400.

—— *Sir Thomas Smith: A Tudor Intellectual in Office* (London: Athlone Press, 1964).

DORAN, SUSAN, *Monarchy and Matrimony: The Courtships of Elizabeth I* (London: Routledge, 1996).

DORIA, MARGARET, 'The Providential Plot of the *Old Arcadia*', in Dennis Kay (ed.), *Philip Sidney*, 83–102.

DOYLE, BRIAN, *English and Englishness* (London: Routledge, 1989).

DUFFY, EAMON, *The Stripping of the Altars: Traditional Religion in England, c.1400–c.1580* (New Haven: Yale University Press, 1992).

DUNCAN-JONES, KATHERINE, 'Philip Sidney's Toys', in Dennis Kay (ed.), *Philip Sidney*, 61–80.

—— *Sir Philip Sidney, Courtier Poet* (London: Hamish Hamilton, 1991).

EDWARDS, PHILIP, *The Making of the Modern English State, 1460–1660* (Basingstoke: Palgrave, 2001).

EKWALL, EILERT (ed.), *The Concise Oxford Dictionary of English Place Names*, 4th edn. (Oxford: Oxford University Press, 1960).

ELSKY, MARTIN, *Authorizing Words: Speech, Writing, and Print in the English Renaissance* (Ithaca, NY: Cornell University Press, 1989).

ELTON, G. R., 'Parliament in the Sixteenth Century: Functions and Fortunes', *Historical Journal*, 22 (1979), 255–78.

—— *Reform and Reformation: England, 1509–1558* (London: Edward Arnold, 1977).

—— (ed.), *The Tudor Constitution: Documents and Commentary*, 2nd edn. (Cambridge: Cambridge University Press, 1982).

—— *The Tudor Revolution in Government: Administrative Changes in the Reign of Henry VIII* (Cambridge: Cambridge University Press, 1953).

FENNELL, BARBARA A., *A History of English: A Sociolinguistic Approach* (Oxford: Blackwell, 2001).

FOWLER, ELAINE W., *English Sea Power in the Early Tudor Period, 1485–1558* (Ithaca, NY: Cornell University Press, 1965).

FOX, ALISTAIR, *Politics and Literature in the Reigns of Henry VII and Henry VIII* (Oxford: Blackwell, 1989).

GELLNER, ERNEST, *Nations and Nationalism* (Oxford: Blackwell, 1983).

GENETTE, GÉRARD, *Narrative Discourse: An Essay in Method*, trans. Jane E. Lewin (Ithaca, NY: Cornell University Press, 1972).

—— *Paratexts: Thresholds of Interpretation*, trans. Jane E. Lewin (Cambridge: Cambridge University Press, 1997).

GILLINGHAM, JOHN, 'The English Invasion of Ireland', in Bradshaw et al. (eds.), *Representing Ireland*, 26–42.

—— 'Images of Ireland, 1170–1600: The Origins of English Imperialism', *History Today*, 37 (1987), 16–22.

GOODMAN, ANTHONY, 'The Anglo-Scottish Marches in the Fifteenth Century: A Frontier Society?', in Roger A. Mason (ed.), *Scotland and England, 1286–1815* (Edinburgh: Edinburgh University Press, 1987), 18–33.

GRAFTON, ANTHONY, and LISA JARDINE, *From Humanism to the Humanities* (Cambridge, Mass.: Harvard University Press, 1986).

GRAFTON, ANTHONY, and LISA JARDINE, ' "Studied for action": How Gabriel Harvey Read his Livy', *Past and Present*, 129 (1990), 30–78.

GRAY, HANNA H., 'Renaissance Humanism: The Pursuit of Eloquence', in Paul Oskar Kristellar and Philip P. Weiner (eds.), *Renaissance Essays* (Rochester, NY: University of Rochester Press, 1968), 199–216.

GREENBLATT, STEPHEN, *Renaissance Self-Fashioning: More to Shakespeare* (Chicago: University of Chicago Press, 1980).

GRENDLER, PAUL F., *The Roman Inquisition and the Venetian Press, 1540–1605* (Princeton: Princeton University Press, 1977).

GUY, JOHN, *Tudor England* (Oxford: Oxford University Press, 1988).

—— (ed.), 'Tudor Monarchy and its Critiques', in id. (ed.), *Tudor Monarchy*, 78–109.

—— (ed.), *The Tudor Monarchy* (London: Arnold, 1997).

HADFIELD, ANDREW, *Literature, Politics and National Identity* (Cambridge: Cambridge University Press, 1994).

—— *Literature, Travel, and Colonial Writing in the English Renaissance, 1545–1625* (Oxford: Clarendon Press, 1998).

—— 'Translating the Reformation', in Bradshaw et al. (eds.), *Representing Ireland*, 43–59.

HAIGH, CHRISTOPHER, *English Reformations: Religion, Politics, and Society under the Tudors* (Oxford: Clarendon Press, 1993).

HAMILTON, A. C., 'Sidney's *Arcadia* as Prose Fiction: Its Relation to its Sources', *ELR* 2 (1972), 29–60.

HARRIS, JESSE W., *John Bale: A Study in the Minor Literature of the Reformation* (Urbana: University of Illinois Press, 1940).

HAY, DENYS, *Polydore Vergil: Renaissance Historian and Man of Letters* (Oxford: Clarendon Press, 1952).

HEALE, ELIZABETH, *Wyatt, Surrey and Early Tudor Poetry* (London: Longman, 1998).

HELGERSON, RICHARD, *The Elizabethan Prodigals* (Berkeley: University of California Press, 1976).

—— *Forms of Nationhood: The Elizabethan Writing of England* (Chicago: University of Chicago Press, 1992).

—— *Self-Crowned Laureates: Spenser, Jonson, Milton* (Berkeley: University of California Press, 1983).

HENINGER, S. K., *Sidney and Spenser: The Poet as Maker* (University Park: Pennsylvania State University Press, 1989).

HOAK, DALE E., *The King's Council in the Reign of Edward VI* (Cambridge: Cambridge University Press, 1976).

—— 'The King's Privy Chamber, 1547–1553', in Delloyd J. Guth and John W. McKenna (eds.), *Tudor Rule and Revolution* (Cambridge: Cambridge University Press, 1982), 87–108.

—— 'Rehabilitating the Duke of Northumberland: Politics and Political Control', in Jennifer Loach and Robert Tittler (eds.), *The Mid-Tudor Polity, c.1540–60* (London: Macmillan, 1980), 29–51.

HOBSBAWM, ERIC, *Nations and Nationalism since 1780: Programme, Myth, Reality* (Cambridge: Cambridge University Press, 1990).

HOGREFE, PEARL, *The Sir Thomas More Circle* (Urbana: University of Illinois Press, 1959).

HOWELL, WILLIAM, *Logic and Rhetoric in England, 1500–1700* (Princeton: Princeton University Press, 1956).

HUDSON, WINTHROP, *The Cambridge Connection and the Elizabethan Settlement of 1559* (Durham, NC: Duke University Press, 1980).

HUNTER, G. K., *John Lyly: The Humanist as Courtier* (London: Routledge & Kegan Paul, 1962).

HUTTON, JAMES, 'John Leland's *Laudatio Pacis*', *Studies in Philology*, 58 (1961), 616–26.

JAMES, MERVYN, *Society, Politics and Culture: Studies in Early Modern England* (Cambridge: Cambridge University Press, 1986).

JARDINE, LISA, *Erasmus, Man of Letters: The Construction of Charisma in Print* (Princeton: Princeton University Press, 1993).

—— and WILLIAM SHERMAN, 'Pragmatic Readers: Knowledge Transactions and Scholarly Services in Late Elizabethan England', in Anthony Fletcher and Peter Roberts (eds.), *Religion, Culture and Society in Early Modern Britain* (Cambridge: Cambridge University Press, 1994), 102–24.

JONES, NORMAN, *God and the Moneylenders: Usury and Law in Early Modern England* (Oxford: Blackwell, 1986).

JONES, R. BRINLEY, *The Old British Tongue: The Vernacular in Wales, 1540–1640* (Cardiff: Avalon, 1970).

JONES, RICHARD FOSTER, *The Triumph of English: A Survey of Opinions concerning the Vernacular from the Introduction of Printing to the Restoration* (Stanford, Calif.: Stanford University Press, 1953).

JORDAN, W. K., *Edward VI*, i: *The Young King. The Protectorship of the Duke of Somerset* (London: George Allen & Unwin, 1968).

—— *Edward VI*, ii: *The Threshold of Power. The Dominance of the Duke of Northumberland* (London: George Allen & Unwin, 1970).

KAY, DENNIS (ed.), *Sir Philip Sidney: An Anthology of Modern Criticism* (Oxford: Clarendon Press, 1987).

KEDOURIE, ELIE, *Nationalism* (London: Hutchinson, 1960).

KEMILAINEN, AIRA, *Nationalism: Problems concerning the Word, the Concept, the Classification* (Jyväskylä: Jyväskylän Kasvatusopillinen Korkeakoulu, 1964).

KENDRICK, T. D., *British Antiquity* (London: Methuen, 1950).

KIDD, COLIN, *British Identities before Nationalism: Ethnicity and Nationhood in the Atlantic World, 1600–1800* (Cambridge: Cambridge University Press, 1999).

KING, JOHN N., *English Reformation Literature: The Tudor Origins of the Protestant Tradition* (Princeton: Princeton University Press, 1982).

KNOWLES, DAVID, *The Religious Orders in England*, iii: *The Tudor Age* (Cambridge: Cambridge University Press, 1959).

KOHN, HANS, *Nationalism, its Meaning and History* (Princeton: Princeton University Press, 1955).

KRISTELLER, PAUL OSKAR, 'The Cultural Heritage of Humanism: An Overview', in Albert Rabil Jr. (ed.), *Renaissance Humanism: Foundations, Forms and Legacy*, 3 vols. (Philadelphia: University of Pennysylvania Press, 1988), iii. 515–28.

LAKE, PETER, and MARIA DOWLING (eds.), *Protestantism and the National Church in Sixteenth-Century England* (London: Croom Helm, 1987).

LANHAM, RICHARD, 'Sidney: The Ornament of his Age', *Southern Review*, (1967), 319–40.

LENNARD, JOHN, *But I Digress: The Exploitation of Parentheses in English Printed Verse* (Oxford: Clarendon Press, 1991).

LEVY, F. J., 'Philip Sidney Reconsidered', *ELR* 2 (1972), 5–28.

LEWIS, C. S., *English Literature in the Sixteenth Century, excluding Drama* (Oxford: Clarendon Press, 1954).

LEWIS, CHARLTON T., and CHARLES SHORT (eds.), *A Latin Dictionary* (Oxford: Oxford University Press, 1879).

LEWIS, G. R., *The Stannaries: A Study of the English Tin Miner* (Cambridge, Mass.: Harvard University Press, 1908).

LOADES, DAVID, *England's Maritime Empire: Seapower, Commerce and Policy, 1490–1690* (Harlow: Longman, 2000).

—— *John Dudley, Duke of Northumberland, 1504–1553* (Oxford: Clarendon Press, 1996).

—— 'The Origins of English Protestant Nationalism', in id., *Politics, Censorship and the English Reformation* (London: Pinter, 1991), 39–55.

—— *Politics and the Nation, 1450–1660: Obedience, Resistance and Public Order* (London: Fontana Press, 1974).

—— *Two Tudor Conspiracies* (Cambridge: Cambridge University Press, 1965).

LOEWENSTEIN, JOSEPH, *Ben Jonson and Possessive Authorship* (Cambridge: Cambridge University Press, 2002).

LOVE, HAROLD, *The Culture and Commerce of Texts: Scribal Publication in Seventeenth-Century England* (Amherst: University of Massachusetts Press, 1998).

—— *Scribal Publication in Seventeenth-Century England* (Oxford: Clarendon Press, 1993).

LUBORSKY, RUTH SAMSON, 'Allusive Presentation in *The Shepheardes Calendar*', *Spenser Studies*, 1 (1980), 29–67.

—— 'The Illustrations to *The Shepheardes Calendar*', *Spenser Studies*, 2 (1981), 3–53.

LUIGI, PIERONE, 'La Paternità Machiavelliana del *Dialogo Intorno all Lingua*', *Studium*, 72 (1976), 715–20.

MCCABE, RICHARD A., ' "Little booke: thy selfe present": Spenser's Politics of Presentation', in Howard Erskine-Hill and Richard A. McCabe (eds.), *Presenting Poetry: Composition, Publication, Reception* (Cambridge: Cambridge University Press, 1995), 15–40.

MCCONICA, JAMES KELSEY, *English Humanists and Reformation Politics under Henry VIII and Edward VI* (Oxford: Clarendon Press, 1965).

MCCOY, RICHARD C., *Sir Philip Sidney: Rebellion in Arcadia* (Hassocks: Harvester Press, 1979).

MACCULLOCH, DIARMAID, *Thomas Cranmer: A Life* (New Haven: Yale University Press, 1996).

MCEACHERN, CLAIRE, *The Poetics of English Nationhood, 1590–1612* (Cambridge: Cambridge University Press, 1996).

MCFARLANE, I. D., *A Literary History of France: Renaissance France, 1470–1589* (London: Ernest Benn, 1974).

MACKIE, J. D., *The Earlier Tudors, 1495–1558* (Oxford: Oxford University Press, 1994).

MCKISACK, MAY, *Medieval History in the Tudor Age* (Oxford: Clarendon Press, 1971).

MCRAE, ANDREW, *God Speed the Plough: The Representation of Agrarian England, 1500–1600* (Cambridge: Cambridge University Press, 1996).

MALEY, WILLY, 'Spenser's Language: Writing in the Ruins of English', in Andrew Hadfield (ed.), *The Cambridge Companion to Spenser* (Cambridge: Cambridge University Press, 2001), 161–79.

MANLEY, LAWRENCE, *Convention: 1500–1570* (Cambridge, Mass.: Harvard University Press, 1980).

—— *Literature and Culture in Early Modern England* (Cambridge: Cambridge University Press, 1995).

MAROTTI, ARTHUR, *Manuscript, Print and the English Renaissance Lyric* (Ithaca, NY: Cornell University Press, 1995).

MARTIN, FRANCIS-XAVIER, 'The Image of the Irish—Medieval and Modern—Continuity and Change', in Richard Wall (ed.), *Medieval and Modern Ireland* (Gerrards Cross: Smythe, 1988), 1–18.

MASON, ROGER A. (ed.), *Scots and Britons: Scottish Political Thought and the Union of 1603* (Cambridge: Cambridge University Press, 1994).

MEDINE, PETER E., *Thomas Wilson* (Boston: Twayne, 1986).

MITCHELL, R. J., *John Tiptoft* (London: Longman, 1938).

MOLEN, RICHARD L. DE, *Richard Mulcaster (c.1531–1611) and Educational Reform in the Renaissance* (Nieuwkoop: De Graaf, 1991).

MONTROSE, LOUIS A., 'Interpreting Spenser's February Eclogue: Some Contexts and Implications', *Spenser Studies*, 2 (1981), 67–74.

—— 'A Kingdom of Shadows', in David L. Smith, Richard Strier, and David Bevington (eds.), *The Theatrical City: Culture, Theatre and Politics in London* (Cambridge: Cambridge University Press, 1995), 70–86.

MORRIS, GEOFFREY, *Political Thought in England: Tyndale to Hooker* (Oxford: Oxford University Press, 1953).

MUELLER, JANEL M., *The Native Tongue and the Word: Developments in English Prose Style, 1380–1580* (Chicago: University of Chicago Press, 1984).

MUIR, KENNETH (ed.), *The Life and Letters of Sir Thomas Wyatt* (Liverpool: Liverpool University Press, 1963).

MULDREW, CRAIG, *The Economy of Obligation: The Culture of Credit and Social Relations in Early Modern England* (Basingstoke: Macmillan, 1998).

MURPHY, JOHN, 'The Illusion of Decline: The Privy Chamber, 1547–1558', in David Starkey et al. (eds.), *The English Court: From the War of the Roses to the Civil War* (London: Longman, 1987), 119–46.

NEEDHAM, PAUL STROPE, 'Sir John Cheke at Cambridge and at Court', unpublished Harvard dissertation (Harvard University, 1971).

NICHOLSON, GRAHAM, 'The Act of Appeals and the English Reformation', in Claire Cross, David Loades, and J. J. Scarisbrick (eds.), *Law and Government under the Tudors* (Cambridge: Cambridge University Press, 1988), 19–30.

NÍ CHUILLEANÁIN, EILÉAN, ' "Strange Ceremonies": Sacred Space and Bodily Presence in the English Reformation', in Piesse (ed.), *Sixteenth-Century*, 133–54.

NORBROOK, DAVID, *Poetry and Politics in the English Renaissance* (London: Routledge & Kegan Paul, 1984).

OLIVER, REVILO P., 'More's Latinity and the Strictures of Brixius', in More, *Latin Poems*, 22–32.

ONG, WALTER, *The Presence of the Word: Some Prolegomena for Cultural and Religious History* (New Haven: Yale University Press, 1967).

The Oxford Classical Dictionary (Oxford: Clarendon Press, 1949).

PARKER, ROBERT W., 'Terentian Studies and Sidney's Original *Arcadia*', *ELR* 2 (1972), 61–78.

PATTERSON, ANNABEL, *Reading between the Lines* (London: Routledge, 1993).

PAYTON, PHILIP, *The Making of Modern Cornwall: Historical Experience and the Persistence of 'Difference'* (Redruth: Dyllansow Truran, 1992).

PIESSE, A. J. (ed.), *Sixteenth-Century Identities* (Manchester: Manchester University Press, 2000).

PIGGOTT, STUART, *Ruins in a Landscape: Essays in Antiquarianism* (Edinburgh: Edinburgh University Press, 1976).

POCOCK, J. G. A., *The Machiavellian Moment: Florentine Political Thought and the Atlantic Republican Tradition* (Princeton: Princeton University Press, 1975).

PROSPERI, ADRIANO, 'Una esperienza di ricerca nell' archivio del sant' uffizio', *Belfagor*, 53 (1998), 309–45.

QUINN, D. B., 'Sir Thomas Smith and the Beginnings of English Colonial Theory', *Proceedings of the American Philosphical Society*, 89 (1945), 543–60.

RAAB, FELIX, *The English Face of Machiavelli: A Changing Interpretation, 1500–1700* (Toronto: University of Toronto Press, 1964).

RASMUSSEN, CARL J., 'A *Theatre for Worldlings* as a Protestant Poetics', *Spenser Studies*, 1 (1980), 1–28.

REBHORN, WAYNE A., 'Baldesar Castiglione, Thomas Wilson and the Courtly Body of Renaissance Rhetoric', *Rhetorica*, 11 (1993), 241–74.

RENAN, ERNEST, 'What is a Nation?', trans. Martin Thom, in Homi K. Bhabha (ed.), *Nation and Narration* (London: Routledge, 1990), 8–22.

REX, RICHARD, 'The Role of English Humanists in the Reformation up to 1559', in N. Scott Amos, Andrew Pettegree, and Henk van Niewp (eds.), *The Education of a Christian Society: Humanism and the Reformation in Britain and the Netherlands* (Aldershot: Ashgate, 1999), 19–40.

RICHARDS, JENNIFER, *Rhetoric and Courtliness in Early Modern Literature* (Cambridge: Cambridge University Press, 2003).

ROBERTS, P. R., 'The Union with England and the Identity of "Anglican" Wales', *Transactions of the Royal Historical Society*, 5th series, 20 (1972), 49–70.

ROSS, TREVOR, 'Dissolution and the Making of the English Literary Canon: The Catalogues of Leland and Bale', *Renaissance and Reformation*, new series, 15 (1991), 57–80.

ROWSE, A. L., *The Expansion of Elizabethan England*, rev. edn. (London: Macmillan, 1969).

SAUNDERS, J. W., 'The Stigma of Print', *Essays in Criticism*, 1 (1951), 139–64.

SCATTERGOOD, JOHN, 'John Leland's *Itinerary* and the Identity of England', in Piesse (ed.), *Sixteenth-Century Identities*, 58–74.

SCHMIDT, ALBERT J., 'Thomas Wilson and the Tudor Commonwealth: An Essay in Civic Humanism', *HLQ* 23 (1960), 49–60.

SETON-WATSON, HUGH, *Nations and States: An Enquiry into the Origins of Nations and the Politics of Nationalism* (London: Methuen, 1977).

SHRANK, CATHY, 'Civil Tongues: Language, Law and Reformation', in Jennifer Richards (ed.), *Early Modern Civil Discourses* (Houndmills: Palgrave, 2003), 19–34.

—— 'English Humanism and National Identity, 1530–1570', unpublished Ph.D. dissertation (University of Cambridge, 2000).

—— ' "These fewe scribbled wordes": Representing Intimacy in Early Modern Print', in Alexandra Gillespie (ed.), *Early Tudor Manuscript and Print*, *HLQ*, special issue (2004).

SIMPSON, JAMES, 'Ageism: Leland, Bale and the Laborious Start of English Literary History, 1350–1550', *New Medieval Literatures*, 1 (1997), 213–35.

SKINNER, QUENTIN, *The Foundations of Modern Political Thought*, 2 vols. (Cambridge: Cambridge University Press, 1978).

—— *Reason and Rhetoric in the Philosophy of Hobbes* (Cambridge: Cambridge University Press, 1996).

—— 'The State', in Terence Ball, James Farr, and Russell L. Harris (eds.), *Political Innovation and Conceptual Change* (Cambridge: Cambridge University Press, 1989), 90–113.

SLACK, PAUL, *From Reformation to Improvement: Public Welfare in Early Modern England* (Oxford: Oxford University Press, 1999).

SLOANE, THOMAS O., *Donne, Milton, and the End of Humanist Rhetoric* (Berkeley: University of California Press, 1985).

SMITH, ANTHONY D., *The Ethnic Origins of Nations* (Oxford: Blackwell, 1986).

SMITH, BRUCE R., 'On Reading *The Shepheardes Calender*', *Spenser Studies*, 1 (1980), 69–93.

SPITZ, LEWIS W., *The Religious Renaissance of the German Humanists* (Cambridge, Mass.: Harvard University Press, 1963).

STEIN, DIETER, 'Sorting out the Variants: Standardization and Social Factors in the English Language, 1600–1800', in id. and Ingrid Tieken-Boon von Ostade (eds.), *Towards a Standard English, 1600–1800* (Berlin: Mouton de Gruyter, 1994), 1–17.

STEIN, DIETER, and INGRID TIEKEN-BOON VON OSTADE (eds.), *Towards a Standard English, 1600–1800* (Berlin: Mouton de Gruyter, 1994).

STERN, VIRGINIA, *Gabriel Harvey, his Life, Marginalia and Library* (Oxford: Clarendon Press, 1979).

STOYLE, MARK, *West Britons: Cornish Identities and the Early Modern British State* (Exeter: Exeter University Press, 2002).

STRANG, BARBARA M. H., *A History of English* (London: Methuen, 1970).

TALBERT, ERNEST WILLIAM, *The Problem of Order: Elizabethan Political Commonplaces and an Example of Shakespeare's Art* (Chapel Hill: University of North Carolina Press, 1962).

THOMPSON, E. MARGARET, *A History of the Somerset Carthusians* (London: John Hodges, 1895).

TYACKE, NICHOLAS, 'Introduction: Re-thinking the "English Reformation" ', in id. (ed.), *England's Long Reformation, 1500–1800* (London: UCL Press, 1998).

VICKERS, BRIAN, *Classical Rhetoric in English Poetry* (London: Macmillan, 1970).

WACQUEATH, FRANÇOISE, *Latin, or the Empire of a Sign from the Sixteenth to the Twentieth Centuries*, trans. John Howe (London: Verso, 2001).

WALKER, GREG, 'Dialogue, Resistance and Accommodation: Conservative Literary Responses to the Henrician Reformation', in N. Scott Amos, Andrew Pettegree, and Henk van Niewp (eds.), *The Education of a Christian Society: Humanism and the Reformation in Britain and the Netherlands* (Aldershot: Ashgate, 1999), 89–111.

WALL, WENDY, *The Imprint of Gender: Authorship and Publication in the English Renaissance* (Ithaca, NY: Cornell University Press, 1993).

WEINER, ANDREW D., *Sir Philip Sidney and the Poetics of Protestantism: A Study of Contexts* (Minneapolis: University of Minnesota Press, 1978).

WEISENGER, HERBERT, 'The Self-Awareness of the Renaissance as a Criterion of the Renaissance', *Papers of the Michigan Academy of Science, Arts and Letters*, 29 (1943), 561–7.

WILLIAMS, GLANMOR, *Welsh Reformation Essays* (Cardiff: University of Wales Press, 1967).

WILLIAMS, NEVILLE, 'The Tudors: Three Contrasts in Personality', in A. G. Dickens (ed.), *The Courts of Europe: Politics, Patronage and Royalty, 1400–1800* (London: Thames & Hudson, 1977), 147–67.

WHEELIS, SAM, 'Ulrich von Hutten: Representative of Patriotic Humanism', in Gerhart Hoffmeister (ed.), *The Renaissance and Reformation in Germany: An Introduction* (New York: Ungar, 1977), 111–27.

WILMOT-BUXTON, H. J., *English Painters* (London: Sampson Low, 1883).

WINSTON, JESSICA, 'Expanding the Political Nation: *Gorboduc* at the Inns of Court and Succession Revisited', *Early Theatre*, 8 (forthcoming).

WITHINGTON, PHIL, 'Citizens, Community and Political Culture', *Historical Journal*, 44 (2001), 239–67.

—— *The Politics of Commonwealth: Citizens and Freemen in Early Modern England* (Cambridge: Cambridge University Press, 2005).

WOOD, ANDY, *The Politics of Social Conflict: The Peak Country, 1570–1770* (Cambridge: Cambridge University Press, 1999).

WOOD, DENIS, with JOHN FELS, *The Power of Maps* (London: Routledge, 1993).

WORDEN, BLAIR, *The Sound of Virtue: Philip Sidney's Arcadia and Elizabethan Politics* (New Haven: Yale University Press, 1996).

WRIGHTSON, KEITH, 'Estates, Degrees and Sorts: Changing Perceptions of

Society in Tudor and Stuart England', in Penelope J. Corfield (ed.), *Language, History and Class* (Oxford: Blackwell, 1991), 30–52.

ZEEVALD, W. GORDON, 'The Uprising of the Commons in Sidney's *Arcadia*', *Modern Language Notes*, 48 (1933), 209–17.

ZIM, RIVKAH, *English Metrical Psalms: Poetry as Praise and Prayer, 1535–1601* (Cambridge: Cambridge University Press, 1987).

Index